YOUNG
BOBBY

BRIAN BELTON
YOUNG
BOBBY

Volume 2

Boleyn to Bratislava, the Rise
of England's Greatest Captain

First published 2023 by DB Publishing, an imprint of JMD Media Ltd,

Nottingham, United Kingdom.

ISBN 9781780916330

Printed in the UK

CONTENTS

ACKNOWLEDGEMENTS

The author thanks Terence Brown for gifting access to the entirety of the Charles Korr research recordings. These include numerous in-depth interviews with former players and staff of West Ham United, encompassing the entire era this book focuses on.

All images presented in this book have been taken from the author's collection. While every effort has been made to trace the relevant copyright holders, this has not been possible in some cases, and copyright owners are invited to contact the publisher.

FOREWORD BY GEOFF PIKE

I started as what is now known as a 'scholar' at West Ham in 1966. It was just after the World Cup when my school teacher contacted West Ham advising that they needed to have a look at me. I got an invite to training; John Lyall was the youth team coach at the time. He asked my name, and how old I was, and I said, 'I'm ten.' He said, 'You're a little bit young, but join in while you're here.' Afterwards he told me, 'Make sure you're here next week.'

I was in the Academy at West Ham, taking part in training on Tuesday and Thursday nights. Being associated with a football club that had the three stars of the World Cup Final in its ranks, Bobby, Geoff Hurst, and Martin Peters, gave youngsters like me something to aspire to.

During the school holidays the Academy kids – teenagers, but sometimes younger lads too – would get to go over to the club training ground in Chadwell Heath. My family lived in South Ockendon at the time, and as both my parents were working, I had to get three buses to get there. The first time I made that journey I was about ten; you probably wouldn't let a kid of that age do that now. But then, you either got on with it or you didn't. You learn to stand on your own two feet a little bit.

At that time, Chadwell Heath had an old wooden shack that served as the changing rooms. There was a full-size football pitch, but the goals were two big green boards, basically flat walls with a white line around the outside.

We sometimes got to play 15- or 16-a-side games with a few first-team players. One time I recall Bobby, Geoff and Jimmy Greaves were playing. Jimmy had not long joined the club. To be in that company, that environment, to get on the same pitch as those people, at such a young age, was an amazing thing.

When I came into the club on a full-time basis, as what they then called an apprentice, it was just before Bobby went to Fulham and Geoff moved to Stoke. I played in a reserve fixture at Cardiff; Bobby was playing behind me, I was in midfield, and Geoff Hurst was in front of me. To be in that scenario was unreal, but it was all part of how the club was run at that time – its traditions; older, more experienced players, playing a part in younger players learning about the game. This was the order of things. It was not just expected, it was the nature of the culture.

Many years later, I was playing in a charity game in Basildon with Martin Peters, so in the end I played with all three of the players whose names became synonymous with West Ham and the 1966 World Cup Final. If, as a young player, you couldn't pick up something from players of that ilk, then there was something wrong with you.

I was having a conversation with Nemanja Vidić, when he was doing his Pro License with the FA. I was saying reserve-team football is part and parcel of what the game should be. He said, 'I'm not interested in reserve-team football' – but two people who had won the World Cup for England were prepared to do just that. It's going to be hard for younger players to learn about playing competitively with and against experienced, top-quality professionals, if that isn't going to happen in reserve football.

It was during that game at Cardiff that I made a challenge for a ball and ended up getting kicked in the head. I remember Bobby being the first person on the scene to check if I was all right. He had empathy for everybody. That sort of attitude has an impact, certainly when you are looking to work as a team; that people genuinely care about what is happening to each other.

As I got to be more involved in first-team football, quite often Bobby would come over to watch West Ham play. I think the club didn't treat him as well as it perhaps should have. He would often exchange a few words with people. I remember him walking up to me and shaking my hand, wishing me all the best. He didn't have to do that, and again, that sort of thing has a positive effect on your approach to your work; how you understand the game and how you treat others. I think that indicates how important the game was to Bobby. Even when he had stopped playing, he seemed to want to do what he could to make the game just that bit more civilised and decent.

When I got the opportunity to go to the US and play in the North American Soccer League, I was playing with people like Pelé, Franz Beckenbauer, Eusébio, and George Best – it was all part of my football education. But growing up, always having Bobby in the background, partly prepared me to be able to learn from that environment, and contribute to it. He was part of the spirit of West Ham at that time. Out of that you build insight, and with insight comes the potential to be inventive, innovative, and creative – the ability of individuals and teams to make something attractive, even beautiful; to interpret what might be practically straightforward into something exceptional.

At West Ham you were allowed to develop, to have a level of creativity; it wasn't regimented. One time all the apprentices were under the stand, John Lyall was there, and although he was with the first team at that time, he still had the interest in the younger players and youth development. He got us to just kick the ball up against the wall. I learned to play the game like that, kicking the ball up against a wall of my mum and dad's house; to master the ball. A couple of us, after a while, got bored of simply kicking the ball against the wall, and started to lift it to strike the wall, then control it and lift it on to the wall again. That was myself and Alan Curbishley. John never said, 'No, don't do that.' He allowed us to keep experimenting and innovating based on what he had at first told us to do. That's the sort of space that's needed to learn and develop.

For me, giving people that room to learn is part and parcel of coaching. I'm fortunate to know Paul Gascoigne quite well; he was never scolded for trying to beat someone instead of passing the ball – he was encouraged to try and beat them again – that made him the player he was.

Over the years people have talked a lot about the 'West Ham Way', without perhaps having much idea of what it is or was, so it has become a bit of a cliche. For me, Bobby personified the 'West Ham Way'. It was part of our learning about football and how it *should* be played, to approach the game in a certain way, but also understand its broader context and influence on people. Perhaps the two considerations went hand in hand to some extent. You are taught to do and think about things in a creatively positive way, which means you build an attitude to the game that makes it something more than just people kicking a ball around.

We were encouraged to coach at local schools. A little bit before me Pat Holland did that – and he has had a good career in coaching. Paul Brush was similar. Working with the Spurs Academy, he followed those principles, what you might call the 'West Ham Way'; the culture, which included thinking about what you could give back. It was instilled in us as young players and professionals, that it wasn't just about us. In the contemporary game it concerns me that, that is not so much the case. Retrospectively this was part of an ethical tradition, but it was also a practical and sensible way to grow the game, build good performance and promote support of the club. If you give people something, they are more likely to want to give something back.

It stands to reason that if you are going to play football to any positive effect, you need to achieve two basic things; find a way of getting the best from the player as an individual, but at the same time getting each individual to operate as part of a team. If you think about it, it might feel as if there is a bit of a contradiction in those two aims, but they really are the same aim – all groups, organisations and teams are made up of individuals.

From a learning perspective, in coach education, teaching coaches how to coach, I start from the basic principle of play; enabling individual players to perform to their potential, which means the team can operate to maximum positive effect. That doesn't change, regardless of age or gender considerations. It applies in and out of possession. It's not too grand to think of this as the fundamental philosophy and ethics of the game, which is based on transitions of either losing the ball or winning the ball.

People have asked me many times, 'What's the West Ham Way?' I ask them, 'What do you think it is?' They usually say something like, 'Play football – pass it around.' I let them know the basics I was told about as I learned to play in midfield: hit the player furthest forward, as quickly as possible, with quality, and get early support. When in possession, in control, the team spreads out, get the full-backs to go wide and high, and the centre-backs will split. When the ball is delivered, the quality of the pass or delivery is critical, as is who it's being delivered to. Then there's the receiving skills. The person who picks up the pass needs to receive it in a way that they can do something with – either to go backwards or come forward. Away from the ball, where the support from the rest of the team comes from, is another factor.

Regardless of context, this is what is foundational to the game played in the most positive and progressive way. My job, over the last nearly three decades, has been to teach coaches how to teach these principles. It's not just as simple as teaching a mechanistic system; it requires that people adopt a particular kind of attitude or mindset. That was the sort of thinking about the game at West Ham. These were the principles that Ron Greenwood, John Lyall and Bobby Moore and all the players at West Ham in their eras developed and followed, and of course many of them went on to be very successful coaches and managers.

For me, this understanding was motivated by John Lyall, and before him there was Ron Greenwood. That approach and consciousness really is an incarnation of 'all for one, and one for all'. Bobby Moore embodied it.

When I watch the game played nowadays, when I see the ball played sideways and backwards, I fall asleep! It takes so long to get forward. What we tried to do was to get sideways on, so you can look to play forward. When I was working for the FA, I was at St George's Park, when Gareth Southgate, a good friend, had just had his interview for the England job, after being caretaker manager for the team. I asked him how the interview had gone, and he said, 'I think it went all right.' I said, 'Well, do us a favour, if you get the job, get Eric Dier to play the ball forward.' We had a bit of a laugh, but it's so frustrating to see players just looking to up their passing statistics rather than, at times, risking trying to play the ball forward when they can.

Others have also carried the 'West Ham Way' forward. The many managers and coaches who came out of the club were produced on the foundation of the principles of what the club wanted us to do.

There was a guy who came on a UEFA B course I ran at what was the David Beckham Academy, over at Greenwich, before they took it all down. He walked in the room on day one and I thought, 'Oh my god, I got one here!' Some of the questions he asked made me think, 'You're going to struggle' – he didn't have much of an understanding of the game. You had three years to complete the qualification and then the final assessment. I got an email from him, two weeks before the three years was up, saying he'd achieved the qualification. He'd taken everything on board and worked hard.

By chance, after my wife and I had been to the theatre in London, we were at Stratford station and as we walked down to the platform, this same fella was standing there. He'd had a few beers with his mates, and most people tend to tell the truth when they've had a few. He walked over, totally ignoring me, and said to my wife, 'This man changed my life.' He was on the wrong platform (he was drunk). I've worked with people like Nemanja Vidić and Gianfranco Zola, but when people ask me about my memories of training coaches, I always bring this story up. We ended up directing him to the right platform and he just shook my hand and disappeared. He had achieved something he might have never achieved – and he valued it so highly. It was moving. But that's why I do the job – not to work with the top names, but the help people get better at what they do.

That too is the 'West Ham Way'. It's what West Ham did – it wasn't necessarily the aim to be the best club in the country and win every title, it was to make the players better at what they do. Probably that is what is going to make a club or a team the best they can be. That's the legacy of being at West Ham; it was the way they brought the players up. Bobby was one of those players, as were John Lyall and Malcolm Allison. In my second year out in the NASL Malcolm Musgrove was my manager, and was cut from the same cloth.

Brian Belton's book is an intriguing and valuable work. A study of the 'West Ham Way' in many respects, endeavouring to explore and explain much of what I have written above. It does that job by articulating and analysing how Bobby Moore was moulded and emerged from his education at Upton Park. It indicates, usefully, that while football is not life, it is and has been part of billions of lives, and so plays a big part in who we are and/or can become, as individuals and as a society. This is the true treasure of the game as an education, a path of learning that has the potential, at almost any level, to enrich personal, group and community worlds. Like Brian, I am an educator, and if education means anything, it has to be about that.

Geoff Pike

Geoff Pike made his debut for the West Ham first team in the 1975/76 season, at Upton Park, coming on as substitute for Yılmaz Orhan against Birmingham City on 6 March 1976.

Over a dozen years in the ranks of the Irons, Geoff was a committed and talented midfielder, but his pedigree is longer than that. He comes from a family of West Ham supporters and had been wearing the Hammers over his heart since 1966, when he first came to Upton Park at barely ten years of age.

Geoff played his childhood football in Thurrock and later joined Gidea Park Rangers. After almost a decade at the Boleyn Ground, he ran out with the West Ham 1975 FA Youth Cup Final side alongside the likes of Alan Curbishley, Alvin Martin, and Paul Brush.

In 1976 Geoff went on loan to Hartford Bicentennials of the North American Soccer League, playing alongside and against some of the greatest names in world football of the second half of the 20th century. He was with the club in 1977 when they relocated to become Connecticut Bicentennials.

Geoff was a member of West Ham's FA Cup-winning team in 1980. That side reached the last eight of the European Cup Winners' Cup in 1981, going out to the eventual winners of the competition that season, Dinamo Tbilisi. The following year Geoff gained a League Cup runners-up medal, as West Ham were in the process of winning the Second Division championship. He amassed 372 appearances in claret and blue, scoring 41 goals along the way

Before becoming an international consultant, focusing on the development of coaches and managers, Geoff gained the UEFA Pro Licence in 2004, and worked for the FA as the national coach developer lead. He transformed the programme into three international licence courses (for overseas candidates) – foundation, intermediate and advanced.

Geoff has worked in Dubai, delivering an international licence course, equivalent to a UEFA B qualification with Chris Brown Football (CBF).

I met with Geoff about writing this foreword on the day West Ham qualified for the semi-finals of the 2021/22 Europa League. I was keen for him to undertake this task as his career overlapped with that of Bobby Moore; as Geoff followed his football education at Upton Park, he experienced the immediate legacy of Moore's influence, the system of learning that blossomed during Bobby's very first years at the Boleyn Ground. By the time Geoff walked through what would be the John Lyall Gates in Green Street, this had become the established culture of the 'West Ham Way'.

Geoff was part of the third generation of the West Ham Academy and is well placed, as an international coach educator of renown, to commentate on the structure and attitude to the game Bobby was so much part of, and so to provide a direct insight into how the likes of 'a' Bobby Moore was and might be made – the subject of both this book and *Young Bobby*, the first book I wrote about Moore's early years.

I thank Geoff for his time and contribution here, but also down the years.

PREFACE

I started writing about the early life of Bobby Moore just over half a century ago. The work grew and grew as the years went by, and about the time of the first Covid lockdown it was clear that what I had was at least two volumes. The work fell easily into two distinct periods. The first volume deals with Bobby's most formative years, when and how he came to be who he was. This second part of the biography focuses on the time when Bobby started to demonstrate his development, and express the attitudes and attributes that were nurtured by and with him, and the personality he had grown, the qualities and considerations that took him to the zenith of his career, at the very top of the game he had devoted his whole life to.

The preface of the first volume of *Young Bobby* tells the reader something of the writing journey (or more realistically 'journeys') looking at, investigating, and analysing the life of England's greatest skipper, so I will not reiterate that confession here. However, as was the case with that first book, I have called upon my own experience, as well as that of my family, friends, and associates to give the picture presented more context and depth; a 'view from the terraces' if you will, that I think helps draw fellow supporters and others into the expedition. This 'intelligence' adds to what I have learned from former players, managers, and other employees of West Ham United.

I was once told that great works of art are more made by their audience than the artist who initially created and exposed his or her impressions to the gaze of the world. The scrutiny, emotions, moods and ultimately the collective opinion or judgement of the viewer are what continually define, refine, and evaluate the presentation; it grows in that process of continued reinterpretation and analysis. Much the same might be said of sport and sportspeople; the 'great' competitor or player is, by the continued expansion of the perception of their qualities, confirmed, or sometimes depreciated. What we write, say, and even think about the likes of Bobby Moore elaborates his life's performance, thus the view of the audience is crucial for a better understanding of him, and how he honed his exceptional talents and unique mind. So, the effort to keep looking is probably justified as it respects and honours the life lived.

As was the case with my first book, what I here present to the reader is a collective understanding, a bevy of views, shared analysis, and insights. Once more I thank everyone concerned. I am particularly grateful to Terry Brown, former chair and Life President of the Hammers, who passed on Charles Korr's recordings of the dozens of interviews he carried out in the writing of his seminal sociological history of West Ham (published in 1986), certainly the most intelligent and thorough study of the inner workings of the club, perhaps any club. This precious record includes employees of the club, both on the pitch and behind the scenes, whose association with the Irons spanned four and five decades up to the 1980s. Listening to and studying this treasure was both an education and a privilege

What follows would not have been the rich expedition it has proved to be without the contribution of the hardy and brave brigade of authors, journalists, historians, sociologists, and artisan leisure time writers who have followed a similar path to my own down the claret and blue chronicles. From Tina Moore and Charles Korr, they have taken up the pen with love, passion, and compassion. I have appreciated every sentence, thoughtful comma, and definite full stop. I here acknowledge their combined knowledge and endeavour, as I have done what I can to not weigh the story down with endless citations and 'for their own sake' references. As a dyslexic, but also a working-class academic, with secondary modern roots, I have always found such convention a labour for both reader and writer; a messy diversion, a 'look how much I've read' exercise, flaunting a species of trite scholastic pomposity. For me it's the VCR of the textual universe – it gets in the way in order to give an illusion of getting things right – futile conventionalism that puts no faith in the generosity of knowledge shared for its own worth and no more. Believe me, no one has made any money from writing books such as the one you are reading; they are a labour of loving obsession that will take more out of the pocket than they might return. That said, no other football club has had as many words written about it between covers as West Ham – that is testament to the craft of the wordsmiths involved and a tribute to their readers. I am forever indebted to those on both sides of the page.

As I warned in the first volume of *Young Bobby*, I deploy the words I have been given. Some will find a selection of them 'too long' (me and my extra syllables, eh?). Others might take elements of my lexicon to be offensive, but all these words are who I am; if you want others, or can't accept them, there is little I can do about that, except maybe offer you a few words from Stephen Fry, in *I saw hate in a graveyard*, The Guardian, 5 June 2005

"It's now very common to hear people say, 'I'm rather offended by that.' As if that gives them certain rights. It's actually nothing more... than a whine. 'I find that offensive.' It has no meaning; it has no purpose; it has no reason to be respected as a phrase. 'I am offended by that.' Well, so fucking what."

As always, after writing quite a bit about West Ham, you deserve my thanks for opening this book, even if you decide it's not for you – I try these days to never talk anyone into anything. In this world we are at our best when we stand where we want to, and to do that with as much grace as we might muster. In part I learned that from Bobby Moore.

CUMM ON UUU EYE-ONZZZZ!

INTRODUCTION

The year 2023 marks the 30th anniversary of the passing of Bobby Moore. It is also 65 years since he made his first team debut for West Ham United and 60 years after he first captained England.

This book, alongside *Young Bobby*, is a celebration of the legend that was and remains Bobby Moore as he moved towards the peak of his shining career

I am a lifelong West Ham fan. From the late 1950s on, and like so many others, the Hammers have accompanied my every day. This second book looking at the young life of Bobby fulfils a decades-long ambition to write about how he came to be, but while the first and this second volume looks to fulfil that goal, together these books are something more and less than that. A life exists in a time. To understand any existence, an understanding of the wider context, including the influence of others, is crucial. Thus, the perspective I offer is broad, taking the reader into another era and other places: the years – and locations that defined and refined Moore.

No one can say everything about anything, but I have worked to say something unsaid previously about Moore by focusing on his life before the 'glory years', the time that encompassed what are usually depicted as his greatest triumphs. The period prior to his three Wembley finals in two years is where the Bobby who is often close to overlooked or even forgotten resides. However, that alone isn't enough reason to undertake what was an exhaustive endeavour. Why look at the days of struggle and doubt, when the focus on the 'glittering prizes' is what we are inclined to want to relive, reiterate and celebrate – why 'go back to basics'?

Well, firstly, many dozens of books and millions of words have been spoken and written about Moore. Film and television, drama, biography, and documentary have portrayed the now well-known 'legend' of England's 'Golden Haired Hero'. But, exactly how did the storied paladin emerge? His whole development has been, for the most part, almost a footnote, or something that sometimes feels like it is an inconvenient necessity that needs to be got out of the way as succinctly as possible.

For me, someone who has spent the best part of five decades learning about and working with young people, their communities, training youth workers, studying and teaching human psychology and development, all the material covering the well-trodden highway of the mature Moore, at best, tells us only part of the story. At worst, lack of an understanding of the foundations on which Moore was 'built' constitutes the construction of a fable, akin to an idealised statue or a protracted homily to a fallen idol. That aside, the glory and glitter are but the tip of the proverbial iceberg.

Who we are by our late teenage years represents what we have learned to be, and we look to confirm that being. We act according to behaviour we have found to be successful and/or rewarding. *Young Bobby* drew a focus of Moore's early socialisation and learning, how the foundations of who he was were laid. This volume offers a vista on the next stage, the embedding of his personality and the elaboration of his talents and extension of his skills.

This portrait is enveloped in the seminal games Moore played during the period focused on. Because of this, this book has quite a different character from the first volume; I have set Bobby much more in the context of his art, of doing what he did. That has been necessary to exhibit how he expressed and honed his previous development.

The 'road less travelled' starts when the boy Bobby first came to football, the tubby kid who didn't know what his left foot was for. He couldn't tackle and seemed unable to head a ball. His lack of pace, a handicap he shared with his mentor Malcolm Allison, meant, at top speed, he did little more than lurch around the pitch at what was a relative amble. He seemed to have nothing much going for him, and less to offer the game. But what Bobby did have was a good brain and a determination of mind. He also possessed a seemingly indomitable spirit. Out of this blossomed a personality and an imagination that allowed him to turn each of his apparent weaknesses into strengths. *Young Bobby* surveyed how and why all that happened.

After Moore broke into the West Ham first team on 8 September 1958, he accomplished a series of achievements, wrought out of a lot of small victories, and a few significant setbacks. These experiences set his future path into immortality in his chosen sport and over the wider horizon of history. It was the years of the late 1950s and early 1960s, a time characterised by hard work and trepidation for Moore, and most people living in and around East London, where the kernel, level and meaning of his making was realised.

Given this, tapping into on the memories, insights and experiences of supporters, scouts, Bobby's managers, coaches, friends, and former players who lined up with him from his earliest years in the game, I examine the part of Moore's life wherein he found his feet and, literally, his place in football. It is in that block of years that most of us think of being, in the days before colour television, in black and white, that Bobby emerged as the harbinger of England's footballing hopes and forever, captain of all the Hammers. This story is of the flowering of the greatest defender football has known, his influences, teachers, and mentors, many of the same people he was to rebel against, mostly silently but sufficiently to beguile them. It is about the context out of which he, an able and intelligent teenager, became the young man, who personified the coming of a new tomorrow for his country's 'Saturday passion', the game that is a shining element of the soul of Britannia.

Presence

Very few players have sparked the imagination of Hammers supporters close to the manner that Bobby commanded and continues to evoke. There have been half-arsed attempts to name a 'second Bobby Moore' coming through the ranks, and to compare him to other former heroes at the club, but he wasn't a goalscorer, and you couldn't claim he had anything like an overt or consistent air of approachable conviviality about him. What Moore possessed was perhaps the most obvious aura to identify, but probably the most difficult ethos to explain: he had 'presence'.

His persona, his aura on and off the pitch, was out of the ordinary. Almost his every movement transmitted poise, but also purpose and this inspired confidence in those around him. The central aspect of Bobby's personality was that he was, almost invariably, in control of himself, radiating the surety that he knew what action to take and would find a means of bringing it into the world. Ron Greenwood, his long-term manager at West Ham, often had it that Moore's timing was immaculate in everything, and that was his 'superpower'.

The boy from Barking rose to the status of a national hero following the 1966 World Cup, and it was the local sports journalist Trevor Smith who was to argue that Moore's background was not a primary source of pride to West Ham supporters, that he would have been just as popular if he had not been an East End lad. Maybe that's true. Smith was something of a local soothsayer with that estimable periodical, the *Ilford Recorder*. He was born in East London; however, unlike Bobby and his family, and my father and his mum, who remained in London throughout the Second World War, Trev was evacuated to the Berkshire countryside to escape the Blitz at the age of seven. Later Smith moved to Ilford, what was then the leafy borders of East London and Essex. He retired in 1999 to begin a new life in Tunisia. I'm not sure he was as in touch as he might have been with the 'grunts' (like myself) on the terraces, for whom Saturday afternoons and Upton Park, was a deep-set cultural consideration. Certainly, in my puff I can't recall anyone reverting to 'Smugger' as a local identity compass. Eminent scribbler though he was, I'm pretty sure 'social anthropologist' didn't figure in his CV.

When I grew up, the municipalities around the docklands and the north Essex Thames estuary, from where West Ham drew support, were among the poorest in the UK. Relatively few people emerged from the area as 'greats'; when they did they were lauded, celebrated, and acted as beacons of hope, especially for the young. That someone had made a success of themselves was immensely important, saying, 'Something good can come out of this place.' To dismiss that feeling, that hope, is not to know the people who possessed it. At the same time, Moore was and is something more than 'popular' to those of us whose lives have the Hammers woven into them; Bobby is a figure, something beyond a Beckham or a Best, and represents the soul of the district, the people, the streets, and communities that nestled round and yonder from the Boleyn Ground; those thought of a thousand years or so ago as the 'Water People – North of the River, East of the Tower'. That he was, that he is, 'of us', matters. It matters a fucking lot.

Trevor Smith passed away in Tunisia and was buried in a French cemetery there; God bless him, may he rest in peace. Me? My ashes will be scattered at the mouth of Bow Creek, at its confluence with the River Thames, at Leamouth Wharf (often referred to as Blackwall), the east side, at Canning Town, where Thames Iron Works once stood. West Ham 'til I die (and after).

As a childhood supporter, born a short bus ride from where Bobby Moore was born, the area where my paternal grandmother came into the world, as I grew with him as a consistent figure in my life, I could have never envisaged being a professional, academic and author in multiple fields. However, like Moore, I remain an East Londoner, and a Hammer. These lives and their shared context mediate the journey you are here invited to walk. At times, this is a challenging voyage; not all heroes are flawed, but the real ones are imperfect as all humanity is. However, it is that panoply, the light and shade of all our lives, that gives our existence meaning and colour and, at points, funny, sad, romantic, stirring and hopefully informative elements. Along the way, we can all 'walk' with Bobby, sharing the intersections of our own life experience. For me, and maybe for some of you, this includes growing up in East London in the warm shadow of Boleyn Ground, something of a similar path the youthful Bobby followed. This brings a personal understanding of the setting or stage on which he evolved from being just another kid on the pitch to England's most storied captain.

So this is a portrait of the young man more than the myth of a footballing saint; the adolescent, his environment and character, who made the saga possible. Here is the complex and intriguing process of growth and development, from West Ham's elevation to the top flight of the English game, after decades in the wilderness, to the point when, for the first time, the leadership of his country was entrusted to Moore; when the whisper of greatness fluttered from the easterly banks of the cockney river to the rolling waters of the mighty Danube.

Emergence

Over the second half of the 20th century East London changed, but even today, well into the first part of the 21st century, it remains the same. The district, steeped in a dark, historic romanticism, abides both at the centre and on the edge of things, part of the most vibrant city on Earth, although essentially separate from it. While embracing dozens of cultures, it endures as just one place, although seen through millions of eyes, the area's homogeneity is contradictorily characterised by the prevalent heterogeneity. London is a patchwork matrix of diverse villages, made up of peoples who are as various in almost every sense of what it is to be human. The docklands are a microcosm of its great, bustling parent, the rumbling and roaring capital of the world.

We go to and come from places. Usually, any location is more than just a single place. The Boleyn Ground is no more, but it exists in these words I have, and in the hearts of millions. As before, now still, minutes can change years, and years seem to be gone in minutes. The institution that was, is and will continue to be West Ham United; its fans, players, and managers, even grounds, have been a continuous stream in my life, as they have for the place where I was born. This entity includes games played at Upton Park and my journeys, amounting to probably hundreds of thousands of miles, following the claret and blue dream that has yet to fade and die.

Matches, speaking to former players, ex-managers, and supporters (they are never 'former' or 'ex') has underwritten all my learning, from the pagan years at Burke Secondary Modern School in Plaistow, West Ham College of Further Education, into the legacy of the ancient and noble Saddlers Guild that is City University, and Master's study in Essex, through to doctrinal studies in the sacred city of Canterbury. In this ceaseless dialogue I have been educated, inspired, saddened, angered, and enchanted by *Days of Iron*. Conversations (in-person, electronically and by telephone). The exchange of correspondence with some marvellously informative and insightful people has been an enriching, dialectical experience, '*Founded on Iron*'. But I have also met my share of idiots too, and been sent down enough blind alleys and block turnings to challenge my sanity (and lose it at points).

Amazing though it seems to me now, over the expanse of weeks, months, years and decades the two volumes I have devoted to Bobby Moore have been fermenting. As they have emerged, I have managed to grasp something of what happened to just one of the hundreds of Hammers who have been good enough to give me something of their time and a few echoes from their lives. To capture just an essence of the development of the young Moore, piecing together impressions from those who played alongside him and those, who like me, were fortunate enough to watch him, could not be achieved just be the usual telling of *Roy of the Rovers* tale; a sort of fictional hagiography – that would never do the man justice. Part of the mission of both books has been to make that point and chart a life voyage. Moore did not appear from nowhere, a prêt-à-porter genius. He was a figure wrought out of the fecundity of the dark dirt of the game.

Phil Sammons, general secretary of Essex County Schools FA, and the county archivist, kindly drew my attention to the Home Counties Cup Final of 8 May 1956, wherein Middlesex were beaten 3-1 at Green Pond Road, Walthamstow Avenue. The Essex under-15 team that day was:

M. Leigh, B. Moore (Leyton); K. Pearson (Walthamstow), H. Cripps, E. Proctor, C. Norcott, F. Mercer, L. Harvey (West Ham); M. Everitt, G. Lawrence (Colchester), A. Reed, A. Smillie (Ilford); D. Carver (Chelmsford), J. Wells, J. Phillips (East Ham).

Aficionados of West Ham United will recognise some of those names, who made it into the professional ranks – Harry Cripps and Andy Smillie for instance, and the (seemingly oddly positioned) centre-forward for that game, Bobby Moore.

From such grassroots origins, there can be few who would have envisaged that Moore was to become a consummate captain, the class of on-field general able to take responsibility as the 'master and commander' of his team. When Bobby was entrusted to skipper England, he had already captained West Ham, as well as the England youth and under-23 sides; he knew how to do it. He was in the second half of his teenage years when he made one of many visits to see his friend and mentor, Malcolm Allison, in hospital. This was the man who had stuck with him from boyhood. Allison had been struck down with tuberculosis, then a life-threatening disease. On this occasion Bobby told the ailing Hammers club captain that he had been selected to play for the England youth team. Malcolm was pleased for his progeny, and told him, 'You must be the captain.' Moore would ultimately lead the youth team, but at that point he corrected his teacher, 'I'm not captain, I'm just in the team.' Malcolm was quick to reply. 'No,' he said definitely, 'you must be the captain – when you are centre-half, you've got to be the captain … You can read the game, you know what to do, so when you are a centre-half, you tell everyone else what to do. It doesn't matter who goes up to flip the coin, you be the captain in your own mind! Be in control of yourself – take control of everything around you – look big, think big and tell people what to do. Be in command!'

Bobby laughed softly, slightly self-consciously, but he took that advice and equipped himself well in that game.

Although early on Moore was sometimes amazed at his own ability to influence others, he was, all through his career, to lead by example rather than instruction, rant, or nagging persuasion; he didn't use his voice much, although when he did, he made it count. Bobby would take control, assume authority. At his most animated his arms would signal his commands, sometimes this would be accompanied by the barking of a one or two word direction. However, all this was, to a certain extent extraneous, because the man had an aura, and definite style. In lesser individuals this might be a stage on which narcissism can flourish, the ego suffocating any creative force outside of the self. However, Moore had ideals, which were perhaps the source of his clear pride and integrity as a leader. Never performing less than superbly on the pitch, and regardless of the challenges, rising above the temptation to cheat and the opportunity to smother the spark of what it is to be a team. These factors defined Bobby as a professional.

Moore rose to the occasion; he liked the big games and seemed to find an extra gear for such challenges. He just got better when it mattered. That said, whatever the match, Bobby hardly dropped below those standards he consistently set himself. Although he was recognised as quiet, and sometimes noticeably secretive, no one had a bad word to say about him as a person. At the same time, although on occasion he was able to express doubts about some of those in authority, Bobby never bad-mouthed owners, supporters, managers or other players, no matter what their sins, flaws, or frailties.

For all that, people knew when he felt critical of an action or personality – a look or stance (such as hands on hips) would give that away – but it was probably harder to know when he approved of someone. Bobby generally kept his emotional cards close to his chest, and his opinions closer still. He said little in the dressing room. At West Ham he allowed Ron Greenwood to do all the talking, although he was known to have a quiet, instructive, or supportive word with individual players, sometimes in stark contradiction to the directions of management. Greenwood hardly ever openly asked Moore his view on things in front of players, but manager and skipper had frequent, if brief, informal chats about opponents and strategy. My guess is that Bobby and Ron had such a comprehensive idea of one another's perceptions about the game that they were unlikely to have had huge differences that needed to be handled by more than Moore's on-field 'modifications' to Greenwood's plans and tactics. Given the chasm that existed between them in terms of personality, there was a synergy between the pair.

From then to thereafter

Most of the readers of this book will be familiar with the above outline of Moore as a captain and player, but for most he came into consciousness 'ready-made'. In the first volume of this biography I highlighted how he might have never made top-class football, that the fates played their part in Moore's emergence and road to greatness, not least the tragic and early death of Duncan Edwards. However, the journey was only starting when Bobby broke into the Hammers team to face Manchester United on 8 September 1958.

The morning after that West Ham victory, Bobby's debut game, Sam Leitch wrote in the *Daily Herald* of the 'contemptuous' way the Hammers had 'toyed with Manchester United' and how 'the East End boys' were perched atop of the First Division. Others sang the praises of West Ham's brand of football, seeing it as the future of the game. There was something to this; it was the first glimmerings of a new era, but the road ahead of Bobby would hold more and greater challenges than he had previously faced.

Although he was to say he never consciously copied anyone's playing style, when Bobby was first getting noticed he was being hailed in some quarters as the 'new Duncan Edwards'. He was to say, 'Like all things in football, you learn to accept the differences and leave the comparisons to other people.'

However, crudely, Edwards was the more 'complete' footballer; at the top level he was more adaptable than Bobby. Moore was never the 'natural' that Edwards was. For me, while there are similarities, I believe these two majestic players to have been quite different in terms of personality, capability, and role. As is constantly reiterated in this book and the first volume, it was Bobby's mind and his qualities of perception that set him apart. Edwards was a force of nature, albeit one blessed with balance and grace.

Like myself, from boyhood Moore had learned to be cautiously doubtful of comparisons. When he started to break through into the West Ham first team, and even before, in youth internationals, he was being hailed as an incarnation of Edwards. This sort of pressure takes its toll. For instance, Kevin Lock, in the early 1970s, when he was an England youth player, was not the first or last to be hailed as the 'new Bobby Moore'. Sadly, as with all the other candidates to fill those boots, that hope was never to transpire. Kevin gave good service to West Ham and Fulham before finishing his career with ten games at Southend United, but he was never in contention for a full cap.

In his later teenage years Moore was big, strong lad and had played at left-half, but he saw the reason for the type of adulation heaped on him as an embodiment of the hope people have to find another great player – the likes, in Bobby's case, of Edwards – regardless if the contrast is accurate. We have often been told of the emergence of a 'new George Best', Peter Marinello's arrival at Arsenal in 1970 being a case in point. With all due respect to the diminutive Scotsman, that was an anticlimax of monumental proportions (now there's an oxymoron to be envied!). The boxing public have never really given up the desire for a 'second Ali', but as the faithful remain expectant of the second coming, the fraternity of the noble art are still waiting. But there was and will be only one Bobby Moore, *The First and Last Englishman.*

Moore saw Edwards once before he was killed in that tragic Manchester United air crash at Munich, playing at White Hart Lane against Tottenham. He recalled, 'We had a day off school for the game, so it must have been a midweek afternoon match. Ted Ditchburn was in goal for Spurs and what really impressed me was Edwards' fantastic shooting.'

Edwards, 'The Tank', had scored two goals from outside the area, neither the result of fortune. For Moore the name of Duncan Edwards would for ever invoke images of those goals. The mention of Bobby was and never will be synonymous with the ball bulging in the back of the proverbial onion bag; his is a much more nuanced legacy .

Bobby was also named as the 'new Billy Wright', particularly after he became captain of England. He admitted to being flattered, but of course he was to make a far more indelible and enduring mark than the man who was managing Arsenal by the time Moore was made England skipper.

In the late 1950s Moore was evolving into the footballing giant he would become, forged by a context of the place and time. Yet to be recognised as the spiritual loadstone of Hammers history, his tale, here told, is a portrait framed in the landscape of mid-20th century West Ham United, the club's staff and supporters, as well as the setting of East London's docklands, as it continued to recover from the ravages of war, to enter the first stirrings of the liberation decade and the 'permissive society'.

If you look at most West Ham XIs or squad photos that include Moore, he'll very likely be standing in the back row, on the far right of the shot, often not looking directly at the camera. Mostly his pose will be dominated by a 'thousand-mile stare' away to his right. There have been one or two guessed explanations for this, but he had been advised by the young David Bailey (from Leytonstone) that we, in the west, 'read' pictures differently from how we read words. We take in images not from left to right, but from right to left. Thus, while you might not be conscious of it, the first person you will register in most West Ham team photos of that era is Moore himself. It was also Bailey who told Bobby that to look away from the camera creates interest or intrigue, because it hides part of the face, but, at the same time, it motivates the viewer to ask a 'what's he looking at?' question – albeit not totally consciously. The positioning and attitude Moore adopts both draws and diverts the attention of the viewer. This sort of sums up Moore's public persona; he wanted to be noticed, but he didn't want to be the centre of attention.

In the popular mind of the English, Bobby Moore has a place in the canon of the Albion. As such he rubs shoulders with Robin Hood, Winston Churchill, Elizabeth I, St George, Uther Pendragon and Boudica. Globally his name can sit comfortably in the same breath as Muhammad Ali, Pelé, the Beatles, Frank Sinatra, Albert Einstein, and Marilyn Monroe. However, in reality, he was an extraordinary ordinary lad.

That said, it is hard to think of Moore as a young man working during the summer in the William Warne rubber factory[1]. His mum had a job there and 'got him in', along with other young Hammers' stars of the future. After the collar at the factory the young footballers would be filthy, but they took home more in a week than they did in payment for their on-pitch talent. Often, on leaving work, they'd all stop off at the Moores' family home for tea. That was 'ordinary' life around the environs of the Boleyn Ground, and Bobby was of that world as much as any other.

Then there is another ecosphere. The constant portrayal of Moore's life and achievements over decades, via a universe of multimedia, amounts to a plethora of eulogy and biography; actual, wished-for and made-up dramas, played out for any and all reasons. This has made him one of the best-known figures in football. From the first organised incarnation of the game on a national basis in the mid-19th century Moore stands tall in the collective annals of sport. This notoriety has added to a propensity, in the mind of many, perhaps principally those of us who watched him play, particularly for West Ham and England, to see the man as variously a 'legend,' a hero, an unjustly un-dubbed knight, a saint or god of the 'hallowed turf' of the Boleyn Ground and Wembley, the famed 'twin towers' standing in his shadow. For the modern player, Moore might be a fabled role model, but contradictorily one it is impossible to emulate.

All these imagined incarnations are personal and group archetypes, the kind of narratives that we use to grasp (or convince ourselves and/or others we understand) a person of Moore's undoubted stature in the beautiful game, the broader prospect of sport and popular culture. However, this book does not seek to add too much to those popular and mainstream allegories.

---

1   This was based at India Rubber Mill on Abbey Road in Barking.

Bobby was just a man, and before that he was a kid, then the young bloke who became the adult, who has become the very stuff of romantic myth; a storied existence. Moore was a figure who will only grow as the past, yesterday and the present become history. This said, as someone who, for the better part of half a century, has been concerned with the growth and development of the young, and been part of the education and learning of many thousands of people who have gone into the world to devote their lives and careers to the same vocation, it is young Bobby who most interests me, probably more than the figure of fable, although even a survey of the first third of his life has its fair share of parables, the salutary anecdotes that might be thought of as the 'lessons of life'.

What I have sought to do on this voyage through the second part of Moore's early life is analyse his nascent development. My endeavour has been to gain insight into the foundation of the personality that, deity-like, has been able to breach the barriers of eternity to represent part of the spirit of a game. At the same time, I have worked to study a figure who has become a symbol of a place, a time, and a world of feeling that has transcended his era and context.

This is Bobby's story up to the start of the pinnacle of his fame, the foothills of his Everest of achievements, his metamorphosis into an English lionheart – the finest, most elegant defender football has known. It is an epic journey, populated by heroes and villains, teachers, gurus, champions, liars, shysters and conjurors, giants, dwarves, the helpful, the scurrilous, the hopeless and the hopeful, *Bubbles, Hammers and Dreams*.

Back to basics

Moore was to say that he understood tackling as a skill, 'Any time I see a defender just whacking through the back of a forward's legs to get at a ball, that to me is ignorance. You can't win the ball if you've got a body in front of you. You don't have to go around kicking people up in the air to be a good tackler. The art is to deny a forward space and force him to knock the ball away.'

Bobby's adherence to a considered approach to the basics of this type, outside of the England setup, was not always totally shared by those who surrounded him on the pitch, but to his credit he found a way, which demonstrated his getting and giving of wisdom; something more than knowledge. This is awareness, consciousness given dimension.

For all this, mid-20th century football, which lacked the Premiership's preened, billiard-table playing surfaces, the tailored, ballet shoe footwear, and the cosseted, effete, manicured mannequins that pass for the modern game's gladiators, was an exacting time for sophisticated consideration more generally according to Bobby, 'One of the problems was that sometimes West Ham didn't do this as a whole. They were so obsessed with creating space for themselves that they could not or did not recover when moves broke down.

'That failing conspired with a lot of northern antagonism to undermine West Ham. The delicate football they played and the glamour of our surroundings, some of their players made them bear the brunt of the anti-London feeling which exists in most football centres outside the capital.'

Moore noticed this even before he got into the first team, 'I was a reserve standing in the tunnel at Upton Park one day when Bolton Wanderers came down with a team of hard nuts. They were all saying, "We're going to wipe the field with you pansies." Every team seemed to feel the same. Wherever we went they seemed to want to get stuck into us; got all steamed up about giving West Ham a kicking. We were everybody's London hate team.

'Maybe we brought it on ourselves. In midwinter, we'd get to some of those tough, cold grounds in the north and we'd upset the locals by going out to play wearing gloves. They just thought we were a bunch of fairies. It was like a red rag to a bull with their players. They couldn't see the sense of it. Ron [Greenwood] used to say, "Put the gloves on; you can't concentrate on playing football when you've got cold extremities."

'The teams lower down the league were as bad. All wanted to stuff West Ham.'

Yes indeed, English football is its own worst enemy. The top end suffers different maladies now; infantile cheating, feigned hurt, and the whining we might expect from a realm populated by a callow, spoilt breed of man-child popinjays, but it remains a self-destructive environment, no place to cultivate 'the getting of wisdom', and so we get what we deserve perhaps and that can't include another Bobby Moore. The women's game looks more hopeful, but that is yet to be beset by the same destructive parasites that plague men's football, the ilk of agents, legitimised money-launderers and media hangers-on.

Each of us are, to a significant extent, made by other people and sculptured by our environment – the space we live in and occupy; our brain, in a very literal sense, plays out this truth. Areas of our brains that are stimulated by our early experience develop, while those that are neglected wither; we actually shed what proves to be unwanted (unused) brain matter. Yet we also enter this world with both similar and varying potential capacities, which are honed or abandoned by those around us and so ourselves. The old question asking what is mostly pertinent in terms of impact on human achievement or otherwise, 'nature or nurture', has long been answered; neither and both.

It is the interaction between these considerations that, at the same time, limits and expands our potential. The narrative of this interplay, for each and every one of us, is the personal biography and the wider story of who 'we' individually and collectively, are or might be, or might have been. Yes, this encompasses our identity, but the examination of any young life, such as Moore's, will add to our generic picture of how the ecosystem of human development works.

American author and lecturer Alfie Kohn has had a lot to say about how children learn. He has written, 'To take children seriously is to value them for who they are right now rather than adults-in-the-making.'

This is a principle that has guided my work. You see, external force can't make people wise. For sure you can instruct and indoctrinate, and people will act according to the script they have memorised if they are obliged to. This is the type of learning you might expect of a parrot. But if you can thoughtfully foster conditions for people that are optimal for their development, they will learn what they want to learn, and even look to teach others what they have learned; the words from Bobby above illustrate this – we can create situations and circumstances that foster wisdom. My efforts to write about Bobby Moore's early experience is foundationally a study of that process. I'm inviting you to look out on this panorama with me, thinking about how we can and do fashion ourselves, and how people are and might be wrought by their experience of and in the world, and what they make of it.

You can take the youth worker out of youth work, but it seems difficult to take youth work out of the youth worker.

'West Ham fans are not born,
Nor are they manufactured.
We do not choose,
We are chosen.
Those who understand need no explanation,
Those that don't understand,
They don't matter.
We are never beaten;
We only win and learn.'

1
SUMMONSED TO CAPTAINCY

Towards the end of the 1962/63 season, the matchday programme at Upton Park noted that Bobby Moore had been named Hammer of the Year, writing, 'Our congratulations are extended to Bobby Moore on being voted "Hammer of the Year" in the annual ballot organised by the *Stratford Express*. Bobby has been a "regular" in our line-up all this season and has been selected five times for the England under-23s, skippering them on the last occasion. He will be playing on Friday next at Stamford Bridge for Young England against the current international side in the annual Eve-of-the-Cup Final Match, and Early in May departs for Australia and New Zealand as part of the FA touring Party. We wish him the best of luck on these latest ventures.'

In May 1963, singer-songwriter Bob Dylan released his influential studio album *The Freewheelin' Bob Dylan* . The recording included the seminal track 'Blowin' in the Wind'.

The Monaco Grand Prix was won by British driver Graham Hill. He would win this race five times between 1963 and 1969, a record only bettered by six-time victor Ayrton Senna.

In the USA, attorney general Robert F. Kennedy invited James Baldwin and other Black leaders to discuss race relations in Manhattan. The turbulent meeting gained wide publicity and had a significant impact on the brother of the president to be.

NASA launched astronaut Gordon Cooper into orbit on Mercury 9, the last mission of the Mercury program. Thirty-four hours later he returned to Earth safely after making 22 orbits and travelling 546,167 miles in spacecraft Faith 7.

The Rolling Stones signed their first recording contract, after being asked (on the advice of Beatle, George Harrison) to audition for Decca Records by talent scout Dick Rowe. Dick allegedly rejected Jimi Hendrix and the Beatles, saying, 'Guitar groups are on their way out.'

After 18 years of denial, the Soviet Union confirmed that it had recovered and identified the charred remains of Adolf Hitler on 30 April 1945.

In the UK, Sir Winston Churchill announced his retirement from politics at the age of 88, for health reasons. He pledged that he would remain an MP until Parliament was dissolved, but would not stand for re-election.

'She Loves You' by the Beatles was the biggest-selling single of 1963 in the UK, it was also the best-selling single of the decade. 'From Me to You', also by the Fab Four, was the second best selling single.

Much of the football season was postponed for several months because of the 'Big Freeze' of that year, when temperatures fell as low as -22ºC. Ultimately Everton won the League Championship, six points clear of runners-up Tottenham Hotspur. It was the Toffees' first postwar title. With 40 points West Ham finished the season in 12th place, nine points ahead of relegated Manchester City, who were ten points ahead of bottom club Leyton Orient.

The Hammers might be said to have been unlucky in the last eight of the FA Cup, but it was Manchester United, captained by former West Ham skipper Noel Cantwell, who would win it, their first major trophy since the Munich air disaster in 1958, while Birmingham City became the new League Cup holders. Spurs were victorious in the European Cup Winners' Cup, becoming the first English side to win a European competition – unlike West Ham's victory (see Belton 2013b) in the same competition a couple of years later, Spurs, with two Scots and a Welshman, were really a 'British' team. Oxford United were elected to the Football League to replace the defunct Accrington Stanley, who had resigned the previous season.

The Football Writers' Association named Stanley Matthews of Stoke City as its Footballer of the Year. The country's top goalscorer was Spurs striker Jimmy Greaves, with a total of 37, and at the end of May, Bobby Moore took up the captaincy of England, pretty much accidentally, although there was likely to have been an element of design in the pattern of destiny.

Moore was offered the role, standing in for church organist incumbent Jimmy Armfield, the successor to Johnny Haynes (the Fulham man had led the national side since October 1962) for the previous half a dozen games. Armfield had been the on-field leader seven times in all after his first run-out as skipper in September 1961. He was not able to play in what was the opening match of England's 1963 summer tour of eastern Europe, on 29 May, because of injury.

Bobby was young and relatively new to the England senior side. He took up the task of captaincy after his club had failed to have the most notable of campaigns. West Ham's mid-table finish in the old First Division could not be said to have placed East Londoners as anything other than 'also-rans' over 1962/63.

England's most recent match a few months earlier ended in bitter defeat at the hands of the forever bitter French, not the best start for the new manager, Alf Ramsey. At the same time, it had been two years since England had won in Europe, when beating Italy 3-2 in May 1961. However, during that summer tour, Ramsey would predict, 'England WILL win the World Cup.' The expedition was the start of the groundwork of building a side able to take on the best national teams the planet could offer.

Ramsey, in the absence of Blackpool captain Armfield, turned to West Ham's youthful defender because he saw Moore as having innate qualities of leadership. Bobby had played under the authority of Armfield, and the skipper during the 1962 World Cup, Johnny Haynes, the most sophisticated passer of a ball in the English game during that era, who had suffered serious injuries in a car accident and had struggled for much of the season to find his fitness.

Ramsey's choice of the 22-year-old Moore exhibited remarkably discerning judgement. He had seen Bobby lead at under-23 level and at West Ham, and understood that Moore relished knowing that if something happened on the field, he had to make a decision. Bobby found that the role caused him to be a lot more conscious of what was happening 'inside' a football team. Ramsey recognised that this consciousness was an asset to any manager. Tellingly, Bobby was to reflect, 'We'd all like … to make decisions instead of always having to do what other people tell us.'

Being the captain suited Moore. He was never to forget how, when he was a young player with West Ham, the way the likes of Noel Cantwell and Malcolm Allison had helped him and he was to declare that he wanted, as the captain of West Ham or of England, to do the same for those going through the same experiences.

However, to believe that anyone having won, and successfully exercised, authority is going to straightforwardly and consistently conform to the will of others is a mistake. Ramsey, like Ron Greenwood, was surprised, perplexed, and hurt when he found that ultimately, more overtly post 1966, Moore would not exhibit the kind of compliance that Armfield had. Jimmy did not show the capacity for dissent that had always been part of the character of Haynes, maybe part of the reason why Ramsey called on the Blackpool skipper in preference to the 'Pass Master', consideration of the car accident notwithstanding. Former England manager Walter Winterbottom, the consummate educationalist, had valued the propensity Haynes had for questioning received wisdom and presenting alternatives, the very stuff of constructive argument and analysis that is the essence of scientific management. Relatively, Alf leaned much more towards the 'what I say goes' school of leadership

For Moore, the captain was not necessarily just the outstanding player in the team. Handing over leadership to someone simply because others might be impressed by their raw skill is demonstratively stupid; you do not task your strongest and most able warrior to operate behind the lines, to sweat over strategy and maps of the battlefield in the war room.

In Bobby's mind, captaincy was more than a title that allowed someone to tell others what or how to do things. He argued that rank meant more than just a label; it had to be given to someone who could take and use authority. So, the skipper would be the type of individual who others were prepared to give authority to. However, the person given the captaincy would also need to possess the means to apply that authority constructively for those who had given it up (else they would just take it back). The captain would thus be a person whose play and conduct set an example to the others to the extent that they would follow that example – conferring and confirming trust or if you like inspiring faith in the captain's vision and decisions.

Captaincy is thus hybrid of leadership and management; it is neither but it is both. It is a role that exerts control, but motivates collaboration; it is directive and collaborative and works to encourage others to manage themselves and each other. Leaders come and go. A good manager is anonymous, a captain stands out, and stands back; they fill the breach, hold the line and are the fulcrum around which people regroup and advance.

Ramsey was in harmony with Moore's thinking in some of these respects. He recognised the young man's composure that distinguished him from other players. Alf had also been struck by the way Bobby handled himself when watching his first game as England manager. Bobby had been one of the few players to stay totally focused during the defeat to France in Paris. On the coach to the airport after that game, Ramsey had sat beside the West Ham youngster, asking about the way things had been done under Winterbottom. Alf appreciated Moore's knowledge and insight.

Three months later, just before facing the 1962 World Cup finalists in Bratislava, Alf Ramsey had told Moore, 'I'd like you to be my captain against Czechoslovakia … I will understand if you prefer not to at such late notice. I've captained England and know it can be an ordeal.'

Moore didn't miss a beat in answering, 'I'd be honoured.' He took it that he had been chosen on a short-term basis, but as he was to say it was 'a dream come true' for him.

Ramsey told his new skipper, 'Whatever you do on the field, whatever decisions you think are necessary, you'll have my full backing.'

This was not a snap decision on Alf's part. He had, for some time, thought of Bobby as his potential lieutenant on the pitch . He saw that Moore was thrilled to be asked to take on the role and he sensed the youthful Hammer had a liking for taking responsibility. In a brief conversation I had with Ramsey in the mid-1970s he told me that he didn't think he was taking a chance asking Moore to lead the team. 'He was the obvious person,' he told me, adding that he had 'no doubts that it would be just a matter of time before Moore would make the captaincy his own'.

Ramsey had perhaps felt the determination and ambition Moore quietly possessed. Both men understood the onerous prospect of leading an England squad that included much more mature players, with far greater international experience than the Hammers' captain.

It was quite something for Alf to turn to a player with the intention of handing over authority. His habit was to keep tight control of the team and everything to do with it. He missed no opportunity to exert his influence. Before the 1963 summer tour the players were fitted for suits at Simpson's, in Piccadilly. The whistles were heavy-worsted jobs. Moore was among a group of players who asked Bobby Charlton, as one of the team's old hands, to go to Ramsey and ask permission for players to wear lighter clothes for travelling, given that the temperatures in central Europe were going through the roof.

Charlton agreed, and approached the manager. The customary uncomfortably pregnant pause followed before Alf said calmly, 'All right, Bobby, I'll think about it.' Charlton wasn't out of the door before Ramsey said, 'Bobby, I've thought about it, and I've decided we'll wear the suits.'

On reporting back to the team, several players, including Moore, were stifling laughter. But it was clear that Ramsey was the governor, at least for the time being.

When the squad got to Bratislava, Alf impressed the players with his approach to training and preparation. Before each session he would say, 'I want you all to go to the positions you would naturally take up once the match starts.' When this was done, he looked around for a few minutes and then announced, 'Right, now I'll tell you where I want you to be.'

Position by position Alf, very swiftly, outlined what he expected from each player. He made it clear this was about attention to detail. Nothing was too small to be overlooked. He did all he could to make sure his players, while in action, would avoid being confronted with needless problems and confusion. This was something he had learned and practiced as a player and a serviceman. Like Moore, Ramsey made himself a player of the quality who could captain England, and he had achieved this by way of devotion to getting the detail right, with all functions and expectations understood, and enacted.

Ramsey insisted players familiarised themselves with those parts of the pitch on which they would most probably operate. Those he chose to play for England understood they would get all the support in his considerable arsenal. From the start of the European tour, he started to build his World Cup-winning team in his own image, and right at the centre of it was Bobby Moore.

Big little city

Bratislava, since 1993, has been the capital of modern Slovakia, but less than 20 years after the Second World War it was (as it remains) a compact little city. Its population during the early 1960s was less than a quarter of a million, about the same as what was then East and West Ham (the areas that would become Newham in 1965), on the border of which the Boleyn Ground stood. So compared to London, Bratislava is a hamlet.

Straddling the great rolling Danube, the 'little big city' has a centuries-old history. At the start of the 1960s it was still overshadowed by the memory of wartime atrocities. Thereafter it was, until 1991, locked into the ambit of the control of the Warsaw Pact and the influence of Soviet Russia, which seemed to exacerbate the scars of conflict.

Then, as now, the cityscape was dominated by Bratislava Castle and St Martin's Cathedral, both reminders of the city's rich past. Eleven Austro-Hungarian emperors and seven royal wives were crowned in this precinct and, despite the decades of assault and threat, the echoes of their awe and splendour continue to resonate.

Bratislava's squares are linked by a multitude of alleys and snickets, which, in the mid-20th century gave the city the character of a place plucked directly from another time, although for Tottenham's Bobby Smith it looked a bit like 'toy town'.

Along the banks of the Danube lies the oldest public park in central Europe. When the England team visited the city in 1963 this was probably its main attraction, along with the cathedral and the castle. Sad Janka Kráľa traces its history back to 1774–1776, during the reign of Maria Theresa, when it first opened as a public park. The original landscape was influenced by the Baroque style of the time. So, it's a bit like West Ham park. Well, a little bit.

The white fury

Prior to 1963 England had met Czechoslovakia only twice before. The first match, in May 1934, had ended in a 2-1 home victory at Stadion Letná, Prague. The wonderfully named Tommy Cooper of Liverpool had skippered England (presumably 'juz like dat'). Manchester City's Fred Tilson had scored the visitors' goal. The second game, in 1937 at White Hart Lane, had been a 5-4 win for England, with Manc Blue Sam Barkas leading the side on to the field. The line-up included a couple of Hammers. Len Goulden's assist led to England's opening goal – Arsenal's Jack Crayston, moving up the field, sent the ball across to Goulden, who returned it for Crayston to drive a waist-high, right-footed shot from outside the penalty area into the far corner of the net. Goulden's fellow Iron, John 'Jack' Morton, scored the home side's second goal – a close-range shot after 20 minutes. After being put through, Morton cleverly beat his man, and finished with a fine drive just out of the visiting goalkeeper's reach. On 44 minutes England had been 3-1 up. However, it was Stanley Matthews' hat-trick that was to make the headlines.

Langenus

The referee for that game was John Langenus from Belgium. My grandfather had met him when playing a game for the Middlesex Regiment against a French Army side during the First World War. Langenus was the Pierluigi Collina of his day. After that conflict he became well-known, popular, and well-respected throughout the sporting world. Langenus was a striking figure on the field. Tall, with slicked-back hair, he ran out in a shirt, tie, jacket, and a pair of plus-fours. He was to officiate for FIFA in three World Cups, including the first final in 1930. He later wrote three books: an autobiography, *Whistling in the World*, and two other football-related works of non-fiction.

A fluent English speaker, in addition to his native Flemish, Langeuus also spoke French, German, Spanish and Italian. He and my grandfather struck up a friendship based on their shared interest in politics. They were to exchange correspondence for many years, which included an invitation by John for my grandfather to accompany him to Uruguay for that first World Cup.

Youngest ever skipper

The 1963 encounter was something of a prestige game, and all eyes were on the visitors' new national manager. That, seemingly without hesitation, he had passed the captaincy to a man with just 11 caps to his name raised more than a few eyebrows. This was more than an unusual move at the time. Indeed, it was seen in some quarters as bizarre. Yes, Moore had demonstrated leadership qualities at club and at junior levels internationally, but he was still young, and really had not been fully tried as a player worthy of a place in senior international football. At 22 years and 47 days he became England's youngest ever skipper, 53 days younger than Tinsley 'The Lawyer' Lindley of Cambridge University, Nottingham Forest and Corinthians, in 1888.

For all this, 43-year-old Alfred Ernest Ramsey, steely eyed and unhesitant, was never going to be swayed by the mere opinion of nondescript others.

Some have had it that Moore had admired the England captains of his youth, the likes of Billy Wright and Johnny Haynes, but the reality was he didn't rate the Wolves skipper at all, and had only started to be impressed by Haynes when he began to train and play alongside him in 1962. For Bobby, for a long time, England had chosen the wrong players, although it is true that for him there was no greater honour in football than leading one's country. But he was also motivated by liking the role of captain and the feeling that he could do a job that others had largely failed to do. Thus, it was predictable when asked about the lack of accomplishment of his predecessors, he would be critical.

Bobby would recall, as he walked out at the head of his nation's team for the first time, he had never been so proud. As he was to later say, 'I loved the experience of just leading the side out,' but he was aware that England 'were not meeting a poor team'.

Bobby was certainly correct in that brief assessment. Czech boss Rudolf Vytlačil had a massively experienced playing background compared to Ramsey, and his half-decade as an international manager looked like a lifetime alongside Alf's nascent career. The appointment of the England boss had gone through on 25 October the previous year, and although he had been effectively working part-time from 31 December, he had only gone full-time in the same month as the game in Bratislava. Up to that point his record with England read no wins, one draw and two defeats, with eight goals scored and ten conceded.

As we say down in the old East End, that was 'a bit shit'.

The awesome Josef Masopust stood in the Czech ranks. He alone was a foreboding presence in midfield. He had been a key player for Czechoslovakia for a dozen years, helping them reach the 1962 World Cup Final, and would be capped 63 times, scoring ten goals for his country.

Masopust had been crowned as European Footballer of the Year in that World Cup year. He predicted, in 1963, that after his Dukla Prague side met West Ham in the Challenge Cup Final in America, the Hammers would win a major European trophy within two years. He was, of course, proved correct. In November 2003, to celebrate UEFA's Golden Jubilee, Masopust was selected as his country's 'Golden Player' by the Football Association of the Czech Republic – that body ranked him as its most outstanding performer of the previous half a century. He was named by Pelé as one of the top 125 greatest living footballers in March 2004, and is today regarded as being among the greatest midfielders of all time.

Taking the field, the home side, *Bílá zuřivost* ('The White Fury') looked strong in their kit of white jerseys, white shorts, and white socks. They didn't seem to have too many weak points at all. Bobby, in the face of a major battle in a foreign land, carried a huge burden of accountability, not only for the day but the start of the future of English football.

However, turned out smartly in the 1962 Bukta away kit – red v-necked short-sleeved continental jersey, red shorts, red socks – Moore was conscious that he wanted to make the most of, justify and keep the position, responsibility and authority Ramsey had given him. As such, his sense of determination was understandable. As the roar of the 60,000 fanatically partisan crowd hit him, much more raucous than what he had expected, he told himself, 'If the Czechs are going to win this match it will be over my dead body.'

Cometh the hour, cometh the Hammer.

Why Bobby?

According to England's 1962 World Cup skipper, Johnny Haynes, following his time as captain, Moore was the 'obvious choice' to lead the country on the pitch, 'No one else came close … He was a great user of the ball, which became far more important than it had ever been before. It's important for a captain to be in the right sort of position on the field and he was perfect being in the middle at the back. He was never too loud, but, nevertheless, there was a lot of authority about him.'

The initial challenge of England's European peregrination was the first time that the incoming manager had sole responsibility for team selection. Alf Ramsey understood how his predecessor had been undermined by the intrusion of the FA's dated selection bureaucracy and, for Alf, its concomitant, largely clueless, mandarins. Taking the England reins with the proviso that he, and only he, would pick the team, was perhaps the prime move that would ultimately lead to victory in the World Cup.

In taking advantage of his new powers and turning to Bobby Moore to take on the captaincy, Ramsey had not opted for an obvious candidate. Bobby Charlton had 42 caps by that date, but no one questioned the offer made to Moore. Why might that have been the case and what was Alf's motivation? Well, one shouldn't count out, at least in part, the idea that the choice was a demonstration of his power (a bit of a 'fuck you' to the ghost of the selection panel). While the players might have been good with it, the functionaries of the FA would, almost without doubt, have vetoed the promotion of one so young and inexperienced. However, Moore mirrored much of Ramsey's vision of football, but so did Charlton. Certainly, for Alf, Moore's apparent solemnity and discipline resonated with the newly installed England manager, but again, Charlton showed much the same qualities.

Following England's World Cup win just three years after the game in Bratislava, Ramsey named Moore as 'my captain, my leader, my right-hand man'. Alf called Bobby 'the spirit and the heartbeat of the team' and 'a cool, calculating footballer I could trust with my life'. Ramsey said, 'He was the supreme professional, the best I ever worked with.' He went on to state that without Moore, 'England would never have won the World Cup'.

Ramsey's use of the word 'cool' summed up the essence of Bobby as a player. On and off the field he looked, and was taken to be a calm, natural leader, who exuded authority and balance. He never appeared to be under pressure. Where did this come from? His long-time team-mate in defence for the Hammers, Jack Burkett, had it that Moore was 'like Dr Who' having 'a brain like a time machine' because he was able to see things before they happened. If you have that ability it's going to make you more confident and so give you more time for calculation and forethought. But this poise and surety camouflaged a drive and ambition to prove and improve himself. These qualities made him, what in my professional sphere we might call a 'reflective practitioner', but out of this he emerged as an inspirational skipper who scaled the peaks of his chosen occupation and passion.

Relative to Charlton, Moore was charming, and possessed of a warm smile; he had a more convivial, *bon viveur* relationship with most other players than Charlton commanded. Like the Manchester United man, Moore could appear detached, but his demeanour had more of a diplomatic touch. His capacity to listen and demonstrate genuine concern and interest made him approachable. There was always a frisson of northern dourness about Charlton for some. Unlike Moore, Charlton was not a 'party animal', less than comfortable at the local bar or the patrician cocktail parties. His natural skill and athletic prowess, which outshone what Moore had to offer, might have caused him, albeit unconsciously, to appear superior to some less-experienced or less-able players. At the same time Moore was professional, not disposed to fostering closed circles of players based on 'special friendships' or regional similarities. He mediated with Ramsey more as a thoughtful adviser, and player representative than a quasi-managerial quisling. People trusted Moore and Alf recognised that and understood the power such confidence could harness.

Gordon Banks summed all this up succinctly. He was to have it that Bobby 'had a bit of that London swagger' that made others feel good. He was 'Mr Cool', never letting things get to him. Banks played alongside Moore in more than 70 games, and couldn't recall him ever appearing ruffled. For England's World Cup-winning goalkeeper Moore was consistently nothing less than composed. According to Banks, 'It was a pleasure to play with him and count him as a team-mate and pal.'

Moore had a clear view of what a captain had to do and how someone in that position had to conduct themselves to the best effect. He had been tutored to captaincy and had taken the part hundreds of times at every level before taking on the role with the senior team. He saw the task as encompassing 'special responsibilities', principally to 'set a high standard of behaviour on and off the field'. For Bobby, the skipper needed to offer 'the right example' more than set about 'bossing the team about'. He was to tell how on the park he had little difficulty taking on the challenge of leading the side, enjoying the responsibility, and being motivated to play as well as he could, while keeping the team 'on the right lines'.

Malcolm Allison made the point when he asked me, 'Why do you think that Bobby Charlton only captained the England side three times in over 100 games? It wasn't just that Moore was consistent. The players wanted him in that position. They knew he wasn't "the manager's boy". He handled Alf brilliantly, but he never took his side over the rest of the team. I'm not sure you could say the same for Charlton.'

Moore saw his off-the-pitch responsibilities as being potentially more complicated. He reflected on being criticised for being stand-offish and spending too much time with some players and not enough with the others, but called such accusations 'too silly for words'. He argued that players spent more than enough time together living, training, playing, sitting through team talks, going to the cinema, and attending functions as a group. In the few spare hours left, individuals made up their own mind about what they did. Some went shopping, some played cards, while others sat reading in the hotel lounge, wrote home or went to bed. Moore remonstrated, 'No captain can be everywhere, but I can honestly say I made sure I didn't develop any cliques of my own.'

Although Moore most certainly was choosey about the company he kept, and unlike Charlton he wasn't averse to the odd protracted visit to a bar or club with team-mates, he was always seen to be nothing less than fully supportive of other players, often actively sticking up for their interests.

There have been endless eulogies about Moore as a leader, but few have put a finger on what this meant in practice. It has been devalued as a title because of that. For sure, Bobby was a leader, but a great deal of his feelings for taking on captaincy coagulated around the need to be accountable, assume authority (take control) to grasp, hold on to and use responsibility. All this implicates the application of rational capacities, the deployment and interpretation of logic into action; this is a description of 'management'. Leaders cultivate followers, usually via manipulation or coercion. That is partly why most leaders don't last too long relative to managers; they are deposed. Looking at Bobby, his attitude and action was that of a manager. It was probably this that caused Ramsey, likely unconsciously, to name him as his representative on the field of play. Alf, who had more characteristics of leadership, needed him to underwrite his ideas and direction. Moore did just that, but he was not blindly following directions. He and Ramsey shared a similar vision of how the game should or needed to be played – it was that coincidence that caused the relationship to work, at least on the pitch.

Every England player, including Charlton, liked, but more importantly looked to Moore for direction and guidance. However, whether they were fully cognisant of it or not, they gave him the authority to *manage* the side on the field . For the most part Charlton, while being highly admired and respected as a player, lacked the charismatic, magnetic personality of Moore, framed as it was in sophisticated good looks, a dry sense of humour and incisive social intelligence. His fellow players saw him as both likeable and authoritative to a measure that Charlton could not match. Bobby's charisma outshone the impression the Northumberland man made, but more importantly perhaps, the belief Moore commanded was unmatched, and to be a good manager you need those you look to manage to have faith in your judgements and actions. He looked unshakeable and indomitable; the best of English spirit,

As time went on, Moore also was able to maintain Ramsey's faith in him – although there were points, from the late 1960s, when that was touch and go. At the same time Moore, while having the players' confidence, also had a rapport with them that allowed some familiarity, although he was always able to preserve his integrity as first among equals.

This said, Charlton was perhaps more of a 'boss's man'. If some of the squad broke Alf's code of conduct, Moore would deal with that in his own way, although often he was an instigator of the dissidence. Charlton was inveterately compliant and more likely to make Ramsey aware of any would-be clandestine transgressions that came to his attention.

There is much to be written and discussed about the Moore-Ramsey relationship, but guess what, that's another story. As it was, in Bratislava, history awaited. But as was the case with his amazingly successful crusade at Ipswich, as England manager Alf's focus was wholly on producing a winning team. The wider aspects of the English game, so beloved by his predecessor, were of no interest to Ramsey, perhaps even potentially a distraction. This was made clear from the moment he was offered the job by the FA, when he stressed that he was not going to take on Walter Winterbottom's director of coaching gig. He dictated that his concentration would be entirely on putting the England senior side back where he believed it belonged, and Moore was, in his mind, crucial to this. Indeed, for Alf, Bobby personified what he wanted English football to be.

The Brick Field

Moore's first game as England skipper was played in the Tehelné pole ('The Brick Field) stadium in Bratislava. The original structure was built during the First Slovak Republic, when Nazi Germany occupied Petržalka, the city's largest borough, in 1938. Bratislava had lost almost all of its sporting facilities in the conflict. The construction lasted from 1939 to 1944. The stadium was officially opened in September 1940 with a capacity of 25,000.

The old stadium underwent reconstruction in 1961. Just before the breakup of Czechoslovakia in 1993, it was the country's largest stadium in regular use, and was the home ground for the Czechoslovak national team.

The original architect was Kamil Gross, who also worked on the nearby Winter Stadium and other notable projects. The Tehelné pole, between 1940 and 2009, was also the home of the famous Slovan Bratislava. The first international match played there took place on 27 October 1940, with the 'Bieli jastrabi z Tehelného poľa' (White Hawks from Brickfield) meeting Hertha Berlin. That encounter produced four goals and ended honours even. Then, as now, Slovan Bratislava were the most successful team in the nation's history, having won the most domestic trophies, and are the first – and so far only – club from Slovakia (as well as the former Czechoslovakia) to win a major European competition, defeating Barcelona in the 1969 European Cup Winners' Cup Final in Basel.

In 1963 the Tehelné pole presented a fascinating, if awesomely dark, mixture of postwar architecture in state-socialist Czechoslovakia and the original Fascist influences. It also reflected the political developments and processes going on in the Eastern Bloc, but there was a hint of light from a few nods to inspirations filtered in from the other side of the Iron Curtain. All in all, the dominant feeling it might inspire in the less-than-stoical visitor was somewhere between whispered threat and grey despondency.

Cap 12

The two sides lined up before the match with the officials sandwiched between the teams. It was a warm, dry evening, pleasant enough for Ramsey to be in shirt sleeves on the bench. The pitch looked hard.

England kicked off at 5pm BST. As was usual at that time only the final 20 minutes of the game were broadcast live by the BBC, admirably, if predictably, commented on by the immortal Kenneth Wolstenholme.

Czechoslovakia 2 England 4
Wednesday, 29 May 1963
Friendly
Tehelné pole
Attendance: 50,000
Referee: Bertil Lööw (Sweden)

Czechoslovakia: Schrojf, Lála, Novák, Pluskal, Popluhár, Kvašňák, Masopust (Titus 43), Štibrányi, Scherer, Kadraba, Mašek.
England: Banks, Shellito, Wilson, Milne, Norman, Moore, Paine, Greaves, Smith, Eastham, Charlton.

The game, refereed by Sweden's Bertil Lööw (who would officiate at the 1966 World Cup), demonstrated that the Czechs were never going to be less than a challenging test, but Ken Shellito and Terry Paine were impressive debutants, and overall the visitors appeared to be a well prepared unit.

The athletics track around the stadium looked as if it should have had a detrimental effect on the spectators' perspective of the game, but unlike West Ham's London Stadium in its initial incarnation the sight lines were such that a good view of play was had from every standpoint .

The first meaningful shot of the game, from about ten yards outside the penalty area, caused Gordon Banks, who seemed a long way off his line, to parry the drive away. Luckily it fell to an English defender and the ball, a couple passes later, came back to the keeper who sent a long throw into the home half.

The opening goal, after 18 minutes, started with a Moore pass to Bobby Smith, who sent it to his Spurs team-mate Jimmy Greaves. The Manor Park E12-born genius cut through three defenders to tuck away a left-footed strike that was by that time seen as typical of Greaves. He made it look easy, but the almost imperceptible feint that fooled goalkeeper Viliam Schrojf was a little piece of art that allowed Greaves to trickle the ball in from just a few yards out.

The next chance was a Smith screamer, practically from the middle of the top line of the Czech penalty box. Schrojf pushed the ball away at full stretch.

Masopust had to be substituted just before half-time – he had not been at his best in the first-half, somewhat tellingly the home side seemed no worse for his absence.

The Czechs probably should have scored following a second-half scramble, hitting the woodwork twice before the ball was carried safely away by the England defence.

When the home side finally got the ball in the net it followed a sort of scrabbling race between Adolf Scherer and Banks from which the ball bobbled up to the striker's head for him to nut home in the 52nd minute.

Moore, who by the conclusion of the European tour was the only player in the side to have taken part in every England game of the post-1962 World Cup season, had felt that his promotion to captaincy signified that the winds of change were blowing. His sense of things was confirmed as Greaves, once more with his deadly left foot, completed his brace with nine minutes remaining. Between his contributions Smith (on 46 minutes), from a Greaves pass, and Bobby Charlton (71 minutes) demonstrated the power of England's attack. The Czechs decreased the deficit through Josef Kadraba just a minute after Charlton's goal.

Both sides were guilty of missing chances, but England were able to take more of the opportunities presented to them. The match was a much closer contest than the scoreline indicated, but the victory seemed to whisper a signal that a new age of hope and ambition for England was dawning.

Banks was to have it that the game against the Czechs laid the ground for 'the club-style spirit'. This approach would be a feature of Ramsey's reign as his nation's footballing supremo. The team looked to have found some bravery and the pride to inspire unwavering force in competition.

It was to be a huge loss to England and Chelsea when a knee injury virtually put an end Shellito's career within the year of the game in Bratislava where he had shown himself once more to be a sublimely balanced player. He demonstrated alacrity of thought and physical pace that at times amazed. But as the door closed for Shellito, it opened for Fulham's George Cohen.

England had won on the back of determined running and skill. George Eastham filled the calculating role formally undertaken by Johnny Haynes, and as a consequence of Ramsey's efforts in training, each player had a firm grasp on where their team-mates were on the pitch and what was expected of each of them, and as a team.

The Czechs worked hard, seemingly defending their standing so hard-won in the world game. Tough tackling while keeping pressure on the English defence, they had been no pushovers. However, a sense of confidence had grown in the collective heart of England, and a feeling that they had worked out the way they wanted to play.

Ramsey lays down the law

Following the game, Alf was explaining to the players that the coach would be departing in three-quarters of an hour, stressing, almost menacingly, that the whole England party would return to their hotel together.

It was Greaves who spoke up, asking if a few of the players might go for a drink before going back to the hotel. At the start of the 21st century he told me, 'Bobby [Moore] put me up for it. He said as I'd scored a couple of goals Alf would cut me some slack. I should have known better … As I started speaking it even sounded a bit cheeky to me! It all went a bit quiet and Alf looked at me as if I'd suggested we all go out and get pissed! He said, "Gentlemen, if some of you want a fuckin' beer, you'll come back to the hotel to have it." It makes me smile now, but at the time it was bloody uncomfortable.'

Ramsey's response symbolically marked the difference between him and his predecessor. His authoritative leadership style was going to be unwavering, with none of the leeway characteristic of Walter Winterbottom's 'friendly schoolteacher' approach. Alf was from the same neck of the woods as Greaves and Moore, and unlike Winterbottom, he spoke their language.

There was a hint of shock and awe in this for some of the younger players like Greaves, but Moore, usually quietly skeptical about managers, said of Ramsey's start, 'For the first time since I'd come on the scene, England were really getting organised. I don't mean that to be disrespectful to Walter, but I'd come in at the end of his reign, when he'd done it all. Alf was fresh and full of ambition.'

I wonder now if Bobby wasn't testing his new manager by putting his long-time pal in the firing line, knowing that Greaves was least likely to be taken as expendable by Ramsey. But Alf had nipped in the bud an idea that he might countenance any snipping at his authority. In his first few years under Alf, Bobby kept his powder dry when there was any sign of resistance to the manager's authority. Maybe he was sussing him out, looking for weak points, avoiding exposing himself to Ramsey's appetite for vindictive action. Moore rarely moved unconsidered.

Ray Wilson was a great defender, probably less celebrated than others in Alf Ramsey's England team of the early to mid-1960s. For me, he had been one of the most outstanding of performers in Walter Winterbottom's 1962 World Cup side. Remembering the game in Bratislava he said of Moore, 'I was six years older than him and I wouldn't have wanted the captain's job. Alf made him skipper … and there was no objection, because when Alf made a decision, it was usually pretty sound. No one disagreed and most of us thought Bobby was the best choice.'

Gordon Banks would years later say that it had been clear to all of the England boys that Moore was their captain in waiting. As such, they were among the few less than surprised when the manager put him up to lead the team out to face the Czechs. For the world's finest ever keeper, Bobby never failed to have a 'bearing about him that made him a natural leader'. According to Banks, Moore wasn't a 'fist-pumper' – he used his own performances to point the way. This gave the side great confidence to follow him out on to the pitch.

Moore captained the team with distinction, appearing to be made for the task. For most of us, we enjoy what we do well, and Bobby was to confirm that he had loved his first experience of being England's 'chef de mission' on the field. He was to say of the moment, 'The atmosphere was magic. The crowd are fanatical in Bratislava … The Czechs were still a great side. It had taken Brazil to beat them in the World Cup Final the previous summer and the stars were all there; [Ján] Popluhár, [Ladislav] Novák, and the magical man [Jozef] Masopust.'

Moore savoured pitting himself against the very best, but as he was to recall, the side believed they could be successful, 'There was a good feeling in the squad … a level of confidence that was something new; it hadn't been that way in Chile in '62. We were a different side really, and under Alf it was a new start. We didn't feel 'patched up', the way we seemed to see things in Chile, with all the illness and injuries.'

Almost certainly, the only way one can promote oneself into the ranks of the best is to raise oneself above the station of the ordinary. Those who aspire to excellence must test themselves in the heat of competition against and alongside the exceptional. Our bravery is defined by the level of temerity we express by being prepared just to step into that arena. In that company, however, even those able to summon the most extraordinary courage, without wisdom and poise, will be the first to fall.

Past, present and future

Just a few days before England's third meeting with Czechoslovakia, the Liblice Conference took place in Liblice, near Mělník, a town north of Prague. It looked to discuss and promote the 'cultural democratisation of Czechoslovakia'.

The Liblice meeting proved to be the first stirrings of what became known as the Prague Spring, which flowered five years later, a brief moment of political liberalisation and hoped for freedom of expression and independence.

Representatives from all Eastern Bloc/Walsall Pact countries were invited to Liblice; only the Soviet Union did not send a representative. The conference had a revolutionary impact and paved the way for a range of political, social, and artistic reforms.

On 20 August 1968, the Soviet Union led Warsaw Pact troops in an invasion of Czechoslovakia to crack down on reformist trends in Prague.

After the invasion, the Soviet leadership justified the use of force in Prague under what would become known as the Brezhnev Doctrine, which stated that Moscow had the right to intervene in any country where a Communist government had been threatened. This doctrine also became the primary justification for the Soviet invasion of Afghanistan in 1979.

Because the United States interpreted the Brezhnev Doctrine and the history of Soviet interventions in Europe as defending established territory, not expanding Soviet power, the aftermath of the Czech crisis also lent support to voices in the US Congress calling for a reduction in American military forces in Europe.

The conference of May 1963, the seed of the Prague Spring, directly and indirectly led to events and situations that included to the fall of the Berlin Wall in 1989, which marked the start of the end of the Soviet Union two years later, the rise of Vladimir Putin, the decades long war in Afghanistan, the destruction of New York's World Trade Center, Russia's annexation of Crimea and the war in Ukraine, the seeds of which were sown in 2014.

Moore of the same

In Bratislava, England discovered that their interdependence was going to be the key to progress. Bobby Moore had captained the team and had grown into the role from the first minute, seemingly without effort, reflecting his customary application on the field. The only West Ham player to have been called up more times for England was the legendary Len Goulden (14 caps).[2] Bobby had carried a mighty load of expectation, but he lifted it with aplomb and a typical calmness.

Bobby's tenure as England's captain had started in fine style, and Ramsey's first win as boss illustrated Moore's capacity to rise to and be inspired by the big occasion. His performance elicited positive reviews in the English press, although the mercurial Greaves, weaving his genius in the penalty area to notch up an international double, inevitably dominated the headlines. However, the ousting of World Cup finalists on their own turf would prove a seminal moment for Ramsey, Moore, and the team.

For Bobby, the moment of victory marked the release of an optimistic spirit of expectation, and audacious ambition seemed to enter the psyche of the side. The squad had forged some courage, the means to straighten their resolve and dig pride out of their combining. Although he might not have been fully aware of it, or keen to accept it, that 1963 encounter in Bratislava can be understood to have been a seminal and significant step for Moore on the road to a status in

---

2   Goulden played his last game for England (v Yugoslavia) in 1939 although he also turned out in wartime internationals (caps were not awarded for those games). Moore had equaled Tommy Moroney's dozen caps for the Republic of Ireland. Up to the spring of 1963 Noel Cantwell remained West Ham's most capped player with 17 international appearances for the Republic. Bobby played his 15th game for England (v Wales) in October 1963 and gained his 18th cap (v Scotland) in April 1964.

football, sport and popular culture that would live and grow in history. He had made the time to watch every European tie at White Hart Lane in Tottenham's run to victory in the 1962/63 Cup Winners' Cup. By the time he had achieved the rare feat of captaining England sides at youth, under-23, and senior level, he knew continental football well.

England would play the Czechs nine more times before that country ceased to exist, winning five, drawing three and losing just once, during qualifying for the 1976 UEFA European Championship.

I have, along with many others, including his contemporary playing colleagues, said that Moore was to come to play better for England than he did for West Ham. That is not saying he didn't endeavour to give his all in both contexts. He once had it he had badly wanted a league championship medal and would have hoisted the Hammers to that aim single-handedly if that had been within his powers. I totally believe that, but firstly, the Irons could not surround him with the talent available to England, so any adaptable player was bound to look better in the international team. However, watching him on both stages many hundreds of times, his feelings and experience playing for West Ham, the way he was treated and the relationships at Upton Park, did not, certainly after 1966, draw from him what the England stage managed to. Something of this situation is examined later in this book.

England's three-match European expedition of 1963 was a great success, one they needed after their unsatisfying World Cup experience a year before. They beat East Germany 2-1 and Switzerland 8-1 to complete the tour. The squad returned to England to be hailed by the media as 'buoyant' and 'full of confidence'. Throughout the tour Bobby had exuded class, and while not notably quick, he appeared to have no end of time, almost capable of stretching the seconds and minutes. In those times most people would have considered him to be not much more than a kid, but his maturity was astounding.

For all this, by the close of 1963 many continued to urge Ramsey to reinstate Johnny Haynes as the team's captain. The Fulham maestro was still not out of his 20s and had been a cornerstone of club and country for years. However, Alf didn't think he was fit enough, or at least that was the line he stuck to. Haynes was very likely past his best, but he was still a player of exceptional ability, although way too much his own man for Ramsey's liking. At Craven Cottage he had acquired this sense of himself; what he said went on and off the field. He was a big fish in a small pond and was revered. Jimmy Hill would later point out that it was he who did all Haynes's running for him. Haynes would often stand still, shrug, moan and become visibly fed up when things didn't go his way. That wasn't the kind of attitude Alf could accommodate. Haynes's England team-mates would protest that this wasn't a true reflection of what he was like, but from Ramsey's perspective he was not the archetypal team man – the quiet and gentle spirit, say, of Bobby Charlton, who became the rock of experience in England's World Cup-winning team.

Thus it was the safe hands of Jimmy Armfield that took the captaincy for England's next five games until Moore was reinstated for the long haul in May 1964. However, Bobby Moore was the future. When Ramsey made Moore captain on a permanent basis, after Armfield lost his place to George Cohen, it was in his 18th cap. Bobby Charlton had 49, Greaves 33 and Ray Wilson 24, but no one in the England squad, for one minute, questioned the thought of Moore leading England out at Wembley to face Uruguay. His side left the field 2-1 winners; he was 23 years of age.

That was a year on from the victory over Czechoslovakia in Bratislava. By then Bobby had led West Ham to FA Cup glory, and had been voted Football Writers' Association Footballer of the Year. He also had another battle to win against testicular cancer.

Now and then, Bobby would approach a young debutant looking anxious during their first match and quietly tell them, 'Block out the noise, it's just another game of football in the park,' or just before that inaugural game assure them that, 'When you cross the white line, you are as good as anyone else … you are equal to everyone else on the pitch.' However, no one was equal to Bobby Moore.

2

'COLTIVATING' YOUTH

As detailed in *Young Bobby*, in the last part of the 1950s West Ham became a pioneering club with regard to the development of local and homegrown talent. Under the scouting and coaching structure that Ted Fenton initiated, Malcolm Allison and Noel Cantwell built, and later Ron Greenwood developed and extended, the reputation of the Hammers grew into part of the mythology of the Boleyn Ground, and the identity of the East London Irons, 'The Academy' and The 'West Ham Way'.

While the youth policy started out as an adaptation of the precedent set at Manchester United, and proceeded alongside a similar programme being introduced at Chelsea, no contemporaneous club was to match the cultural and organisational impact the youth scheme had at Upton Park. Certainly, no club outside the top tier, even come close to the culture of fostering youth. West Ham's success rate in terms of the movement of young players groomed by the club into the professional ranks was, for the best part of a decade, unparalleled, certainly taking into consideration the relatively modest resources the club was able to devote to this part of its operations.

West Ham tasked professional players to 'spread the word', many devoting part of their week to coaching in local schools. Clyde Best was assigned to Burke Secondary Modern at the time when this was my own seat of learning. He was accompanied by a young Scottish player, George Andrew . Such was the diversity of my teenage community, and so the school's population, Clyde's broad but silky Bermudian accent was universally understood, even though he spoke relatively quietly almost the whole time he was on the pitch with us. Sadly, the same can't be said for his Caledonian colleague, who constantly roared in an incomprehensible Glaswegian intonation. The only instruction that was anything close coherent was the repeated, exasperatedly questioning entreaty, 'WILL YE NAY STOPP PHOKIN' SHOOTIN'!?'

It's a straightener to look at any life journey from the vantage point of childenood. Andrew began his career in the youth ranks at Scottish club Possilpark Juniors, before joining West Ham United in August 1963. He was obliged to wait nearly four years for his first team debut, deputising in a defence without West Ham stalwarts Bobby Moore and Ken Brown, in a 2–2 draw against Sunderland on 11

February 1967. Andrew made one final appearance for the club, a fortnight later in a 4–0 loss away to Everton. In July 1967, George signed for Crystal Palace. He stayed with the (then) Glaziers for a year, failing to make a first team appearance. In 1968 he dropped down into Non-League football, playing for Romford. Following his retirement, Andrew went into teaching and osteopathy. George died 30 July 1993 in Edinburgh aged just 47.

The organisation and nurturing of young cockney talent came to be a significant factor of the Hammers brand that would be replicated by other clubs over the years, producing some of the best young players and youth sides.

It's hard now to imagine the transition from school football to the 'big-time' game of the late 1950s, when it was a buzz for lads like Bobby Moore to be summoned to don the claret and blue for midweek matches, often at hallowed historical sites of the game, like Clapton's Spotted Dog ground in Forest Gate. Not unusually they would be watched by a clutch of first-team players, which was taken to be something of a compliment by the kids. But the process was animated by the achievements of West Ham's young players, exemplified by the FA Youth Cup winners of 1963, 1981 and 1999, but perhaps the most outstanding side was the one that didn't quite claim the same triumph.

Floodlit to Berkshire

In 1959 the West Ham youth team was captained by Bobby Moore. Six months after he broke into the first team in the Football League, he was leading the young Hammers in the Southern Junior Floodlit Cup – at that time a trophy, at youth level, second only in stature to the FA Youth Cup.

After pushing aside Millwall and Fulham, at 7.15pm on Wednesday 4 March, West Ham faced Reading in the semi-final. The Irons (detailed as being kitted-out in claret and blue shirts and white 'knickers') lined up as follows, 'P. Reader, H. Cripps, J. Burkitt, G. Hurst, B. Keetch, B. Moore, W. Woodley, J. Cartwright, M. Beasley, A. Smillie, Scott.'

As was the wont of whoever wrote the match programmes, some players were given initials and not others, a habit that is a tiny bit bewildering, but misspelling of Jack Burkett's name remains a disappointment.

The Reading team included one or two names of the future – see if you can spot any: Arthur Wilkie, Bruce Dorrell, Keith Rumble, David High, Gordon Neate, David Grant, Stan Turner, Alan Fielder, Terry Warth, Peter Shreeve, Gordon Buck.

Although playing in the wilds of Berkshire, West Ham came out of an avalanche of goals as 6-3 winners.

The reserves

The bread and butter for most of the young Hammers was the reserve team fixtures. This was hard, slogging football that made or broke players, mixing it with men either desperate to get back into first-team football following poor form or injury, or often those jadedly just seeing out the end of their careers in the shadows of the game. This mixture often made for treacherous opposition and sometimes not the most generous of team-mates.

A fortnight after the Floodlit Cup semi-final against Reading, Moore was in the reserve side that played host to Bristol Rovers. The matchday programme report of the game told the dismal story, 'The reserves had only one holiday game, an attendance of little over 1,000 seeing Bristol Rovers Reserves gain a 1-0 Combination victory at Upton Park on Saturday against the following line-up: Rhodes; Cripps, Lyall; Pyke, Moore, Lansdowne; Wragg, Cartwright, N. Bleanch, Hills, Scott.

'It was probably the dullest game seen at the Boleyn Ground this season, and there was little real football. Aimless midfield play too often ended with attacking movements petering out after a couple of passes and even the visitors showed little spirit despite the fact that their foot-of-the-table position made the points at stake extremely valuable to them.'

The 'glory game' is sometimes little more than a monotonous test, but without these trials few lessons can be learned or character made.

FA Youth Cup

In the third round of the FA Youth Cup Bobby notched up a rare goal, from the penalty spot, in the 6-0 win over Eastbourne United. He was almost a constant presence for the young Irons in that season's competition, apart from a couple of early games. Youth-team football was always well supported, but was also something of a marketplace for younger players.

As the 1950s was fading into the panoply of history, the youthful Hammers reached the final of the FA Youth Cup for the second time. They had been unsuccessful in 1957 against a strong Manchester United outfit, but the XI Moore led looked to be a more sophisticated line-up, although it is entertaining to imagine a match between the two groups of young Irons – despite there being only two years between the them, they were the same in terms of the general spirit of their game, but very different in character and demeanour.

The journey of the 'Boys of '59' that led them to their encounter with the Blackburn youngsters, saw the claret and blue kids overcome some stiff opposition.

In the last eight Aston Villa stood in their path. The subsequent matchday programme report of this tie reveals something of the extent to which Moore was developing as a player and a leader, 'Our Colts had a very hard struggle against a strong Aston Villa Colts team when they visited Villa Park in the fifth round of the FA Youth Cup on Wednesday, 18 March.

'A 6,500 attendance saw our lads get away to a flying start when Andy Smillie scored within 90 seconds of the kick-off. The Hammers maintained this pressure and for the first quarter of an hour were rarely out of the Villa half. However, the Midlanders gradually came into the game, and asserted themselves by equalising through Tindall three minutes before the interval.

'The second half found Villa again in the ascendancy and our defence was hard-pressed to keep them at bay. Hero of the Hammers was Bobby Moore, whose performance at centre-half had all the hall-marks of greatness upon it; he certainly "earned all his salt" and the remainder of the team accorded him the fullest praise.

'Nevertheless the rest of the boys in the XI must not be forgotten and although one or two had an "off night" they are to be congratulated on holding a team which contained seven professionals.

The Hammers' complete line up was: F. Caskey; Cripps, J. Burkett; E. Bovington, Moore, G. Hurst; D. Woodley, Cartwright, M. Beesley, Smillie, Scott.

'It was originally hoped that in the event of a draw the replay would take place last Monday. However, this was not practical as three of our players would not have been available due to their selection to travel with the England youth party to Bulgaria. Consequently the replay will not now take place until sometime next month.

'The winners of the tie will enter the semi-final, which is played on a "two leg" basis. The other teams already in the semi-final are Arsenal, Blackburn Rovers and Manchester United.'

During that tie with Villa a confused melee ensued in the Hammers' penalty box, a moment of intense danger and so stress for the young Irons. Bobby Moore emerged from the maul, cleared the box, and sent a 40-yard pass directly to the chest of striker Mike Beesley. Watching England's final goal at Wembley in 1966 is almost a rerun of the same situation. That moment in the early spring of 1959 exemplified the class, poise and promise of the vernal Moore.

On 9 April 1959 the Irons beat Villa 3-2 in the replay; the reward for their victory was a meeting with Arsenal. The defeat of the Gunners paved the way for the two-legged meeting with Blackburn Rovers on 27 April 1959, a side that had beaten Manchester United in their semi-final, watched by an Old Trafford crowd of 30,000.

West Ham 1 Blackburn Rovers 1
Monday, 27 April 1959
FA Youth Cup Final first leg
Upton Park
Attendance: 10,750
Referee: Unknown

West Ham: Caskey, Cripps, Burkett, Bovington, Moore, Brooks, Woodley, Beesley, Smillie, Cartwright, Scott.
Blackburn: Griffiths, Wells, Pickering, England, Newton, Leach, Ratcliffe, Bradshaw, Jervis, Daly, Mulvey.

An attendance of 10,750 was by far the best turn-out of the four FA Youth Cup games at Upton Park hosted that season. The tie was an energetic encounter with both sides crafting chances.

Geoff Hurst, usually a half-back at that time, was crocked so Micky Brooks stepped in, giving the lad his only outing in the competition. Brooks was a fine midfield player. He had played for Tottenham Schools and England Schoolboys, but he never made the senior grade. One or two of his peers thought that he might have found the game too easy. Micky, like a lot of good young players, had all the potential, but not that certain something that enables them to break through. It's hard to know at an early age that more than talent is needed to make the professional game. Few had the application of Bobby Moore, who had far fewer natural gifts than many of his peers.

The Hammers were something north of unfortunate to be denied a penalty before going a goal up after half an hour. Their luck got no better as the athletic John Cartwright struck an upright, so it was fitting that it was the future England under-18 manager's lofty long cross that dived into the Rovers penalty area for the waiting noggin of the slick and agile Andy Smillie (who had by this time played as a senior Hammer).

Talking with Smillie many years later he remembered the goal, making the point, 'As soon as John kicked the ball for the cross, I knew I'd score. John was a great passer of the ball and it was a simple move we had practiced over and over. Do simple things well!'

Harder than it sounds, but words to live by, straight from the Malcolm Allison playbook.

Thereafter, it was Rovers' turn to be foiled by the stubborn goal frame. However, with half-time just a linesman's fart away, Alan Bradshaw's left foot brought the lively lads from Lancashire level. Smashing through the centre, he sent the ball high into the West Ham net.

Coming out after the break West Ham were a player short. Noticing this, the referee asked the Hammers' skipper about it. Bobby looked around, asking team-mates, 'Where's Derek?' When Woodley eventually returned to the pitch it was revealed he had been taking a particularly protracted dump. Apparently, that failed to be included in the referee's report.

After the striker had cleared the basement, during the second half of the match the goalkeepers weren't too busy, but it was in that period that the industrious Hammers were refused what was a painfully, preposterously, palpable penalty. Andy Smillie, right of Blackburn's penalty area, touched the ball beautifully beyond their goalkeeper. As the Ilford kid went to gallop through, the Blackburn stopper upended him. A free kick was (to say the very least) something well short of anything close to justice for what was a deliberate foul.

With ten mean minutes left Billy Jervis, with just Frank Caskey in front of him, lobbed his shot over the West Ham custodian. It was a smart move, but the ball went out of play after bouncing off a post.

This game did not see Bobby at his best; probably his less-than-impressive performance was related to a robustly strapped right ankle. However, West Ham's inside-right, John Cartwright, shone out among all the youngsters. He, along with Smillie, had deserved more for their endeavours. At the back Harry Cripps and Jack Burkett had been as solid as the best of hopes might hope for. Harry was to let me know decades after, 'We was robbed. Blackburn weren't better than us for a minute.' He had a way with words, did H.

Certainly, David Wells and Fred Pickering did a stoical job protecting the Blackburn goalkeeper Barry Griffiths, but West Ham, while never bettered, had been held by Rovers in what had been a game decided by the respective defences. Keith Newton gave Mike Beesley not an inch of room. Looking back, Mike confessed that Newton 'played a blinder'.

The day after the game the *Blackburn Evening Telegraph* hailed John Cartwright with rather laboriously awkward praise, saying it was the Brixworth-born boy 'who caught the eye more than anyone'.

That notable tome of the Blackburnian locale of the time, the *Blackburn Times*, bugled the central injustice of the game in its report on 1 May, 'Smillie, charging after a loose ball down the right side of Rovers' penalty area, was bowled over by Griffiths … The referee awarded an indirect free kick when, quite frankly, a penalty looked the more just decision.'

Blackburn Rovers 1 West Ham 0
Tuesday, 5 May 1959
FA Youth Cup Final second leg (Blackburn win 1-0 on aggregate)
Ewood Park
Attendance: 28,500
Referee: William Clements

Blackburn: Griffiths, Wells, Pickering, England, Newton, Leach, Ratcliffe, Bradshaw, Jervis, Daly, Mulvey.
West Ham: Caskey, Cripps, Burkett, Bovington, Moore, Hurst, Woodley, Beesley, Smillie, Cartwright, Scott.

The gate of 28,500 for the second leg showed the exceptional interest and considerable status of the competition at the time. As was customary with any West Ham side visiting the north, the players were jeered as 'soft cockney fairies' when they trotted out on to the pitch in their light-brown tracksuits 20 minutes prior to the kick-off to warm up, a nod to the influence of Malcolm Allison. That practice hadn't totally arrived in much of the macho world of British football.

The secretary of the Football Association, Sir Stanley Rous, along with the mayor of Blackburn, alderman George Haworth, met both teams prior to the start of the match. George, who had left school at the age of 12, was a sometime president of the Blackburn and District Master Butchers Association; maybe he was invited because there was so much at stake, but he had risen from humble origins to be a cut above the rest, although he eventually got the chop.

The Hammers XI for the second leg was bolstered by Geoff Hurst's return from injury, taking back his left-half place from Mick Brooks.

Documents are not monuments

This situation has failed to be noted in several West Ham handbooks and other publications, seemingly replicating each other's inaccuracy or oversight (this happens a lot). Hurst was recorded as being involved in the second leg in both local and national newspapers of the time. An article on Hurst in the home programme of 21 April 1962 for a game against Arsenal seems to confirm these earlier publications, stating that Geoff did return from injury for the Ewood Park leg and that he got his runners-up medal. Oh, and my great uncle Bronco was at the game and had always insisted that Hurst played … but no one ever believed him about anything.

For all this, up to the start of the Second World War, records of clubs like West Ham were some way short of accurate; sometimes they are totally unreliable with precision in mind. Newspapers of the era were no better when it came to details about football. While things weren't quite so bad in the immediate postwar years, expectation of exactness in sports like speedway and football before the mid-1960s is a matter of a fair bit of hope and a modicum of blind faith, rather than living up to anything like a mirror of reality. I have been into the reasons behind this in other publications, and as such it would be redundant to repeat the same. However, it is as well to say that right up to the present day, authors, bloggers, amateur historians, and journalists have, predictably, taken such accounts (and that is what records are; not some sort of indelible photographic proof) as gospel and repeated them as 'facts'. This sort of 'received wisdom' is what becomes thought of as, and is too often taken for 'history'. To paraphrase French philosopher, historian of ideas, writer, political activist, literary critic and supporter of 'Les Dragons' of Stade Poitevin, Michel Foucault; documents are not monuments, they are just documents.

Thus, my own approach to research of this type is, while taking any record into consideration, in the last analysis, to rely more on the predominant personal testimony of players and supporters, many of the latter being my close immediate or extended family. More than a couple of the players of that era have corroborated Hurst's presence in the second leg of the FA Youth Cup Final of 1959, as have multiple contacts with fans who were either at the game or had close family who attended the match. And then there was Bronco.

What might have been

What was pretty much for sure was that the game was an exasperating encounter for the fledgling Irons. The pitch was in an awful state, and while it was said the home side were somewhat handicapped by the hard ground, preferring a heavier playing surface, after the first quarter of an hour they looked to be the livelier outfit on the night. Blackburn striker Alan Bradshaw's passing was deadly dangerous, but it seemed certain that West Ham would take the lead when centre-forward Beesley picked up a pass that left him in a one-on-one situation with Griffiths. Mike tried a crafty chip but it wasn't pitched high enough; the Blackburn goalkeeper simply plucked the ball out of the air. The lost chance can't be laid totally at the door of the young Hammer as the surface didn't favour anything too cleaver

The full-time whistle signalled the conclusion to a goalless stalemate aggregate situation. Thus tolled the allegorical bell of destiny that is extra time.

As 1965 FA Cup Final referee, West Bromwich-born Bill Clements' sublimely synchronised watches ticked the 11th minute of added time, Blackburn's Paddy

Daly struck the fateful if dubious blow; VAR would have shown him offside by a street today. Maybe.

The attack came from the left, the ball being pushed to Daly, probably something more than a couple of feet ahead of any Hammer. Cutting around Moore's attempt to stop him, he smacked the ball wide and to the left of Caskey. If the West Ham keeper had not been on the 'height-challenged' side for his position he might well have got to the shot, but he wasn't, so he didn't.

Retrospectively, the Hammers' cause had been lost with four minutes of the first half remaining. Rovers skipper Fred Pickering, a 1964 England hat-trick hero[3], handled the ball and the predictable penalty was awarded. Griffiths, who had previously played for Sheffield Wednesday, flinging himself right, had shown his anticipation to be equal to inside-left Smillie's powerful effort. Griffiths produced what was called in subsequent press reports a 'wonder save' and 'the finest of saves' in response to the neatly crafted strike by the promising young Hammer. The keeper's fist was to mark the end of West Ham's hopes. The bitterness of this blow was exacerbated by the denial of a clear penalty when, in the fourth minute, future Spurs defender Mike England had clearly handled the ball. But the luck of the Druids was with the Welsh lad who would win 44 caps for the land of his fathers, the match officials being blind to his sin.

One can speculate about what might have happened if the gods of the penalty box had been kinder to West Ham, allowing them to finish one or two goals ahead of their opponents, giving the Irons an aggregate victory. However, in terms of scoring opportunities the home side had done better in the second leg.

For all this, even Blackburn's local press gave the East Londoners a deal of credit. For example, one report told how the Hammers had the 'better footballing formation' and were 'clean cut in approach and more capable of finding their men'.

As it was, despite the combined and individual pace of the West Ham lads, the unarguable talent in their ranks, and the experience of the likes of Moore in the senior side, shots were noticeable by their lack. Certainly, it might have been hoped that the Irons would have taken greater advantage when, Bradshaw being distinctively physically shot with eight minutes left to play, Rovers had a player carried from the field. Billy Jervis, a 5ft 6in, slightly built Scouser, had been hobbled by severe abdominal cramp. Although Moore (who one local hack noted was possessed of 'a commanding physique') had been assigned to marshal him, Jervis had been as annoying to the West Ham defence as a wasp at a picnic.

At the same time, Beesley, while a constant threat to Rovers, was once more blunted by the commanding attention of Keith Newton.

---

3   A 10-0 drubbing of the USA in May of that year at Downing Stadium, Randall's Island, New York City

Thus, it was Pickering, in front of the thousands of supporters who populated the pitch after extra time was brought to an end, who received the trophy from Sir Stan. It must be said that West Ham had really lost the FA Youth Cup at least as much as Blackburn had won it, and sadly all the evidence points to that conclusion.

Totally out of character, Moore was enraged at the end of the game. The allowing of the 'offside' goal looked and felt profoundly unjust. His team-mates needed to drag him away from the referee, such was the ferocity of his protestations. As far as Bobby and the rest of the West Ham side were concerned, Daly hadn't been anywhere near being onside.

The Hammers, in both legs, had looked the slicker, classier outfit; for example, Woodley, with an amazing turn of speed, had more than tested the home defence, but sadly not much came of the dominance of the Isleworth boy. Cartwright, Beesley and Smillie combined well, moving the ball forward, but in the second leg they made little significant impression in dangerous areas.

Nevertheless, while Barrie Ratcliffe wasted opportunities for Rovers, being slow to shoot, lacking the pace that the Ewood supporters had come to expect of him, and Paddy Mulvey's performance was at best sporadic, the forward line failing to get it together, both sides had defended with tough, uncompromising brilliance. Moore had been on song as his side's pivot – the post-match reports noted his capacities and predicted a promising future for the sturdy blond boy. Right-back Cripps and goalkeeper Caskey were heroic, West Ham's custodian had twice charged off his line to save the Hammers, but it was Blackburn who had the defensive edge. England was dominant in the air, Newton shone, David Wells tackled like a demon, making a string of telling clearances, while Vincent Leach was the best wing-half on display that evening. However, Griffiths had been the ultimate obstacle to the young Irons. His denial of Smillie was to be the apogee of his footballing career. He made just two senior appearances for Rovers, before moving to Altrincham.

It has to be said that Blackburn had some outstanding players such as the likes of Mike England who later went on to have an exemplary career, while Keith Newton and Fred Pickering were both future England players; Newton played in the 1970 World Cup in Mexico.

The claret and blue boys were collectively sickened by the result, in particular Bobby Moore, but he knew that he and his players needed to learn from the defeat. He didn't believe Rovers were the better team, although he was to recognise that his side had not quite clicked in the way that they were capable of. Football is an atmospheric game; much is dependent on the collective mood of those interacting on the park. The Hammers had just not been 'on it' – sometimes there is little more explanation than that.

The *Stratford Express*, one of the top local newspapers on the West Ham patch, before naming Cartwright and Smillie as the stars in attack, with special mentions for impressive full-backs Harry Cripps and Jack Burkett, emphasised on 8 May 1959 just how close the Hammers had gone to ultimate victory, 'West Ham may well go down in history as the unluckiest FA Youth Cup finalists of all time … they lost by the only goal scored, somewhat desperately and with a strong suspicion of offside, in the tenth minute of extra time.'

Fourteen kids

West Ham called on 14 players throughout the tournament. As well as the dozen who turned out in both legs of the final, Bobby Keetch and Peter Reader appeared in prior rounds.

The young Irons played ten games during their run, scoring 27 goals while shipping just seven. Smillie and Beesley combined netted 21 times. Beesley's dozen, getting on the score sheet in every round before the final, made him his side's top marksman in the competition. Smillie trailed his strike partner by just three hits, the Arsenal keeper being the only one of his ilk not to be beaten by the blonde boy from the west Essex/East London borderlands.

The second leg of the final was the only match in which the Irons failed to score.

West Ham United in the FA Youth Cup 1958/59					
Date	*Opposition*	*Result*	*Round*	*Scorers*	*Home/ Away*
4 Oct 1958	Leyton Orient	7-0	First	Beesley 3 Smillie 2 Woodley 2	A
1 Nov 1958	Eton Manor	4-0	Second	Beesley 2 Smillie Cartwright	A
20 Dec 1958	Eastbourne United	6-0	Third	Beesley 2 Smillie 2 Bovington Moore (pen)	A
2 Feb 1959	Charlton Athletic	3-1	Fourth	Beesley Scott Smillie	H
18 Mar 1959	Aston Villa	1-1	Fifth	Smillie	A

11 Apr 1959	Aston Villa	3-2	Fifth (replay)	Beesley 2 Smillie (pen)	H
14 Apr 1959	Arsenal	1-1	Semi-final first leg	Beesley	H
23 Apr 1959	Arsenal	1-0	Semi-final second leg	Beesley	A
27 Apr 1959	Blackburn Rovers	1-1	Final first leg	Smillie	H
4 May 1959	Blackburn Rovers	0-1	Final second leg		A

Goals: Beesley 12, Smillie 9, Woodley 2, Bovington 1, Cartwright 1, Moore 1, Scott 1.

Appearances: Cripps 10, Burkett 10, Woodley 10, Smillie 10, Beesley 10, Cartwright 10, Scott 10, Hurst 9, Bovington 9, Moore 8, Caskey 6, Reader 4, Keetch 3, Brooks 1.

Of the dozen lads who donned the claret and blue in the FA Youth Cup Final in 1959, half of them would be eligible to turn out for the 1959/60 campaign. Geoff Hurst took over as skipper of a side that also included Beesley, Mick Brooks, Burkett, Caskey and Woodley.

Most of that team were England youth internationals: John Cartwright, Geoff Hurst, Bobby Moore, Peter Reader, Tony Scott, Andy Smillie, Derek Woodley.

Together they amassed 57 England youth caps. Moore, with 18 appearances, led the pack. No one had played more games for the young Lions, a record that endured 23 years until fellow Hammer Paul Allen broke it, winning 26 caps. Tony Scott (12 caps) and Reader (11 caps) were also a credit to their club.

All the achievements of West Ham's youngsters were formally overseen by Bill Robinson, designated by the club as the manager of the youth side, but the team was the creation of Malcolm Allison, together with the likes of Noel Cantwell and John Bond (as covered in *Young Bobby*). It is a testament to their contribution and efforts that of the 14 Hammers who did themselves proud as 'the lads of '59', only one, Frank Caskey, would fail to become a professional player. Nine would wear the crossed Hammers over their hearts at senior level. Out of their ranks emerged the core of West Ham's 1960s 'golden era'.

Together, Moore (647), Hurst (503), Burkett (185), Bovington (184) and Scott (97) contributed 1,586 first-team appearances for West Ham.

Beesley, Cartwright, Smillie and Woodley also got to make the first team at Upton Park. Beesley and Woodley both scored in their first outings.

Most of that FA Youth Cup Final team felt that they were the best youth outfit in England, but their loss was an important moment for Moore. It was the most significant game he'd played in for his club that far. Defeat was a blow for all concerned, having an impact on a lot of futures. Many years later, in a too-brief conversation about his work at Southend United, Bobby told me of something Noel Cantwell had said to him not long after that fateful game, 'If you fail to lose well, you lose the chance to learn how to win.'

If we can accept and use loss, not be drowned in it, all that's left to do with it is learn from it. Bobby elaborated, 'It's not the way you lose that's most important, it's what you learn from losing. Winning and losing are the same in as much as they both offer opportunities to learn how to win and how not to lose.'

You never saw Moore crying after a defeat, but if you took even a cursory look at his expression, you would know he was thinking; you would almost hear him learning, going over what he had experienced. To give a modern example, any F1 racing driver worth their salt is trained and trains themselves to do just that.

Derek Woodley, a team-mate of Moore's from the FA Youth Cup Final side, said Bobby

'was the best player I saw at Upton Park'. He added, 'I can't say I liked him as a bloke. He didn't have a football body, but he had a marvellous mind for the game.'

3
FLOODLIGHTS AND FIRST LOVE

The Southern Floodlight Cup semi-final was played out between the two legs of the FA Youth Cup, on 6 April 1959. With a plethora of absentees, Bobby was brought into what was a first-team game to face a strong Arsenal side. The Gunners would finish third in the First Division that season, behind champions Wolves and runners-up Manchester United.

The tournament, which had a deal of prestige and attracted some impressive crowds, ran from 1955 to 1960. Over those five competitions clubs from London, south-east England, and a small number of teams from the Midlands took part. The inaugural tournament was contested over the 1955/56 season, with the first teams of ten clubs involved . West Ham won the trophy that term. In its final season, 1959/60, the number of entrants had increased to 18. The other winners were Luton Town, Portsmouth, Arsenal, and Coventry City. In 1960, the competition gave way to the Football League Cup, which was open to clubs throughout the Football League.

The Southern Floodlight Cup operated on a straight knockout basis, with all ties being decided by single games, with replays if necessary. The final was fought out on the home ground of one of the competitors. From 1955/56 to 1958/59, there were four rounds including the final with an extra round in 1959/60 to accommodate the additional entrants.

Sixteen clubs took part in 1958/59: Aldershot, Arsenal, Brentford, Charlton Athletic, Coventry City, Crystal Palace, Fulham, Luton Town, Millwall, Orient, Portsmouth, Queens Park Rangers, Reading, Southampton, Watford, West Ham United.

The match report of the semi-final, headlined 'Lucky Arsenal!' appeared in West Ham's programme against Bristol City on 11 April 1959. It read, 'Despite some very wet weather a 15,681 attendance was at the Boleyn Ground last Monday evening to see the Southern Floodlight Cup. Undoubtedly many of them were attracted by the prospect of seeing Mel Charles make his first-team debut for the Gunners, although this to some extent did not fulfil the expectations of many of those present. However, Charles scored two goals (the first a 30-yard "dipper" after 25 minutes' play, the other with a "toe ender" in a goalmouth duel ten minutes after the interval) and these sufficed to give his side a 2-0 victory.

'However, the "lucky Arsenal" tag was very much in evidence on this occasion, for they not only survived two woodwork-rattling drives and a couple of goal-line interceptions, but had also to thank goalkeeper Jim Standen [a future Hammer] for a sterling display that kept his charge intact.

'On paper the North Londoners appeared to have a distinct "edge", for we were without three of the XI which had defeated Everton two days earlier, Noel Cantwell not being back from his Eire international duties, John Dick being "rested" for today's England v Scotland game and Johnny Smith being absent through army duty. We were further handicapped through an injury to Johnny Lyall which left us virtually "ten men" after 50 minutes, and knocks sustained to John Bond, Joe Kirkup and Andy Nelson only added to our disadvantage. Nevertheless, the whole of the Hammers XI put on a good show, and Ted Fenton was rather pleased with them for a performance that was by no means reflected in the result.'

Try a little Alps with you friends

The following month Bobby was playing with the Colts in a tournament in Switzerland.

Group games	Score	Scorers	Highlights
FRIBOURG (Switzerland)	2-0	Beesley, Scott	Unusually, Bobby took the corner that Beesley connected with to score the opening goal. The game was much closer than the eventual score suggests, Moore clearing off the line before a goal was scored.
West Ham: Reader, Cripps, Burkett, Bovington, Moore (c), Hurst, Woodley, Cartwright, Beesley, Smillie, Scott			
ZÜRICH (Switzerland)	2-1	Beesley, Scott	This was an exciting, back-and-forth game that could have gone either way, and it was probably West Ham's defence, with Moore holding the line, that was the difference between the sides.
West Ham: Reader, Cripps, Burkett, Bovington, Moore (c), Hurst, Woodley, Cartwright, Beesley, Smillie, Scott			

semi-final			The Hammers were desperately unlucky to lose this game. Both Moore and Scott were denied by the woodwork, while Beesley's perfectly good second was, grossly unfairly, called offside. The winning goal was something of a freak, a wicked deflection off Harry Cripps, effectively deciding the game late on. This was after keeper Reader was obliged to leave the field (feeling dizzy after a clash of heads) with Bobby putting on the gloves. Moore had made a couple of impressive saves before what turned out to be the winning goal.
VERONA (Italy)	1-2	Beesley	
West Ham: *Reader, Cripps, Burkett, Bovington, Moore (c), Hurst, Woodley, Cartwright, Beesley, Smillie, Scott*			
Third Place Match			Demonstrating a great deal of character, coming back from a morale-sapping defeat, the young Irons completely overwhelmed the opposition. Hurst's goal was ripe from the Grange Farm training ground, Geoff's timing was perfect moving on to Moore's 30-yard free kick.
ZÜRICH BLUE STARS (Switzerland)	4-1	Smillie 2, Beesley, Hurst	
West Ham: *Reader, Cripps, Burkett, Bovington, Moore (c), Hurst, Woodley, Bickles, Beesley, Smillie, Maxted*			

A couple of friendlies were played, The first with the tournament runners-up

Friendlies	Score	Scorers	Highlights
RUTI (Switzerland)	3-2	Beesley, Moore, Smillie	Against the tournament runners-up, any of West Ham's goals might have been rated the best of the Colts' tour. Beesley was impressive, keeping up his record of scoring in every game in Switzerland that far, while Smillie looked a class above any striker the lads had seen since leaving London. However, it was Moore's 25-yard drive that drew the sides level – described by the Rüti manager as a 'breathtaking effort'.
West Ham: Reader, Cripps, Burkett, Bovington, Moore (c), Hurst, Woodley, Cartwright (Brooks), Beesley, Smillie, Scott			
VADUZ (Liechtenstein)	5-0	Scott 2, Hurst, Smillie, Woodley	The very best of West Ham craft was presented in this game. Without taking anything away from the opposition, the Hammers made an exhibition of how the game should be played. The Irons' final goal tally could have stretched into double figures, but collectively they demonstrated what they had learned to become over the season, being almost liquid in their movement. Moore looked every inch the captain, seemingly at the hub of everything. His assists led to goals scored by Hurst and Woodley.
West Ham: Reader, Cripps, Burkett, Bovington, Moore (c), Hurst, Woodley, Brooks, Beesley, Smillie, Scott			

In Switzerland the Hammers' Colts finished in third place, playing against some estimable sides. They equipped themselves well, winning all but one of their games, and that to the eventual winners of the tournament.

It proved to be an invaluable experience for Bobby and the rest of the team, and he showed himself to be outstanding, playing at centre-half. Jack Burkett was to say how Bobby always appeared to have plenty of time on the ball and his distribution was 'immaculate'. For Jack, Moore was not prone to wasting passes; even as a teenager his economical but authoritative game made him an imposing presence.

Like many, Burkett has recalled that Moore, as a young man, was quiet, keeping himself to himself, but he was also a 'prodigious trainer'. Jack has told of how when training with the senior players, Bobby always listened, looking to pick up on things from more experienced colleagues.

According to Burkett, Bobby was able to 'see and interpret everything that was happening on the pitch in front of him', constantly seeking out space to pass into, freeing a team-mate and building play. For Jack, Moore was, from his earliest years at West Ham a 'great interceptor, one of the best of all time and that was an outstanding facet of his play'.

Urban spaceman

One of the most reoccurring themes in Moore's footballing life was that of 'space'. It is expressed as an aspect of practice, but also as a theory relating to strategy and tactics. The finding and using of space was a constant in Bobby's development as a player. The subject was central to Malcolm Allison's understanding of football, and something that Noel Cantwell, worked to make young players mindful of (both men were West Ham captains during Bobby's formative years). From Moore's time as an England youth player, Ron Greenwood reiterated, confirmed, and advanced the same approach: a consciousness of the pitch as a place where space is sought out, created, and used as traction, particularly when looking to convert defence into attack.

Space was a central feature within Moore's broad, mostly unspoken, philosophy of football as a game, but also as a confluence of intellect and physicality. This might be understood as being akin to a 'chess mentality' – the endeavour to put oneself in the best possible position, relative to where other players (pieces) are at any given moment.

Space might be taken as a metaphor of a view of the game as a multidimensional stage, more a theatre of ideas or opportunities than dreams. Like chess constitutes thousands of games within one game, football is a space full of shifting, transforming spaces, coming into, and going out of existence. As such, it reoccurs consistently in the analysis of Bobby's story.

This kind of perspective was something that Greenwood fostered. He spent more time than anyone else accompanying Moore on the road from good to exceptional.

For Ron, space didn't just appear – it had to be 'made'. Just waiting for a gap to arise is too much a matter of chance, according to Greenwood. That opportunity might not arise, so players were obliged to work to create room, to actively seek out and even create space. One way of doing this was by a side's attacking players making diversionary runs, causing opposing defenders to follow them. These 'runners' understood they were unlikely to receive the ball – the purpose was to be a lure for defenders, thus plying areas of the field open. This is something practiced across professional sports like basketball, American football and rugby, and has long been part of professional soccer. However it was Greenwood who made it a major factor of West Ham's play, turning the strategy into an orchestrated, crossfield, multifaceted practice.

Lightfoot Len

Moore had learned some useful things about movement from a champion ballroom dancer (although Bobby was tone deaf himself), Lennie Heppell. Len was featured on the BBC's *Nationwide* show in 1974 at the nightclub he and his wife and former dancing partner Molly ran in Hexham, Northumberland, the Fandango. Len, a mere 5ft in height having never previously touched a golf club until his 30s, had taught himself to become a leading player after his dancing career. He then went on to become accomplished at table tennis, ultimately coaching his daughter Maureen to international level.

Len possessed no sporting qualifications at all, but assisted several of the players at Upton Park with running technique. All his life Bobby had been ready to listen, and he would reserve judgement on most ideas until they were verified, so when Ron Greenwood brought Heppell to the West Ham training ground, he gave Len a chance.

Len told Moore he ran upright, like he had a coat hanger strapped to his shoulders. This made his running harder work and slowed him down. He suggested Bobby rolled his shoulders, but not his body. Following these instructions, Moore found he could make more repeat runs, taking less out of himself. Indeed, if you compare Bobby's gait at the start of his career with his later time in football, you can see something of this development. Heppell also taught Bobby to turn by moving his head first. Moore started throwing his head, and rather than falling over, it improved his balance.

Molly and Len were parents-in-law of future Hammer Bryan 'Pop' Robson, who also took advantage of Len's coaching while he was with Newcastle. 'Pop' was considered too slow in the penalty area, until Len took him in hand during the close season – at the end of the following term, Bryan had scored 30 goals.

Greenwood saw the personal attention and 'issue focus' that Len brought to training on an individual level was part of his success. Len helped several West Ham players, including Trevor Brooking. This was a facet of individual choreography, and Ron did something of the same thing with players, both in one-to-one situations (notably with Hurst and Moore) but also on a broader team level. He maintained that space continued to be just space as long as no one moved into it. He would point out that should a gap appear in an opposing team's penalty area, most strikers would be inclined to exploit it, but if a defender followed the attacker then the space no longer existed. Greenwood wanted his players not to make for space until the team were prepared to use it to the best effect – when a team-mate with the ball was in a place to make a pass, and attackers could see how the move would benefit the team's cause. This was a demand for 'intelligent,' 'synchronised runs', all over the pitch, avoiding thoughtless (merely hopeful) through balls and ultimately pointless, wasteful activity.

Greenwood drilled such underlying principles into his teams. What Ron was positing was an animated philosophy about the importance of taking up good positions and how critical that is. Together with the need to be continuously thinking about the whole game situation, this was a demand for a collective 'mindfulness' and interconnected awareness. The aim was for the players on the park to develop a 'hive mind', to work organically as a unit.

Hell for rubber

When the young Hammers got back to Upton Park from Switzerland, most were quickly brought down to earth (literally) as some went to work at the City of London cemetery in Manor Park, digging graves and looking after to the gardens. Bobby, Eddie Bovington, Andy Smillie, Jack Burkett, Tony Scott, Brian Dear, John Charles and future Millwall legend Harry Cripps all at some point worked at a company called William Warne Ltd, at the India Rubber Mills in Barking. The firm had been around since 1882. Over the years lots of young people from the district were to find work there, until in June 2000, when Icon Material Technologies (Holdings) Ltd purchased William Warne, changing the company name to Icon Warne. At the time there were 140 employees at the Barking site. The latter was closed in 2002 when Icon Warne based its production in Retford, Nottinghamshire. I was taken on for a while, but was sacked after a few weeks. I soon bounced back though.

When Bobby told Harry Cripps he was going to work in a rubber factory, Harry initially thought he meant the factory was made of rubber. In fact, it was involved in the manufacture of rubber products. Bobby's mum Doris had a few connections with the company and it was she who got the West Ham lads summer employment there. The plant wasn't far from the Moores' family home, so the boys would go back to Waverley Gardens for tea after they knocked off for the day. They all had great affection for Doris and Bobby's dad, 'Big Bob'.

Warne produced everything from tyres to the heavy-duty, industrial-strength condoms of the early 1960, but also some better than tidy footballers it would seem. Bobby also worked with Harry Obeney, a talented centre-forward and wing-half for the Irons, at the Industrial Hose Company, in Barkingside. A 'joy ride' around that establishment, in a little factory truck, with Andy Smillie and the gifted striker Tony Scott in tow, concluded with damage amounting to hundreds of pounds (Bobby ran over a massive industrial pipe). It's amazing there were no footballer fatalities among these young men indulging in such capers. At Warne, Cripps fell through the roof on one occasion – who knows what he was doing up there. Fortunately, 'Bulky' (as his fellow players knew him) landed on a pile of tyres – if they hadn't been there to break his fall, he would probably have pegged it, or, as Bobby had it, 'Unless he had been lucky enough to land on his head.'

Pat the Hammer

It's a constant fascination how people doing the things of everyday life can transform into cultural and national icons. We are entranced by stories of young people, living for excitement and fun today, undertaking what is necessary, and making what they can of it, transforming over a relatively short span of years to shine as the exceptions of their generation. Bobby was one such young person and Pat Booth, the author, photographer, and former model, was another. Born a couple of years after Bobby, she grew up in the same patch as him. She and her family lived above a pie and mash shop, with an outside loo. She was to remember her younger years as 'tough, cold, damp, and austere'. Her father worked in the docks, boxed at fairgrounds (she carried his towel), and helped her mother with her jellied eel business. As children Pat and her sister served on the stall outside Whitechapel station. When she was 13, her father gave her a gutting knife and told her, 'Now's the time for you to learn.' Pat didn't fancy that though.

Pat left school at 15 to earn her living as shop girl and waitress, until the head of a modelling agency saw her face as fitting the 'London look' of the era. There were the 'dollies', Pattie Boyd and Twiggy; the 'kooks' such as Grace Coddington; and the blonde, blue-eyed, posh-boned 'Chelsea girls', but Pat had something more convincing and unique. The famed snapper David Bailey liked her – her background was far rougher than that of the lad from Leytonstone. She became a Pirelli calendar girl, and adorned the covers of *Vogue* and *Harpers & Queen*, although she was most suited to *Nova*, a magazine for which she was shot wearing only a sheer bodystocking, printed with a tattoo pattern across the front, plus big, feathered wings.

Supported by her ambitious mum, in the 1960s Booth also posed for other top photographers, such as Norman Parkinson, and famously she was the model for Allen Jones's 'table', a woman on all fours, bearing a plate glass tabletop on her back. The image became a powerful metaphor for the budding women's liberation movement, symbolising how females were objectified and instrumentalised.

Later Pat became a photographer herself, taking pictures of such well-known figures as David Bowie, Bianca Jagger and Jean-Claude Duvalier, as well as Queen Elizabeth II and the Queen Mother. Her work has been displayed in the National Portrait Gallery' the *Sunday Times* and *Cosmopolitan*.

A lifelong Hammers fan, in the 1980s Pat turned her hand to writing racy and glitzy romance novels, partly inspired by her own glamorous lifestyle. She was published in both the US and the UK. She was, however, also a devout Roman Catholic and regular churchgoer. She provided assistance to women who became pregnant, but were unable to support a child.

Tina, Bobby's first wife, would become Pat's friend, and a great admirer of her photographic work.

Mummy's boy

Tina knew Bobby before he was hailed and recognised as exceptional. She has memories of him as 'bit of a mummy's boy', and it's true that for most of his life he respected Doris's place as the family matriarch. This was exemplified one Christmas when Bobby and a crowd of fellow Hammers went out at lunchtime to celebrate the festive season.

After Bobby and Tina were married, Christmas Eve always seemed to be a bit of a trial for the first Mrs Moore. There had been a couple of yuletides over the course of their married life when the turkey, in that era West Ham's annual Christmas present to playing staff, would go walkabout instead of coming home. Each time it would be spotted sitting on the bar somewhere, with Bobby ordering a lager for himself and a gin and tonic for the bird. The pairing would eventually find their way home, the turkey propped up in the front passenger seat of the Jag.

On a particular occasion Bobby and Tina were due to go to an evening 'do' in the West End, but by mid-afternoon, when he and the turkey still hadn't made it home, Tina began ringing round all his known haunts. Eventually she tracked him down to the Globe in Stepney and reminded him about the function.

'I'll be home in 20 minutes,' he promised.

Tina waited for an hour, then rang again. 'Don't worry,' said her increasingly merry husband, 'I'll finish my drink and be on my way.'

So she waited for another hour, then rang again. 'If you don't come home right now, I'll tell your parents to come and get you,' she told him. Even that peril didn't flush him out, so Tina carried out her threat. Doris and Big Bob duly set out for the Globe, and on arrival they advanced on Bobby from the rear. Doris laid a hand on his shoulder and said, 'Home, son.'

'Mum?!' exclaimed the errant Bobby as they escorted him out, protesting he wasn't a boy any more. Doris turned to the assembled company, 'He isn't usually like this, you know. He's been under the weather lately.' That was the excuse she always made when trying to convinced others Bobby wasn't pissed.

In her own way, Tina had been also strongly influenced by her very protective mum, Betty. Tina has told how she thought Betty felt guilty about leaving her when she was a child to go to work every day, and consequently Tina was frequently treated to breakfast in bed before her mum set off on her commute to work, so she would have understood a bit about Bob's relationship with his mother.

'The Ghost' cometh

Andy Smillie turned professional about the same time as Moore. This made room for other talented young players to join the ground staff. Among the newcomers were two local boys who had played together for England Schoolboys the previous season. One was the rumbustious attacking player Brian Dear, and the other was a lanky but elegant midfielder from Plaistow. Martin Peters was a player who epitomised everything about the type of football the Hammers were cultivating. He was almost certainly the most technically talented player in the UK of his era.

Peters would be nicknamed 'The Ghost' by Hammers fans, England supporters and the press, because of his penchant for appearing in the penalty box undetected. He was possessed of tremendous innate balance and dexterity, whereas Bobby, and the likes of Geoff Hurst, had to work hard to become the players the world would come to know. It was only when Bobby switched from centre-half to wing-half and later, under the tutelage of Ron Greenwood, moving to a somewhat deeper role, playing alongside the centre-half, that he really bloomed. Hurst started out as a wing-half who showed some ability venturing up the field, However he wasn't a strong defender, seemingly losing track of the ball when it was behind him. Greenwood worked with Hurst to convert him to a front-runner and from there he became the world-class forward we remember. Ron rarely gets any credit for producing England's goal machine, the man ultimately responsible for winning the World Cup in 1966.

When the ground staff boys came back from the dead (or the cemetery) and the world of rubber in July 1959 it was the first time that Moore, Hurst, and Peters trained together. Just seven years later they would be running around Wembley as the core of the global champions of football.

Out with a win

Bobby departed the 1950s with a taste of victory; the Colts had won the Floodlight Southern Junior Cup. The game had been delayed from the previous season because of fixture congestion at the end of the campaign, but only those players eligible for 1958/59 could play in the 14 October 1959 final. The delay allowed Peter Reader, the Hammers' keeper, to return from injury, displacing Frank Caskey.

West Ham lined up as follows: Peter Reader, Harry Cripps, Jack Burkett, Eddie Bovington, Bobby Moore, Geoff Hurst, Derek Woodley, John Cartwright, Mick Beesley, Andy Smillie, Tony Scott.

A Smillie penalty after quarter of an hour was all that separated the sides and gave the Irons a third win in three seasons in their fourth successive final appearance. The greater experience of the Hammers was the decisive factor. By that time they were all professional players; Chelsea fielded just five players from their professional ranks.

West Ham's journey to the final had been impressive. In the quartet of games in this competition the Hammers had conceded just three goals, while scoring 12, beating Millwall Colts 3-0, Fulham Colts 2-0, and then Reading Colts 6-3 in the semi-final.

Goals: Cartwright 5, Beesley 3, Smillie 2.
Appearances: Cripps 4, Burkett 4, Hurst 4, Woodley 4, Cartwright 4, Bovington 3, Beesley 3, Moore 3, Smillie 3, Scott 3, Caskey 2, Keetch 2, Brooks 2, Reader 2, McQuade 1.

As Moore moved into the 1960s he was a maturing player and leader. He had the respect of his peers and the acknowledgement of senior players who recognised his application and determination. For all this, his manager, Ted Fenton, continued to have reservations about the young man from Barking. This is hard to square from a distance; maybe Bobby's growing prestige disturbed Ted, perhaps he just didn't grasp the nature of Moore's drive and style, despite his achievements representing his country, impressing the likes of Walter Winterbottom and Ron Greenwood. I doubt all of this though. Fenton's misgivings were, by the coming of the end of the 1950s, lacking any reasonable explanation.

Courting

By that time Tina Dean, then Bobby's girlfriend, had left Ilford County High School[4] and had started work as a junior secretary at the Prudential Assurance Company in Holborn. Most evenings, when Bobby wasn't playing, he'd go 'up the city[5]' to meet her. Friday evenings during the season were off limits as Moore had to prepare for matches the following day. Sunday, 6 January 1974 was the historic day which saw four FA Cup third round ties played, the first match on a Sunday; Cambridge United v Oldham Athletic, which kicked off in the morning, marked the start of 'sabbath soccer'. So Friday night was when Tina could catch up with friends, but she would drive her mum mad because she'd constantly be on the telephone, talking to Bobby for hours. She understood her boyfriend to be bashful and not altogether confident in the relationship stakes, but they grew closer by the week, and she could see he was resolute in succeeding in football.

There was a lot of fun in their relationship. Bob would kid Tina that the motivation for him asking her to dance when they first met was that her mates were too short for him, and he chose her solely on the basis of her height. Affectionately he called her 'Pet' or 'Teen', later 'Percy', which was usually shortened to 'Perce'. However, as often he would refer to her as 'My Princess', and for sure, Tina ruled Bobby's heart.

For all his macho credentials as a footballer, Bobby was not typical of most young men of his generation or origins. He once gifted Tina with a skirt and paper nylon petticoat, which he had bought himself, something way out of many men's comfort zone at the time. He was also happy long into their relationship, well into his career as England captain, to help Tina do her hair, bleaching her roots and so on. Bobby loved going shopping with Tina, particularly for clothes. Even well into the 1970s, that wasn't a role associated with red-blooded males, certainly not those brought up in postwar, working-class East London.

Tina has had it that Bobby was always 'mannered and manicured', having a strong feminine side. I understand her point. Perhaps this is related to the striving for perfection that is akin to the pursuit of art; very few of us, at core, are psychologically 'unigendered', but men of Bobby's class background and generation, coming out of East London and its environs, would not be encouraged

---

4   Unlike me, but like Moore, Tina took, and passed the 11-plus and got her O-levels – I got barred from even attempting it! Maybe the powers that be thought I'd pass – and that wouldn't have done at all would it?
5   In East London we always went 'up' the city or 'up west', even though it should be 'over' instead of 'up'. One only went 'over' where it was either 'my place' or 'your place'. As far as the East End was concerned, pretty much everywhere else was 'up' except 'down south', which was either a wasteland (like South London, which doesn't really exist, it's 'north Kent') . Anywhere you went on holiday was 'down', even if it was 'up north'.

socially to display any hint of what might be called 'feminine' traits. But my father wasn't too far from what Tina describes in relation to Bobby's 'feminine' side. Dad was a huge, strong, hardworking man, well known and respected in the district, but he thought nothing of buying my mum's lingerie when she just didn't have the time. He painted landscapes and was an incorrigible romantic, readily shedding a tear provoked by sentimental music or a nostalgic moment. Like Moore he came from a very matriarchal family background, and his mum was born in Barking, so maybe that's an influence too.

What is expected of men, maybe particularly those from British working-class backgrounds, was, and really to some extent still is, the very forms of stereotypical behaviour they are often accused of. They are, to an extent, weaned to conform to these tropes of what it is to be 'masculine'. Personally, after a lifetime of consideration, I think it's a crock of shit. A few years ago, I was listening to BBC Radio 4, a discussion on *Woman's Hour*. A section of this was devoted to a rather insistent lady repeatedly stating that 'women think differently to men', that their 'brains are different'. She provided no evidence and no men were included in the conversation. This to me felt incongruous. It echoed what the misogynistic societies of the past and versions of religion have touted for millennia about women – and made the tiny jump from 'different' to 'inferior' possible. As soon as you create such dichotomies, premised on vague biological claims, or really any spurious principle, you create a 'them' and 'us', and in our society this is usually ordered into a hierarchy. This, almost inevitably, pans out as an adversarial situation, couched in prejudice, inequality and the forms of subjugation and oppression that go along with such environments.

But it doesn't need to be this way. Our actions and attention to our emotions can avoid this wasteful way of being. Bobby loved to buy Tina gifts, like the tortoiseshell powder compact he got for her, not long after they had started 'courting' (as dating was called in those days). Once, on the way home from a night out in London's theatreland, the couple found a shop selling tiny glass animals – they were quite fashionable *objets d'art* at the time. Later in the evening the shop was still open, so Bobby went inside and bought one of these diaphanous creatures for Tina. That was the first time he told his teenage beau of his love for her.

In the mists of their amour, the last bus home departed without them. Tina thought Bobby might be frustrated, maybe annoyed, at having to walk her home. It would take a couple of hours, then he'd have another trek of about an hour to get himself back to Waverley Gardens. He told her he was so happy it didn't matter. When they got to Tina's home in Iford, before departing he said, 'Goodnight

Princess,' and announced that he was going to use the route back to his parents' place as a 'training jog'.

Tina has confessed that she found Bobby a bit 'square' when they first met, a term in the last part of the 1950s which meant something like 'conventional' and a little unexciting. This was probably true and perhaps part of the consequence of leading a disciplined lifestyle relative to most East London lads at the time. Sometimes Bobby seemed not much more than a baby compared to other boys Tina had dated. However, although a tad conservative and unworldly, Bobby was a romantic, and he had good taste. He would often send Tina flowers and place little *billets-doux* in the pocket of her coat.

From the start of their relationship, Tina found Bobby attractive; the striking man to be was a good-looking boy. Although he had the odd run-in with a rogue pimple, he didn't suffer the common plague of adolescent acne, so often the curse of young men. He was a good dancer (he strove for perfection in whatever he did) and the couple would kiss in time to the music. It was heady stuff, although it was so innocent. Betty was annoyed when Tina told her about this, saying, 'You weren't brought up to be a floozy!' She was right. Tina was relatively inexperienced, but how does one get experience? She and Bobby did their courting in the pre-contraceptive pill era. A girl she had been to school with died after a back-street abortion. Tina read about it in the local paper and felt horrified and frightened. Betty's cautionary words were echoed by Bobby's mum. The first night Tina stayed at the Moores' home she was put in the 'box room'. Doris let her know that her son was 'a good boy' and said, 'Any girl who gets my Robert into trouble will have me to deal with.' But Tina was never going to make mistakes of that type. She was 17 when she went on holiday with Bobby to Italy, and they slept in separate bedrooms. Tina was always going to keep to the straight and narrow with regard to their relationship, although in fairness, that was the only way he knew.

Tina grew up on the edge of East London. Ilford wasn't that far from Bobby's home in Barking, but that part of Essex was definitely regarded as socially a cut above the areas to the immediate west and south, being quite middle-class (from 1950 to 1966 the Conservatives held electoral sway in the district). In those days its long High Street was looked on as a notable shopping Mecca. About halfway along the thoroughfare was the boy-meets-girl factory, dance hall and theatre of Saturday night dreams, the Palais-de-Danse (or as locals knew it 'Ilford Palais') where Bobby and Tina first set eyes on each other.

Tina's first home was a semi in Christchurch Road, Ilford. Betty and Tina lived downstairs, her aunt Molly, uncle Jim and their three children – Jimmy, Marlene and Jenny – lived upstairs. The house wasn't divided formally into separate flats.

Jenny was three years younger than Tina and more like a little sister than a cousin. Unlike the Moores and my own family, Betty's family were evacuated to Cornwall during the war.

Tina's father had left the family very early in her life, so Betty had to earn a living. Molly returned to Essex to childmind Tina. It was a very female-dominated environment. After Tina's dad departed, it was a long time before Betty had another serious relationship. She was the driving force in Tina's life, and the girl grew up without much experience of men. But Betty was determined to make sure her kid would maximise her chances in life. She had paid for Tina to have elocution lessons[6], and guided her to modelling agencies. There was no doubt that Tina had the right qualities to make it in that sphere.

Tina and Betty's part of the house had a large living room at the front, with a smaller room to the rear of the house, which served as Tina's bedroom. Also on the lower floor was a scullery (that's what everyone I knew as a kid called it – I later learned that others know that room as the 'kitchen'). There was another large room, Betty's bedroom, at the back. This had French doors that opened on to the garden. The place, like many at the time, had a cellar.

With her mum at work, when Tina started school, she was a 'latchkey' kid. For some years she often had trouble reaching the key, so she'd gain entry via the coal hole (a shoot at the front of the house where the coalman emptied deliveries of coal that cascaded into the cellar).

The toilet was outside but the bathroom was upstairs. Betty and Tina would visit Molly to take a bath once a week. On the other days they used a tin bath that needed to be filled by kettles of boiled water. Occasionally mother and daughter would save time and energy by visiting Ilford Baths – which in those days did include actual bathtubs. Tina was to remember the shouts of, 'More hot water for number six!' with a touch of nostalgia – but just a touch.

Tina was raised with love, tolerance, and affection. She remembered her years in Christchurch Road with fondness, a time full of laughs and a lot of fun. Like Bobby, thanks to her mum's efforts, she was well-mannered and polite. Betty also taught her girl the best things in life needed to be more appreciated than expected. However, early on Tina had a work ethic that would always enable her to get what she wanted for herself, but she was good at appreciating the efforts, kindness, and generosity of others. Sir Geoff Hurst recalled a Christmas conversation with

---

6   Today, people often balk at such a prospect, perhaps seeing it as a kind of inverted snobbery, but the nature of British society at that time, dominated by class prejudice, made it sensible to change your accent, because if was anything like mine, it was a disadvantage from the get-go. My manager in my first job in the academic world was keen for me to undertake a similar route to the one Betty sent Tina on. I avoided it sadly and have for ever been the unreconstructed Eliza Doolittle I was and am today.

Bob. Geoff talked about his intention to buy Judith, his wife, a new Hillman Imp (the modest but fashionable run-around at that time). Moore responded saying, 'Bloody hell! 'I'll have to buy Tina a coach.'

Tina was a well-brought-up lass – Betty did a great job, it has to be said, against all the odds. The world was a narrow-minded place when Tina was born, and it stayed that way well into her 20s. People and institutions were cruelly prejudicial and condemning of single parents, and of children without fathers. From this place in time, for me, the likes of Betty were fighters and unsung heroines, the seeds of the nascent feminist movement; they might have deserved a medal, but they certainly deserved better.

Early on in Bobby's relationship with Tina, Betty assessed him to be a decent lad. She soon understood that his parents had a long and committed relationship, so Bobby had the kind of solid family life she wanted for daughter. What she didn't want Tina to experience was the rocky relationships she had endured. The boy was attractive, well-mannered, upright, and respectful. However, he was also charming, with a slightly mischievous twinkle in his eye, which was supplemented by a ready, attractive smile, so unsurprisingly Betty quickly grew to love Bobby, a feeling reciprocated by the young man. Indeed, Tina sometimes teased her fella, telling him she sometimes felt Bobby loved Betty more than her , although Bobby maybe was a little bit in love with Betty.

Betty was a very indulgent mother, but she was close to draconian about table manners. When her girl was young, should Tina foul meal-time decorum, she was swiftly despatched from the table. Bobby, who was dazzled by Betty's clear class, set enthusiastically about brushing up his style in the face of the refinement of his girlfriend's mum. He was very keen to be correct in everything he did, so he taught himself a range of formal etiquette, mostly by watching and learning. He was naturally polite, but now he was adding polish to his manner.

Betty knew things about the world and how to behave in ways that would, 60 years ago, help anyone get on. Bobby had an appetite for learning from others about practically anything, because he wanted to be the best at everything. He realised that Betty was much more erudite and sophisticated than his own family. Born Elizabeth Wilde, she grew into a beautiful and young woman, with an attractive and intelligent sense of humour. Like her daughter, she never really lost her looks. The pair would walk down the road together and men would whistle at her, but later also probably Tina. Bill Larkin, a wealthy West Ham fan whose family had made their money from peanuts and later selling sweets[7], would regularly tell Tina that while she was a good-looking woman, 'You're not a patch on your mum yet.'

Betty was a great cook, bright and a good listener. When the time came for Bobby to introduce his parents to the mother of the girl he loved, he bought gin and wine for them to serve. Betty was alert to the fact that Doris and Big Bob were teetotallers, so when asked if she wanted a drink she replied, 'I'd love a cup of tea.' Equally keen to impress, Doris came back with, 'Cow's milk, sterilised or condensed?' That became a running joke between Bobby and Tina whenever anyone asked what they would like to drink, although until I was about 20, outside of one or two more continental cafes, I was never to drink a cup of tea coloured with anything but sterilised milk!

Tina recognised that Bobby's parents were good people, and she was conscious she would need to put Doris's mind at rest that she was going to look after her boy. It took a while before the two women could feel close to relaxed in each other's company – Tina was faced with the challenge of matching Mrs Moore's standards. Like most people, she got on with Big Bob almost immediately; it was he, along with Doris, who took Tina to Upton Park for the first time. She had never been to a major football match before and was taken by the size of the crowd. It was her first experience of seeing tens of thousands of people in one place. They sat in 'D' Block with all the other players' families, behind the directors' box, in what us North Bank wallahs knew as the posh bit of the Boleyn Ground; the West Stand[8]. She noticed that Doris hardly took her eyes off Bobby throughout the match. She repeatedly yelled, 'Unload him! Unload him!' Tina took this to be technical terminology. I guess in a way it was.

---

7   Joe Larkin started the business with a peanut stall in Rathbone Market, Canning Town, and came to be known as 'The East London Peanut King'. According to my dad, who ran a stall in the same market, Joe was a 'careful' man, not associated with shelling out…
8   Later named the Dr. Martens Stand

4
INTO THE '60S

As the 20th century moved on, and the 1950s, almost inevitably, gave way to the '60s, the price of a ticket at Upton Park was among the highest in the country, something that was to remain consistent into the future.

The Irons had started the 1959/60 season well. Leicester were beaten 3-0 at Upton Park on the opening day, wins over Burnley and Preston followed. The Hammers' first reversal came in September as Leeds visited Upton Park and took the game 2-1. That match was the last for long-term club servant, custodian of the rigging, Ernie Gregory. He subsequently took over as club coach, focusing on the development of the goalkeepers.

The meeting with Tottenham on 9 September at White Hart Lane, which finished 2-2, attracted a gate of 58,909. Ten days on, 54,349 saw West Ham give the blues to the Blues of Stamford Bridge with a 4-2 defeat of their hosts.

November started with a trio of wins for the rampaging Irons; Manchester City were done 4-1, there was a 3-1 victory at Arsenal, and a John Dick hat-trick against Wolves at Upton Park sent the Hammers faithful away with a 3-2 win in their respective 'skys'.

Dick was one of the most 'enthusiastic gamblers' to ever grace the Boleyn Ground. Ted Fenton had arranged for all the players to be provided with luncheon vouchers[9] that were mostly traded in at Phil Cassettari's cafe on Barking Road. The majority of the lads tucked into massive fry-ups, including huge doorsteps of bread and butter, all washed down by bucket-sized cups of sweet tea. The notion of a 'footballer's diet' would have been an anathema in those days, but that aside, for most of the single lads, that was likely to be their only square meal of the day. Bobby however was quite careful about what he ate. He knew he put on weight relatively easily, so would trade a good half of his vouchers for cash, although Dick would exchange the lot and therefore go hungry, but have a couple of more bob to

---

9   A luncheon voucher was a paper ticket used by some employees in the UK to pay for food from cafes and restaurants. It allowed companies to subsidise midday meals (luncheons) for their employees without having to run their own canteens. The scheme dated from 1946, when food rationing was still in force following the end of the war. The government granted an extra-statutory tax concession, believing that this would help citizens afford healthy meals. Under the concession, luncheon vouchers were free of income tax and national insurance contributions up to the value of three shillings (15 pence) a day. The initial level of 2s 3d (11.25p; £5.50 in 2023 equivalent) was increased in 1948 to level of 3/- (15p; about £6 in 2023), but was not later adjusted for inflation. The concession was abolished, 15p per day having become a trivial amount, from 6 April 2013.

have a few extra bets on the greyhounds at West Ham stadium (in Custom House, a brisk 25-minute walk or short trolly bus ride from Upton Park).

Smith

On 17 October 1959, at Goodison Park, Moore was brought back into West Ham's First Division side, covering for John Smith, who was involved in a reserve international at Ninian Park, Cardiff, a meeting with Welsh counterparts.

Five minutes remained of a goalless match when Bobby carried the ball up the right wing. He passed to Andy Smillie, who pushed the ball to Malcolm Musgrove. The winger sent a left-footed shot under the diving body Toffees' keeper Albert Dunlop; perhaps he was 'tiring', but he, along with the rest of his team-mates, failed to bounce back, making the game something of a dead rubber for the home side, giving the Londoners the win.

Smith returned the following week for the 1-0 defeat of Blackpool at Upton Park. Bobby was once more consigned to duty in the reserves, as Ken Brown won what was to be his only England cap against Northern Ireland at Wembley.

By that point it was Smith who stood between Moore and a place in the first team. A thick-set wing-half, as the 1960s dawned Smith was on the cusp of being selected for England. Up to the end of November of that season he, along with the rest of the side, was doing well, and it seemed Bobby was fated to languish in the second string.

However, Moore's next opportunity came by way of a friendly meeting with FC Austria. Smith had been selected by the FA for a game against the RAF. The visitors sent out seven internationals at Upton Park, but the Hammers bettered them, 2-0. Bobby's assist led to a Malcolm Musgrove goal. But once more, the 20-year-old from E1 came back to reclaim the left-half position in the Irons' first XI.

Those were the years when West Ham's reputation for unpredictability was fully justified. By November they were top of the First Division, having lost only four times in 18 outings. But they would do what they seem to have always done and continue to do now; play well when faced with the better sides and fuck up against ordinary and mediocre outfits.

As leaders West Ham went to Sheffield Wednesday with their tails up, but left with their heads down on 28 November. Wednesday had been 4-0 up after the first half; the Irons made their disconsolate way out of the Steel City on the end of a 7-0 drubbing. A fortnight later another journey north ended with Blackburn doling out a 6-2 thrashing.

West Ham's confidence seemed to have been shot after Burnley's 5-2 humiliation of their hosts on the second day of the 1960s. The FA Cup brought no relief.

Following a 1-1 draw at the Boleyn Ground, Huddersfield, relegated the previous term but inspired by the youthful Denis Law, won 5-1 in the replay.

Three days after that debacle, Moore got a game at Elland Road. This seemed to change little as the Hammers went down 3-0. Yorkshire was taking a toll on the East Londoners. Bobby kept his place for the Upton Park encounter with Bolton, but the 2-1 defeat left his side in slough, seemingly having no way out of the losing spiral. However, Bobby must have been doing something right as he hung on to the number six shirt for the match that saw Chelsea venture into East London. Full-back John Bond, in desperation, was shifted into the centre-forward role. He claimed a hat-trick in the 4-2 win over the Pensioners, and went on to get three more goals over the following five games. The *Stratford Express* had it that Bobby and Ken Brown had 'averted disaster'.

For all that, Bobby was dropped for the encounter with Newcastle that saw West Ham beaten 5-3 at Upton Park. Goalkeeper Noel Dwyer was the fall guy and was ousted. Brian Rhodes protected the Irons' nets over the final 15 games of the increasingly fraught campaign. After defeat on the road to Nottingham Forest at the start of March, Moore was again drafted into the side for the Boleyn Ground draw with Everton and the defeat at The Hawthorns.

Something clearly had to be done. As the first whispers of spring crept up the Thames, a cash-plus-exchange deal with Tottenham brought centre-forward Dave Dunmore to East London. This was the arrangement that took John Smith to White Hart Lane. Smith had wanted away for a while, seeing Upton Park as not being the best place to build his future. His transfer request was growing mushrooms by the time he rushed into the arms of Bill Nicholson.

The move to N17 didn't turn out to be the transformative excursion for Smith that he had probably hoped for, becoming one of the most expensive reserve players at the time. The plan was that he would step into Danny Blanchflower's golden boots; however, those clogs were a bit too big for the Shoreditch lad. Smith's departure from Upton Park effectively cleared the way for Moore, although Bobby might have felt a tinge of envy as he had an admiration for Spurs and the football they played. He saw Smith as a good player and wasn't surprised when he made the shift to Tottenham; it was an appreciably bigger club, although the timing was a bit odd. The North Londoners were on the verge of winning their historic First Division and FA Cup double, which would send them into the European theatre, and while Smith was a very good performer there were other perhaps more 'attractive' candidates for the White Hart Lane stage.

If Smith had not traversed the babbling waters of the Lea, he would have likely proved a big obstacle to Bobby's continued advance at West Ham. Moore was himself to assert, 'If John hadn't have gone to Spurs I might have been a reserve footballer who threw in the towel.' However, when the man who had won an England under-23 cap against France in November 1959 moved to Tottenham to contest for the role of displacing the player who in 1958 captained his country to the quarter-finals of the World Cup in Sweden, the first Northern Irishman to achieve half a century of caps when he played against Wales in 1962, with Dave Mackay, the skipper of the Scottish national team, retrospectively a task one might not wish on one's worst enemy, Moore was to once more take his chance. Looking back, he was to say, 'You've got to be lucky even if you know you're good enough, to take the chance if it comes.'

For many of the Irons faithful the loss of Smith was a step backwards, but for Moore it was good news. He later said, 'Once I got back in the team, I was determined never again to be a reserve player. That is soul-destroying.'

Towards the end of 1959/60 West Ham had played some good football, but over the season 91 goals were scored against them. They had lost 16 games after November and only managed one win in the final eight fixtures. Five were lost. Moore played in the last seven matches of the season as the Hammers finished in 14th place. Only eight points separated the bottom nine teams. It was just as well there was so much crap in the First Division that season, as the Irons concluded their efforts just four points clear of relegated Leeds. It had been a disappointing end to what had started as a promising campaign, having been top of the table early on. Promoted Aston Villa and Cardiff City replaced relegated Leeds and bottom club Luton in the First Division.

Malcolm Musgrove was West Ham's top scorer with 15 goals. He missed only one game all season and was named 'Hammer of the Year'.

Lingering doubts

Like many, Moore found himself, at times, feeling that West Ham lacked the ruthlessness that comes from the desire to push forward at every opportunity. On too many occasions the Hammers had literally taken their collective eye off the ball and so the ultimate prize. The team had been persistently playing long balls with unsuccessful results. Moore saw that the club was low on ideas, some thought this was part of the motivation for Smith making his exit. Moore and other Academy graduates became more and more openly critical of strategies, tactics, and the management generally.

Bobby came to Upton Park's senior side with predictable humility and modesty. Perhaps the most enduring image of Moore in memories of West Ham and England fans was of him leading his teams on to the park, but in the early part of his career he had a propensity to be the last man to take to the field.

'Don't ask me why,' he had said. 'It just has to be that way. I am always the last out. I don't know how it began … nor am I normally superstitious. Call it a habit … Things become drill during a successful run.' That's probably true, but success had been a long way off for West Ham as the prospect of the 1960s opened.

As a schoolboy and youth, Bobby had played at centre-half; however, for England and West Ham he was to take the role of wing-half or left-half, although he was quite at home at right-half, the position he would take with credit at the World Cup in 1962. For all this, he will for ever be remembered as a commanding and insightful sweeper, and as the new decade dawned he really started to cultivate that role.

The former winger Johnny Hartburn, who had played with distinction for Millwall, QPR and Orient, after a spying mission to Upton Park a week before West Ham's FA Cup tie at Brisbane Road in January 1964, said of Moore, 'That fellow Moore will be playing until he's 92. He doesn't break sweat – and yet he doesn't miss a thing … there's something different about him that's hard to put your finger on, but he has an effect across the park, on both teams. He's a bit frightening.'

Hartburn was spot-on, but there was more to Moore than this. His integrity was towering. On and off the field Bobby was always perfectly turned out. Never would he be seen playing with his shirt outside of his shorts. This attention to appearance had its origins in the straightforward disciplines he honed from his earliest days. These qualities were the bedrock of his overall surety, which caused others to look to him, follow his direction and lead – but as Hartburn indicated, there was a hint of intimidation about him; detached, aloof, yet taking everything in, and so totally involved.

Breaking into the first team, Moore brought these foundational assets with him; such attitudes (like less positive ones) tend to fill the void in moral and ethical vacuums. All groups, but especially teams, to function at a high level, need a 'way of being' – a clear boundary around their behaviour and the means they require to strive to realise objectives. This is what Moore started to bring to the West Ham side.

Over the years, I have wondered if this fuelled Ted Fenton's unease about Moore. He would not be the only one to see the germ of greatness in the young man, although people with such insight were rare during Bobby's earliest years at Upton Park. In terms of attitude, Bobby carried with him something of the legacy of Malcolm Allison who, even after he left the club, maintained contact with and influence over an appreciable number of the playing staff, and especially Moore. Allison had always been something of a potential nemesis to Fenton, but at the same time he was central to any success West Ham had achieved while Ted was manager; for Fenton 'Big Mal' played the role of both angel and demon

Allison's departure from West Ham, which coincided with Moore's rise to first-team status, left a definite leadership vacuum. Many involved with the club, outside the boardroom, would have been in favour of Allison taking over the manager's role sooner rather than later, so any potential or actual ally of his could easily have been seen as a 'fifth columnist' in Fenton's mind. While Ted might not have been totally conscious of this, as the decades overlapped, the ignominious end-of-season results, coupled with player dissatisfaction, would have logically stoked any potential paranoia, a condition that any top-flight manager may need to learn to live with. As many others however have buckled underneath the burden of the insecurity the threat of usurpation engenders.

More subtly, Bobby represented the future, while Fenton had become a relic of the past, having probably gone as far as he could go in the modern game. Somewhere in his mind and the collective consciousness of the club, while this might have been resisted, it would have been understood. Organisations have elements of their culture that are unconscious; the way things are done dominates what can be achieved.

'Football's is all about goals' (?)

When I was young, one of our teachers took PE lessons. I'll call him 'Mr Koch'. He wasn't really a PE teacher as we didn't have one, he just oversaw the cricket and football – nearly always in a brown three-piece suit. In truth though, apart from being obliged to do handstands, cricket and football was about it for PE for boys at Greengate Primary, West Ham.

Mr Koch sort of adopted one of the more outstanding sports stars in our 200-strong ranks. The lad was making his mark in the junior football scene from about eight years old. Let's say his name was 'Frank'.

Frank and his parents started to become 'special people' in the school, and Frank, who in all fairness wasn't at the front of the queue when the raisins were being added to the bread pudding, was summoned to the front of almost every event.

Once, the assistant deputy to the chair of the board of governors (who knew that such a dignitary existed?) presented the school with about a dozen multi-coloured plastic buckets. The bloke's name was Fred Finn, I recall because he had a 'bric-a-brac'[10] stall in Rathbone Market, Canning Town. He was, to put it mildly,

---

10   A term that covers a multitude of sins, but what my plain speaking paternal grandmother would call 'a load of old shit'

a 'portly' figure, known locally as 'Fat Freddy Finn'. I wasn't that impressed with the donation to be honest – they were the sort of thing my dad gave away as a trader in Queens Road Market[11] (a three-minute walk from the Boleyn Ground) when people bought a mop and a bar of carbolic. But during the school assembly we were all called to applaud, showing our gratitude for said buckets. Well, what does it take to show a bit of appreciation? Buckets don't grow on trees do they!

Frank got called up to say a few words, and then good old Freddy asked him what team he wanted to play for eventually. Without missing a beat Frank piped up 'Man U' to the shock and consternation of the bucket-giver, who started to rattle on, tongue-in-cheek about 'the good ol' Ammers' and local support, jumpers for goalposts etc. Mr Koch interceded, relegating local fidelities to their place in the reality stakes by stating, 'Football's all about goals. We know that don't we Frank!'

Even at that tender age, for me there was something wrong about this proposition. Perhaps I was already imbrued in the 'West Ham Way' (we had just won the FA Cup after all), but I was brought up with loyalty as probably the central tenet of personal and family values, so I guess it was inevitable that Mr Koch's footballing philosophy was not going to sit well with me. I wouldn't have been in a position to articulate my entire value system at that point, what football is and has always been for me, something personal, but also communal, solidly related to identity – who 'I' and 'we' are, and want to be. But how do you express, in a few words, that at its best, played by its best, the game, like any collective activity, can offer a part of the means to learn how to live? It's more than goals, if it isn't, then it's not much, and we know that's not so. If it were otherwise no one, at the time of writing, would support any club but Manchester City (or 'Oil United' as they are becoming known).

All that is a tad pretentious maybe, but as kids we use what is around us to shape our values, our hopes, and our being. That isn't just about gain and doing others down; there is something about being impacted by why and how things are done, how they look and work.

Ultimately, Frank spent his school years doing not much else other than scoring goals. His family kicked up a fuss when he was sent to the same seat of childhood learning as me. Burke Secondary Modern was shit at football (and most things other than causing trouble) so he was consigned to the other side of the borough to play for the 'big' footballing school.

The next time I saw Frank was when Burke played his side in the early rounds of a local school cup game. As it was taken from the get-go that we were doomed, few of our better players (I not only use the term relatively, but permissively;

---

11   He also traded at Rathbone Market

hey, that's just the way I roll) turned up for the match, so the desperate and the deadbeat were recruited to the Burkeian cause. In truth the only reason I was there was as punishment for collective study-based misdemeanours – under the watchful eye of Mr Peters, a radical, left-wing teacher, with severe Mod overtones (dark-haired, good-looking bastard, of the Scouse persuasion, the girls swooned over him).

As we were gathering at the hub of junior football in the manor, Southern Road playing fields in Plaistow, while I was having a fag on the touchline, for some contorted and perhaps debauched reason, or maybe just thinking I needed humbling, Mr Peters informed me that I would skipper our side of dimwits and reprobates.

The recourse of 'Fuck me sir!' having fallen on deaf ears, I looked for the worst player of all the worst players in East London lined up for my selection to play in goal. I chose Timmy Scobie, a little, scrawny kid, who was known, for obvious reasons, as 'Skinny Boobie'. He was the clear choice, being readily kitted out with a pair of driving gloves, either one of which he could have used as a sleeping bag, and a huge flat cap, reminiscent of tweed duvet (to keep the non-existent sun out of his eyes).

As we strung ourselves across the pitch in my famous 8-1-1 formation, some old guy watching from the touchline with a dog, that looked like a cross between a cocker spaniel and a pork pie, maybe with a touch of possum thrown in, shouted, 'No fuckin' chance!' – always good to have critically analytical support.

Well, from the first whistle, Frank was at us, marshalling an all-out attack, bearing down on the evermore vulnerable looking Boobie. Shot after shot went in, but it seemed on that day, in that place, our trusty custodian was determined to keep a clean sheet. In fact he was like a very short, scrawny Lev Yashin (or a frail bird in big hat and gloves). The will-o'-the-wisp-like Timmy flew around his goal like an emaciated, but demonically possessed sparrow, time after time denying access to his domain.

As the final whistle went the tie was goalless.

In such games, in such times, the facilitating adults were in no mood to hang around any longer in the frozen, mud-ladened winter of the steel-grey docklands than absolutely necessary, so not only was extra time never on the cards, the drama of a protracted penalty shoot-out wasn't going to happen either. The match would be settled by the captains taking sudden-death penalties! Me v fuckin' Frank. Great!

So, up marched Frank, ball under his arm, to face our undernourished champion of E13, who now looked microscopic between the posts – like a starving ferret framed in the entrance to a cathedral.

The gifted striker, armed with his dreams of greatness, placed the ball carefully on the smudge in the mud that passed for the penalty spot. He struck a powerful drive high and left of our trusty if gaunt stopper. The effort had 'goal' stamped all over it in bold gold leaf capitals, but Timbo rose like a famished phantom, stretching towards Frank's cannonball. The world stood still; seemingly only our scraggily diminutive keeper moved on the entire face of the planet – sending the ball over the bar with the very tip of the well-clad fingers of his tiny left hand.

Frank was crestfallen as we mobbed our heroic insect.

However, it wasn't over. Now the pressure was on moi! I really hadn't asked for any of that! Responsibility hung on me like a fever bounded by a tractor tyre. The opposing goalkeeper was a monstrous giant of a kid – with hands like shovels, bolting black eyes, redolent of Beelzebub's headlights, and a head like a bricklayer's bucket – my last hope of physical threat/intimidation was thus ruled out.

But I had my Gypsy guile, which blended with generations of cockney bullshit, and this social/genetic mélange offered a resource of fissile proportions. I took a run-up of about 20 yards as the Forest Gate Goliath squatted on his line, set between the posts, evoking a container lorry parked in a beach hut. I tore at the ball like a rocket, but as I reached it, I pulled up sharp – and as the juggernaut of the keeper crashed to the left of his line as a downed B36 might (the ground actually shook) I tapped the ball straight into the centre of the goal. As it crossed the line I heard Mr Peters, in his stark Liva-pud accent, utter, 'You cunning little bastard.' That made me rather proud of myself.

That goal shouldn't have counted as the keeper had moved before the ball was struck, but despite Frank and his team's protests, the ref, Padraig O'Cohen, who doubled up as the local lollipop man and rabbi, was clearly late for his daily date with the Belisha beacons, telling his picketers, in his thick Cork brogue, to 'Feck orf? Tá sé déanta! Es iz dernakh![12]' So, Burke notched up a rare victory.

In time Frank signed apprenticeship forms for Ipswich, but like the vast majority of youngsters he failed to make the grade. Last I heard of him he was working in a soap factory in Silver Town; ultimately that's where goals got him – nowhere, but he did finally end up blowing bubbles.

Mr Koch remained a Koch to the last, venting his dislike of me by joining the staff at Burke, where he was let nowhere near any responsibility for the physical education of us doughty scholars as we pursued our handful CSEs (a sort of National League O-levels).

---

12   This is two versions of 'it is done' and I only can tell you that thanks to the wonderful cultural and ethnic mix the scholars of Burke were

You see, Moore, Allison and Greenwood were right; football is more than a game. For a lot of us, it's part of who we are and how we become what and who me might or can be.

Managers are not always right

The 1960/61 season saw Moore take his next chance to step up; his first full season in the first team at Upton Park. He was to miss just a handful of games over the whole campaign. The Hammers travelled to Molineux for the opening fixture with Noel Cantwell at left-half, while Bobby played left-back. He recalled, 'We were playing the way the players wanted: 4-2-4, with plenty of good football.'

The Irons didn't play badly, but lost 4-2 and as Moore was to relate, 'It went that way for a few games. Playing well, but no breaks. Then the manager had his say. He wanted us to hit long through balls from the halfway line. We became the world's best hitters of long through balls to nobody from the halfway line. We seemed to lose every match 4-0.'

Certainly, West Ham were producing some attractive football, but Fenton's revision to the long-ball game was tantamount to a white flag; a desperate lack of ideas and inspiration dragged the team down, so by the concluding games of their schedule the hapless Hammers looked to be just about where they deserved to be. Moore had by this time long been disabused of his youthful faith in managers, convinced not only that they were not always right, but often they proved themselves to be totally wrong.

The way the players had wanted to play was a nascent prototype, and the first time it had been fully implemented in the top end of the British game. From the outset however the experiment was the subject of a tsunami of misinformed criticism. West Ham were accused of polluting English football with new-fangled, somewhat effete, alien notions, derived from iffy continental backstreets, when what was said to be needed was 'back to basics', the 'good old days' mentality – dashing, goal-grabbing wingers, the 'W' formation (with full-backs, wing-halves and forwards etc.), the 'meat and two veg' that had made England supreme. Who needed a cold beer when you could have warm ale? The Irons were branded cowardly theorists, traitors abandoning cherished customs and 'manly' virtues for the sake of 'Johnny Foreigner' gimmicks.

These were the days when, for most of the population, even the thought of the UK being part of Europe was an anathema swathed in a contradiction of terms. Anything imported was understood to be second best, and the notion of 'overseas ways' an abomination. 'Little England' persisted by keeping the 'aspidistra flying', as fish and chips remained the height of culinary delight for most West Ham supporters (the concept of a 'fan' was a crude Americanism). This was a place that Jacob Rees-Mogg would have been very at home in.

For all this, Moore's critique of Ted Fenton was to be indicative of the doubts he would develop about all the managers he would work with. This was probably something to do with his seminal relationship with Malcolm Allison, but his extraordinary insight into and instinct for the game was likely the major factor of his heresy.

For a while, West Ham's fortunes were definitely hiding while performances had been mixed. At the Boleyn Ground the Irons could look a solid enough unit, but on the road too often they were something more than shaky. Half a dozen defeats in the first ten games told the story, and letting four goals against Wolves and Everton and six at Old Trafford turned up the volume on the negative vibes.

England – the next steps

On the last eastbound tube train on a mid-September evening in 1960, Bobby and Tina were heading back to Ilford following a visit to a cinema in Leicester Square. He had picked up an evening paper for the longish Central Line and overhead journey. As is and was the wont of many young men, he first turned to the sports pages. However, it was Tina who spotted some exciting news and exclaimed, 'Look, Bobby! You're in the under-23s!' Bobby read the headline, 'MOORE CAPPED BY ENGLAND'.

A confirming FA missive winged its way to Barking a couple of days later (it addressed Bobby in Etonian tones as 'Dear Moore'). The letter included what he needed to know about arrangements for travel, and informed him that the third-class rail fare would be covered. I'm sure I must have travelled third-class as a lad, having a fourth-class attitude and an underclass background, but retrospectively I can't think what third-class might be today – clinging to the outside of the train perhaps?

The FA epistle also detailed a range of instructions, including how players should present themselves: shoes polished, boot laces washed 'bearing no unseemly marks of mud'. All that suited Bobby only too well.

At that point Bobby had featured in just 26 league games for West Ham.

The Germans but not the Germans, the Danes but not quite the Danes

Of the half a dozen new caps selected to meet East Germany at Maine Road, Manchester, in September 1960, Moore was the only Londoner. Indeed, there were just two southern-based players in the team.

Bobby was surprised by his selection as he was still getting accustomed to first-team duties at Upton Park. The inferiority complex groomed in his childhood years (see *Young Bobby*, 2022) was still with the 19-year-old.

Moore's under-23 debut was something of an odd affair. A few hours before the game the team sat in a Manchester hotel waiting to be told about the side they were about to encounter at the home of the Manc Blues. It was the first international of the season, but all the England lads knew of it was that they were going to play a Danish select XI instead of their East German counterparts who they had been scheduled to meet.

The Cold War was raging and just four days prior to the game, the German Democratic Republic FA announced that they could not obtain the necessary travel documents. Travel restrictions relating to access to Berlin had caused them to pull out of the match. It turned out the British government had dragged its bureaucratic feet failing to issue the appropriate visas. However, the English FA had been loath to entirely scrap the fixture, so had hastily arranged stand-in opponents. All that was known about the replacement opposition was that, like the bacon in the rolls from Phil Cassettari's cafe, they would probably be Danish.

There had been an ongoing dialogue with London all day, but there was no idea exactly who the opposition might be. There was some talk of the Danish Olympic silver medal-winning team, but ultimately it transpired that England would meet the club side Vejle Boldklub. When the lads' manager, Ron Greenwood, informed his players of their opposition there was stony silence, until Barnsley's Dave Barber uttered, to the amusement of all and sundry, with the exception of Ron, 'That's easy for you to say!' Dave would never again be selected to play for an England team.

It had been Greenwood who had saved the day. His relationship with Frits Gotfredsen, Vejle's manager, led to VB making their way to Manchester at the last minute. Gotfredsen had developed the attacking style of play that made Vejle the most popular club in Denmark during that era, although like Barber, few people had heard of them in the UK. The *Jyllands Rubin* ('Ruby of Jutland') had, in 1958, claimed their first national championship, and went on to 'do the double' by winning the national cup competition, the only Danish team to have achieved such a feat to that date. Vejle retained the cup in 1959, and at the Olympics in Rome four VB players were selected to represent the Danes. The team finished runners-up. Poul Jensen captained the Olympian Danes, and was joined in the squad by club-mates Henning Enoksen, Tommy Troelsen and Poul Mejer.

Despite some seeing the game as meaningless, Walter Winterbottom, who oversaw the whole development of English international football as part of his role as senior team manager, denied this, saying that the players would be able to make a case for full international honours. In particular, Everton's Brian Labone was a prospect. For all this, it had been Greenwood who had baulked at the prospect of the game being scrapped, telling both Winterbottom and the FA that scratching the fixture altogether would make all concerned look amateurish, and passive victims of circumstance. For Ron, England needed to show that they were able to adapt.

During the 1950s and 1960s match preparations for England games often encompassed behind-closed-doors practice matches. Before the meeting with the Danes the under-23s, including Bobby, faced a senior England side at Loftus Road. Winterbottom witnessed the younger players beat the full international XI 2-1 - a tough, star-studded crew: Ron Springett (Sheffield Wednesday), Jimmy Armfield (Blackpool), Graham Shaw (Sheffield United), Ron Flowers (Wolves), Bobby Robson (WBA), Peter Swan (Sheffield Wednesday), Dennis Viollet (Manchester United), Ray Pointer (Burnley), Johnny Haynes (Fulham), Maurice Setters (Manchester United), Norman Deeley (Wolves), Brian Pilkington (Burnley).

Winterbottom had high hopes for Moore. He had been assured enough by Greenwood not to be concerned about him coming to his debut from the Hammers' 4-2-4 game into the conventionally set-up England side, saying, 'Moore is an intelligent player … With West Ham he is virtually a full-back who attacks when it's on.' He went on to say that with England, Moore would be a wing-half who, when the opportunity arose, could reinforce the forward line. Eddie Baily, who played for Spurs and England and went on to become a renowned coach, was to tell me that later in his career, when playing at international level, such was the acknowledgement of Moore's influence on offensive play that opponents were assigned to mark him. There can be no greater flattery for a defender than being regarded not only as an obstruction, but also an offensive threat.

Ultimately, the programme for Moore's first under-23 game labelled the visitors a 'Danish XI'. They arrived in Manchester very much up for the short-notice challenge, but the English had a good record against Danish sides, having won their two previous encounters with the national team.

Vejle were not exactly a like-for-like substitution for the East Germans, but they were a better than decent outfit. Olympic silver medalist Poul Jensen also skippered his side at Maine Road. The Danes had tasted defeat just once during the Olympic tournament, being betted only by the impressive Yugoslavs in the final, which had taken place just 11 days prior to the game in Manchester. On their way to the gold medal game they had put aside strong Hungarian, Polish and Argentinian opposition, as well as a stoical Tunisian team, managed by Frane Matošić, who is regarded as one of Hajduk Split's greatest players and is that club's all-time leading goalscorer.

One newspaper headline pre-match had it at 'No Moore Problem', telling how Bobby would have no issues slotting into the under-23 team. That was pretty much the case. He was reported to have been 'one of the players who did well'.

England U23 5 Vejle Boldklub 1
Wednesday, 21 September 1960
Friendly
Maine Road
Attendance: 11,800
Referee: Pieter Paulus Roomer

England U23: Banks, Angus, McNeil, Barber, Labone, Moore, Paine, Hill, Baker, Burnside, Charlton.
Vejle Boldklub: K.H. Sorensen, Johansen, Jensen, K. Sorensen, Petersen, Foulsen, Anderssen, Troelsen, Thomsen, Enoksen, Meyer.

Indeed, both Labone and Moore shone, but it took a fair bit of the first half for the home side to organise themselves as the 1-1 half-time score indicated. England were doing most of the work, and while the wet conditions had made the pitch slippery, the hosts had put some nice moves together early on. However, despite seemingly doing enough to give them more than an edge in terms of partially developed chances, England were achieving little more than getting not very far. As the first period wore on their style degraded, and the Danish goalkeeper was, for the most part, untroubled.

David Burnside seemed to be wandering aimlessly, while Fred Hill was showing a distinct lack of form. Joe Baker, a full international by that time, was unimpressive, while Bobby Charlton appeared intent on winning the game on his own, which amounted to a lot of effort with no reward. Terry Paine was, as usual, driving like a train, focused, and determined, but halfway through the first half, as Bobby recollected, 'England looked more like a crowd than a team.'

Fortunately, the Danes posed little threat to the England defenders for the most part, although Greenwood's boys habitually passing back to their keeper, sometimes when there was not a Dane within half a street of the ball, did not endear the youngsters to the Moss Side audience.

Before England went in front Burnside trashed a golden opportunity, failing to control Charlton's centre in front of the visitors' goal, but he managed to tap the ball to Paine although the young Saint cannoned his shot over the bar.

With 17 minutes played, a shot from 20 yards by Barber was parried, the keeper forced into a full-stretch save. The subsequent powerful Paine drive was then blocked but Baker took full advantage, ramming the rebound home.

Moore was largely responsible for breaking up some good Danish build-up play, but his passing out of defence hadn't been up to his usual standard. However, he took a chance from long range, and the subsequent header by Hill seemed certain to hit the mark but on the line Kai Johansen got his head to the ball, the clearance hitting the angle of the crossbar and post.

A dozen minutes from the break the Danes equalised after Moore brought Thomsen down, just outside the penalty area. Henning Enoksen hit a 25-yard rocket straight to the right of Gordon Banks. The keeper had no chance, with the ball entering the net just inside the near upright. That free kick was the best shot of the game.

Charlton, by then a relative old hand at under-23 level, went into overdrive, firing a trio of long-range efforts, making long 40 yard runs as a preamble, but all to no avail before the half-time whistle.

The start of the second period saw England swing the ball about with artistic abandon, bombarding the Danish goal. The commanding play culminated in Charlton scoring twice in a golden seven-minute spell; the first going in off the foot of a post, the second a conversion from a Burnside pass.

Moore, looking an enterprising figure, picked up a pass in the 66th minute from Hill to put his name on the scoresheet, striking the ball a width of an Olympic swimming pool from the goal line (bet you've never come across that simile in the context of football before!). The home side's fourth goal was the first of Bobby's four in an England shirt.

With a 4-1 lead England appeared to relax into the game. Following a ferrous shot from Burnside that was well saved, Paine concluded the scoring for the night with a quarter of an hour remaining on the referee's trusty Ingersoll.

In truth, the visitors never looked capable of worrying Greenwood's boys, who probably could have scored more than the handful claimed on the evening. The youthful Banks was rarely troubled in goal and the Danish XI was well beaten. Charlton's brace in the 53rd and 60th minutes had killed the game. He had thus polished his chances for selection for the senior team the following week with a dollop of Brasso.

Of the team that beat the Danes so comprehensively only Barber and Burnside were to fail to win full England honours. The match allowed the home side to perform something of an exhibition, and even given the ample time and space the visitors allowed them, the young Lions demonstrated a deal of potential and promise in terms of the national team's future.

In the last analysis England had dominated, but the critics were correct to ponder how the East Germans might have taken advantage of their first half disorganisation. The demand in the press was for more direct play, but it nearly always is.

One of the most memorable aspects of the event was the whistling of the Dutch referee. The volume of his mouthpiece was deafening, and might have interfered with other games being played over a radius of three miles.

After his encounter against the Danes, Bobby achieved FA representative honours. On 21 October 1960 he was part of an FA XI that defeated an Army Representative side 2-1 at Hillsborough, Sheffield. The FA fielded a team that included three full internationals and six future caps, including Banks and Moore. The Army Representative XI featured two internationals-to-be in Alan Peacock (England) and Ron Yeats (Scotland). Burnley's John Connelly and Johnny Fantham of Sheffield Wednesday scored for the FA XI, while Geoff Strong, at that time an Arsenal player, replied.

This was the first season of the League Cup, and while some of the bigger clubs turned their backs on the competition, on 26 September Upton Park entertained Charlton in that competition. The hosts won 3-1 and John Dick became West Ham's first League Cup goalscorer. Musgrove also netted and Moore got the Irons' third in the 64th minute, driving home a classy, low first-time shot from a point almost dead centre of the goal, outside the box.

Jubilation soon gave way to humiliation as the Hammers hopes for the new tournament were dashed when the travelling Irons were bettered 3-2 at Fourth Division Darlington. This was one of the rare occasions a mascot was included in the spectacle. This really didn't become a 'thing' until more than a decade later. The hosts had a bloke parading round the pitch dressed as a quaker, although his garb didn't look that well-researched; while being a tall, thin individual, he got taken as an undertaker or Abraham Lincoln. The fact that he also had a fag hanging out the corner of his gob and gave every impression of being, at least in good part, Brahmsed, didn't add to his 'act' (the 'followers of Fox' being big on abstinence from both the 'milk of Saturn' and the 'puff of purgatory'). The whole charade concluded untidily. Having suffered protracted piss-taking from the crowd, Abe got into an altercation with a small clutch of the Feethams congregation, which came to a head with him losing his shit and laying into them. Ultimately the dishevelled talisman was carried away by the combined forces of the local rozzers and the noble practitioners of St John's Ambulance.

Disappointment was followed by disbelief when the news broke that West Ham's club captain Noel Cantwell had been sold to Manchester United. It felt to most of the Upton Park flock like an act of betrayal on the part of the board.

The £30,000 income meant nothing to the supporters; they had lost a man and a player they regarded as one of their own. The club's tsars appeared to see this act as little more than good business, looking to John Lyall to slot into the Irishman's place. Lyall himself told me that was wishful thinking at best, saying, 'Noel and I were very different types of defenders … I was, at the time in "they shall not pass" frame of mind, whereas Noel was one for playing out from the back, one of the original "attacking full-backs".'

While Noel was a resilient craftsman, there was an intelligent guile and finesse in his play. John was a tough, no-nonsense player in the tradition of the Irons – an honest, robust, no quarter asked for, and certainly none given bombardier, as fit and muscular as a drayman's hound. Lyall was professionally close to Moore; the future manager-to-be was to tell how he and Bobby had 'grown up together' and named Moore as the individual he most enjoyed working alongside, describing how Bobby was 'a dream to play with' and adding, 'He spoke to you every minute of the game … He had time to play your game, as well as his own.' However, Bobby's relationship, although built around football, was, at foundation, personal. Like Moore, Cantwell, exuded a calmness, an ability to think and act at the same time. Lyall's bottom line was to act as a tank trap, then rise out of the carnage and 'Charge!' He was the broadsword to the Cork man's Scimitar – John was the thumping howitzer, while Noel was the guided cruise missile.

Ted Fenton was likely relieved to see the back of Cantwell. He and Malcolm Allison had, in different ways, usurped Ted's authority and dwarfed any influence he had among the players. Cantwell's departure might have thus seemed like a chance for the manager to take a firmer grip on the reins of his club's destiny.

Ernie Gregory's testimonial was played in October against Liga Deportiva Alajuelense, a Costa Rican side famous in their own backyard, but no one had heard of them around East London at that time (or likely at any time), the central American state being known more for pineapples than football. Not a great pick for one of West Ham's longest-serving stalwarts. However, while the 'Men from Del Monte' might well have said 'yes', West Ham beat them 3-2.

Preston were defeated 5-2 on 22 October in East London, Malcolm Musgrove registering a hat-trick. This match saw a debut for 17-year- old Ronnie Boyce, who went on to make more than 300 appearances in the West Ham cause. That was the team's 14th league fixture of the season and their sixth win, while seven had been lost, with 31 goals scored and 35 conceded. That record demonstrates the inconsistency of the side, and while a lack of predictability offers the excitement of jeopardy in football, the stop/start character of West Ham was also frustrating for someone like Moore, and nerve-wrecking for Fenton and his board.

5

CAPTAIN KID

At the tail end of 1960, Dave Dunmore netted in seven consecutive First Division fixtures from late October to mid-December. The run included a hat-trick in the 6-0 destruction of Arsenal at the home of the Hammers on 5 November, which certainly turned out to be fireworks (sorry, couldn't resist that) and was just one goal short of West Ham's record First Division defeat of Arsenal, the 7-0 trouncing in March 1927. Vic Watson got a hat-trick then – he sold the match ball to my granddad for 15 bob (75p – apparently his airing cupboard was full of them). Jim eventually auctioned it for charity in the 1960s.

The 1960 meeting with the excoriated Gunners exemplified West Ham's form at the start of the season. The side seemed to be sturdy enough at Upton Park; the conquest of the hapless Highburians was the Irons' seventh win in eight outings at the Boleyn Ground (the 3-3 draw against Blackpool was the only dropped point in that run). Bobby had been involved in every game as his side hit 30 goals, letting just 14 go by them. Poor results on the road, however, had registered only a single point in eight outings, a catalogue of failure only equalled by a struggling Manchester United side.

The North Londoners arrived at Upton Park ten days after the Hammers' League Cup embarrassment against Darlington.

Goalkeeper Jack Kelsey, probably Arsenal's best performer on the day, likely kept the score down to single figures. The Welsh international, who couldn't be faulted for any of the goals conceded, made a series of crucial stops. Seemingly unflappable, he cut out much of the rain of crosses that the Gunners rearguard seemed unable to quell.

An attendance of 29,375 was the highest of the term that far. The Irons were buoyed up from the first moments as Dunmore struck with under 200 seconds played, capitalising on an error by the Gunners' defence. A 20-yard left-footed shot notched up his second, and the Hammers' final goal in the last minute gave Dave the match ball.

Although the playing surface was akin to Everglades of Florida, Phil Woosnam (who had left his job as a physics teacher at Leyton County High School for Boys to turn professional) and his allegedly webbed feet (rumoured to be a 'Caersws thing' on the terraces) had a good game. One hack eulogised that the very Welsh

Welshman had put on a show that was the best he had 'ever seen from an inside-forward' (perhaps he was a teenager though?). Phil the Boyo was central in carving out four of his side's haul; the other one was scored by the Powys Pedagogue himself in the 78th minute.

Andy Malcolm, Ken Brown, and Bobby Moore collectively looked an exemplary half-back line, and as an added bonus, Andy Malcolm claimed what was to be his only top-flight goal. Keeper Brian Rhodes showed his handling skills, frustrating the impressive Arsenal strike force, which included David Herd of Scotland, Wales's Mel Charles, and England youth and under-23 international John Barnwell.

The Irons scored five goals on succeeding Saturdays; an extraordinary ten-goal draw at St James's Park was followed by a 5-0 victory over visiting Wolverhampton Wanderers. Playing at left-half, Moore contributed to that total. Hurdling a tackle from Wolves' pivot man Bill Slater, Bobby dribbled passed right-half Eddie Clamp and kicked on wide of goalkeeper Geoff Sidebottom to score his first league goal. There were some accusations that he had made contact with Sidebottom, resulting in the stopper having to be stretchered off the field, but Moore was adamant there had been no contact between him and the Mapplewell man. It seems Sidebottom's last-gasp dive ended with him colliding with a team-mate.

Italy – ain't nothing like the real thing

Two months after making his under-23 debut Moore was called on again, this time to face the Italian under-23s in Newcastle. It was quite a game. Although the encounter with the Danes had been, in almost every sense, an England under-23 match because of the East German no-show, the meeting with Italy, under the floodlights of St James' Park stands as Moore's first cap and official debut at that level.

England U23 1 Italy U23 1
Wednesday, 2 November 1960
Friendly
St James' Park
Attendance: 15,064
Referee: Lucien Van Nuffel

England U23: Macedo, Angus, McNeil, Mullery, Labone, Moore, Connelly, Dobing, Baker, Fantham, Charlton.
Italy U23: Anzolin (Albertosi HT), Burgnich, Trebbi, Micheli, Salvadore, Trapattoni, Mora, Rivera, Nicolè, Bulgarelli (Ferinni 29), Rossano.

The sides had met three times previously; England had won two and lost the other. Post-match reports and memories were dominated by a melee that ensued after the home side pulled level. In the 14th minute, Joe Baker, England's centre-forward who sported a solid Scottish accent, noticed Roberto Anzolin, the opposition keeper, standing on his line with the ball gripped to his chest. Regarded as one of his country's best goalkeepers of his generation, Anzolin was to play for several Italian club sides, but is best remembered for his successful time with Juventus. At international level he was capped by Italy and was a member of their squad at the 1966 World Cup.

Baker, who would play part of his career in Italy, shouldered Anzolin, still clinging to the ball, into the net. At that time such an act was viewed a perfectly acceptable and fair barge in the British game. The Belgian referee was OK with it too, immediately pointing to the centre spot. The Italians on the other hand went ape shit. Charging keepers wasn't a thing then in Italy, it seemed. Players of the ilk of Sandro Salvadore, Giovanni Trappatoni, Bruno Mora, Giovanni Rivera, and Bruno Nicolè, all of whom went on to achieve full international status, surrounded the referee, screaming and gesturing, and that wasn't a thing in Britain then.

The man in black was bustled to the spot where the offending incident had taken place, all the while the Italians continued protesting loudly and waving their arms about. The demonstration carried on for minutes. At one point the battered Belgian almost had his jacket ripped off (many referees, especially those with continental origins, wore a black blazer in those days, sometimes a dinner jacket even!).

The Italian team was managed by a police sergeant, who jogged on to the field ostensibly to restore order, although he also was extremely animated and hollering.

Bob asked Brian Labone, whose family had Italian roots (a relative called Nicholas Antonio Labone taught various foreign languages in Glasgow) if he thought the ref might call the game off. Labone was of the opinion that if the official did get the game restarted it might never finish.

After the linesmen, the Italian backroom staff, the police, perhaps the tea lady and 'Why aye' the St James' Park cat, were pulled into the fray, the visitors calmed down and the goal stood. The game ended in a draw with Nicolè scoring for Italy.

Back in the First Division, the tide seemed to turn yet again for West Ham when Spurs performed a double over the drooping Irons over the Christmas period. This proved to be the *hors d'oeuvre* for the White Hart Lane luvvies' historic First Division and FA Cup double.

Engagement

Boosted by Bobby's newfound career stability, Tina and Bob got engaged on Christmas Day, 1960. Bobby was 19 and Tina was 17. Naturally for Bobby, the proposal was meticulously planned and carried out in style. He'd even asked Betty's permission beforehand. That meant Tina had an idea what was in that big parcel, with her name on it and tied with a huge bow. She had been prodding it expectantly ever since it had appeared a few days earlier under the Christmas tree in Christchurch Road.

The pair were due to go that night to a party, but Tina had a terrible cold and wasn't really looking forward to it. She pointed out that her nose was red and she had nothing to wear. Resisting the predictable reference to Rudolf, Bobby grinned, then picked up the parcel and placed it in her arms. She opened it to reveal a burnt umber and black check mohair skirt, along with a mohair jumper.

'I want you to wear those,' Bobby said, 'when you put on what's inside that.' He pointed to another box, a very small one, nestled in the folds of the outfit. Tina opened the diminutive case and inside was a ring with one dazzlingly faultless diamond.

Half-joking, Bobby went down on one knee and announced, 'Tina, I'd like us to get married.'

Tina's cold was miraculously cured. She and Bobby went off to the party in Cranbrook Road, Ilford, Tina flashing her engagement ring and wearing the mohair outfit, despite the fact that it made her look ever so slightly like the Michelin Man's better-looking Mrs.

When they got to the do they found that Tina's cousin David, a trainee plumber, had brought along (uninvited) a crowd of his mates from East Ham, then the municipal borough east of West Ham.[13] One of this group was his best friend, also named David, who had dreams of making it as a celebrity photographer. Tina vaguely remembered him asking her, a couple years previously, if she would let him take some photos of her in Epping Forest. Betty, deeply and probably understandably suspicious of his motives, had said, 'Over my dead body.' If she hadn't guarded Tina's virtue so closely, she would have been able to boast of owning a set of portraits of her as a kid by David Bailey.

By the time Tina and Bob got engaged, Bobby was experiencing his first full season in the West Ham first team. For this he was paid £8 a week, which these days wouldn't buy a cheap Alice band for Jack Grealish. At the time, players were still paid according to the Football League's notorious maximum wage limit of £20 a week during the season and £17 a week during the summer lay-off. That

---

13   When the two boroughs merged in 1965 the strikingly creatively and pungently imaginative provincial politicians decided not to adopt the obvious Forest Gate and take an existing parish name within the area. Instead they came up with not 'Docklands' or 'River Town', but 'Newham' for the resultant local authority. If there was a competition for bland and uninspiring place names, that would have been an all-time winner. Next door is Tower Hamlets, a relatively attractive appellation.

didn't change until 1961, when Jimmy Hill, then a Fulham player and chairman of the Professional Footballers' Association, forced through its abolition after threatening a players' strike.[14]

To give an example of how comparatively low footballers' wages were, Bobby's £8 a week was £3 less than Tina was earning at Prudential Insurance, so you could say that she was the main breadwinner at that juncture. Most of their money went into saving for their first home, but life was still a lot of fun. The couple went round in a crowd of other young West Ham players like Alan Sealey and Tony Scott, and their girlfriends – Janice, who went out with Alan, was that year's Miss Dagenham and very glamorous.[15] After games they would go to a private club, Harlene, in Forest Gate, where the ladies drank Bristol Cream sherry, that particular tipple being taken as 'a bit posh' around the area. To be fair, in that neck of the woods then, when the favoured poison was the likes Toby Ale, it was. I recall ordering a larger and lime in a local hostelry and being told they didn't 'do cocktails'!

After the club the happy band would move on into Essex and the Room At The Top. Further east was another hotspot, the Dick Turpin, then 'the' place to be on Thursday nights. There they would bump into other up and coming young players, the likes Terry Venables and Brian Dear, as well as occasionally future screen legends Terry Stamp, Jim Booth and Barbara Windsor. The landlord would facilitate a lock-in, being glad to accommodate their needs because that 'set' (there's a verb not much used since the 1960s) were their best customers.

Early in the new year Moore made his FA Cup debut against Stoke City. The Potters put an end to any West Ham ambitions in that competition with a third-round replay victory by the only goal of the night, following a 2-2 result at Upton Park four days previously.

Welsh squelched

A month later Moore was back on international duty. England had only met Wales once before at under-23 level, a 2-1 victory for the Welsh (Brian Clough scoring England's goal in April 1958). At Goodison Park on 8 February 1961 the home side had prepared to use a modified 4-2-4 system devised by Ron Greenwood.

The Welsh came to Liverpool with three full internationals in their ranks, but it was Moore who was to stand out. It was his name that dominated the match

---

14   Many players regarded the maximum wage part of the 'slavery of the contract' that kept them in the position of the indentured labour of the previous century.

15   My aunt Gert had been Miss Dock Road in the late 1920s. The prize was a free pie and mash supper for four. Seems she developed a bit of a taste for that delicacy, having it for her dinner every day for the rest of her life (including Sundays and Christmas). She passed away at the age of 98 after being hit by a trolly bus, somewhat ironically (or poetically) on Connaught Road, Victoria Docks. Legend has it that the bus was a write-off.

reports the next day, the press naming him as England's 'bright young star' and trumpeting 'Memo to England – Moore is Ready'.

Already recognised as outstanding as his nation's youth captain, Bob had combined so impressively with Chris Crowe, Blackburn's inside-forward at that time, there was talk of the pair being ready step in for Bobby Robson and Johnny Haynes at full international level, although to say that was a tad previous would be generous. The exuberance of the callow sports journalist then, as now, knew no bounds.

England U23 2 Wales U23 0
Wednesday, 8 February 1961
Friendly
Goodison Park
Attendance: 27,235
Referee: Gilbert Bowman

England U23: Banks, Angus, Byrne, Kirkham, Labone, Moore, Riley, Crowe, Byrne, Allen, Clark.
Wales U23: Hollins, Hughes (Griffiths HT), Williams, England, Nurse, Hole, Barrington, Jones, Moore, Burton, Williams, Jones.

England went ahead from Crowe's penalty, but it was West Ham's teenager who was to pose a series of threats to the Welsh keeper. After having a close-in header miraculously foiled, unusually Moore was a persistent menace in the away side's penalty area, crafting his team's second goal in the 63rd minute. His characteristically swiftly taken 25-yard free kick hit Swansea's Mel Nurse, the visitors' centre-half, before sailing by the Welsh goalkeeper, Dave Hollins. However Bobby was recorded as the scorer.

Beware the ides of March

From the start of February 1961 West Ham experienced a dismal run and with March almost out they had recorded only a single win in eight games, with just one draw.

In that same month the board at Upton Park let it be known their manager, Ted Fenton, was on 'sick leave'. Later it transpired that he had in fact left the club. It was a much-mooted source of pride for the board that they had never sacked a manager, and it seemed that a compromise had been tried to hang on to this myth, even though it was common knowledge that the club's first manager, Sid King, had been booted out in all but name (see Belton, 2003b, 2006, 2014 and 2015). It was also clear to anyone with half a brain cell that Fenton had been dealt with in much the same way, but that's another story. The following month, Ron Greenwood was named as the new manager at Upton Park.

Scotched

As the winds of change were blowing at Upton Park, the young Scots were heading south. The programme named the Wednesday evening encounter in Middlesbrough as an 'Intermediate International'. England had won three of their five under-23 meetings with Scotland, and two had been drawn.

England U23 0 Scotland U23 1
Wednesday, 1 March 1961
Friendly
Ayresome Park
Attendance: 21,858
Referee: Leo Callaghan (Merthyr)

England U23: Banks, Cohen, McNeil, Kirkham, Labone, Moore, Brabrook, Dobing, Byrne, Crowe, O'Grady.
Scotland U23: Ogston, Hogan, Riddell, Crerand, McNeill, Ure, Hilley, Law, Hughes, Gilzean, McLeod.

Scotland started the game disadvantaged by several of their first-choice players being unavailable for selection because of club commitments or injury. But Denis Law appeared prepared to take on England on his tod. With impressive regularity he left the English defenders flat-footed, spraying precision passes round the pitch with alacrity, as well as finding time to do a shift in defence. Moore and co. failed the command the traction on which to build an answer. However, it was hard to blame Brian Labone and Michael McNeil as they did OK, but the wing-halves, Moore, and John Kirkham, looked sluggish.

Crowe, England's outside-left, was all but absent, leaving Johnny Byrne (who came into the team as a late replacement for Joe Baker) to graft alone up front. Indeed, the centre-forward was the only real success story of the night for the home side – Byrne's fellow strikers seemingly being devoid of imagination.

Scotland, from the commencement of play, advanced on their old foe at a furious pace. England, feeling the strain, conceded three corners in the first five minutes, and McNeil was obliged to clear a shot from Law off the goal line. In the early stages the home attack was seldom in evidence, although Peter Brabrook made several swift sorties down the wing, he was too often a lone raider.

Law's work rate gave the visitors a distinct boost, while Crowe was well held by the strongly effective Pat Crerand. Byrne, forced to desperately go in search of the ball, seemed to win back some of the play, but the tartan defence was solid, in no mood to give anything away (no stereotype intended).

Scotland took the lead a minute after the interval. Banks parried a header from Law but Johnny McLeod hooked the ball back, where the 'Lawman' had been waiting, marauder-like, to score the killer goal from eight yards out.

Throughout, Byrne did his best to get the forward line moving, but even Scotland's goal failed to give England any discernible sense of urgency, and the visitors' defence, ably marshalled by Billy McNeill, took almost complete command of events.

Scotland should have increased their lead in the 74th minute when McNeil stopped what looked like a certain goal by handling a Gilzean header, but Law shot wide from the penalty spot (really the only blot on his evening's copybook).

The Scottish victory, their first over England at under-23 level since such games were inaugurated in 1955, was seldom in doubt, but it was seen as one of the biggest surprises of the season. The Caledonians were almost coasting through the final quarter of an hour. Like a pirate raid across the border, they had swashbuckled their buccaneering play to plunder the plaudits, honour, and the ultimate victory.

The encounter was to be Moore's only loss as an under-23 international. He and his team put on a below-par performance, but Law was righteously hailed in the press as the inspiration of the Scots. He had run riot against the English defence, and been pivotal in the match. From then on, as with Jimmy Greaves, whenever they met on the pitch, Moore made sure the lad from Bucksburn was tightly marked, remembering the lesson of that defeat. That said, Denis the McMenace was rarely anything less than irresistible.

Any England manager is going to be less than happy about being beaten, but defeat by a Scottish side will unfailingly cut deep, and as a result of the reversal heads were going to roll.

When Greenwood took over at Upton Park, Moore was both anxious about his future and hurt by how he seemed to have been treated by the club. He shared these feelings with the new manager. Ron had known Bobby for some time from their work together with the England youth and under-23 teams. He told his captain-to-be that his destiny was West Ham's future.

For Greenwood, Bobby embodied the next stage of the game's evolution, the football he wanted to play. Although Moore had failed to gain any major acclaim as a schoolboy, from the first time Greenwood had seen him, he had been impressed by the lad's presence and solidity on the ball. Although West Ham had deployed Bobby as a wing-half, Greenwood brought him into the centre of the defence in the England Youth team.

At Upton Park, playing for the reserves, Bobby could be found wanting; too many goals were conceded with him in the last line of defence. Ron put this down to him being unsure of himself in the air. Moore's team-mates wanted him back at left-half, but this didn't worry Greenwood because the youth team played a lot of continental sides who tended to keep the ball on the ground. Moore coped better than well with that situation .

At the time of Ron's appointment, Bobby appeared to have the potential to be a good, reliable performer, but the same could be said of a lot of other young men around at that time, many of whom seemed better-equipped for future stardom than the ambling Moore. He continued to be pretty much single-paced, and therefore it was argued by more than a few that he would never be able to cope with a 'chasing'.

Moore's critics could only see his weaknesses, partly because they were ignorant in terms of having the means to judge his qualities. There was no one to compare him to and people can only know what they know. But Greenwood, like Malcolm Allison, had seen the Hungarians of the 1950s and this had given him a vista into another dimension of football. Moore certainly was not possessed of the natural talent of the likes of Martin Peters, but few knew of his tremendous dedication, willingness to learn, and towering insight into the shape and direction of play.

The young Moore and Greenwood had few interactions that might reach the level of what might pass for a conversation; their encounters were mostly taken up with Bobby asking questions and Ron doing his best to respond. At that stage Moore was essentially interviewing his mentor. Moore seemed to want to know everything and anything about the game, quizzing Greenwood endlessly and picking his brain. To his credit, Ron was pleased to oblige. He recalled how Bobby 'would slip into the seat next to me, on a plane or coach' and for the rest of the trip would milk his manager's mind.

Greenwood had made a study of Real Madrid, certainly the best club side in the world during the immediate postwar era, and told Bobby how *La Casa Blanca* full-backs played early balls down the line, with the outside of the front foot. This meant their intentions were camouflaged. Moore was to master that move – front foot, outside contact, early ball to a target already in mind; he turned to this technique throughout his career. His front foot was always his right.

Ron was to admit that occasionally he was purposely harsh with Moore. Once he told him he would fail to get a place in the Hartlepool side given that he seemed unable to head the ball. But Bobby got around that, using his brain and feet to get into positions where the ball would fall on to his chest or foot. Generally, early on, Greenwood found him 'difficult to fault' for anything other than his insistence on achieving perfection in almost everything he did.

Bobby's under-23 career had continued his impressive record as an international player, which had started with the England youth team. Following his run-out against Scotland in Middlesbrough, Bobby was drafted into the FA's summer tour.

Kapitän Bobby

The defeat at Ayesome Park saw only four of the team who met the Scots hold on to their places for England's next under-23 game against West Germany at White Hart Lane: George Cohen of Fulham, Johnny Byrne of Crystal Palace, Huddersfield Town's Mike O'Grady, and Bobby. With skipper Michael McNeil of Middlesbrough also absent, Greenwood gave the captaincy to Moore, the only player selected for all the under-23 matches that season.

Because of commitments to the FA Cup semi-finals the following Saturday, together with an agreement with the Germans not to choose players with more than two full caps, the selectors were able to give chances to some promising youngsters. So, Greenwood fielded a somewhat experimental team.

England U23 4 West Germany U23 1
Wednesday, 15 March 1961
Friendly
White Hart Lane
Attendance: 15,632
Referee: Leo Horn (Netherlands)

England U23: Macedo, Cohen, Ashurst, Shawcross, McGrath, Moore, Paine, Hill, Byrne, Barnwell, Harrison.
West Germany U23: Bernard, Neumann, Olk, Sundermann, Wenauer, Porges, Flachenecker, Schuetz, Stehl, Straschitz, Kremer.

In the days prior to the match, Greenwood took the under-23s, including Bobby, to face a West Ham XI at the Boleyn Ground. Ironically it was the same evening that Ted Fenton was exiled from Upton Park. The fixture was played over two half-hour halves, the Irons came out on top with Geoff Hurst scoring the only goal, a 30-yard piledriver. That was the moment Ron grasped what Hurst might be able to do as an out-and-out striker. Unbeknown to anyone outside the club boardroom, Ron already knew he was the Hammers' manager in waiting.

England and West Germany had met at under-23 level only once previously, drawing 2-2 a couple of years earlier in Bochum.

In the fifth under-23 game of the 1960/61 season, for long periods it looked as if Moore and Byrne were taking on the Germans single-handed. Byrne, was inspirational. He and Bobby had moved almost simultaneously into the England under-23 team and they were now building a noticeable understanding. Playing with tremendous grace, judgement and athleticism, Byrne's control and distribution seemed to be the spark of England's offensive potential. Time after time, when Moore moved forward to make a pass, he found that John was ideally placed to receive the ball. The Crystal Palace progeny appeared to have an innate ability to exploit space, showing his fantastic positional sense, but it was Moore who was getting the ball to him. Greenwood started to imagine how the two could become a phenomenal presence in the West Ham ranks.

The Germans were lively and agile, and certainly put in a shift, but they were all at sea for the most part when it came to interpreting effort into attack, particularly after their inside-left, Hermann Straschitz, left the game 25 minutes in with what looked like a rib injury. Heinz Höher, who in total would play nine times for the West German Olympic team, proved an energetic replacement, but his imaginative enthusiasm was not matched by his fellow forwards, who operated in a way that was far too straightforward to worry England.

Cohen dominated Willibert Kremer, the German outside-left, allowing the Fulham lad to make several penetrating raids into the visitors' half. His passing was accurate but Terry Paine and Fred Hill did not make the best of his efforts.

The opening goal, in the 31st minute, was a Byrne conversion of a lofty pass, delivered by John Barnwell from the edge of the penalty area. The left-footed volley was emblematic of Johnny's whole performance. The ball cannoned off the underside of the bar and goalkeeper Günter Bernard managed to grasp the rebound. Although the Germans in the crowded penalty area made avid appeals to the referee, their protestations were to no avail as the man in black deemed that the ball had crossed the line – foreshadowing Hurst in 1966.

Paine and Hill might have increased the lead before half-time, but it was Heinz Strehl, combining with Höher, who netted six minutes from the break. That had been the first incisive move of the match from the Germans.

Paine, who was later accused of being more 'decorative than direct' (that must have been a first and last accusation of its type made about the

Winchester brick shithouse) shot crisply to put England in front from Len Ashurst's 54th-minute cross. On the hour Hill nutted home Paine's corner.

Greenwood's lads were comfortably on top for all but isolated moments of the second half. Chelsea's Michael Harrison, a late replacement for Huddersfield's Mick O'Grady, missed when it would have been easier to score, Byrne also came close before Manchester City's David Shawcross, after calling loudly for the ball, made it four for England.

Byrne had demonstrated the rare combination of power, poise, and subtlety beyond his years. Such was his shine under the White Hart Lane floodlights, post-match he was being touted for the senior team's summer tour of Portugal, Italy, and Austria.

Bobby's first game as skipper was West Germany's first loss at under-23 level in six years. Although the visitors put on a spirited showing, Byrne, Hill, and Barnwell established a solid understanding, while the English defence all but closed down the efforts of their opponents' forwards.

Moore was to remember Byrne's performance that evening as 'outstanding'. His sense of where he was in relation to everyone else on the pitch, even at that early stage, was advanced. Moore believed that anyone watching might have suspected that he and Byrne had agreed to deal with the Germans on their own, so often did the ball go from Bobby to Johnny. But it was down to Byrne's instinctive ability to get into space and Moore's capacity to find the West Horsley scion.

Malcolm Allison had watched the game with French international Raymond Kopa, who Bobby was destined to meet on the pitch in the future. Allison calculated that Bobby had made over 100 passes and only once failed to find a team-mate. At one point Kopa told Malcolm, 'If Bobby hadn't made that bad pass, I wouldn't have known he was playing.' It was Moore's only slip of the game, his percentage of passing accuracy and keeping possession was extraordinary.

Insightfully, Allison was to say of Bobby that he had many innate strengths, elements of his personality and ability that he hadn't learned from anyone. Malcolm was referring to Moore's seemingly natural charisma, his instinct for leadership, and the means to distance himself from the team, while remaining connected to it.

Allison was to recall how when he and Bobby attended matches together, Moore would try to avoid people and duck out of the limelight. He had no yearning for recognition or to be in the public gaze. However, at the same time, he was determined to be central to any side he was part of, and as such, shine.

Over the second half of the 1960/61 season West Ham won just three games, collapsing to 16th place in the First Division in the process. But there was consolation for Bobby as his international career continued to blossom.

On the eve of FA Cup Final day, from the 1950s up to the start of 1970s, it was something of a tradition for a senior England side to test the mettle of an under-23 team, known as Young England. Bobby was picked for Young England in both the 1961 and 1962 matches. On 5 May 1961, at Stamford Bridge, the encounter ended in a 1-1 draw. *The Times* reported Bobby's first appearance for Young England facing the country's senior side, ''Young England took what honours there were at Stamford Bridge last night when they held the England team to a draw. But this was England with a difference, for [Jimmy] Greaves was not playing. If it did nothing else it showed that England can afford to be without a finisher of Greaves's excellent reliability.

'In spite of a brave display by Macedo, the England forwards had enough chances to win comfortably in the second half. Charlton, Hitchens, and Eastham all missed their opportunities, and England's plan of using Eastham as a goalscorer was not a success. England's selectors had a bad moment in the second half when the right-back, Armfield, was helped off with an injured right ankle after a collision with Ashurst. Fortunately, the injury proved to be only bruising. Haynes scored for England, Robson for Young England.

'The teams were:

'England – Springett (Sheffield Wednesday); Armfield (Blackpool), McNeil (Middlesbrough); Robson (West Bromwich Albion), Swan (Sheffield Wednesday), Flowers (Wolverhampton Wanderers); Douglas (Blackburn Rovers), Eastham (Arsenal), Hitchens (Aston Villa), Haynes (Fulham – captain), Charlton (Manchester United).

'Young England – Macedo (Fulham); Angus (Burnley – captain), Ashurst (Sunderland); Kirkham (Wolverhampton Wanderers), McGrath (Newcastle), Moore (West Ham United); Paine (Southampton), Hill (Bolton Wanderers), Baker (Hibernian), Robson (Burnley), Harris (Burnley).'

Bobby didn't get much of a mention in the press, but most who saw the match and voiced an opinion thought he had played solidly enough, although Johnny Haynes had reason to remember the young Hammer's performance. I spent a little time with him when we were both in the bookmaking industry in the mid-1970s and he told me, 'Bobby was really the captain in that game. There wasn't a player on the park who didn't recognise his authority, the quiet way he organised from the middle of the back line. It was striking, but you couldn't put your finger on exactly what he was doing. Jimmy Armfield was a great judge of players, and as we walked away from Stamford Bridge, he said to me, "One day that lad should captain England." I don't think I replied. Bobby didn't drive players on, there was no praise or criticism, a bit of pointing, arm-waving, but nothing else, not even a change of expression. But by the time I got home I was thinking Jim was probably right.'

6

'IF YOU'RE AS GOOD AS TOM FINNEY WAS, YOU DON'T HAVE TO TELL ANYBODY.'

It was on 11 May 1961 that Bobby Moore took off with the FA touring side. They were a very eclectic group of players, the FA needing to draw from across the football panorama (amateur and professional) that they represented. As such, the party must have been a source of a great deal of valuable knowledge and learning for Bobby. The legend who was Sir Tom Finney came out of retirement as player-manager to lead an 18-strong squad on their very extensive six-week journey.

I was privileged and fortunate enough to meet Sir Tom at an anniversary celebration of the 1964 FA Cup Final, which included many former players from both the West Ham and Preston sides that met at Wembley that year. Sir Tom was for me perhaps the finest exponent of the game who ever lived, although he wasn't involved in that historic match of '64. The North End legend was a guest of honour at a reunion event. He remembered Bobby as one of the younger members of the touring party. Sir Tom recalled Moore as having a shy and reserved nature, but despite that being, by a long way, the most studious of the squad in terms of his curiosity about the game. Moore showed great respect for the 'Preston Plumber' and the more senior players. He particularly admired the modesty of the great England international, once saying of him, 'I was in awe of the man … If you're as good as Tom Finney was, you don't have to tell anybody.'

Sir Tom told me how, while on tour, some of the squad were introduced to Jack Sullivan, the former All Blacks player and latterly the national coach of the New Zealand rugby union side. Jack was impressed with Moore's inquisitiveness, particularly about conditioning and diet, but also about the attitude and motivation of high-level rugby players.

The tour was intended to be principally a six-week, ten-match expedition to the Far East and New Zealand, but there was a trip to San Francisco thrown in on the way back to the UK. It must have been an amazing experience for Bobby, perhaps even a life-changing one.

The squad[16] was as follows: Alan A'Court (Liverpool), Colin Appleton (Leicester City), Bobby Brown (Fulham), Lawrie Brown (Northampton Town), Ray Charnley (Blackpool), Fred Else (Preston North End), Johnny Fantham (Sheffield Wednesday), Tom Finney (ex-Preston North End), Mike Greenwood (Corinthian-Casuals), Grenville Hair (Leeds United), George Hannah (Manchester City), Jim L. Lewis Jr (Walthamstow Avenue), Hugh Lindsay (Kingstonian), Bobby Moore (West Ham United), Mike Pinner (Manchester United and RAF), Graham Shaw (Sheffield United), Gerry Summers (Sheffield United), Bryan Thurlow (Norwich City).

The party included three full internationals in A'Court, Finney, and Shaw, three future internationals in Charnley, Fantham and Moore, and six members of the Great Britain's amateur Olympic team who competed in the 1960 Games in Rome – Lawrie[17] and Bobby Brown, Greenwood, Lewis, Lindsay, and Pinner. GB had been drawn in a tough group that included the hosts, Brazil, and China (that was really Taiwan, then known as 'Formosa'). England beat the Chinese, drew with Italy, and lost by the odd goal of seven to the South Americans.

Stan Anderson (Sunderland) and Joe Shaw (Sheffield United) had been included in the original tour party, but later withdrew. They were replaced by Lawrie Brown and Gerry Summers.

In the second match of the tour, played on 21 May 1961, Moore scored one of his side's goals in a 4-2 defeat of a Hong Kong XI. It was a successful adventure for the English, winning all 11 of their games, netting 78 times and conceding just seven.

English Football Association Tour of Malaysia, Singapore, Hong Kong, New Zealand, and USA – May-June 1961

Malaysia			
Date	**Venue**	**Result**	**Scorers**
13 May	Stadium Merdeka, Kuala Lumpur	Malaysia 2 **England 4** [HT:1-2]	Koe, Choe **Charnley (3)**, **Lindsay**

---

16   Corinthian Casuals, Kingstonian and Walthamstow Avenue were part of the Isthmian League during the 1960/61 season.

17   Lawrie Brown turned professional prior to the tour – he would play well over a hundred games for Arsenal from 1961 before moving to Spurs in 1964.

Attendance – 20,000. The tour began with all three England internationals in the side (including Finney) and two of the future caps, one of whom (Ray Charnley) scored a hat-trick. Two of the Olympic team started the match, with Hugh Lindsay scoring, and another, goalkeeper, Mike Pinner came on as a substitute.

Malaysia:

Yusuf Bakar, Seng Chey, Ahmed Nazari, Wal Hong, Kamaruddin, Dutton, Gabrielle, Ghani, Choe, Arthur Koh, Abu Hassan.

English FA XI:

Fred Else (Mike Pinner), Grenville Hair, Graham Shaw, Gerry Summers, Lawrie Brown, Colin Appleton, Tom Finney [c], Hugh Lindsay, Ray Charnley, John Fantham, Alan A'Court.

Referee: T Nadarajah (Malaya).

Singapore			
17 May	Jalan Besar Stadium, Kallang	Singapore 0 **England 9** [HT:0-5]	**Charnley (2), Fantham (2), Hannah (3), A'Court, Finney**

Attendance – 14,294. This time, all six past, current and future England internationals played (Moore had missed the first game). There were no amateurs in the side, but there was one member of the Olympic team, who was by that time a professional (Lawrie Brown)

Singapore:

Idros Albar, Lee Wah-chin, Matmoon Sudasee, M Sutton, Kok Seng, Osman Johan,

Ibrahim Hussain, Rahmin Omar, Sahar Hussain, Kim Swee, Ibrahim Mansoor.

English FA XI:

Fred Else, Grenville Hair, Graham Shaw, **Bobby Moore**, Lawrie Brown, Colin Appleton, Tom Finney [c], George Hannah, Ray Charnley, John Fantham, Alan A'Court.

		Hong Kong	
21 May	Government Stadium, Wan Chai	Hong Kong 2 **England 4** [HT:2-4]	Lau, Yeung **Charnley (2), Moore, Hannah**

The visitors were unchanged from the side that had won in Singapore. Moore scored a stunning goal, dancing round four defenders before shooting home just inside the penalty area. He also had a hand in Hannah's success.

Hong Kong:
Wong Su-woo (Kwok Chow-ming 29'), Lok Tak-hing, Kwok Kam-hung, Wong Man-wai, Keung Ke-pe, Keung Le-chung, Wong Chi-keung, Lau Chi-Lam, Chow-Siu Hung (Yeung Wai 7'), Ho Cheung-yau, Mok Chun-wah.

English FA XI:
Fred Else, Grenville Hair, Graham Shaw, **Bobby Moore**, Lawrie Brown, Colin Appleton, Tom Finney [c], George Hannah, Ray Charnley, John Fantham, Alan A'Court.

Referee: Sammy Tsang (Hong Kong)

23 May	Government Stadium, Wan Chai	Combined Chinese XI 0 **England 3** [HT:0-0]	**Charnley (pen), Fantham, Hannah**

Attendance – 20,000. The hosts kept six players that had finished the first game, two days earlier, and recruited from China to field a combined Chinese XI. England made two changes, including replacing one of their full internationals (Graham Shaw). The Chinese came out all guns blazing in the first 15 minutes and were unlucky not to go ahead when Moore cleared on the England goal line. Thereafter however it was all pretty much one way traffic.

Combined Chinese XI:
Le Takueu, Lok Tak-hing, Tau Mee, Lo Shun-king, Lau Tim, Wong Man-wai, Wong Chi-keung, Lau Chi-lam, Yeung Wai-to, Ho Cheung-yau, Leung Wai-hung.

English FA XI:
Fred Else, Bryan Thurlow, Grenville Hair, **Bobby Moore**, Lawrie Brown, Gerry Summers, Tom Finney [c], George Hannah, Ray Charnley, John Fantham, Alan A'Court.

Referee: I Petrie.

New Zealand			
31 May	Caledonian Ground, Dunedin	Otago 0 **England 10** [HT:0-3]	**George Hannah 10', Alan A'court, Colin Appleton 2, Bobby Brown 3, Hugh Lindsay 3**

Attendance – 7,500. The squad had flown almost six thousand miles to visit New Zealand for the first time. They made five changes from their last game in Hong Kong and fielded their three full internationals, but none of their future caps. Three of the Olympic team were in the side; two of them scoring hat-tricks against a team representing one of the largest area of the South Island

Otago:
E. J. Stephenson, A. Young, H. Sperandio, D. Downie, J. Ferguson, John Rae, W. Berry, George Cuthill, G. Little, Duncan McVey, Charlie Steele Jr..(guest player. His home province was Southland)
English FA XI:
Mike Pinner, Bryan Thurlow, Graham Shaw, Colin Appleton, Lawrie Brown, Gerry Summers, Tom Finney [c], George Hannah, Bobby Brown, Hugh Lindsay, Alan A'court.

3 June	English Park, Christchurch, South Island	Canterbury 1 **England 11** [HT:1-6]	Durant **Hannah, Fantham (4), Lewis (2), Charnley, Finney (2), L.Brown**

Attendance – 12,500. Ontago's neighbours fared no better under a merciless England attack, although the tourists made six changes, including their three future internationals coming back and one of the full internationals (Alan A'Court) left out. Two of the Olympic team played and both scored
Canterbury's goal came after Appleton handled the ball in the penalty area when trying to halt a run by Verham. Canterbury were awarded a penalty. Durant's initial kick was blocked by Else but the ball rebounded to Durant who managed to score. At that stage the match was standing at 1-3.
All the second half goals (5) were scored in the last ten minutes of the match!
D. Chapman, P. Frost and P. Saunderson played for Canterbury in this match. It is likely, but not confirmed, that those players are Derek Chapman, Phil Frost and Peter Saunderson.

Canterbury:
Derek Chapman, Kevin Hendy, Phil Frost, Dick Durant, Dave Simmonds, Hiram Taylor, A. Verham, Paul Rennell [c], Edward Charlton, Terry Haydon, Peter Saunderson.

English FA XI:
Fred Else, Grenville Hair, Graham Shaw, **Bobby Moore**, Lawrie Brown, Colin Appleton, Jim Lewis, George Hannah, Ray Charnley, John Fantham, Tom Finney [c].

Referee: D. Welham (Otago) – assisted by L. J. Tointon and J. A. Davidson.

5 June	Basin Reserve, Wellington, North Island	New Zealand 0 **England 8** [HT:0-2]	**Charnley (2), Fantham (3), Lewis, Finney,** *Middleton* **(OG)**

Attendance – 19,000. The tourists made three changes to face the national side as they arrived on the North Island for the first time. A'Court returned to the team to bring back a full complement of six full internationals (previous and future), alongside three of the Olympic team. Moore's long and swiftly taken free kick was picked up by Finney, who scored with a beautifully executed lob from 30 yards out, catching Whiting off his line.

New Zealand:
Peter Whiting, Jim Middleton, Arthur Leong, Jim Warrender [c], John Kemp, Ken Armstrong (also the New Zealand coach), Gary Eccles, John Wrathall, Rodney Reid, D Buller, Robert Ormond.

English FA XI:
Mike Pinner, Grenville Hair, Graham Shaw, **Bobby Moore**, Lawrie Brown, Gerry Summers, Tom Finney [c], Jim Lewis, Ray Charnley, John Fantham, Alan A'court.
Referee: Dickie (New Zealand).

7 June	McLean Park, Napier, Hawke's Bay	Minor Provinces 0 **England 13** [HT:0-4]	**Tom Finney 3, Bobby Brown 3, John Fantham 2, Jim Lewis 2, Hugh Lindsay, Lawrie Brown, Graham Shaw**

Attendance – 6,000. A third game in five days didn't stop England hitting double figures once again. They had scored 42 goals in a week.

Minor Provinces:

R. Leakey, T. Henderson, K. Eyles, J. McGhie, Arthur Leong, P. Marshall, Jim Bell, E. Bellchambers, K. Polyansky, E. Stewart, Robert Ormond.

England FA XI:

Mike Pinner, Grenville Hair, Graham Shaw, **Bobby Moore,** Mike Greenwood, Bobby Brown, Tom Finney [c] Jim Lewis, Hugh Lindsay, John Fantham, Lawrie Brown,

The New Zealand Minor Provinces line-up given above is based on information which was published about a week before the date of the match. Some late changes may have been made to the line-up. The source listed the following as reserves: W. Clarck (goalkeeper), W. Webber, J. McMillan.

10 June	Epsom Showgrounds, Auckland	New Zealand 1 **England 6** [HT:0-3]	Duncan McVey 87' **Jim Lewis 15' pen, Ray Charnley 18', Alan A'court 30', Tom Finney 54', 82' John Fantham 62**

Attendance – 15,000. Both sides made only two changes from their meeting in Wellington, five days earlier. England had one less Olympian in the side as a result.

New Zealand:

Peter Whiting, Jim Middleton, Arthur Leong, Jim Warrender [c], John Kemp, Ken Armstrong, Gary Eccles, Arthur Inglis, Rodney Reid, Duncan McVey, Robert Ormond.

English FA XI:

Fred Else, Grenville Hair, Graham Shaw, **Bobby Moore,** Lawrie Brown, Colin Appleton,

Tom Finney [c], Jim Lewis, Ray Charnley, John Fantham, Alan A'court.

Referee: Williams (New Zealand).

14 June	Epsom Showgrounds, Auckland	Auckland 0 **England 8** [HT:0-4]	**Tom Finney 4, Bobby Brown 2, Lawrie Brown, OG** Wallace

Attendance – 8,000. England made two changes for their final match in New Zealand, giving them three full internationals, two future caps and three Olympians.
The first four goals of the game were all scored in the first 20 minutes. The Press (a Christchurch newspaper) credited Bobby Brown with three goals.

Auckland:
A. Cozens, B. J. Wallace, G. Kaiser, Ken Armstrong [c], W. G. Ward,
John Kemp,Gary Eccles, John Wrathall, L. Polyansky, R. J. Cochran, P. Oden.

English FA XI:
Fred Else, Grenville Hair, Graham Shaw, **Bobby Moore**, Lawrie Brown,
Gerry Summers, Tom Finney [c], Jim Lewis, Bobby Brown, John Fantham,
Alan A'court.

Referee: Morrie Swain – assisted by Les Coffman and Barry Wilkins.

USA			
18 June	San Francisco, USA	San Francisco 1 **England 2**	Helmut Bicek **Lindsay, Charnley**

Attendance – 10,000. Another 6,500 mile trip took the squad to San Francisco, where they played one last game before heading for home. The home city goalscorer, Helmut Bicek, spent most of his career with the Los Angeles Soccer Club. He earned five caps, scoring two goals, with the US national team between 1960 and 1965. Bicek scored on his international debut in a 3–3 draw with Mexico on 6 November 1960. He played again seven days later; that time Mexico were victorious. That defeat kept the US out of the 1962 FIFA World Cup. Bicek did not play for the national team again until 7 March 1965, another draw with Mexico – once again Bicek was on the scoresheet. His last cap came ten days later in a 1-0 victory over Honduras. Both games in 1965 were qualification games for the 1966 FIFA World Cup.

English FA XI:
Fred Else, Grenville Hair, Graham Shaw, **Bobby Moore**, Lawrie Brown, Colin
Appleton, Tom Finney [c], George Hannah, Ray Charnley, Hugh Lindsay,
Alan A'Court.

Referee: R.Spath

With four under-23 caps to his name at the time, just a month before landing in Malaysia for the first match of the tour Bobby had celebrated his 20th birthday. By the end of the tour it was clear to Sir Tom that the most consistent player had been Moore, but above and beyond that he told me, 'From just before Christmas 1960 the FA were looking at who might go on tour. Bobby was talked about on the back of some good reports about him from the likes of Ron Greenwood and Water Winterbottom, but strangely not so much from his club. So, I knew he was going to be handy, although as we went on, I found him to be something special. I told anyone who asked just that. While he couldn't have been considered the "star" of the tour, he was too modest for that, he was by far the most committed trainer and team player. He made everyone look a little bit better for him being on the park. Moore was obviously a new type of defender; we had not seen anyone quite like him before.'

Iron evolution

Ron Greenwood's first full season working alongside Moore was a time for laying ground, although everyone was pretty much finding their feet. The Irons were still new to top-flight football, and had done well to maintain their place, but the transition from old traditions to new methods and ideas about the game, although much spadework had been done by Malcolm Allison and Noel Cantwell, was a cultural shift of some proportions. Greenwood brought with him more of a demand for something that looked and felt beautiful. At Upton Park, the days of the 'agricultural artisan' player were done.

A high priority was to find someone to fill Ernie Gregory's sizeable brogues, and the first shot at this was shipping in Scottish international Lawrie Leslie. Seemingly knowing no fear, the Caledonian custodian was soon to be a favourite at the Boleyn Ground.

During the summer of 1961 a roof was added to Upton Park's North Bank, so for the new season there would be cover on all four sides of the ground. For those who never lived through those days and have been acclimatised to 'luxury football', you have missed something in the working-class culture of the game. Sitting hygienically in your plastic seat has little comparison to the traditions of support; no one sits to fight. Having your arse cosseted is more being supported than supporting, but it's too late to do a thing about that. We are softened by the armchair 'pay-to-view' indulgence and stadiums that feel more like a furniture warehouse outlet, or the lobby of a budget tourist hotel at the dodgy end of Cancún, than a place, in the heat of competition, to *stand* behind your team. Yes, there are, at the time of writing, some experiments with bringing back standing, but this is little more than 'novelty' value, its resemblance to the traditions of watching football is slight. I guess song sheets will be next.

Moore would miss just one game over the 1961/62 season, (Eddie Bovington stepped in for the league victory at Bolton Wanderers) making 44 appearances in total.

In August, reigning league champions Tottenham were twice opponents for the Irons. It was all square at 2-2 in North London, but back in the East End Tony Scott opened the scoring for the Hammers and Alan Sealey (pleasingly, nicknamed 'Seal') sealed a 2-1 win for the hosts.

The game goes on and Bobby goes off

In the League Cup, Plymouth Argyle were defeated 3-2 at the start of September 1961 but the capriciously irreconcilable Irons then went out 3-1 at home to Aston Villa.

West Ham wended their wobbly way to Maine Road on 4 November. By the break the disoriented Boleyn boys were 3-1 down, a Peter Dobing hat-trick doing the damage. However, in the second half City's guests got their proverbial shit together to hit their hosts four times to take the game 5-3. But the historic moment of the match was Bobby Moore's sending off for a foul on winger Dave Wagstaffe. It was Moore's first and last dismissal in the top flight as a Hammer, and he became the first West Ham player to receive their marching orders under the stewardship of Ron Greenwood (save that one for the pub quiz).

The referee, Chesterfield's very own Ken 'Friar' Tuck, had simultaneously blown his whistle for the offence and for full time (and probably at the same time farted – talk about 'multitasking'). As the only red cards around at that time were those sent by the Young Communists to express solidarity with fellow workers on Lenin's birthday, the dismissal didn't become apparent until after the match. The incident was to be the exception that was to prove the rule in terms of Bob's lofty professionalism, and yet another reason it was natural for his fellow players to look up to him in a special way.

Looking back some years on, Bobby recollected that from the very start of the game it seemed like a certainty he and the fiery flanker were destined for something of a battle. Youth and enthusiasm playing its part, Moore recognised that both he and his opponent were determined to 'come out on top'. He said, 'In the first minute I took the ball from him in a tackle,' which would have wound up Wagstaff, who was justifiably proud of his dribbling skills.

Bob and the outside-left went on into the game fighting for advantage over each other, and Moore probably had got the better of the ongoing tussle in the second half. Thus, predictably the frustration overtook the lad who in 2013 would be inducted into Wanderers' Hall of Fame. Moore described the incendiary situation, 'For the whole of a 30-yard run up-field he kept after me, trying to get the ball back – and almost ripping the shirt off my back … The referee blew us up and gave West Ham a free kick. For the rest of the match there was a bit of what players call "atmosphere" between us, but it didn't flare up until the last minute of the game.'

Wagstaffe had lost the ball to Joe Kirkup, who in turn sent it to Bobby, who continued, 'I was out on the touchline when Joe Kirkup pushed the ball forward.

As I was collecting it, I sensed someone coming at my back, so I played it on to one of our forwards as quickly as possible.

'The ball was just away when I felt Wagstaffe's boot coming in sharp contact with the back of my leg. I spun round and gave him a vicious kick. The referee saw my retaliation and sent me off.'

Moore had got by Wagstaffe when the City man, from behind, got that crafty boot on the Hammer, clogging him across the back of his calves while pursuing him along the touchline. Thus a few good old cockney genes fired and the future steward of the Bispham Conservative Club in Blackpool was paid back about twice as much as he gave out. It has to be said that Moore placed his retaliation very well, causing the Openshaw assassin to fall like a sack of shit to the dirt.

For all this, Bob immediately regretted his action. Referee Tuck ('Shop' as he was sometimes referred to by players) didn't see the initial assault, but he saw Bob retaliate. What made matters worse in those days when conduct was probably more important than form was that Moore was due to be on England under-23 duty at Leeds the Monday after the game. Within the corridors of the FA, fired up by the media, Moore's temperament came under the metaphorical microscope that concluded with the FA suspending him for a week. He remembered his feelings. Youth and the concomitant lack of experience in disciplinary matters left him anxious about what the selection panel would make of his actions, 'I also felt very guilty about the whole business but everyone seemed very understanding about it.'

Typical of Bob, he took practical advantage of his seven-day suspension, having the smallpox jab required for some overseas trips. Such vaccines were relatively primitive compared to today and, as Moore told me, this one resulted in 'a dirty great lump'. He said, 'I doubt if I would have been fit to play that week in any case.' He confirmed however that he had 'learned a very good lesson. What had I gained from the momentary satisfaction of having a kick at a bloke? Nothing. What could anyone gain? Nothing.

'I thought about the whole business of petty fouling and retaliation. There are players who make a point of trying to annoy you from the kick-off, either by physical or verbal niggles. An angry player is less effective, and there is something to be gained in pushing a bloke until he is so incensed, he loses his temper.'

Tuck had made a bit of a name for himself the previous January, abandoning an FA Cup tie between Luton Town and Manchester City. Denis Law had scored all his side's goals as City stormed into a 6-2 lead, but Tuck stopped the game with just over 20 minutes to play due to heavy rain. For rain to stop play in a football match in that era was about as common as the Queen Mother nutting the

Archbishop of Canterbury during a Buck House garden party spat (she only ever did that the once, and he asked for it). City were to lose the rearranged fixture 3-1 with Law scoring their goal. While Mrs Tuck might have been looking for Ken's betting slips, the then most expensive player in Britain had his incredible feat from the first game wiped from the records.

In the light of his dismissal, Bobby was given a serious dressing-down by Greenwood in the shape of a protracted lecture about the necessity to control his temperament. Bobby was to ultimately put his hands up to the offence, admitting the old red mist had got the better of him, but almost immediately after the event he was to vow never again to give in to provocation, developing a notion that the best way to deal with provocateurs was seeing reprisal as compromising his own integrity and focus.

Bobby, throughout his career, was a target for opposition intimidation. Boots, insults, and elbows were aimed at him regularly. He was to say he realised that he was commonly taken to be something of a 'tame character'. He partly believed that this perception might have been connected to his role as his national team's captain, and the thinking that such responsibility would only be taken up by a 'Holy Joe'. According to Moore this made thuggish antagonists take him for a 'stuck-up snob', marking him as a target for coercion, which would then lead them to lose control. But Bobby had his own means of winding up aggressive opponents, 'I'd pretend they don't exist. "I'm not coming down to your level, mate" is the attitude I try to convey and this infuriates the niggler … so much he loses his temper, or drifts away to try his tactics with someone else.'

For all this, Moore was familiar how the media magnifies any controversy and how this impacted on player conduct, 'I and the rest of West Ham's players seem to escape the huge publicity which surrounds the odd brawl on football fields. For some reason what is actually a tiny number of "incidents" is thought to be of fantastic interest to the public. I know for a fact that being involved in a scuffle and getting suspended adds to the amount a player can ask for his life story … I have made it a personal rule not to have anything to do with the kind of petty niggling that can lead up to fights on the field.'

For Moore, cheating and poor discipline or dirty play was at the very least a waste of time that usually led to incidents that did nothing for the game. He saw the player being sent off as letting his own team down, both for that game and for the length of any suspension. Bobby looked to garner the same sort of respect bestowed on Stanley Matthews and Tom Finney by way of their unimpeachable comportment. Moore saw that their ilk had not needed to stoop to foul play or questionable tactics of the kind that demonstrated irresponsible immaturity or just straightforward bloody-mindedness – they would see such behaviour as beneath their dignity.

This said, according to Moore he was not a 'goody-goody'. He explained, 'It's a cold-blooded decision made from a very practical point of view; a player who has complete control over his emotions has a great advantage over a player who may lose his head. By staying aloof from "all that" you plant the idea in their heads (or hope to) that you are superior all round. It's like psychological warfare.'

An example of this was when once, during the course of a game, a particular twat spat in Bobby's face. Moore wiped the gob with his shirt sleeve and offered the spittle back to the uncouth lout who had dealt it saying, 'I think this belongs to you.'

A fellow Hammers fan, Stephen Infield, recalled a meeting with Newcastle at Upton Park on 2 December 1972. The clubs were in eighth and ninth respectively in the old First Division. In Stephen's words, 'Bobby's foot had brushed the defender Frank Clark's heel as the ball went off for a goal kick at the North Bank end. Clark jumped up and got right in Bobby's face. Bobby just gently cupped Frank's face with both hands, smiled and then went back to upfield for Newcastle to take the goal kick.

'It was on *The Big Match*, and Jimmy Hill in the post-match analysis, specifically commented on it after the game, admiring how a classy player reacts to provocation … Bobby Moore, Proper class!'

Highlights of the 1-1 draw – Trevor Brooking scoring for the Irons – can be found on YouTube. Stephen let me know that those moments about Bobby cupping Frank's face are at 18 minutes 47 seconds. Hill's analysis of Bobby Ferguson and Moore starts at 34.08. His comment on Bobby's reaction to Clarke can be seen 37.40 in. Hill gives a glowing critique of Bobby Ferguson that is also worth a watch 34.08 in.

Moore understood the need for hard men, such as Nobby Stiles, but felt that players needed to know the difference between that and needlessly uncontrolled belligerence. He also saw that footballers, to maintain the spectacle of the sport, need to be prepared to face and deal with its physicality, 'It's a man's game and if you can't take hard, jarring tackles you should try hockey.'

While he believed that there were 'no full-time cloggers in the game', he argued that spending any time in football during his era would mean coming across sides that played hard, that there were some defenders who just waited for an opportunity to 'flatten you with a good hefty charge' and others with tempers that would be easily provoked into retaliation 'but the fault there is of temper, not dirtiness'.

If Bobby responded at all to a snarl it would be with a smile. During a game at Bolton on New Year's Eve 1960, John Higgins, an old-school central defender, persistently yelled at his team-mates, alluding to Moore, 'Send him over here, I'll kick the bastard.' No reflection on John there, his attitude was pretty much indicative of his position in that era, but Bobby was an artist in comparison. At the same time, if Higgins had got the chance to kick the Barking boy, the 'Macclesfield Masher' himself might have felt the swift presence of another 'southern softie' in the Hammers' ranks that day, Upton Park-born Andy Malcolm. The Bakewell tough guy would almost certainly have been proved a bit of a tart by maleficent Malc.

While I was writing this in the summer of 2022, Sajid Javid was busy resigning from then-PM Boris Johnson's government. During his parting shot he said, 'One thing we can control is our own values and behaviours.' I can't say I'm a big fan of the Javster or his political persuasion, but that contention struck me as poignant when thinking about Bobby Moore. If you are out of control, you can't follow a plan or a strategy (being able to make and follow a plan and strategise is what control is). Lacking direction or aim, what can you really achieve of any meaningful and enduring merit – other than the remote chance that the inevitable catalogue of accidents that result will include one or two happy ones? Perhaps that'll be one of the parables/cautionary tales that will endure from the mess Saj, late in the day, bailed out of?

The next time Moore was dismissed was 6 October 1976, and by that time he was skipper of Fulham. It was amid extraordinary scenes at the end of in a League Cup third round replay against Bolton Wanderers at Burnden Park. Now that's an interesting, but another, story.

Professionality

I have used (and will continue to refer to) the much overused and widely misunderstood word and concept of 'professionalism' in relation to Moore. His professional discipline has never really been deeply analysed and so it has failed to be entirely understood in print. Perhaps that's because one would not only need a model of professionalism, but also Bobby's interpretation of professional deportment and attitude. I have spent many years on the global stage working to define the nature of professional practice and conduct. This is certainly not the place to present any lengthy conclusions, but ideas about 'integrity' and 'decency' prevail in the analysis.

Ron Greenwood, in a nutshell, saw Moore's professionalism as underpinning of what he wanted to create in football. Without a grasp on what professionality might be I can understand how one might see Moore as 'unemotional' or even 'cold'. But when someone dies, say in hospital, good nurses don't weep along with all the family and friends round the bed. They will tend to the body in a calm and systematic way; they will click in to comforting the family, perhaps offering a cup of tea etc. In short, they will control their emotions and by extension the situation; they will extend professional care. That doesn't mean they don't empathise or feel sad – in my experience most do – but their role, their function is bound by procedures and codes of practice. They have a job to do and doing that job defines their professionality. They couldn't do this if they collapsed in grief with the family of the deceased.

In something of the same way, Moore's job was not to let go of his emotions and, say, wildly celebrate a goal, do what he could to influence a referee to send an opponent off, feign injury, or lash out at opponents when foiled or fouled. All of these 'performances' constitute unprofessional behaviour. The concept of the 'professional foul' muddied the waters for a time, a sort of excuse to cheat, but Moore took his role to encompass the avoidance of intimidation, exaggeration, fake consternation, and not giving way to tears, fears, demonstratively reacting to jeers or cheers on the field. His first duty (being imbrued by Malcolm Allison's doctrine, to 'take' responsibility) was to save or win the game, but crucially without compromising his leadership, dignity, and integrity by way of infantile, irresponsible, and irrational behaviour. This was the spine of his professionalism.

Bobby's own shorter explanation for such behaviour was looking not to lose concentration at crucial moments – such as the minutes after a goal is scored, a vulnerable time for most teams (from the point of view of a supporter maybe this might be particularly true of West Ham). For the players, for the club, for the fans that is as caring as you can get. It is more caring than carelessly dancing round kissing the bloke next to you for instance. One can be emotional and remain in control of one's emotions. What is selfish (cold) is just doing whatever it is that occurs to you and fuck everyone and everything else.

Application to task overriding anger, applying logic, rationality, intelligence, or 'sense', tempering raw emotional and subjective reactions – these are pivotal considerations when looking at what constitutes professional behaviour. In short, professional conduct is a melding of logic, dignity, and wisdom – indeed, like love and marriage, they go together like a horse and carriage (and 'you can't have one without the other').

As outlined above, Moore didn't see his reactions as some attempt at sainthood; it was about making professional and so rational decisions. But he also understood that his response, or lack of it, to abuse and intimidate gave the bullies and cheats the idea that he felt he was superior to them, or that they were inferior to him. And he was, and they were. As he mentioned to me once, 'It's like psychological warfare.' I never got the chance to give a useful response to that, but as usual, on the drive home I thought of one – 'It's professionalism.'

Others have picked up on this sort of response, Glenn Hoddle being one. He gave a gorgeous example of an opponent getting in his face, screaming, and threatening. Hoddle looked at him askance and asked, 'Err, who are you?'

Hard men are rarely the mouthy wanker who pretends to be one. Plaistow's own Martin Peters was the hardest of players you might meet. You won't find many incidents of the likes of Tommy Smith, Norman Hunter, or Ron 'Chopper' Harris laying into 'The Ghost' – just as he produced 'goals from nowhere', he could inflict pain in much the same way. Hence the so-called 'mad dogs' gave him a wide berth for the most part. In much the same way Denis Law, while complaining about the praise Moore got for his 'sporting' attitude, said, 'But you're not there when he's standing on my fucking feet.' Peter Osgood recalled, seemingly still feeling the bruises, how Bobby 'had a way of sticking his knee in your groin with that face-on tackle he had … it not only stung at the time, it gave you a headache until the next day'.

Moore was clever – he went along with the folklore about him – but he was as solid as a rock and as sharp as the sharpest of blades. When it came to covert aggression, well, look no further than Cantwell and Allison – Moore's teachers. I'm pretty sure the likes of skinny-arsed Roy Maurice Keane, and dainty Duncan Ferguson, before being conscious of it, would have been trampled into the 1950s mud of Upton Park by either and perhaps both.

There is a root to anger. It is not a base emotion, it comes from something; humiliation, anxiety, misery, fear, resentment, feelings of ineptitude, a need to compensate or disguise feelings of inferiority or failure and so on. Once this is understood, one can see that anguish, as a standalone response, is incomprehensible, and only slackened (never sated) by its expression; the expression of anguish does not cause the anger to disappear – it is a 'cathartic' act, temporary, just letting off pressure, that will, until the actual base cause is addressed, build up again. This repetitive and vicious cycle is what makes for what we call 'angry people' – individuals trapped in the prison of their own anger. Bobby did not let this loss of control happen to (and so dominate) him, even in the face of continued provocation, intimidation, and injustice. If he had habituated getting involved in that dance, it would have literally been professional suicide.

Anger tends to provoke anger in others, to the point where we all destroy each other. Moore's response (an apparent non-response) to persistent violations had two outcomes: either the anguish was defused in the resulting puzzlement of the assailant, or the angry aggressor defeated themselves by way of their anger bouncing back on them via Bobby's refusal to reciprocate that anger.

This attitude does not rule out considered retaliation though. The professional has an obligation to teach others the consequences of both decency and abuse – this is part of the integrity of the professional role. For instance, there was an occasion when Bobby was thumped twice in quick succession by an opponent. He made a point of showing that he was checking his attacker's number, although the bloke had one of those 'bulldog with a mouth full of spanners' faces – you were not going to forget a fizzog of that sort. However, it was the deliberateness of the action that would have an impact. The thug came at Bobby a couple of more times, but on the next occasion, the one Moore had lured him into, the geezer eventually got to his feet on the terraces. The moral of this tale? Well, if you act instantly the referee will link action 'A' with reaction 'B' – so wait! What you might call the 'Wagstaffe lesson' – revenge is a dish best served cold, but it can also be an edifying desert.

Integrity

For all this, integrity, perhaps the foundation of professionalism, feels like an increasingly rare quality, not only in football but more generally. Literally it means being honest, having strong moral principles, but in professional contexts it relates also to being 'integrated', like holding yourself together, staying in control. This involves maintaining poise, or straightforward dignity, that necessarily encompasses appreciable moral fibre. The late and lamented Terry Neill, the Northern Ireland international who played for and then managed Arsenal, told of the respect Moore had for his friends on the pitch. 'Bobby and I grew up together as teenagers in London and at a very early stage, we agreed on a pact … We decided that if we were playing against each other, whatever side won a corner, neither of us would go up to intimidate the other. It was a pact we never broke. I miss him now like hell.'

Terry told me after he had left Highbury, 'Bobby was always polite, to anyone and everyone. That's a massive strength that's rare today. Sure, it's showing respect for others, but the key is, if you are unable to respect others, how are you going to respect yourself? It's a discipline, but with Bobby it was innate. Like me, it was something implanted in him as a kid. You'd rather have taken a kick in the shins than have someone take you as ill-mannered or rude. That's a good thing for the world, but it's also good for you; hanging on to your decency, your integrity as a human being.'

Taking Terry's logic a step further, one's behaviours or conduct constitute the physical playing out of one's attitudes, that are held together by personal values.

What you do reflects who you are, to others but, perhaps more importantly, yourself. No one had to tidy up after Moore; not his mum, wife, or fellow players. Never seen any other way than immaculately turned out, on and off the pitch, Bobby was also zealously neat. He would arrange everything in order and just so. The clothes in his wardrobe were lined up as though they had been prepared for inspection; his jumpers were hung in sequence from dark to light. It was almost an aesthetic pleasure to open his wardrobe. This precision and organisation translated into his football.

Ray Wilson won 68 caps for England – I've never seen a better full-back – he remembered the way Moore used to make the most of the ball, never content to waste a pass or make a clearance for the sake of it if the ball could be played instead. He explained, '[Bobby] would use it so well … If I had won the ball in a tackle, he always made himself available, so I would always be free of trouble once I got it. Sometimes he would even knock me off the ball to be in there first to play it away. He was remarkable for a defender in the way he distributed it.' There was no messiness in Bobby's play. Everything was 'together', ordered – 'integrated'.

Wilson's description reflects Moore's generosity, the heart of his on-field management qualities. This is not a sentimental thing, not a sort of inclination for piecemeal and pointless charity. It was perhaps similar to how Bill Shankly understood football, as 'a type of socialism'; a practical reaction to life and its tasks, which grasps that almost any ambition is better, sooner, and more morally achieved if it can be undertaken collectively, drawing on 'all the talents'.

As mentioned above, leadership is grossly misunderstood. What is so often called Bobby's leadership was really his gift to manage himself. His self-management caused and inspired those around him to manage themselves. If there is such a thing called 'empowerment' (a word I detest) then what Bobby did on the football field was 'it.'

When Malcolm Allison and Noel Cantwell left Upton Park, Ken Brown was to fill part of the void left in Bobby's world. Although not so much as the father figures these men had been for Moore, Ken was more of a surrogate on-field big brother. He was to be with the Hammers for 17 years; no one played alongside Moore more often or as effectively than the man who progressed to become a successful manager at Norwich. Ken often recalled what Bobby sometimes put him through, saying, 'Bobby used to give me kittens most of the time.' He explained, 'We covered at centre-half for West Ham. I was the stopper and Bobby was the playmaker. My strength was heading and safety first, his strength was control and weighted passing. He could volley or one-touch a pass without looking, and you wouldn't struggle to reach it, it would drop at your feet, or to be exact, he'd put the ball where he knew you would be.'

Brown felt it was 'bred' into him to go behind Moore, 'My natural instinct was to cover him in case he missed a ball, but I can't remember him ever bloody missing it. He was so consistent.'

Ken was to describe Moore as 'unique' because, 'Every ball that used to come down to Bobby, I used to go behind him because he was never going to whack it, he wanted to use it all the time … I was there as a stopgap that never had a gap to stop.'

Moore referred to this partnership from his point of view, 'Ken Brown was far from being everyone's ideal at centre-half, but he was right for us. He was powerful in the air and his priority was always to get the ball the hell out of the danger area.'

Brown commented on this arrangement, 'While Bobby was all style and elegance, I was more of a no-nonsense player and concentrated on getting the ball out of harm's way. Sometimes I would bash it up in the air and Bobby would give me a sidelong look. I would say, "Well while it's up there it's not going into our net!"'

Bobby was to confirm this, saying of Ken, 'Sometimes he would whack it away when I thought we should capitalise on a situation … I'd say, "Brownie, what are you doing?" He'd say, "Don't worry, it's out of trouble up there." But he was always positive and it took a long while to replace him. He had a good understanding with John Bond.'

Brown knew his own strengths and Bobby's weaknesses, but he always took pains to emphasise Moore's extraordinary abilities, 'Bobby was an absolute master of positioning and his passing was always thoughtful and positive. It's no secret that he was not the greatest at heading, but I took care of that and won most things in the air.

'While the rest of us were sometimes dashing around like headless chickens, Bobby would just stroll into position and sort things out with a few barked commands and a perfectly timed tackle. He was a captain who led by example, never bullying, but quietly demanding extra effort. There have been few better defenders in the history of the game.'

You can see how both Moore and Brown analysed the properties of a team and their respective and joint roles; how people fit together, collaborate, give what they've got to make something more than the sum of its parts. To see and understand the concomitant patterns, shapes and horizon of interaction, realised in real time via recollection and imagination.

As Bobby managed Ken, so Ken managed Bobby, and West Ham, with Bobby at the helm, replicated this throughout the team and its play. It is this that Allison,

Greenwood, and Alf Ramsey wanted to foster, but to do it, you needed to flood the side with integrity and the thoughtful, pragmatic generosity that is necessarily part of an 'integrated' team, and to do that a Bobby Moore was required.

I'm not claiming Moore got up in the mornings with a clear intention to 'be' or 'do' any of this. If he did, well, he wouldn't have been that good at it – but it was the way he learned to 'be' and 'do' things. You might call it the 'West Ham Way.' Perhaps it was best described by Noel Cantwell when he had it that when he looked at Moore as a man, he could sense the presence he had seen in him as a youngster a decade earlier. To the erudite Irishman, Bobby felt like another England captain, Billy Wright. Moore had 'a sense of occasion about him'. Noel recollected how Bobby came out of the tunnel 'with such pride in his build … When Bobby walked out, you could tell his proud manner with the ball under his arm. He was a better captain at Wembley than he was at Upton Park, where it all became a bit too familiar to him. Wembley was him all over.'

The presence Cantwell was describing was Bobby's integrity – something that shines out in common parlance as 'pride'. It incorporates a confidence in self, and a surety of purpose.

7
AUTOMATIC CHOICE

England U23 7 Israel 1
Thursday, 9 November 1961
Friendly
Elland Road
Attendance: 12,419
Referee: Menahem Ashkenazi

England U23: West, Kirkup, Jones, Labone, Moore, Deakin, S. Hill, Farmer, Harris, F. Hill, Byrne.

Israel: Hodorov (Nossovsky HT) Aharonov (Grundman 38), Levkovich, Tisch, Tendler, Peterburg, Levi, Rosenboim, Menchel, Stelmach, Young.

On 9 November 1961, now a seemingly automatic choice for the young Lions, Moore and his men were pitted against the full Israel team (the game is in fact listed by the Israel Football Association as a full international).

Eighteen months earlier the visitors had torn England's youngsters apart in Tel Aviv, beating them 4-0 in what was the only previous meeting between the sides, but Ron Greenwood – at that time in situ as West Ham's manager – was not going to allow a similar result at White Hart Lane. Thus, he wanted his skipper on the field and let it be known that Bobby would turn out against the Israelis regardless of a nasty gash on his left knee.

For all this, inside the first ten minutes, Israel looked capable of pulling off another convincing win. Despite the recent disappointment of a 6-0 drubbing by Chile-bound Italy in the World Cup qualifying stage, the visitors, with just two changes to that side, were well supported by a cacophony of bells and bugles, which was accentuated when Shlomo Levi gave them the lead with only seven minutes played.

However, thereafter the home side dominated what was to be a proper rout, with Moore at the industrious heart of the storm. Together with the deadly feverish play of Johnny Byrne, they set about the destruction of their opponents. Both looked every inch much-needed good news for England's international prospects. Ultimately every England forward would get the better of the Israeli defence, taking revenge for the debacle in Tel Aviv during the summer of the previous year.

The Israelis were all amateurs, their best performer being their skipper Nahum Stelmach at inside-right, a clever, neat player. He seemingly covered the field, but was unable to shore up his team at the back. His side showed some good touches. They were optimistic, prepared to shoot from long range. One 25-yard strike from outside-right Avraham Mentechel struck the angle of Gordon West's goal not long after the opening whistle, but after England drew level, the outcome didn't appear to be in question, with the Israeli defence looking entirely square.

Byrne and Steve Hill, who was the successor to Stanley Matthews on the right wing at Blackpool, ran amok, doing pretty much what they wanted. The Seasider had a foot in each of the first four goals – three before half-time – totally ditching his full-back and sending in a series of centres that hung in the air while his team-mates lined up to take advantage. Byrne was the first to benefit from Hill's service, then Ted Farmer, and Fred Hill (no relation) nutted home via his namesake's assist.

Ya'akov Grundman was brought on for Eliezer Aharonov at right-back and the second half saw Yair Nossovsky take over in the visitors' goal, but both Hills, plus Byrne and Harris, would put past him. However, it was Gordon Jones, having played only 30 games for Middlesbrough, who caught the eye, standing in for club-mate Michael McNeil.

Unusually the match referee was not a neutral. Menahem Ashkenazi hailed from Petah Tikva in central Israel. Born in 1934 in a Jewish Sephardic family in Bulgaria, during 1936 he emigrated with his parents to Mandatory Palestine. As a kid he was an accomplished footballer, distinguishing himself as a 16-year-old in the youth team of his local club, Hapoel Petah Tikva, the captain of the Israeli team Stelmach played for the same club. However, after breaking a leg badly, Ashkenazi moved from playing to refereeing .

Ashkenazi had a long and distinguished career as a FIFA official, supervising international matches as a referee or linesman for 15 years starting from 1961. He officiated in the final of the 1964 Olympic tournament (the only Israeli ever to do so) and in the 1966 World Cup. He was in charge in one of the most memorable matches of that tournament, Portugal's 5-3 win over North Korea in the quarter-final. Of course, Bobby's England defeated Portugal in the last four.

Stelmach had received offers to sign for Arsenal and Fenerbahçe. However, it was Greenwood who went close to bringing him into the English game, making a bid to bring him to Upton Park, but problems with the FA and his loyalty to Hapoel meant his destiny was to lead his club to five national championships, four of them in consecutive seasons. Nicknamed the 'Golden Head' in Israel, Stelmach netted what is thought by many the finest goal ever scored by an Israeli international. His equalising header during an Olympic qualifier against the Soviet

Union beat the legendary keeper Lev Yashin at Tel Aviv's Ramat Gan Stadium in 1956. Although Israel lost 2-1, Nahum's goal is widely considered a defining moment in the history of the national team's early years.

Mándi

Israel were managed by Gyula Mándi, a former Hungarian international, who won ten league titles with the great Magyar Testgyakorlók Köre (MTK) side, the Budapest club he would go on to successfully manage. He was also the Hungarian manager from 1950 for six years.

Mandi was of Jewish extraction and had survived the Holocaust with the assistance of his Christian brother-in-law, György Szomolányi, who was the managing director of a paper mill that had been converted to produce wooden stocks for rifles to support the Nazi war effort. He was able to employ whoever he wanted, and in 1942 he saved Gyula from a Jewish labour detail by giving him papers to work in his factory. Two years later, however, Mándi could no longer avoid labour service. He was sent on a train bound for Ukraine, but wrote a postcard to Szomolányi and, in desperate hope, threw it from the train. Someone found it and mailed it, but when it arrived it had been so badly torn and defaced, all that could be read was the word 'KELPUSZTA'. Szomolányi realised this referred to Ekelpuszta, where a transit camp had been set up. He donned his First World War officer's uniform, strode into the camp, and demanded that he be given five men for an essential task. Intimidated, the guards told him to take his pick. Szomolányi selected Mándi and four others.

After retiring as a player, Mándi became a coach. He took over the Hungarian national team during the era of the Mighty Magyars, the side that humiliated England at Wembley and changed the future of the game in Britain, influencing so many who would shape English football over the following decades, including Ron Greenwood, Walter Winterbottom, and Malcolm Allison.

The training regimen Mándi deployed was revolutionary for the time. He encouraged his players to practice athletics and mountaineering, and to train with the ball, including in match situations. Mountaineering aside, Mándi's approach was to a large extent mirrored in the approaches of both Allison and Greenwood, the men who were most influential in Bobby Moore's development

Football is a globally connected and interactive pursuit, sailing through times and places. Life stories and history coalesce in its embrace, while destiny, hope, fear, and joy are pulled into its ambit. As a spectacle it arises from and within a universe of phenomena, but just a single game can remind us that we are all linked, no individual fate is hygienic from the fortunes of others or the providence created by world events and movements. You might be able to see that Bobby, as a footballer and probably as a person, was a child of this oceanic, intersectional environment.

Dutch destruction

Netherlands U23 2 England U23 5
Wednesday, 29 November 1961
Friendly
Stadion Feijenoord
Attendance: 3,000

Netherlands U23: van Zoghel, Flinkevleugel, Laseroms, Schrijvers, Bergholtz, Nuninga, Borghuis, van de Luijt, van Miert, Villerius Visschers.
England U23: Grummitt, Kirkup, Labone, Moore, Jones, Mullery, S. Hill, F. Hill, Byrne, Farmer, Le Flem.

On 29 November 1961, when the English under-23 side faced their Dutch counterparts in Amsterdam, Johnny Byrne was the only full international in the visitors' ranks.[18]

This was Bobby's only overseas trip as an under-23 international. It was not a surprise that he and Byrne were kept together again, Greenwood becoming ever more keen to transplant the pairing at the Boleyn Ground.

The next day Jim Farmer's hat-trick (coming in the sixth, 49th, and 75th minutes) was rightly lauded, but Moore was being hailed in the press as 'English soccer's future'. He looked a natural as the skipper and had grown in the role.

With Klas Nuninga (who would represent his country 19 times as a senior player) netting for the Dutch in the 21st minute, the opening 45 minutes was less than an impressive period for Greenwood's lads. Some poor passing was an obvious drawback, but in the second half Bobby clearly pulled his side round and was brilliantly instrumental in two goals, including Byrne's effort. He kindled the play that saw Fred Hill find Byrne, who sent the ball gliding beyond the Dutch goalkeeper van Zoghel. NAC Breda striker Jacques Visschers, who in 1971 would become manager of that club, was the Netherlands' other scorer.

The only previous meeting between the two nations at under-23 level had taken place at Hillsborough in March 1960 – it had resulted in an identical scoreline.

In the dying days of 1961 Andy Malcolm, whose persuasion for 'muscular' play was never going to fit neatly into Greenwood's playbook, moved to Chelsea in

---

18   Byrne won his first cap v Northern Ireland just a week earlier

an exchange deal that brought centre-forward Ron Tindall across London. Ron scored both West Ham's goals in the 2-2 draw at Arsenal in December. However, Tindall was not destined to find a regular place in the Hammers' first team, ultimately moving to Reading.

The Irons were at Manchester United on 16 December, having made a decent start to the season, pushing themselves into the top six as November closed. However, recent results against the Manc Reds had been mixed. While over the seven confrontations since the Boleyners rejoined the footballing elite United had penetrated the East Londoners' onion bag 20 times, West Ham had replied with 13. Busby's team had won and lost three, the sides had drawn once. Thus it was honours even in terms of points, so Bobby and his team-mates travelled north hopefully, especially because their opponents hadn't had the best of league campaigns so far that season, although visits from Fulham and Real Madrid (talk about from the ridiculous to the sublime) had given them two welcome victories.

A dozen minutes in, West Ham, having filled the United rigging, were disappointed by the referee's offside decision. Six minutes on, the negative feelings were exacerbated when the home side went ahead; the appeals to cancel David Herd's goal went unheeded, although it was a fish carter's furlong offside.

Keeper Lawrie Leslie kept the Irons in the game with a series of scrotum-shrinking saves, while Moore, returning from suspension, was also demonstrating his ample worth. At the same time Phil Woosnam repeatedly bettered his marker to maintain a good understanding with centre-forward Ron Tindall.

Having held off the crimson wave, late in the game, as the floodlights were plugged in due to poor visibility, West Ham bounced back off the ropes. In the 75th minute John Dick equalised, then ten minutes later, picking up a cutting pass from Musgrove, the Scotsman hit his second to bring up his 16th goal of the season.

United goalkeeper David Gaskell had got in Dick's way on a trio of occasions, else much more damage would have been done to local pride.

The match was part of a great Hammers run. In the six games before the trip to Cottonopolis they had only lost once, dropping just four points. This decent form was capped by a 4-2 home trouncing of Wolves on an ice rink of a pitch two days later. After that game, a week before Christmas, West Ham were second in the First Division. Two Bobby Moore goals had helped the Irons prevail in the freezing conditions. The first was hit home after just four minutes when Bobby intercepted England international keeper Ron Flowers on the edge of the penalty area and placed the ball high into the net. His second came 24 minutes later, after Musgrove back-heeled a Woosnam pass for Moore to slip the ball home from five yards. He had scored his first Football League goal against Wolves at Upton Park on 17 December 1960, a year and a day earlier. Musgrove and wing-half Geoff Hurst, with his first goal in the league, were the other scorers.

Pelé said of Moore, 'He defended like a lord and he was definitely the greatest defender I ever played against', and he certainly was not famed as a goal-getter, but from his days playing at youth level with the Hammers Moore demonstrated that he knew where the back of the net was, using both feet, and even his nut now and then. In all, Moore scored 61 times during his West Ham career, including a converted penalty. His record shows he notched up five goals in an England shirt (including FA sides).

As is often the way with the fickle Hammers, on Boxing Day 1961 in East London, the claret and blue bubble popped. On the icy surface they pissed away a two-goal lead gained in the first quarter of an hour, as 17-year-old John Byron carved a hat-trick into his career record. Blackburn had leaked 20 goals in their ten previous away matches, resulting in them being firmly ensconced in the bottom four of the division.

Almost predictably, West Ham were involved in a shock FA Cup result when Second Division Plymouth dumped the travelling Hammers out 3-0.

As the winter continued to, well, be winter, the First Division brought little joy with just a couple wins during January and February. One was at Stamford Bridge, where Bobby scored the only goal of the game with 11 minutes of the first half left to play. He hit a first-time ball with his right foot from outside the penalty box that Peter 'The Cat' Bonetti couldn't get his paws to, and thus the streamline feline was reduced to a spectator as the ball sailed into the far top corner of his cat flap.

Pittodrie revenge

Scotland U23 2 England U23 4
Wednesday, 28 February 1962
Friendly
Pittodrie
Attendance: 25,000
Referee: R.E. Smith

Scotland U23: Ogston, McGillivray, Aitken, McLintock, McNeill, Higgins, Henderson, Hunter, Gilzean, Hughes, Robertson.
England U23: Bonetti, Angus, Moore, Jones, Crawford, Hinton, S. Hill, F. Hill, Greaves, Byrne, Harrison.

Although Bobby had captained the previous three under-23 games, John Angus of Burnley was given the skipper's role on his return to the team for a match against Scotland on 28 February 1962. The change was the upshot of events the previous evening.

After visits to a few rather dead drinking holes, Moore, along with Johnny Byrne and Jimmy Greaves, had by about 8pm found themselves ensconced at the Palais de Danse in Diamond Street (later to be known as Raffles). This was about the most 'happening' place among the fleshpots of Aberdeen on a winter Tuesday evening in the early 1960s.

In the days before the internet, when not everyone had a television even, young footballers could often walk the streets, use public transport and go to a pub or a club while for the most part remaining practically anonymous. Only the really 'big' names, regular internationals and so on, would sometimes be recognised, and then only by the most observant of aficionados. Among the youthful cockney trio trolling around the Granite City just Greaves might have been known enough to draw any attention. However, on that cold February evening in the far north-east of Scotland, Jim could have gone unnoticed even if he had been wearing his Tottenham kit, with a cockerel under his arm. As it was, the Italian-cut mohair suit, while it turned heads, was enough to camouflage his notoriety.

Byrne had widely introduced himself as Billy Fury's agent[19], Dave Dobalot, who was on a talent-spotting tour. As a consequence, he commanded an almost continuous supply of drinks being bought for him and his 'business associates' Dr Ron Flange (Greaves – who had added to his anonymity by wearing a stray pair of pebble glasses picked up in the snug of one of the grim hostelries the triumvirate had visited) and Group Captain Colin Carsey (Moore). As you might imagine, time passed pretty swiftly, so the trio got back to the team hotel well after the 9pm curfew – sometime post-midnight no less – to find Greenwood waiting for them in the lobby. Ron's clerical take on pissed-offedness, together with Greaves continuing to wear the grotesquely chunky specs that all but blinded him to the world, had caused the troika of tipsy talent to fall about in hysterics, while straining to repeat their apologies and repentance.

Greenwood would have dropped all three players, but the incident happened too late to allow him to bring in adequate replacements, so Bobby effectively took the hit for the team and said the expedition had been undertaken on his suggestion, which was in fact the case.

The game was perhaps the most dramatic Moore had played that far in an England shirt. It was watched by the biggest gate of that season at Pittodrie,

19   Fury had been riding high in the charts that month with 'I'd Never Find Another You'.

25,000 turning up. The meeting between the two sides coincided with Greaves's return to English football, having had a miserable time playing in Italy. Bobby and Jimmy went way back, being lifelong friends. While Moore had been obliged to struggle to get out of the Hammers' reserve side, Jimmy was a young star of the game, who had turned down overtures from Ted Fenton, lured by the westerly promise of Stamford Bridge.

When Chelsea had been the visitors in an FA Youth Cup match at Boleyn Ground, Moore was given the job of marking Greaves, who had already made the Blues' first team and was having the praise of sports writers heaped upon him, being hailed as the new wonder boy of English football. Jimmy got one goal in that match. Without Moore on his case he would likely have claimed a hat-trick. But Jimmy kept Moore preoccupied at a cost, weakening the link between Bobby and the West Ham attack; Chelsea won 3-1. Moore had long known what Greaves could do, what it took to face him, and what was needed to make the most of the man's genius.

Moore and Greaves in the same team would for ever be amazing theatre, only matched by the games in which they were obliged to do battle against each other. I have been fortunate enough to see many of these encounters.

The meeting with the young Scots had hardly got going when Jimmy gathered his first pass, halfway inside the hosts' half. He went by four blue shirts with seeming ease before scoring the opening goal. He caressed the ball in for his second, following his kill of a chest-high pass from Byrne.

While Scotland did their utmost to stem the tide, Willie Hunter and John Hughes netting for the homesters in the second half, along with two goals from Mike Harrison, Greaves tore the heart out of the fighting Jocks.

Burn, Johnny Byrne (football inferno)

Being cautious by nature, although groundbreaking in his tactical awareness, Ron Greenwood did not make wholesale personnel changes in the first part of his reign at Upton Park. Nevertheless, after the Irons were put out of the League Cup in early October, beaten in the second round by holders Aston Villa and were humbled by a 4-0 league defeat at Birmingham City, Ron was concerned enough to alter his intended schedule. He marched off to Wembley on 22 November to see England draw 1-1 with Northern Ireland. The purpose of this excursion was to take a gander at Johnny Byrne as he gained his first full cap.

The following March, Greenwood suffered as his side were treated to a trouncing at Turf Moor. Burnley were at the top of the First Division and won 6-0, with some ease. The Lancashire Clarets had scored 51 goals in 13 home games. In the midst of the maelstrom, Bobby was almost sent off after he pushed the referee over (it was eventually understood as accidental). Less than 100 days later Ron whacked out £65,000 to make Crystal Palace centre-forward Byrne a Hammer. It was a record signing for West Ham and the biggest deal ever done between two English clubs.

Byrne had just won promotion from the Fourth Division with Palace, but Greenwood had made his mind up previously after seeing him on fire in the 4-1 destruction of the West German under-23 side at White Hart Lane. Ron saw Byrne as 'beautifully balanced, a short-strider and a master of the ball. He seemed to need no space in which to turn … He could change his mind or his direction in a blink and was almost impossible to anticipate … The bigger the centre-half against him, the better he seemed to play … But although he was an individualist, he led his line well and was always looking to bring his team-mates into the game. He made us tick, and when Budgie played well, we played well.'

Byrne's starting salary was £40 a week (equivalent to about £800 today). It was Greenwood who was to dub Byrne the 'Alfredo Di Stéfano of British football'. This 'twinning' with the Argentinian 'White Arrow' of Real Madrid was to be repeated at various stages in the press, and there were strong likenesses, Johnny, being short for a centre-forward but able to play in any of the central attacking positions. Everyone else knew him by the less illustrious moniker 'Budgie' as he always, on and off the pitch, seemed to be talking.

Although just 5ft 7in tall, Byrne was sturdy, well able to endure the physical assaults handed out by the clogging centre-halves of the time. His low centre of gravity and perfect balance, together with immaculate ball control, short stride, and quicksilver mind, made him an invariable asset to the Irons' cause. He had a bewildering capacity to outmanoeuvre and outsmart defenders with pure skill and rare artistry. He was seemingly made for the football Greenwood wanted to play. Budgie made his debut in the goalless game at Sheffield Wednesday on 17 March 1962.

Turkey shoot

England U23 4 Turkey U23 1
Thursday, 22 March 1962
Friendly
The Dell
Attendance: 18,478
Referee: Jim Barclay (Scotland)

England U23: Bonetti, Kirkup, Moore, Jones, Hinton, Deakin, S. Hill (Paine 28), F. Hill, Byrne, Burnside, Harrison.

Turkey U23: Arkoç, Yelken, Yanardag, Atsuren, Altiparnak, Korsoy, Özkefe, Özkarslı, Czceri, Gokdel.

Moore's last under-23 cap was marked with a creditable victory against Turkey on 22 March 1962. England and Turkey had never met at under-23 level, and the game was the first time that three Hammers – Byrne, Joe Kirkup, and Moore – had appeared in an under-23 international.

By that time Greenwood had initiated the innovative training regimes he had developed with the England youth and under-23 teams at West Ham in a fresh context, the club having moved to their new training ground in Chadwell Heath.

Moore was not at his best against the fervent but inconsistent opponents. However, Byrne was more than on song, both in defence and attack, creating one goal and claiming two of his own in the second half, linking brilliantly with Fred Hill for the second. Hill's pass was taken by Byrne on an impressively extended run before he put it away. Hill and Terry Paine would complete the scoring.

The referee for the game was James Philip 'J.P.' Barclay. From Kirkcaldy, Scotland. 'Barkers' as he was known in most football circles, was a FIFA official from 1958 until the end of 1962. He also appeared on the FIFA list in 1953 as a 'deputy referee'.

According to Byrne, as the players walked off at half-time, he approached Barclay asking if he spoke Turkish. The referee, perhaps predictably, said he didn't. 'Oh, in that case,' said Budgie, pointing to Bobby, 'If you need any help, Bobby speaks the lingo … his dad's from East Hambul.'[20]

During the second half, Barclay blew for offside against the visitors, and almost instantly he was surrounded by bewildered, impassioned and turbulent Turks. Following a couple of minutes of mutual consternation, the referee called Moore over, and asked him to explain the situation to the apparently bemused progeny of Osman. However, not quite being able to make sense of Barclay's request, together with finding Barkers' Fife accent a tad incomprehensible, the East Londoner decided to shake everybody's hand, concluding with the ref and the linesmen (who had come to their gaffer's assistance) nodding, smiling, with the odd thumbs-up thrown-in for good measure. Byrne and Mike Harrison had also joined in to make for a full Marx Brothers vibe. Happily, it worked because the Turks eventually dispersed to allow Bobby to take the free kick that, four passes later, led to England's final goal.

Moore had skippered the under-23s on four occasions, and played alongside Byrne seven times in the team. They had combined well facing foreign competition, and the

---

20   As Hammers fans well know, this is just down the Barking Road to 'West Hambul'.

two had become firm friends as room-mates on international duty. Budgie had been taken with the idea of a move to Upton Park partly because Moore was there, and in the last few months of the season, as fellow Irons, they had started to replicate their understanding fashioned with the 'panthera leo passant' over their hearts. By the end of Byrne's debut season as a Hammer he and Moore had forged an almost telekinetic link on and off the field, building on the understanding they had first forged in England shirts. Their friendship had, at least in part, reinforced their on-field partnership. Indeed, it would have been difficult to have cemented the kind of understanding Moore and Budgie had on the pitch without the solid and mutual affection they had for each other. Ultimately, their relationship was practically brotherly.

The former West Ham defender, coach, and manager John Lyall (who, as a young player, also doubled up as a plasterer in the summer months) was always impressed by the Moore/Byrne partnership. He said of Budgie,

'He took up such marvellous positions that Bobby Moore could find him in the dark. As people they were chalk and cheese, but what they had in common was they were special. They were interested and excited about doing things differently, and they shared a sense of wanting to play the game in an attractive way. They were inventive, but more what you'd call sophisticated.'

The artistic and gifted Byrne was to tell of how Moore's influence ran right through the West Ham side, 'Wherever you were, Bobby could get the ball to you. Like Johnny Haynes, Bobby led by example and people learned from playing with him. Also like John, Mooro was a great leader. Haynes led by word of mouth, but Bobby was calmer. When we first started playing together regular Bobby was a wing-half, but he didn't quite have the pace for that position. As a double centre-half he was the best I ever saw, better than even Franz Beckenbauer. Both had a bit of an aura, but whereas the German used to glide like a swan, Bobby was like a well-oiled train; he had a stronger physical presence. His greatest asset was his reading of the game, but the way he made use of the ball from the defence marked him out as a player.'

For Byrne, in common with countless others, Moore was one of the true greats of English football. Bobby's opinion of Budgie pretty much mirrored John's own thoughts about his colleague, calling Byrne a 'one off' with a 'total footballing mind … a forward who had the talent of a skilful midfield player, but was able to defend like a wing-half might'. Although Jimmy Greaves was Moore's partner in mischief at England level, Byrne took that role with Bobby with West Ham, the innately extrovert plotting and performing alongside the natural introvert; nearly always an indomitable combination. As Budgie had it 'Bob liked a bit of naughtiness and the same things made us smile…he was naturally shy, but that can be charming too, There was more to him than you might think on first meeting. He was deep…'

Off the field of play Bobby's relaxed cool demeanour was the perfect fit with Byrne's exuberance; they complemented each other as players and as social companions. On the pitch together they made a kind of whole, a sublime and seamless conduit between defence and offence. Off the park, the dark trickster and the fair-haired mischievous angel. They were also bound by a deal of mutual affection and respect, sharing a taste for the pleasures that living and working close to what London's West End could offer, including regular visits to places such as Carnaby Street and the Café Royal, taking in top-level boxing at the latter venue. Bobby loved boxing. As Budgie had it 'If you wanted a chat with him, boxing was the best start.' He recalled, 'We'd go to the 21 Club in Great Chesterfield Street, the White Elephant in Curzon Street. At the Churchill Hotel, where we'd sometimes meet up, the piano player always played "Bubbles" as he came in. Bobby liked Langan's restaurant too.

'When we went away, either with West Ham or England, Mooro's suitcase would be tidier coming home than mine was going out. He was always more disciplined than everyone else in the way he looked, trained, and applied himself. That discipline was there in other parts of his personality. For instance, he never put anyone down and no one said a bad word about him. But people never knew how naughty he could be. He was a very private man, but when he knew you well he was a lovely fella and a real laugh.'

It is a presumption to draw too many conclusions about relationships of which one is, at best, just a spectator. I have been somewhere in a triangle of an enquirer, a 'non-participant observer' and an interested (if not entirely innocent) bystander. Thus, my view is entirely a product of what I have understood and saw, what I have been told, often second hand, the product of memory and emotion (affection and otherwise); that's the source of these perceptions and the limit of the stories I relate

The claim of a knowledge of 'truth' about how any one person might feel about themselves or others is by definition very likely spurious. I have grown to have no faith at all in the various therapists and rune-readers who pretentiously claim such knowledge to any definitive extent; to me they are just another incarnation of mumbo-jumbo fortune tellers, pliers of 'psycho-bollocks'. In the end, all of us are left to deal with our own impressions and conclusions, and they tell another story about any and all stories.

That said, my work and study over more than half a century has involved the effort to mine tangible reason and meaning from observation or human association; the multiverse of ethnography[21]. This is not speculation, but neither does it have

---

21   The rational observation of people in their own environment, focused on the effort to understand their experiences, perspectives and everyday practices, which can give in-depth insight into individuals and any

any pretensions to the veracity of a gospel about the experience of others. It is what it is; the evidence of 'reflexion'. That's as good as it gets folks, there is no 'horse's mouth,' regardless of the claims of those soothsayers who would have you believe they have been privy to the oracle of the same.

People tend to reveal more in their actions and dispositions than by way of wordy explanations. My view of Moore, and those in his orbit, as well as the inter-relations between relevant individuals and groups, has been pieced together by being in the same places and times, extended and limited conversations with many who were directly and indirectly held in and pulled into his immediate social context. The millions of words I've read relating to these same people and that period, while sometimes germane, tell less than the collective looks, tells, body language and what on first hearing might be taken as unrelated nostalgic ramblings, milked from the first- (and second-) hand memories and impressions of 'witnesses', 'suspects' and other 'informants'.

For instance, one can posit that Johnny Byrne wasn't exactly Malcolm Allison's cup of tea. Although Bobby didn't see as much of Allison after Malcolm left Upton Park, they would continue to be friends right up to Bobby's passing. They would meet up now and then, and sometimes, up to the mid-1960s, Moore brought Byrne along. While there was no actual deep or ongoing animosity between these two close friends of Bobby, Allison was never totally comfortable when Budgie was around. He was to tell me that John was 'a handful' socially. Budgie spoke highly of Allison, almost on a par with his view of Arthur Rowe, who was to him close to the sensei Malcolm had initially been to Moore. Perhaps it was Byrne's unpredictability, or Malcolm being less than up for being on the end of the kind practical jokes Johnny enjoyed inflicting on all and everyone.

On occasion Big Mal was the butt of John's sense of humour (as were most people). He once, on Malcolm's birthday, went to the trouble of getting a huge industrial sponge decorated with cake icing, sprinkles, candles, the whole works. It looked amazing. Byrne had the creation carried into the West End bar where Allison and many of his followers, admirers, and more general hangers on were celebrating. As the band played 'Happy Birthday' for everyone to sing along to, Budgie danced in with the 'cake', bedecked with candles, the kind that you can't blow out. After Malcolm put in a deal of concerted puffing, replete with some embarrassing effort, that part of the ruse was taken to be the end of Byrne's jolly jape. But after Budgie gave Malcolm the splendidly shiny knife to cut the supposed gateau, as Allison laboured to cut it, to the accompaniment of general hilarity, the outer coating predictably crumbled into a chaotic mess. The only person unsmiling was Big Mal. He didn't mind a joke, but he detested being made a clown.

particular context, group or culture.

Although Allison would never start to do anything like that, there were, maybe, too many ways in which he and Byrne were alike. They were probably equals in terms of football acumen, but while Allison might be thought of as 'flash', he also bore a distinguished air, more James Bond than Budgie's 'Jack the Lad' persona. Johnny was almost a *Carry On*-level practical joker; Malcolm was the doyen of the intelligent but often blunt put-down, delivered with a swift erudition. It was close to slapstick versus satire. This was no basis for the kind of 'buddydom' that existed between Moore and Allison.

While Jimmy Greaves and Allison could have a fascinating duel of wit and light-footed repartee, Budgie just took the piss, although to the heights of an art form. Greaves however was a decent foil for Byrne in that respect too, being able to give back close to what he got. Budgie was wary of crossing swords with either Jimmy or Bobby, knowing full well they would likely conspire to gain revenge and some.

There were moments when the non-stop chatter, the inspiration of the 'Budgie' nickname, appeared to rub Allison up the wrong way. The gatling gun banter could get to Malcolm, while Allison's barbs just bounced off Byrne like so much confetti. There might have been some jealousy on Allison's part of the Byrne/Moore double act, or perhaps it was just irritation. Budgie on the other hand, in terms of who Bobby did or didn't mate up with, appeared not to give a shit; they were all potential targets for his metaphorical jester's pig's bladder. As Tony Scott recalled, Bobby wasn't so hot in the repartee stakes. For Scott, Bobby was noticeably quiet until he'd had a few drinks and 'got caught out in conversations', unlike the likes of Brian Dear, who was quicksilver when it came to badinage. Perhaps that's one reason why Moore knocked around with Budgie, who was the world champion when it came to raillery. Anyone looking to wrong-foot Bobby while Byrne was his wingman would be in for double what they dished.

Byrne had exceptional energy when it came to the capacity for theatrical humour, and the practical joke culture was endemic in the professional game at the time. This is perhaps hardly surprising, given crowds of young men were asked to spend quite a bit of their time not just in disciplined training, but also in one way or another, at a loose end, in hotels or on long journeys to and from games.

I wonder though if the thing about Byrne that really got to Allison was related to his natural ability as a footballer. Unlike Moore and Malcolm, Johnny seemingly came into this world to kick a ball. Although he had a good footballing mind, able to make the most of the company and teaching of the likes of Rowe, Winterbottom, Greenwood, Ramsey, and Allison, he was not the most dedicated trainer. He was not an adherent of the 'death or glory' attitude and exertion of the last drop of blood Malcolm demanded, the cut of the likes of Manchester City legends Francis Lee and Colin Bell, players Allison cultivated, for instance. Indeed,

Budgie probably underachieved as a player partly because of his deficits in terms of his application and dedication to physical fitness. As outlined in *Young Bobby*, wasting or not cultivating such talent was a cardinal sin for Big Mal.

Them's the breaks…

West Ham supporters had a bit of a wait for Johnny Byrne's first goal for the Irons, until the 4-1 Boleyn Ground victory over struggling Cardiff City on 20 April 1962, Budgie's seventh outing for the Hammers.

The next day (yep, two games in two days) West Ham played host to Arsenal. The sides had shared four goals at Highbury earlier in the season, at a time when the idea of a former affiliate of the Gunners taking the reins in East London would have been thought unconscionable at Upton Park. As it was, Ron Greenwood, formally a denizen of the Arsenal parish, and his Irons were chasing a top-six place, and looking to start the end-of-season run-in with something of a flourish in front of a congregation of almost 32,000.

The late-season derby match generated an electric atmosphere as the sides ran out. Ron had stayed loyal to the youngsters with Martin Peters, Bill Lansdowne, Tony Scott and John Lyall all retaining their places in the side.

From the off the teams tore into each other on the bumpy surface and to the consternation of the home supporters teeming behind the goal on the North Bank, Arsenal took an early lead. Scott's equaliser lifted the mood, but it was an injury to goalkeeper Lawrie Leslie that altered the course of the match in the North Londoners' favour. He broke a finger diving at the feet of the pacy winger, Danny Clapton. Peters shifted into the left-back role as Lyall took over in goal.[22]

The tough Scot did manage to return to the fray, heralded by a hero's welcome, as he adopted the left-wing slot for what remained of the second half, proving to be a pain in the arse for the visiting defence. Outside of practice sessions, Lawrie had not played outfield since childhood park games.

West Ham found themselves 3-1 down with 20 minutes to go. But Moore was an inspiration, winning his personal contest with the impressive George Eastham, as the home side laid siege to the Arsenal goal.

It was the admirable John Dick who, nodding home a precise cross from Peters, pulled the Irons back into the match. With just five minutes left to play emergency wingman Leslie artfully stepped over a pass from Scott, and Lansdowne was left to slide in the equaliser.

Greenwood's youthful side, covering a plague of injuries to senior players, had demonstrated commendable spirit to swipe a point in what was a thrilling

---

22   Substitutions during matches in the Football League were not permitted until the 1965/66 season.

confrontation. Ron was delighted that his young Hammers, led by the immaculate Moore, had proved their worth.

Just two days later, at Ninian Park, Brian Rhodes was the goalkeeper casualty. Around the hour mark he crashed into a Cardiff forward and dislocated his collarbone. With Lyall not in the side, the candidates to take over between the posts were Moore and Peters. It was Bobby who said, 'Go on, Mart, you played in goal last week.' Peters had also taken over from Rhodes in the reserves previously. So, with Cardiff two goals up, Martin pulled on the green jersey. Derek Tapscott, the ex-Arsenal man, stuck one past him with a diving header, but to his credit, the lad who had started the day at left-back managed to keep the score down to the final 3-0 outcome.

Fulham went down 4-2 at the Boleyn Ground on the last day of the season. Dick got half of the West Ham haul against the Cottages (his fellow Scot, Ian Crawford, bagged the other two), concluding the season as the Hammers' top scorer with 23 goals. So it was haggis all round at Phil Cassettari's cafe that day! Actually, Wall's pork sausages had to suffice as the E11 wild hagi, that had once roamed free on Wanstead Flats, was by that time all but extinct.

The Irons finished eighth that season. It's satisfying to think that the point won from Arsenal pulled them two places above Gunners. Without that result it would have been mid-table and not the top half for the East Londoners.

Term of Trial

A prelude to the groundbreaking cinema of the 1960s was doing the rounds over the summer of 1962 with E13-born Terry Stamp included in the impressive British cast, directed by the innovative Peter Glenville. *Term of Trial* was based on the novel by James Barlow, that tells the cautionary tale of a British high-school girl (played by Sarah Miles) who becomes infatuated with her English teacher (Laurence Olivier), but after he rejects her amorous advances, she goes to the police and accuses him of indecent assault. It's still worth a watch today.

The season would be a term of trial too for West Ham. They started their 1962/63 schedule with four losses and a draw. Thus, before their first win of the season, when Liverpool were defeated by Tony Scott's only goal of the game at Upton Park following Malcolm Musgrove's free kick, the Irons were sitting in the basement of the First Division, looking lost and disoriented. Wingers Scott and Musgrove, right-back John Bond and Geoff Hurst had been brought back into the first team for Liverpool's visit. Greenwood, for the first time, plugged Hurst into the attacking role that would make him an immortal of the global game.

Tim Bowler has had a long-term involvement within the annals of Upton Park. He has strong memories of what a great player Byrne was for West Ham. He told me, '[Johnny] helped make Geoff Hurst the world star he became. If it was not for Budgie, Geoff would have still been missing barn doors … I spent a whole season watching Hurst missing the goal from two yards virtually every game and then hearing him booed off the pitch. It was painful for him and for us fans. Then along came Budgie Byrne during the summer transfer window and straight away Geoff could not stop scoring. He was brilliant and it never stopped.'

On 8 September, at Maine Road, Hurst vindicated the work his manager had done with him in a 6-1 obliteration of Manchester City, who were also having a bad time in the league. With the score at 4-1 the blue defence froze, expectant of an offside verdict, as Musgrove latched on to Scott's cross to head home the fifth goal.

Former *Jungvolk*[23] recruit, East London bombing Luftwaffe bod and paratrooper in Hitler's war machine, Bert Trautmann, went up the wall, chasing the referee as a Messerschmitt might have only 20 years earlier pursued a Lancaster Bomber. In the ensuing bull and cow, Bert picked up the ball before kicking it into the Bristolian arse of Mr Yates. Brooding Bert then tore off his green jersey, threw it to the dirt and goose-stepped off the field, seemingly intent on heading for the Sudetenland. Which of course was no help at all to City.

In that same month the then secretary of the Football League, former Hull City defender Alan Hardaker (a man once sacked by his own father for playing dominoes instead of working) was having a protracted moan about players wanting too much money for their services. No one took much notice, least of all the players. Brian Cearns joined his two elder brothers on the board, exemplifying West Ham as a 'family club' (or as a seething cauldron of nepotism).

Harry 'Poplar prefab person' Redknapp came into the Boleyn Ground fold as an apprentice professional, thus the starting gun was fired on that saga of ginger ignominy.

With only five wins in 22 outings West Ham shared eight goals at White Hart Lane three days before Christmas, a real treat for the 44,000 present. The North Londoners were sitting second in the table, while the Hammers were sloshing about in 14th – so the yuletide bonus was on Tottenham to do the business, and after 20 minutes, with the home side 2-0 to the good, it looked like Santa had converted to spudoom. The depressing situation was made worse as the scoring had been opened by John Smith, a last-minute inclusion for Spurs at right-half. The former Iron thus netted in his first appearance of the season. Dave Mackay had scored the other goal from 20 yards out with a deadly left-footed drive.

On the half-hour Martin Peters gave the Hammers some hope, hitting home from close range having made the most of a typically intelligent Moore pass.

---

23   The junior section of the Hitler Youth.

After the break the fired-up Irons went for Spurs big time. The equaliser came when Peters' strong effort was parried by Bill Brown, Tony Scott gathered the loose ball, and again the Tottenham keeper got in the way, but Joe Kirkup had placed himself well enough to make the most of the rebound.

From the restart, the home side came forward and a cross from Greaves came off Jack Burkett's feet for Mackay to pick up and score.

The Hammers came back again in the 65th minute. Byrne turned Alan Sealey's throw over his head for Ronnie Boyce to run on to, and 'Ticker' slipped the ball by Brown.

A few minutes later Boyce was again on the move after supplying Burkett on the overlap. Jack's deep bending cross was slammed in by Scott and West Ham were in front the first time in the match.

Spurs looked to be on the ropes, with Brown obliged to perform miracles at the behest of Scott and Sealey. Moore did get past the custodian but his effort was deemed offside.

Byrne and Boyce were destroying Spurs at the very heart of the play, seemingly in on every move, but typical of the dour Scot, Mackay fought on, and well into the last minute of the game, from the centre of Jim Standen's penalty area, he rounded off his hat-trick, smacking the ball beyond the goalkeeper – who had signed for West Ham in 1962 following Lawrie Leslie's broken leg – from ten yards and saving Tottenham's blushes.

West Ham might have claimed the 'moral victory' or a 'win on points', but the result was some compensation for a 6-1 pasting doled out by the FA Cup holders at Upton Park early in August.

January saw football brought to a frozen halt. This was the winter of the 'Big Freeze', arguably the most devastating weather event to hit modern Britain. Snow began falling on Boxing Day 1962 and barely stopped for the next ten weeks. It was the coldest recorded winter in the UK since 1739, as temperatures plummeted to -22°C. However, as spring peeped over the Ziff Meats slaughterhouse in Custom House, West Ham found themselves in the last eight of the FA Cup for the first time in seven seasons, and on the road to Liverpool. Although Bobby was inspiring in the land of the 'Wet Nelly', the Hammers were unlucky to be eliminated by the only goal of the game.

The FA Cup run had made the season a bit better than average. There had been little joy in the League Cup as after the 6-0 rout of Plymouth in East London (Byrne claiming a hat-trick), Rotherham did for the Irons over at Millmoor in mid-October. The side that would conclude the season 14th in the Second Division sent the Hammers home on the end of a 3-1 defeat. This was the low point of

West Ham's calendar. Their fixtures concluded with the defeat of Manchester City in East London by the same score that had pertained at Maine Road in September. Moore's soft back-pass gifted Alan Oakes the consolation goal for the Blues – it had been Oakes who had pulled on the keeper's gloves earlier in the season when Trautmann pre-empted his sending off.

West Ham's modest 12th place in the First Division was compensated a little by the FA Youth Cup win. The Colts were 3-1 down after the first leg at Anfield, but ultimately beat Liverpool 6-5 on aggregate. A couple of days later the side defeated Chelsea Colts to win the London Minor Cup. The youth system that had opened the world to Bobby was flourishing under Greenwood, and even if the summer of 1962 had brought some despondency the future looked promising.

Dreaming of Chile

In the nine games Moore played for his country at under-23 level the side scored 32 goals and conceded just nine, winning seven and losing only once. On 4 May 1962, at Highbury, Moore played his final match for the under-23s (although this was officially a 'Young England' XI) the evening prior to the 1962 FA Cup Final. He captained the side against the full England team in what was then an annual exhibition match. The encounter was played in a thunderstorm and ceaseless rain, which turned the pitch into a quagmire. No Tottenham or Burnley players were included as those clubs were playing the Wembley final the next day, and had several England players in their collective ranks.

As Bobby sploshed around Highbury, he and others could not have helped but have the thought that the game, played in intolerable conditions and without some of England's best players, didn't really smack of the best preparation for the World Cup, which time-wise was just around the corner. The younger men lost 3-2.

Following that game, the initial squad was named for the 1962 World Cup. The players were taken to Roehampton to begin preparations for Chile. Bobby knew that England manager Walter Winterbottom had been watching him play for West Ham and the under-23s, although he also understood that he had been looking at quite a few players.

The selection system was such that members of the 'probable' squad were named first and then other players were added as the 'possibles', to bring the initial squad as a whole to 40 strong. Of course, Bobby was delighted when he found out he was one of the possibles, although he was sure he 'probably' wouldn't be among those who would go to the World Cup (although it was 'possible' he might).

8
ENTER THE BISHOP

On 13 April 1961, when Ron Greenwood first rocked up at Upton Park, he wasn't much of a fan of East London. He saw those of us who lived where I was born, brought up, schooled, and appalled as 'swaggers' (although, predictably, I'd say we have something to swagger about). To be fair, it was just his initial assessment, but it was pretty excoriating, after all, he was talking about the people who were to pay his wages, 'They would love somebody like [Malcolm] Allison … They don't understand sincerity and intelligence. This community and this area doesn't understand or appreciate anything that this club stands for. Put this club in another area and the appreciation would be tremendous … People just don't have the same standards or respect … They just want to be the biggest and the best and to boast.'

Delicious. Now these were the days when 'customer service' amounted to little more than free salt and vinegar (up to a point) on your chips, but most of us would find that assessment a bit much. However, Ron wasn't done. In his next breath he continued to make groundless assumptions, adding to his contemptuous accusations and prejudicial evaluation (he knew little or nothing about East London). It does however say a lot about him at the start of his tenure at the Boleyn Ground, when he admitted, 'Success at a club like this is frightening. It would attract a lot of the wrong people, the kind of people who will disappear as soon as you're not at the top any longer.'

Although his apparent envy of the status of Malcolm Allison was painfully obvious, he was totally wrong about Big Mal's relationship with the supporters. Allison's abilities were recognised, but no one beyond the senior playing staff really knew about his role and intentions regarding remaking the club. Malcolm had not been overly popular with the Upton Park crowd because of his 'South London swagger' (swaggering was endemic all over the Smoke, must have been something in the water) and sometimes tangible (even at a distance) seriousness – generally he played with a look of intense gravity etched across his square-jawed, film star-like eke. His entire demeanour was one of blinkered determination, in the sense that everything outside the field of play appeared to be close to contemptuously shut out.

However, Ron's rant was out of character taking his life as a whole. First and foremost, he was a rational human being, driven by evidence and experiment more than crude assumptions and prejudices. His apparent view of Allison in this statement contradicts his admiration for him as a coach; Greenwood wanted him back at Upton Park when he first took over as manager. As soon as he got his Clarks Cordovans under the table at Upton Park, Greenwood looked to bring Malcolm back as the club's youth coach.

Ron was to say of Allison that he had been involved in effectively 'preparing the way' for him, and that he 'inherited fertile ground' by way of the fruits of Allison's endeavours. Ron named Malcolm as 'a natural coach, a man with real insight into the game', who had 'proved his ability with youngsters right from his early days with West Ham'. For Greenwood, Allison, who was then playing non-league football for Romford, would have made the 'ideal' youth coach at Upton Park, but when he put the proposal to the board he was surprised by their reaction. They were firmly determined not to allow even the notion of Big Mal returning to torment them to see the light of day. As Ron put it, 'They told me one or two things had happened which would not make it a good idea and they were clearly not going to change their minds.'

If the board had not been so short-sighted, scared, or vindictive, the job would have been the first full coaching post for Allison. Until his final days Greenwood believed Malcolm would have been 'perfect for the job'.

A repeatedly reported segment of one of Greenwood's first talks to his players at Upton Park tells how he, with 'a wry grin', came out with, 'Let's face it, you are a team that is just like your theme song. You're always promising – and then the bubble gets burst before you win anything.'

My adolescent 'Canning Town' response to that would have been predictably coarse and immoderate. Of course, such has been my admiration for Greenwood throughout my adult years, I understand what he *might* have said, and how he was *reported* to have said it, was not what he meant. For all that, I'm fairly sure no one in the team might have felt any great or serious connection with 'Bubbles', although any supporter will understand the ditty more as a sort of 'ode to realism over hope' – there's a languid defiance in it, like 'glory is an illusion' and 'it's the journey that counts more than the destination'. That's less the case today. My sad trawling of West Ham related Facebook pages shows a section of supporters prepared to trade watching attractive football with any old pot that might be going. The money-making machine of the international industry of the game appears to invent competitions for the sake of it. Any time now I'm expecting the Euro 'Opps, Just Avoided Relegation Cornflake Alliance Hub Cap' tournament.

Either way, Ron's very literal interpretation of the Hammers anthem shows both naivety and a hint of over-compensation for self-doubt. He'd been given his first big job and he was talking to some very experienced players, as well as a clutch of talented and determined youngsters. Part of him would likely have felt he needed to big himself up somewhat. He went on to inform his, I guess, quite perplexed, audience, 'That's what my job is – to stop the bubbles being burst.' The adroit response to that is of course, 'How does anyone stop bubbles from bursting? That's what bubbles do.' It all comes over with more than a fission of David Brent.

Given what is known about Ron, his attitudes and deportment, one can only suspect these early impressions were more related to opinions he had picked up from the board, certainly the view of Allison, and that he took it he needed to underwrite them. He might have just been taken in by such bigotry, but perhaps more likely he felt it to be expedient to endorse them.

Initially Ron hadn't been overly keen to park his caravan in the docklands. Although his guru, Walter Winterbottom, had given him a nudge in the direction of the easterly reaches of the District Line, he had protested he was happy at Arsenal; he got a subscription to the *Daily Herald* from the club, and free tea and bacon sandwiches at the workers' cafe in Upper Street. On top of that, he thought that the way Ted Fenton had his P60 shoved up his jacksie didn't suggest West Ham was a 'happy club'[24].

For all this, although Ron would miss the gaudy emporiums of consumer fetishism offered along Holloway Road, the exotic delights obtainable from the mystic bazaar that was Queen's Road Market, E13 more than compensated, while not having to listen to what Bob Bellinger[25] was getting up to on his Evershot Road allotment any more would have been a definite bonus.

These considerations, together with the prospect of working with the likes of Bobby Moore and being within a few minutes' walking distance of Nathan's Pie and Mash shop, the initial views, and accusations he once voiced, did not endure (the *Herald* was to go down the lav by 1964 anyway). Ron was undoubtedly better than his early disparagement of the Irons and their flock might have made him look.

In all my conversations with former players and others involved with West Ham I have never heard anyone say that Greenwood was, fundamentally, anything less than a good person. The two or three times he spoke to me and in his answering of my correspondence, I found him to be a decent, polite, massively intelligent, good-humoured and generous individual. There has never been any doubt in my

---

24   I will be looking at Fenton's departure in greater detail in an upcoming publication.
25   One-time Lord Mayor of London, on his retirement as a director of Arsenal, Bellinger was appointed life president of the club. He died in 2002.

mind that he was a visionary, and the hundreds of players I have communicated with and spoken to over the years have had little negative to say about him. He has a massive legacy; the training techniques, and methods he introduced into football in the 1960s continue to be deployed today globally – some have been developed and reinterpreted, but the principles will remain similar or the same.

By the time he got to Upton Park, Ron had worked with coaches and seen the game all over the world, experiencing different and novel types of play and approaches to football. This gave him an advantage over most managers.

Intrigued by European styles and attitudes, Greenwood wanted to realise the best of his experience with an English club in order to be able to compete with the top continental teams. In the 1960s his ambitions were both rewarded and vindicated, not totally necessarily in the currency of silverware, but by a status that came to be universally recognised.

Greenwood set standards, seeing that he had players capable of achieving them. Many other clubs later attempted to replicate what the Hammers were doing; most lacked the personnel with the appropriate skills, but perhaps more importantly, the willingness to learn and try new things. Alf Ramsey and England were not however limited in terms of talent or the determination to break the mould, and the national side would benefit from the innovation Ron crafted with his team that was almost wholly made up of English players.

Geoff Hurst became a massive presence up front, while Ronnie Boyce was the engine of the midfield. Martin Peters was to give more dimension to the mix. At the back, Moore would lead along the line, while covering the entire last third of the pitch. The whole team was a tight unit, pushing forward, with Bobby playing loose and free at the back. As such, the Hammers advanced with the confidence that their captain was always covering them in defence, reading anything coming through, cleaning up.

I watched all this happening and can tell you that while it was demanding, implying a fine balance of daring and rationality, when it all came together, it was delightful and exhilarating to watch. Dozens of former players have told me it was a joy to be part of the 'West Ham Way'.

Fundamentally there was no concrete system, more than a commitment to everyone being involved, moving forward together, and when called upon, retreating in coordination. The organisation of the team was flexible, placing an emphasis on mobility. Liverpool, at their best (which isn't 'now') played in much the same way – three at the back and two wide wing-backs.

It's both easy and complex, and as the periods of inconsistent form evidence, West Ham could be prone to obviate, when it didn't go right it could really go wrong. But everyone was alive to that, which is partly why it was worth watching; jeopardy and glory are bedfellows in the pursuit of entertainment and art. The Hammers pioneered total football, the game the Germans first put together on the international stage. It was exemplified by the great Dutch sides of the Johan Cruyff era; players interchanging positions, strikers moving back if needed and defenders going on the attack.

The interest in West Ham's play drew coaches and players from other teams, and every footballing culture, asking to watch the Hammers train, something unheard of in the 1960s. The British especially were often astonished by how much work was focused on using the ball. At that time, in much of the domestic game, laps and sprints still played a significant part in most training regimes, ball skills often being just taken for granted – you either had them or you didn't.

Ron was a quiet revolutionary. He would never contemplate putting in place what others might have seen as 'real' training. His approach was closer to how musicians might rehearse a performance; breaking routines into basic elements and practicing them over and over, varying situations and conditions, tempo, cadence, and rhythm. The team was his orchestra, he their conductor, Bobby the concertmaster. Play was made up with melodies and harmonies of both innovative and well-practiced movements. It didn't always 'work' but it was hardly ever dull, never predictable, and at times, breathtaking.

All of this met a ready mind in Moore. It was very much in the Allison mode he had adhered to since boyhood. The likes of Dave Sexton, who became one of Chelsea's most successful managers in the early 1970s, often picked Bobby's brains about Greenwood's approach, replicating it with the exciting sides he developed at Stamford Bridge.

West Ham's studious manager hardly ever viewed games from the dugout like his contemporaries did and the current crop of detached Premiership journeymen do, although the majority of the latter spending most of the time lurking like caged porcupines around their 'technical area'. He would sit, practically immobile, in the front row of the main stand, around level with the halfway line. Looking down the pitch provided him a broader perspective of play – which really is just common sense.

Ron did recognise that the aspects of West Ham he respected were a product of the connections between the club and its context, something that Moore personified. Greenwood often had it that the hardest things in football were the easiest, and the easiest were the hardest. Bobby took this notion a step further, developing the knack of finding the best way to do things, which usually started by getting the basics right – more often than not, control of the fundamentals bolstered his confidence. The more he practiced envisioning how things might happen before they happened, the better he got at it; the more you consider what is complicated the less complex such issues seem or feel. This meant, almost invariably, that he remained in control of situations and control is fundamental in the achievement of one's objectives and aims. To control is to manage, so to not manage is being out of control.

Whatever his opinion of Allison's personality, Ron recognised the man's influence and talent. Greenwood practiced many of the same disciplines that were introduced to West Ham by Allison, notably the requirement for players to know, or be conscious of, what was going on around them, using insight and foresight, playing with awareness and intelligence; looking to predict moves and plays to be ahead of the opposition. He ingrained one-touch play that was reliant on this; every player, at any given point in a game, constantly developing a perception of where everyone on the pitch is prior to receiving the ball. Thus, the whole team pretty much knew what they were going to do with the ball before they got it. One of Ron's mantras was, 'Get a picture! Get a picture!'

When Greenwood got to Upton Park, Tom Russell oversaw the youth team on a part-time basis. He was by then headmaster at Tom Hood, the school Moore had attended. Ron couldn't grasp what Russell was doing there, not having any background in the professional game. However, he was also aware, by way of Bobby, that Tom was nowhere in terms of understanding modern coaching methods.

The problem was solved when Russell took up a teaching post in Uganda, but a replacement needed to be found. Predictably, Ron wanted someone with a relevant background in the game on a full-time basis. With the block put on Malcolm Allison, Greenwood turned to John Lyall, who had been obliged, following injury, to give up playing. It turned out to be a wise move.

Not too long after Greenwood instigated his new regime, few players were unhappy with his appointment. The demise of Allison's influence and the departure of Cantwell had left the club with a leadership vacuum. Ron's approach confirmed Allison's training philosophy, and from the get-go he offered the players new ways of doing things and ideas about the game that most approved of and enjoyed, bringing the breath of fresh air that was much needed. His approach, principally being grounded on using space, involved ample opportunities to use and be creative with the ball.

Other than under Allison, Fenton and the other club trainers had asked much the same routine from players day-to-day, emphasis being placed on physical development, with military routines such as stretching, leg, arms and shoulder strengthening. Players had been obliged to do a lot of running, including sprinting, replete with spikes. The latter were soon binned because, as Greenwood pointed out, 'You can't kick a ball in running spikes.' The only footwear to be worn in training was to be football boots, and all training would include balls.

The first thing Ron spent an appreciable amount of money on was footballs. The club had less than a dozen from the Allison era, not all of which were in good repair. The new stock was required because of Greenwood's focus on passing and holding the ball, encouraging players to use and seek out space and move when out of possession. While this had a heritage at Upton Park, most of the West Ham professionals had experience of this sort of emphasis since their earliest days at the Boleyn Ground, under the influence of Allison and Cantwell, but Greenwood took it on, embedding it in every aspect of training and strategy. He organised and developed the West Ham game and made it work in the 4-2-4 system.

'Never wore the shirt'

A good proportion of supporters had been taken aback when a man, besmirched by the whiff of Highbury, had been put in charge of the Irons. This situation was not helped by the rest of his life history. He was a northerner. He had been part of the Chelsea side that won the championship in 1955. He was the first West Ham manager not to have played for the club. For many supporters, having worn the shirt was a prerequisite for anyone to be considered to lead the Hammers, and it remains that way for a lot of us in 'the old guard'. Probably counterintuitively managers since the departure of Harry Redknapp seem slightly out of place. The incumbent at the time of writing, David Moyes, feels about as West Ham as 'Och, Loch and two smoking tatties', or caber tossing[26], while Frank McAvennie, Łukasz Fabiański and Saïd Benrahma well, any of them ranks as 'one of our own'.

All that Ron's CV needed to make the picture complete was a part-time job selling peanuts at White Hart Lane. But Greenwood had worked with the England youth and under-23 teams which, together with the fact that Ted Fenton had, with the help of Malcolm Allison, left Greenwood a decent legacy in terms of the potential of the team, gave cause for some optimism about the future.

To get the gist of the relationship between Moore and Greenwood (or the lack of such a thing) you need to know a bit about Ron's background. There is more to the man than he gave away in his rather restrained and somewhat sanitised autobiography from 1984. He was a church-going, self-educated, football intellectual, out of the same school of the game as his mentor Walter

---

26   Which really should come under as the Labouchere Amendment – Section 11 of the Criminal Law Amendment Act 1885, as 'gross indecency'

Winterbottom, who had been at the rudder of the England team since 1946 as Greenwood took over at Upton Park. Winterbottom might be considered to be the 'Father of English coaching' and Ron was his number one disciple.

Born in Burnley in 1921, the young Greenwood spent his early years in a terraced house in the village of Worsthorne, close to the outskirts of the Lancashire mill town of Burnley. In those hungry 1920s days, the kids of the family wore clogs with iron bars on the soles; shoes were only for Sunday best. The Great Depression impacted the Greenwoods severely, enough to provoke a move to Alperton in Middlesex, after Ron's father got a job as a signwriter at Wembley Stadium.

Leaving school at 14, Ron followed his father as an apprentice signwriter at Wembley; however he did a different form of signing for Chelsea. He got to Stamford Bridge just before the outbreak of the Second World War, but soon, what would have been the seminal years of his playing career, were taken up by his wartime service in the RAF. During the time of conflict Ron did manage to turn out for Belfast Celtic and Hull City, but on his return to West London he was almost immediately transferred to Second Division Bradford Park Avenue for £3,500.

Greenwood, a sturdy, creative right-half at Bradford, converted to the role of centre-half before returning to London and Brentford, where he linked up with Jimmy Hill, who was then a dynamic wing-half. Ron found his way back to Chelsea, playing in the 1955 title-winning side under Ted Drake. Thereafter, he once more played alongside Hill back in the Second Division with Fulham, gaining his single England B cap as a Cottager at the start of the 1955/56 season. His transition from playing to management took place about the same time as Hill's as both became dedicated coaches, attending Winterbottom's FA courses.

Influenced by the thoughts and theories of the England manager, having an insatiable thirst for knowledge, Greenwood embarked on his lifetime project of auto-didacticism. He started his coaching journey with the Oxford University team. It was there he met Michael Argyle, who would become a pioneer of social psychology in the UK and Europe, his most renowned work being 1967's *The Psychology of Interpersonal Behaviour*.

Argyle at that time was just starting to form his ideas relating to the 'communication cycle', which involves six steps: someone deciding to communicate an idea, encoding it, and sending it; someone else receives it, decodes it, and understands it. Feedback demonstrates understanding (an action is performed or a reply message is encoded and sent). The theory works to heighten awareness of the possibility of distortion at either the encoding or decoding stage. This fed into Greenwood's coaching, not relying on spoken instructions, *à la* Fenton, but running through ideas and tactics 'live', 'doing' as much as telling. Understanding being established not just by a nod, thumbs-up, or a verbal assurance, but by moves and strategies being realised in action.

Greenwood also spent time with Walthamstow Avenue and Eastbourne, before taking the job as assistant manager to Yorkshire's George Swindin at Arsenal in 1957. Prior to Ron venturing forth to the hedonistic delights of North London, Winterbottom, who rated him as a brilliant young coach, had asked him to take charge of England Youth and under-23s sides.

Moore remembered feeling 'really excited' when he found out that Ron was taking over from Ted Fenton at Upton Park. He saw Greenwood as having 'a vast knowledge of the finer points of the game', saying that he was sure the Hammers 'were going to have success under him'. Bobby recalled, '[at that time he was] still learning, and knew I could pick up lots of good tips from Ron. In those early days I followed him around like a puppy and listened and learned. He trusted me with the captaincy … We got on well during his first few seasons.'

Those initial years of the 'Reign of Ron' proved to be the honeymoon period of the association between Moore and Greenwood. Bobby valued that his manager put the emphasis on thoughtful more than physical play. He saw this confirmed when Greenwood broke West Ham's transfer record to bring Johnny Byrne to East London, importing skill and invention into the team's forward play. However, perhaps the flaw in Greenwood's vision was getting rid of Andy Malcolm. This symbolically and practically demonstrated that the die was cast in terms of West Ham's playing style, ending any prospect of achieving a balance between the perhaps necessary (in the context of the early 1960s) assertive, muscular element and light-footed artistry. More than a few of the men who played under Greenwood have seen this as the piece of the jigsaw that Ron was not able to accommodate and what, in the last analysis, prevented West Ham from realising a headier height in the pantheon of the mid-20th century game.

Almost on arrival, Greenwood started the conversion of the youthful wing-half, Geoff Hurst into a powerful and dynamic striker. With the amazingly talented Martin Peters also coming into the Irons' first team, Ron was presiding over a new West Ham, a team that played cultured football, looking modern and slick. According to Sir Geoff, Greenwood's early days at Upton Park transformed the young side into 'thinking footballers', demonstrating 'that the game was as much about using the mind as the feet'. For Hurst, 'The style of play he developed was attractive to watch … those first few seasons Bobby, along with the rest of us, fully respected Ron and we knew he was making us better, more thoughtful players. Few could match his knowledge of world football, and he deserved to get a crack at the England job years before he finally got his chance.'

You can perhaps see this potted biography in a few ways, but in some respects similar to Allison, there is a bit of the 'nearly man' about Ron's life story as a player. Slices of not the best of fortune had to be overcome with graft and adaptation. However, there was always a sense that he had failed to get what he might have felt he deserved. Certainly, he may have shared this feeling with a whole generation of footballers, but likely Greenwood expected better of himself, and the worst person to be let down by is yourself. That he turned to Winterbottom and coaching as consolation, a man also much admired by Allison, looking to express his aesthetic aspirations through the skills of others, helps one understand the effort he put into developing talents of the likes of Hurst. It also taps into his motivation to build Moore, to some extent, into an image of what he might have been in terms of both footballing and personal principles. This, of course, like most projects motivated by vicariousness, in an effort to compensate for personal shortcomings or failure, was always destined to ultimately fail.

This said, while never quite inspirational, Greenwood's genius as a tactician and educationalist was to make a massive impression on the West Ham players. He encouraged many of them to take FA coaching courses at Lilleshall in order that they could better latch on to his insights, but also develop their own ideas and approaches. This produced a raft of top managers right though the second half of the 20th century, matched by no other club. West Ham was a 'club of coaches', and had a strong Academy, which created a lively and informed discourse about the football, giving rise to innovatory play and game analysis.

Ron arranged for the whole Hammers playing staff to take over Lilleshall for a week at one juncture – no other league club had done this. Every waking hour, Greenwood and the players worked on building knowledge and awareness of coaching purposes and practice. At the end of the week, several players were awarded their preliminary coaching badges, so they were better informed and skilled, but also gained something that might have prolonged their contribution to and rewards from the game.

Greenwood cared passionately about football and the welfare and consciousness of the players in his care. For all his quirks and social shortcomings, he was a great man and gets nowhere near the credit he deserves for his contribution to West Ham, the English game and football more widely.

I have talked to dozens of players who worked under Greenwood, including perhaps his most devoted student, John Lyall. None disagreed with my understanding that he was a true teacher, a great one at that. Many of those players bemoaned the predictability and the concomitant ugliness of the modern game, with its sideways passing, and the fear of losing, that stymies the effort to win, which means so many semi-finals and finals end in stalemates, even after extra time, needing to be decided on the lottery of penalty shoot-outs.

Ron's gospel, at base, was one of adventure and courage, in the pursuit of something beautiful. Just to give an example, Moore was receiving quite a deal of flack in the media after losing possession of the ball while looking to do something he habituated, dribbling his way out of the penalty area. This had become something of a culture at West Ham long before Greenwood arrived; Cantwell, Allison, Bond, and others were all advocates of this possession game, what was the start of a chain that linked defence to attack. This time the cost was a goal scored against the Hammers. Ron refused to castigate his skipper, or even question his judgement publicly, although they had certainly analysed what had happened within the confines of the club. However, as Greenwood was to point out, a couple of games later, when Bobby had emerged from the box with ball at his feet, giving him the ability to make the pass that effectively turned defence into attack, this was progressive play.

Ron never wanted to lose, but he wasn't going to sacrifice the chance of winning beautifully because of the risk of a defeat from which there was the means to learn to win.

Greenwood, Coach.

Garrincha.

Cottager Ron.

First Game Moore Captain's England.

Tina and Bobby, at home at 'Morlands' in Chigwell, Essex (after their move from Gants Hill).

Tina and Bobby with baby Roberta and son Dean (1965).

Leyton Orient

FOOTBALL CLUB LTD.

Leyton Stadium
Brisbane Road
Leyton, E.10

SATURDAY

8th October, 1960

TODAY'S MATCH

England

versus

Switzerland

INTERNATIONAL MATCH   Kick-off 7.30 p.m.

Official **3**^D _Programme_

WEST HAM UNITED

BLACKBURN ROVERS Colts

F.A. YOUTH CUP — Final (First Leg)

MONDAY 27th APRIL 1959 at 7.30 p.m.

No. 58

95
5

OFFICIAL PROGRAMME

FA Youth Cup Final .

A Captain of All the Hammers is born!.

WEST HAM UNITED*

CARDIFF CITY

FOOTBALL LEAGUE—Division One

FRIDAY 20th APRIL 1962 at 11 a.m.

No. 52

OFFICIAL PROGRAMME

Hellier & Sons, London, E.13

Johnny 'Budgie' Byrne scores his first goal for the Irons

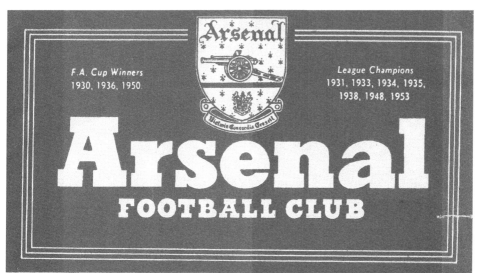

F.A. Cup Winners
1930, 1936, 1950.

League Champions
1931, 1933, 1934, 1935,
1938, 1948, 1953

Arsenal
FOOTBALL CLUB

Season 1957-8

Youth International Match

Tuesday, 4th March, 1958

ENGLAND v. AUSTRIA

Kick-off 7 p.m.

OFFICIAL **3**d PROGRAMME

Bobby Moore shines in 3-2 victory alongside fellow Hammer, Tony Scott. After this game the Gunners manager, Jack Crayson talks to Bobby about potentially moving to Highbury. Until Greenwood moved to Upton Park, this was an on-going possiblity.

Mané Garrincha (Garrincha) "little bird", World Cup Final, 1958, v Sweden, Råsunda Stadium, Solna.

The awesome European footballer of the year Joséf Masopust. He had been a key player for Czechoslovakia for a dozen years, helping them reach the 1962 World Cup Final. He would be capped 63 times, scoring 10 goals for his country.

You don't become a Hammer, it's something you're born to.

Winterbottom and his side arrive in Chile, 1962 (Walt telling an official how short José Gomes Nogueira, the Peruvian manager was) while Ray Wilson and Roger Hunt (shades) sign up to the Santiago Mafia.

Walter Winterbottom and Johnny Haynes with the England Under-23 side in 1957 (at least the cabin crew appear intimidated).

Chile World Cup 1962, Bobby sitting next to Jimmy Greaves with the rest of the England team on the coach that took them from the airport to Rancagua where their group games were played.

2 June, 1962, England v Argentina, Rancagua – England apparently mystified at Ref. Nikolai Latyschev's decision.

On arrival in Rancagua Johnny Haynes leads the England team onto the train to their training camp in Coya.

Bobby and Budgie rip the heart of the Germans.

Another East London star of the 1960s, the original 'Hammerette', Pat Booth at her home in Palm Beach, Florida, 1992. Nice place, but you can't get decent jellied ells anywhere!

Greenwood in his 'Blue Period'.

England v Bulgaria – 1962 World Cup. Springett beats centre-back, Sololov to the ball. Flowers (6) and Wilson (3) in attendance.

Young Bobby.

Garrincha eludes Ray Wilson – Estádio Municipal, Viña del Mar - Quarter-final World Cup 1962.

West Ham at the end of the 1950s.

WEST HAM UNITED F.C. 1958-59

Left to right (Back row) A. MALCOLM, K. BROWN, J. BOND, E. GREGORY, N. CANTWELL
W. LANSDOWNE, M. PYKE, MR. E. FENTON (Manager); (Front row) M. GRICE, J. SMITH
V. KEEBLE, J. DICK, M. MUSGROVE

Quarter-final World Cup 1962 - Wilson with Moore behind him, heads clear to stop a Brazilian attack. Vava (left) and Amarildo are the Brazilians pressurising the English defence.

Bobby and England leave the field following victory over Argentina - 1962 World Cup.

Garrincha's free-kick rebounded off of Springette's chest for Vava to head Brazil into the lead. The disappointment is plainly written in each England player's stance.

Budgie the Hammer.

Moore in action v Bulgaria.

John Lyall – Future West Ham Manager.

Garrincha beats Norman to the ball to head Brazil's first goal to take the lead in the 1962 World Cup quarter-final meeting with England.

Moore of England.

The Czechs team appreciating the 'Cucca' Chilean folk singers.

Ted Fenton - avec tuyau.

Brazil – World Cup Winners 1962: Back (left to right) Dr Hilton Gosling (directory) Djalma Santos, Zito. Gilmar, Zozino, Nilton Santos, Mauro, Moreira (coach) Front (left to right) Americo (trainer) Garrincha, Didi, Pelé, Vava, Zagalo.

*George Cohen –
Fulham and England.*

Chilean kids were given a holiday from school for the duration of the World Cup in 1962 – Pelé finds the time to pass on a few tips.

Bobby Charlton in his pomp.

Greaves in a good position with Naidenov (Bulgaria) desperately diving, but no goal came. Peacock is to the left.

England v Argentina, 1966 World Cup – Hurst is number 10.

England's opening the game of the 1962 World Cup v Hungary – Flowers from the penalty spot beats Grosics.

Charlton (left) and Greaves prepare to cheer a second goal but the Hungarian defenders scrambled the ball away.

Majestic Mooro.

England v Argentina – World Cup 1962. Flowers heads clear, fouled by Rattin (the man was nothing if not consistent).

The National Stadium, Santiago, where group, quarter and semi-finals, and the Final of the 1962 World Cup were held.

Boleyn Days – Boyce attacks as Peters looks on.

England players with Jimmy Adamson training at the Coya Camp, 1962 World Cup.

Chile v Italy – The 'Battle of Santiago' – The first foul occurred within 12 seconds of kick-off. As the image shows, Ferrini (Italy) was sent off in the eighth minute after a foul on Landa, but refused to leave the pitch and had to be dragged off by policemen. English referee Ken Aston did nothing after a left-hook punch by Chilean outside-left Sánchez to Italian right-back Mario David, which had come in retaliation for being fouled seconds earlier. When David attempted to kick Sánchez in the head a few minutes later, he was sent off. In the violence that continued, Sánchez broke Maschio's nose with a left hook, but Aston again failed to send him off. The two teams engaged in scuffles and spitting, and police had to intervene three more times. Ken refereed both of Chile's matches, never oversaw a World Cup match again, becoming a senior member of the refereeing committees of the 1966 and 1970 championships. Later he invented yellow and red cards.

Puskas, the great Hungarian player for Spain, 1962 World Cup.

Andy Malcolm – West Ham.

Hammers into the 60s.

Bobby was voted 'Hammer of the Year' four times 1961, 1963, 1968 and 1970.

Sports Personality of the Year (1966).

Bobby and Ken Brown holding off the Blues.

Byrne on the attack (Upton Park).

Ken Brown.

Shop keeper Bob.

The Barking Boy.

Irons bound for glory.

WEST HAM L. to r. (back): Brown, Hurst, Kirkup, Leslie, Rhodes, Lyall, Bond, Moore. (Middle): Malcolm, Brett, Boyce, Dick, Sealey, Crawford. (Front): Woosnam, Musgrove. (P.A.1.)

Pooch on the pitch – Charlton asking if the pup is a Bulgarian substitute.

Clash of cultures – Garrincha v Charlton.

England 1962 World Cup Squad: Left to Right (back row) Armfield, Norman, Robson, Swan, Hodgkinson, Springett, Howe, Flowers, Anderson, Wilson, Moore; (front row) Peacock, East Ham, Connelly, Greaves, Hitchens, Haynes, Charlton, Douglans.

9

POLES APART, PEAS IN A POD

The two great influences on Bobby Moore's early life, Malcolm Allison and Ron Greenwood were about alike as Frank Sinatra and the Archbishop of Canterbury, Beyoncé and Dame Margaret Rutherford – flagrant flamboyant expression on the one hand, polite, mannered repression on the other. Noel Cantwell and Walter Winterbottom also played significant parts in how Bobby turned out, but Winterbottom was more of a background and relatively brief presence, while Cantwell, certainly a great friend and teacher, was a step behind the two main, more constant pillars of influence.

For a time Allison's other half was a Bunny Girl[27], and he, appropriately, was a playboy; the Great Gatsby of English football. Greenwood, in a nutshell, wasn't. Although Ron was a big influence on Bobby's life, some say equal to Allison, that is looking at things from a long distance. 'Reverend Ron' as players at West Ham, and eventually England, nicknamed him, neither glowed nor shone as brightly as Allison in Moore's life. However, Greenwood was, for a long time, a persistent and righteous preacher of a doctrine Bobby could adhere to, if latterly somewhat reluctantly. His were the kind of words that echo dully in your sleep, somewhere between dozing and unconsciousness.

Allison and Greenwood were both modernisers, both representing and presenting different forms of wisdom; at least in those respects they were truly siblings. Malcolm however ricocheted attractively between a storming force of nature and smiling conviviality, while Ron, possibly out of a need to explain his insights, became associated, probably a tad unfairly, as having a bit too much of a proclivity for delivering sermons on a continuum from the frowning seriousness of a dour politician, to that of a smug schoolteacher with 'I know it all and you don't' half smile. Such apparent arrogance was as much a creation of the brief impressions and imagination of others as any kind of authentic trait of Ron's. If there had been some foundation to accusations of this type, likely it was something of a smokescreen to conceal his inhibitions, and/or feelings of inferiority, perhaps alongside the burden of imposter syndrome. Such frames of mind would be entirely understandable as he was often working with people with a much higher physical capability, skill, and achievement level than he had ever attained.

---

27   His second wife, Sally-Ann Highley.

Both Greenwood and Allison were to mellow with age in their own way. Malcolm became a bit less aggressive and more measured, perhaps accepting the whole world was not going to live up to the standards he demanded. Ron, certainly by the time he became England manager, evolved into the genuinely nice man he probably always was, having lost the defensiveness, likely the source of which was his need to accomplish higher things than West Ham might have been capable of on his watch. He became more confident, able to use fewer words to get more across and occasionally laugh at himself a little.

The bond between Malcolm and Bobby was something rare in life. We really have very few friends in the time given us if we are honest with ourselves, not counting the 'associates' or people we are more or less 'friendly' or 'get on' with, or know on an affable or convivial level. I had occasion to ask Allison about this, in the context of football fame and the perennial 'hangers-on' who are attracted to the bright lights of the game. Of course, there were plenty of such sycophantic desperadoes around Moore, more than a few parasitical in nature. How many articles or books have you read that start out more or less claiming 'I was a close friend of Bobby's'? Malcolm smilingly told me, 'When I was a kid, this duck used to be outside our house, practically every day for ages. I used to feed it breadcrumbs and then it'd piss off. I suppose feeding it made me feel kind or useful, but at the same time, what I also remember is a feeling of being used.'

He chuckled briefly after saying this, and I've taken it that at least the last sentence was irony or satire, but I got the point. The picture of the duck and its impertinent air of expectation stays with me 20-odd years after Malcolm related that parable to me. To be a friend you must have something to offer the person you are notionally friends with; no friendship of any weight meets the needs or wants of just one person, it can't be a one-way street – friendship is, almost by definition, transactional. The idea that you, me, or Bobby might just like someone 'as a person' for 'who they are' (whatever that means) is one thing, but to understand that as the stuff of a lasting friendship is at best fanciful and at worst a lie. What might these self-proclaimed 'friends' have offered Bobby? Would whatever they took from him have been of equal worth to anything they might have offered him?

Maybe I'm just overly cynical, and it has been said (people, eh?). Or perhaps some folk massively overestimate the value of their company to others; sort of just to be with you is doing you a favour, like Malcolm's duck. Then again, who would want to have an ego like that as a friend?

Moore was nothing if not unpretentious, and he found pomposity both amusing and derisible. When researching his life at times I can't help but smile when I find incongruous reporting of 'facts' about his experiences and relationships. For instance,

I have read that his dad was an electrician, a pipe lagger and/or a gas fitter by trade. Although this might be understandable as Big Bob's brother and stepbrother also worked at Barking power station and likely they would have shared tasks and helped each other with a range of work. For all that, it was unlikely that there was enough work for a full-time employee to be involved solely in lagging pipes, for instance. By the early 1970s incidentally he was a railway worker. I have been told by others that Bobby loved/hated/couldn't care less about dogs/cats, that he called his first car 'Sally' (after an ex-girlfriend, although before Tina there is no evidence of such a companion) but also 'Wally' in honour of Walter Winterbottom. I can only too easily imagine the excited fawning, kow-towing journo, feeling oh so pleased with himself, squatting round a table in Phil Cassettari's cafe, in the company of Moore, Johnny Byrne and John Charles, or at the bar in the Moby Dick in Essex's 'West Ham territory', clutching his half of lager top, being told the 'tale of the old iron pot' with stifled laughter in the background as the piss-take proceeded.

One story that must have been hilarious in the telling was about how Bobby, Byrne, and Harry Cripps (by then a fixture at Millwall) bumped into Princess Margaret and jazz pianist Robin Douglas-Home in the Green Gate pub in Plaistow on New Year's Eve 1966, following an Upton Park encounter with Leicester City, Mags being a big Hammers supporter. During the evening Bobby, Harry, and Budgie sang a string of numbers along with HRH, accompanied by Robo on the Joanna. Of course, after banging out 'Auld Lang Syne' at midnight, they all finished off the evening with a rousing rendition of 'Bubbles' followed by 'The Lambeth Walk', the princess pulling off the steps as if born to it. Now there's a cockney fantasy if ever there was one!

Idealism was the factor that linked Allison and Greenwood; Ron had a mission, Malcolm a crusade. Greenwood developed a credo built around a 'way'. He had it that winning was more a possible side-effect of this, but excellence or art was what he was after. So Ron pursued something, perhaps more of the mind than physical factors. Allison was in much the same place, or thereabouts, but he didn't have Greenwood's extreme repugnance of the 'by any means necessary' principle carried by the likes of Don Revie when he was in charge of Leeds. Although Malcolm did seek out beauty in creating patterns of football, something that Revie, a child of the Great Depression, the son of a Yorkshire 'washerwoman', would likely have seen as typical southern effeteness.

As I have in respect of Allison and Ted Fenton, I have also written about Greenwood at some length previously, and again, I don't think you'd be getting your money's worth if I went over much the same ground, but the route Greenwood took to Upton Park is worth drilling down into.

It was while he was coaching at Oxford University that Ron caught the eye of Harold Thompson, who would become the potentate-like chair of the FA. Harry had spent his immediate postwar years swanning around the 'dreaming spires' as a chemistry Don. Later, Thompson, having liked the cut of Greenwood's jib, Aloysius-like, adopted him and supported (or maybe touted for) Walter Winterbottom giving him the job of dealing with England youth setup. Greenwood was doing a bit of looking around in connection with this job when he happened to come across Bobby playing against Glasgow Grammar Schools at Stamford Bridge.[28]

At Upton Park, Moore had been shifted around defence and midfield. This was related to the effort Ted Fenton made to figure out what, if anything, he was. Bobby didn't quite fit into the internal football schemata of the West Ham tradition. Alf Ramsey once said of Martin Peters that he was 'ten years ahead of his time'. In the mid-1950s Fenton wasn't exactly behind the times, in fact in a modest way he was a moderniser of the game, but Bobby was a step outside Ted's peripheral visionary zone – not so much ahead of his time, but in a space all his own. However, Moore's disposition appealed to Ron; the lad seemed to have an integrity beyond his years. This was confirmed as he got to know the boy a bit more. Bobby's penchant for, and fervent interest in, the diligent application of Greenwood's gospel flattered Ron. Greenwood was to recollect that he seldom had a conversation with the teenage Moore as the youngster turned every encounter with his guru into an interview. He just didn't stop asking questions, seemingly looking to understand everything about the game, from defence to passing and bringing the ball out. Like Ron, Moore was a seeker, and deep down, Greenwood saw the hint of a kindred spirit.

It is instructive, when looking at Moore's development in association with Greenwood, to understand something of Ron's playing career. He had done well by most standards, winning the First Division with Chelsea and getting himself a single cap for the England B team, playing at centre-half (an only-goal victory against the Netherlands B side in Amsterdam[29]). However, he was not the only person to understand that while he had been a good player, his own career had been nothing close to star-quality. Greenwood was not the stalwart Alf Ramsey had been both at Tottenham and with England. Ron's career achievements as a player weren't great. Indeed, for a perfectionist like Greenwood, who believed he knew what was needed to create footballing excellence, his track record was not much better than mediocre. He never had the opportunity (or perhaps the ability)

---

28   Moore was playing centre-half for London Grammar Schools. There was no side for London Secondary Modern Schools, but if there had been, I wouldn't have got in it anyway.

29   The first B game was in 1947. There were 54 official and three unofficial B team matches up to May 2007 when the idea lost traction.

to realise and execute his insights and make them part of his own skillset. Thus, coaching was always going to be something in pursuit of what he had not or could not achieve as a player. You perhaps can see, and maybe empathise with, how this might have felt.

Greenwood always had the intention of keeping faith with Moore as he moved into his role with England's under-23 side, and it was no surprise to him when Bobby led West Ham to the FA Youth Cup Final. When the Irons boasted both Moore and inside-forward Johnny Byrne, they looked like a side that had the means to become a club of the future going into the latter half of the 20th century.

Although devoted to taking tactics into all four dimensions, Ron also delivered his share of lectures on strategy, perhaps more than most coaches at the time. Often these left more than a few players lost, bored or both, but at least initially Moore, and three or four others, found these talks both exciting and engaging. Although an innovator, Greenwood did have something of the 'old school' about him. Ron was restrained, in some ways repressed, a bit further down the scale of introversion than Bobby's natural shyness.

Moore was able to change gear in terms of his disposition in a way that was beyond Greenwood (even if it did take Bobby a few drinks to loosen up). One of Bobby's party tricks was to nonchalantly stand behind the bar, seemingly innocuously, trouserless. It is unimaginable that such a gesture might be lodged in Greenwood's social repertoire. He seemed detached to most players, and although nearly all recognised his undoubted wisdom, in the first part of his managerial reign he could come over as taking himself to be superior to everyone else within earshot, although in a few ways he probably was. I have never been convinced this was who Ron was, but retrospectively it furthers the impression that he could overcompensate for some measure of deep lying self-doubt. This did diminish over the years; perhaps as he found less need to prove himself or compensate.

Like Alf Ramsey, during the 1960s Ron had an austere sense of what professionality looked like. He expected players to be disciplined, to live a relatively frugal, abstinent lifestyle. As Moore matured this was most definitely not where he was at. The motto of the West Ham players, as Bobby's good mate John Charles informed me, was, 'Win, draw or lose, we're on the booze.' Moore's taste for a lager or eight was common knowledge. On the train home from away games he would often arrange for the carriage the team were consigned to have a liberal stash of alcohol stowed under the tables. Such antics were an anathema to Greenwood; indeed, on his part, it probably inspired contempt or even disgust.

Just before being confirmed as the new boss at Upton Park, Ron gave up the assistant manager's role at Arsenal (that was his 'day job' alongside taking responsibility for the training and development of England's under-23s). It had become clear that whoever might eventually step into George Swinton's size 12 wellies, it wasn't going to be Greenwood. Bobby was enthusiastic about Ron's appointment, telling players curious about Greenwood that he was 'a proper coach' and if they were keen to understand the game, the new man was one of the best to help with that.

At Highbury, Ron had been pulling down around £1,500 a year. He got another £500 on top of that as West Ham manager, but Greenwood wasn't in it for the dosh. The move to Upton Park engaged his imagination. It was a chance for him to build his vision of football in his own image. For the West Ham board there were several reasons for bringing Ron to East London. Improving results and developing young players were certainly significant motivating factors, but logic tells one that other motives played a part in the post maximum wage era.

On the first morning of his reign Ron called all the playing staff together on the pitch. He told them that he liked 'good habits' on the field (he wanted players to do the right thing without thinking about it). 'Bad habits,' he said, produced inconsistent play. He emphasised the need to surprise other teams, which would mean the players needed to learn to improvise. He also let his players know that everyone would have a chance of first-team football, including the youngest among them.

While his teacherly persona was to prove a blockage for some over time, most were taken with Ron's positive attributes, his forthright attitude and genuineness. This, for me, was the 'real' Greenwood. He knew all the players' names, a courtesy and skill that had not always been shown by everyone in authority roles at Upton Park. For instance, it wasn't unusual for Charlie Paynter to confuse Malcolm Allison with Noel Canwell, and vice-versa, sometimes combinations of both; Noel Allison, Malcolm Cantwell, and maybe Allison Cantwell. He once talked of Cantwell as 'the Welsh fella'. Bill Robinson had referred to Moore on occasion variously as 'Jimmy', 'Jeff' and 'Stan'.

It was Greenwood's training that really brought home the nature of the change the club had instigated. More technical work was introduced, for instance 'phase play' – three-v-three, or two-v-two, four-v-three, seven-v-two, confining play to small areas. He would pit four against three now and then, sometimes, eight against two. This was hard and stimulating training.

The players enjoyed the five-a-side games Greenwood liked to include regularly, pitching strikers against defenders. Ron had it that the defenders nearly always won because they organised themselves better in their own half, so giving themselves a secure platform on which they could put attacks together.

Greenwood encouraged one or two-touch play in practice matches, looking for players to develop positive reactions, honing their technical abilities. To be fair, Fenton by way of his trust in Allison and Cantwell, had prepared the way for Ron, but Greenwood brought a comprehensive change of philosophy, and this was embodied in his training methods. The use of weights was given greater emphasis than the long cross-country runs Ted favoured. The running that was included in training was more intense and over shorter distances, a lot of this with the ball. Greenwood introduced the Scandinavian-type 'interval training', for instance, repeating trots for 50 yards interspersed by 100-yard sprints, combining intensity/recovery training[30]. In the first part of the Fenton era, repeated lapping of the Upton Park pitch, or a six-mile run out at Grange Farm, made up most of the training, while Ted was sitting in his car, puffing on 'Old Mrs Wordsley's slow-release shag' in his briar, watching his squad heaving round the countryside.

Despite the athletic abilities of the younger players, many of the first-teamers, like John Bond, although not the greatest of runners, were often the first to finish the hilly, largely cross-country runs. Those who had been exposed to Fenton's training for some time got to know all shortcuts of course, often knocking three or four miles off the runs.

On one occasion Moore and goalkeeper Ernie Gregory were well in the lead, way ahead of Cantwell and Bond. The players wore roll-neck tops and tracksuit bottoms then , and by the time they reached one of the steeper inclines, sweat was pouring off them. Moore and Gregory were convinced that they might be the first to reach Ted who was waiting at the finish of the run. However, Bond and Cantwell managed to catch a bus and jumped off around 100 yards from Fenton, about the same distance in front of Bobby and Ernie, who were amazed to see their team-mates at the finish waiting for them. This was a trick several of the players repeated time and again; when the bus passed the other runners, the canny passengers would duck down behind the seats.

Unlike the Fenton regime, under Greenwood the manager never failed to turn up for and direct the training, organising the coaching staff, and giving individual attention to players. So there was no opportunity for the kind of skiving, quick fags, or a swift, mid-run half in the Retreat pub, Hainault that Ted's absence facilitated.

---

30   The term for this type of training is fartlek. It comes from the Swedish words of fart (speed) and lek (play). The method was developed by a Swedish coach Gösta Holmér at the start of the 1930s. The training improved both speed and endurance simultaneously without causing significant discomfort and fatigue. The results were impressive, and one of Holmér's athletes, Gunder Hägg, ran a mile in a record time of four minutes and one second. This was a world record that stood for nine years. It's a method I have used myself both as an athlete and a coach, and improvements in performance were always significant and consistent.

Ron was more than devoted; his mind, when it came to football, was like a multidimensional computer. He would often meet a player in passing in and around the Boleyn Ground and say, for instance, 'Two minutes and 24 seconds' – the longest time that player had held on to the ball before passing it during a recent game.

Some players, retrospectively, felt that Greenwood's focus on technique was achieved at the expense conditioning and fitness, but as Noel Cantwell told me, 'If there is emphasis on "this", then there isn't on "that" … sure, in the sprinting stakes Bobby Moore was nowhere, but his muscular strength, concentration on building foresight and working on his attitude more than compensated for that … just as in life generally, you have to make choices in training but you can only do bits of everything … or you can do a fair bit of something.'

However, Greenwood's conditioning had a consequence beyond the acquisition and honing of skill and relevant fitness. He would work hard to develop player potential, but when someone looked incapable of, or found it attitudinally objectionable to play his way, they were quickly shipped out. Primal to his assessment was a player's sense of position and disposition to release the ball thoughtfully and timely; for him this was the oil in the machine. Moore of course was the master of that art.

Not long into Ron's first season, having watched a few games he concluded that the West Ham defence was too focused on marking opponents on an inflexible man-to-man basis. This, for Greenwood, caused them to forget about the ball. He called for more flexibility and improvisation. Soon the side were shipping fewer goals, but also they looked better; although far from perfect, the whole defensive performance was more sophisticated.

Like Allison, Greenwood encouraged the players to talk more during matches. For Ron, calling on the influence of Michael Argyle in his Oxford University days, on-field communication was primary. Off the park he encouraged discussion of tactics and reflection on matches – he wanted the players to come up with their own ideas and practice them in training. All of this was about learning, experimentation and developing innovation as a team. What Greenwood was looking to generate might now be called 'a learning organisation' – a much-used term and strategy in the contemporary management lexicon.

Everything in Ron's football schema was premised on 'pass and hold' while creating space by moving off the ball – it was all about building something aesthetic; for Ron, if it was ugly, it could not succeed, very much in the tradition of the ancient Greeks.

In the first years of the 1960s there were those who saw Moore as a person one might find it hard to have a conventional conversation with, given he was relatively insular and asked so many questions. He was recognised as someone who was hard to get to know. He had a way of keeping people off balance. Bobby was to retain this 'talent' practically all his life. There was an occasion when he sat with João Saldanha, the Brazilian manager, during a long-haul flight. Reflecting on the experience Saldanha said, 'I don't know much about Bobby Moore but he knows a lot about me.' I have often been spoken of in much the same terms and recognise it as a type of guardedness, but in my defence, and Bobby's, I know all about me, and relatively little about you, so the motivation seems obvious from where I'm standing.

For all this, Moore was charming, and had ample social skills, attributes that made him popular with his peers. Perhaps his relative detachment might have caused Greenwood to grasp the root of his intelligence; his curiosity and work ethic – his ability to focus. This was Moore's quiet preoccupation, sociability and seeking out celebrity were not close in terms of his priorities, although, as time went on, fame and notoriety framed Moore in the limelight. Thus, his manager saw in one side of Bobby something of himself that he admired, but at the same time he recoiled at some of Bobby's other proclivities that were utterly foreign to Ron. Not quite 'Jekyll and Hyde' but in that ballpark.

It is puzzling why Bob's liking for a night out received perhaps as much attention as his personal discipline and dedication, what might now be recognised as his professionalism. Indeed, there were many who argued, or implied, he took the latter a tad too far at times. For instance, when a Hammer scored, Moore would usually not be celebrating with the rest of the team; he'd be making his way to take up a place on the field, preparing for the rest of the game. In all the time they worked together Ron only saw Bobby congratulate a goalscorer once, in any manner that might be regarded as remotely ostentatious. Although when Ted MacDougall notched up his first goal for West Ham after moving to Upton Park from Manchester United, Bobby ran the whole length of the field to register his 'well done', but I recall this because it was unusual. So rare was it that Moore would showily recognise his own or others' high points on the field, Tony Scott's debut game stuck in many minds. In February 1960, just prior to the Greenwood era, Chelsea were at Upton Park when John Bond scored a hat-trick and the Hammers won 4-2. As the final whistle blew, Bobby ran 30 or 40 yards to pat Tony on the back. More commonly Bobby would keep his praise quiet. Sir Geoff Hurst recalled such an occasion and a compliment he 'never forgot'. While he was in the bath after a game, Bobby simply remarked, in as subdued but direct and matter of fact fashion, 'Today, you were fucking brilliant!'

Greenwood took it that Moore wouldn't celebrate goals because he regarded it as an unwise use of energy (although he never advised anyone else not to celebrate).

It has been said of Moore that he was a 'calculated footballer', planning his every move on and off the field. This sounds like a description, or maybe an accusation, of paranoiac cunning, a pitifully negative take on the showing of thought and intelligence. It is also probably somewhat tragic to understand composure or poise as 'unnatural' or 'robotic' (other labels applied to Moore in the past).

I saw Moore score a few times. I remember a match against Queens Park Rangers at Upton Park in early November 1968. He came jogging up the field to strike an Exocet drive from just outside the penalty area. It threatened to break through the top corner of the net. He was immediately surrounded by West Ham players only to walk right through them, but not pushing – they made way for him. A flicker of a half-smile flashed for a second, then his face became a picture of something between expressionlessness and serious contemplation. That was not the image of a mechanistic automaton, it was a vision on considered professionalism and exceptional focus. As most encounters between Rangers and the Hammers, it was a good game, better in this instance because of a 4-3 win. Harry Redknapp scored, which convinced me the impossible could happen. Poplar's very own 'ginger ninja' went totally ape shit of course, scampering around the pitch, engulfed in his own apparently boundless glee and utter shock that he had scored a goal.

Moore's stoic attitude was a significant motivation for Greenwood to see him as the pivot point of the changes he wanted to bring to Upton Park. He was to say, 'When I first went to West Ham they employed inside-forwards and wing-halves, but eventually we changed our system to a flat back four to encourage Bobby to play – he was the lynchpin.'

In the first few years under Greenwood he and Moore established a means to make the most of what they had in common; the differences came later. They were something of a 'dream team' in the early 1960s, a thoughtful and intelligent coach, in some ways, with regard to football, picking up the baton from Bobby's early mentor, Malcolm Allison, and a player with innovatory ideas and pioneering ambitions. Ron found Bobby a delight to work with – the young man had a similar hunger to his for knowledge of and about the game. In time that would prove to be an elysian period for manager and skipper, and for a few years they appeared to be the perfect teacher/student pairing. The association was cemented because they shared a belief in how football should be played and how players needed to behave on the pitch if they were to get the most out of their own game and contribute to the team with maximum effect.

Greenwood's desire to 'set standards' was based on his belief in his players; he assessed that they were up to the challenge. Later in life he was to say, 'Our full-backs would push up and get forward … they were more attacking than some present-day wingers.' However, the Hammers also deployed widemen, the likes of Johnny Sissons, Peter Brabrook and Alan Sealey.

Moore was the kernel of the organism Greenwood looked to give life to. Ron once had it that Bobby was 'skill personified', and from a management perspective a complete player. At the peak of their relationship Greenwood took Moore to be a model professional and the template of a captain in football.

The vision Ron enacted was having all his side playing positively and to advance in a concerted and connected fashion, 'Bobby played loose, free, behind everyone else, so the team could go forward with the confidence.' Moore was a constant presence behind the side, analysing anything coming through, mopping up. For Greenwood, 'It was a joy to watch him play.'

Ron had been deeply impressed by the 4-4-2 formation, popularised by Brazil during the 1958 World Cup. He had a clear notion of how he could shape West Ham's play into this novel, fluid, and dynamic structure, placing his captain at the heart of everything. However, prior to 1958, sometime before Moore came into contact with Greenwood, Bobby knew all about the 4-4-2.

West Ham were going to Czechoslovakia on tour at a point when Bobby was pretty much languishing in the reserve side at Upton Park, not making much of an impression at wing-half – his lack of pace and deficits in heading and jumping made him look less than ordinary to many a critic. Malcolm Allison drafted him into the travelling squad as one of the senior players was committed to national service. It was on that tour that Allison initiated Moore into the 4-4-2 system. Those were the days when trainers (at that point in time 'coaches' were a very new innovation as we would understand the role today, and likely a bit 'too American' for those weaned on the pre-war game) and managers didn't shift players around positions; if you were a wing-half, a wing-half is what you would always be. Even if you moved to centre-half, you'd be a wing-half playing at centre-half. Allison breaking that tradition started the transformation of Moore from a prosaic wing-half into the player he would become.

From Moore's earliest days at Upton Park, the influence of world football had been present. For instance, the 1953/54 season saw the Hammers take on several friendly games, making good use of the newly installed Boleyn Ground floodlights. Among those to visit were Olaria of Brazil, who travelled from Rio de Janeiro to East London to meet the Irons on the evening of Tuesday, 27 April 1954. The game ended in a goalless draw.

After Brazil won the World Cup in 1958 their club teams became popular guests. A powerful motivation to transfer the formation into West Ham's first-team game was opened after a friendly against the Brazilian side, Fluminense, at

Upton Park in April 1960. The inspiration for experimentation grew out of Noel Cantwell playing at left-back and Moore at left-half, and agreeing to alter their tactics drastically, as the visiting right-winger played a retractable role in a 4-3-3 setup with the inside-right keeping up the field as a roving striker. Subsequently Moore marked the winger playing wide, while his skipper concentrated on the inside-right. The more they talked about it together and with their team-mates afterwards, the more the players became convinced that this was an effective way of organising their play. As Bobby was to recollect, 'By bringing one half-back into defence we had a lot more defensive power but didn't lose any attacking strength.' The entertaining match saw West Ham run out 5-4 winners.

At the start of the 1960/61 season this new tactical stance was adopted by the Hammers. Initially things didn't go well and a string of disastrous results away from home nurtured seeds of doubt. At Upton Park West Ham won the three games included in the experiment, but on the road they lost their first five matches. Fenton stepped in to end the trial, telling his side, 'We are losing too many goals.' A 3-3 draw at Upton Park against Blackpool had been the straw that snapped the hapless dromedary's spine. Bobby was for ever adamant that Ted had lost his nerve before the tenth game of the season, and that if West Ham had stuck with it, allowing the players to gel with the system, it would have soon come good.

Fenton has been given the credit for initiating 4-4-2 at Upton Park by some writers, but he didn't know much about it. It wasn't his idea and no one asked his permission to run it out. Indeed, by the time the team decided to go with the idea, after years of being effectively undermined by Malcolm Allison, Fenton was more or less ignored when it came to playing strategies. It was really Moore, Cantwell and Bond with previous stimulus from Allison who had innovated in that respect.

Ted was, by nature, a careful man, and fortune favours the brave. He, as such, was much more the man who prematurely, if temporarily, arrested the development of the coming formational revolution than he might have been an innovator of it. Who can say whether, if it hadn't had been for Fenton losing his bottle, England might have been in a better place, come 1962 and Chile, to have handled the likes of Hungary and Brazil more effectively? That's not meant to be harsh; Ted was of his time, like the majority of managers made in the immediate postwar era, likely any other bloke in his position in the First Division of that time would have responded in much the same way. To his credit, unlike many of his ilk and generation, at least he allowed his players to give it a bit of a go, even if it was by way of just standing by, looking, and feeling lost.

Greenwood distanced Moore from the traditional demolition centre-field defender role, as deployed in the tired and anachronistic 'WM' formation. In the latter system (if indeed it could be called that) the function of the centre-half was to essentially nullify the opposing centre-forward. With a few exceptions it was usually a job for the sublimely unimaginative and most brutal of players. As it was, if Moore faced a pacy centre-forward, or one who might pose an aerial threat, he would be exposed, not being too quick over the ground and finding the idea of heading relatively messy. For him 'feet' and 'ball' were synonymous – anything above the neck was for looking, thinking, listening, kissing, and smelling in that order.

Ron had no use for the destructive half-back/harrying midfielder role that Fenton had, albeit half-heartedly, attempted to fit Moore into. Greenwood didn't have much time for the idea of closing play down by any instrument or intention, he was more for overcoming the opposition by sheer craft and/or blinding them with art.

It was before a game with Leicester City in February 1962 that Ron let Bobby know he wanted to pull him back into defence 'to work deeper and looser'. Alongside Ken Brown, Bobby would be a 'spare' centre-half in West Ham's back four.

As Geoff Hurst has suggested, that was Greenwood's 'masterstroke'. Bobby, playing off Brown, fitted into his new task like he was born to it, catching potential issues before they happened, foiling problems as they presented. The war with the centre-forward was left to Ken, a labour he was more than suited to. Moore tidied up (something he was readied for from infancy), organising the defence. Of course, as a child, Bobby liked organising, toys, books and later shirts, suits, and football teams.

His transition to a creative central defender, made in Greenwood's first full season, against the smart and coordinated Leicester side managed by their canny former skipper Matt Gillies, started with Ron's instruction to Moore to drop back, to move back and play more flexibly. The task was pretty much something Bobby had been cultivating most of his life, but Greenwood formalised it.

With Bobby alongside and to the left of Ken Brown, the full-backs were given opportunities to move in and closer to their opponents. Greenwood was to argue that this gave the team more balance. This was borne out as West Ham's performances improved instantly. Bobby had found his position and forte, the role that would eventually open the door to greatness for him with regard to both club and country. In later years, notably 1966, England would owe Greenwood a huge debt for shaping and combining Bobby Moore, Geoff Hurst, and Martin Peters. It is strange this has not been more widely recognised.

10

THE FULL MOORO

As the 1960s bloomed, Bobby was coming to the notice of the world of high fashion. The September 1962 issue of *Vogue* pictured him in his West Ham kit, surrounded by four glamorous models. The rest of the world was discovering that Moore had a uniquely attractive masculine elegance, but unlike many sportsmen, he had no rough edges. There was an aura of intelligent consciousness around him that appealed as much to men as it did to women, although, for the most part, probably in somewhat different ways.

It was also a period when the skills of perception and awareness Moore had honed from the age of 12 with Malcolm Allison came into their own. Falling back from the struggles of midfield gave him the time and room to put his powers of cognisance to their best use. It was this that motivated Jock Stein to remark years on, 'There should be a law against Moore … he can see things 20 minutes before everyone else.'

Ron Greenwood had put Bobby in a place where the game was set out before him and where he could apply his well-tuned judgement to best effect. No one cared or noticed he hardly headed a ball, Ken Brown did that, and if you time dropping off well then the need to use your head diminishes as graceful use of the chest is facilitated.

This was the foundation of liberated football, the kind of game that could accommodate a whole new breed of players and in it, as Ron was to say, 'Moore had found his niche,' but he had also carved out a place for many others as the game became more sophisticated and nuanced.

It has been said, and it is partially true, that without Greenwood and the Brazilians, there may well have been no Bobby Moore as we have come to know him. However, at the same time, without Moore the system, tactics and strategy that gave West Ham their first FA Cup win (the last winners to call on only Englishmen in every round) would likely have not been realised. It also allowed the Hammers to be the first – and last – all-English side to win European honours (again, the Hammers only fielded English players throughout that tournament, see Belton, 2013b) and took England to victory in 1966. None of this could have been fully implemented without Moore, because no one else in the game could do what he did, or be who he was; there was only, and there will ever be, one Bobby Moore.

Exceptional players make positions; to state the 'bleedin obvious' positions don't exist in a vacuum. The success or otherwise of a plan is reliant on someone able to carry it out. Moore fashioned the role Greenwood theoretically developed; Bobby brought it to life by his capacity to take responsibility for, and interpret it into action, and exert his authority to lead his teams from that place.

Bobby named his role as that of a 'sweeper', an appellation few had heard of previously, although it was pioneered by the Austrian manager Karl Rappan. It was he who incorporated it into his *catenaccio* or *verrou* (doorbolt or chain) system with Swiss club Servette during the 1930s. Karl moved one player from midfield to a position behind the defensive line as a 'last man'; this individual would protect the back line and start attacks again. As coach of Switzerland in the 1930s and 1940s, Rappan deployed a defensive player that came to be known as the *verrouilleur* (sweeper), positioned just ahead of the goalkeeper. Generally, the role produced a more versatile centre-back than the traditional position; a player who 'sweeps up' the ball if an opponent manages to breach the defensive line. This was more a fluid function than that of other defenders who man-mark their designated opponents. Because of this, it is sometimes referred to in Italian as *libero* ('free' – see Belton, ibid.).

While the title seems to explain Moore's task, it is just the scaffolding on which he developed what was a methodology. Bobby described the role as 'unspectacular' but went on to talk about positioning, which for him was largely unappreciated by those who watch the game, 'Most watchers keep their eyes on the ball and the player who makes the brilliant pass gets the cheers – few spectators stop to think that the other player had to use even more brains to find the position where the pass was possible. This applies to the sweeper in his job of plugging the gaps. He must read the game so well that he is continually moving to the spot that gives him command of any breakthrough.'

Moore took Rappan's template on to a much more refined and adaptational range of functioning. I can't boast the record for seeing Moore play, although I'm sure I missed very few of his performances for West Ham and England[31] and he just did not sit to the rear of the line, ossified in defensive duties (Italian football generated that kind of operation). Moore played a creative game from the back, to the extent it gave his teams a second engine. He effectively linked the whole side together in a dynamic way, and the thumping heart of this was both proactive and responsive movement. Yes, finding or making space, but also using awareness of space and position.

Greenwood's mantra, referring to opponents, was the question, 'Can you hurt them?' This had nothing to do with physicality, which doesn't touch the best teams. The 'hurt' could be inflicted by players persistently seeking or crafting

---

31   I also took in games Moore played for Fulham, San Antonio Thunder and Herning Fremad.

chances to attack. Moore, occupying the centre of the defence, was the axis of this ask and task. Watch him play on YouTube and you'll see with no longer than 20 minutes of your attention his eagerness to make the swift pass. You'll see, with stunning immediacy, how this transforms defence into attack. For Moore, defence was attack and attack a means of defence; get rid of dichotomies and you have a whole.

Add to this the accurate and precise nature of Moore's placement of the ball and you have something awesome. Observe how Bobby moved into midfield, clipping the ball forward. We often missed the brilliance of this because it happened so often.

In the 4-4-2 formation Moore acted much like a gridiron quarterback, starting plays with well-judged and exquisitely executed passes. In this, Bobby had developed Allison's teaching that he should play from deep. This attitudinal and technical application evolved with Greenwood's attention.

All this required the utmost exactness and so endless rehearsal and refinement. You are always, at some point, going to lose possession if you persistently look to carry the ball out of defence. This however was of little consequence to Greenwood. The search for aesthetic football, for him, was primary. When mistakes were made, he offered little in the way of apology or even explanation. He repeatedly made it clear that his preference was for creative intention, even if it went awry, over the ugly bluntness of the boot to 'row z'.

The horizon of Moore's impact on the field of play remains astonishing even today. It is rare to see a central defender not only audaciously venturing forward, but at the same time forging a game design and trajectory.

For sure, every week in the Premier League you'll see defenders with ball skills, often advancing with offensive intent, but the fully creative centre-half is an anomaly in a game where winning is less than all, because not losing is the principle of everything. While every now and then, in the top-class matches involving continental teams, you might well see a central defender galloping into midfield, in the British game, if you see it at all, it is liable to provoke one, some, or all the following: more criticism than praise, be understood as a mistake, a source of amusement, eccentricity or surprise.

There have been a few 'Moore-likes' over the decades since Bobby left football. Fellow East Ender Ledley King had the same sort of vision and class before tragically being lost to the game through injury, and Italian international Andrea Pirlo, although essentially a midfielder at AC Milan and Juventus, had a similar presence and perceptive qualities. Maybe if one could merge both of these exceptional talents, you'd get yourself a Moore clone. But as Sir Geoff Hurst had it, in the context of English football, the sweeper who might echo Moore's play, the defender who will blend into midfield, is all but extinct; the calm leader, able on the ball, playing with authority. For Hurst we have had instead a production line, a lineage of what are, in the main, markers (from the likes of Terry Butcher and Dave Watson to John Terry).

So, as things stand, we are not going to see another Bobby Moore. The conditions don't exist and nor does an individual with the required authority or persona. Much might be said of Franz Beckenbauer, but finding 'the full Mooro' will likely need a total change in the game that isn't coming any time soon. The era of Dutch 'total football' put the pedal to the metal, but that time has gone. We are now in an age of total paranoia, wherein no manager is going to last long with Greenwood's 'go fuck yourself' attitude toward any suggestion that he or his team should compromise their standards (although he certainly wouldn't have put it quite that way).

During the 2022 Women's European Championship, England's victorious Lionesses adopted Chris Stapleton's 'Starting Over' as their dressing-room anthem. There's a couple of lines in the song that have it:

But nobody wins afraid of losing
And the hard roads are the ones worth choosing

'Who dares wins' – and the women did, but it depends on what you see 'winning' to be. Perhaps it's more than baubles awarded for the 'best in show' from the kind of mechanical mediocrity so beloved of the 'Special One', or the catwalk of the effete global millionaires roadshow currently paraded at the Etihad. Perhaps the 'West Ham Way' was always a myth, but maybe our dreams reflect our better selves, and that might be an excuse not to allow them to 'fade and die'?

As a supporter, blooded in the late Fenton/early Greenwood era, I fully approve and echo the Lionesses' sentiments. In the last analysis I don't care if a game ends with West Ham scoring fewer goals than another side; that's largely irrelevant. We never lose, we only win and learn.

Gerry Rafferty sums this up somewhat from me in his track, 'Get It Right Next Time'.

Life is a liar yeah life is a cheat
It'll lead you on and pull the ground from underneath your feet
No use complainin', don't you worry, don't you whine
Cause if you get it wrong you'll get it right next time, next time.

You gotta grow, you gotta learn by your mistakes
You gotta die a little everyday just to try to stay awake
When you believe there's no mountain you can climb
And if you get it wrong you'll get it right next time, next time.

Those of us who 'are' West Ham will 'get' this, but we're born to it I suspect. You can't really make someone a Hammer. One doesn't choose 'Ironhood', one is chosen. I'm not going to try to explain that to anyone because those who understand it need no explanation, while those who don't 'get' it, well, they never will. Without pushing the proverbial boat out too far, this is reminiscent of a Hammer original, Italian priest and philosopher Thomas Aquinas (1225–1274), and his take on faith, 'To one who has faith, no explanation is necessary. To one without faith, no explanation is possible.'

In the game with Leicester in February 1962, the start of an epoch was witnessed with Bobby slotting in just behind Eddie Bovington, the darting midfield marauder; this was the nascent brand of a revitalised 4-4-2 that would change English football and win the World Cup.

Bovington was not alone when he confessed to sometimes feeling that Moore got all the accolades while the likes of Eddie were also grafting on tight marking, Bobby getting the seemingly less-onerous task of tidying up behind. He did, however, qualify this view by saying that complaint wasn't appropriate as Moore was a one-off, having 'a special quality of making time on the ball'. For Bovington that was a mark of a great player; Moore *took* control (it is never given) while his team-mates operated within his organisation of play.

From that 1962 encounter with the Foxes onwards, Bobby was established in the ranks of the Irons, a place fashioned by Greenwood but wrought by his own talent and will. To achieve this both Moore and Ron had to have a mindset that embraced the proposal that people can be made (trained/educated/coached) to be 'better'. Moore was to affirm, 'A boy who won't make the effort to think and study the game will not go very far.' It was the continuation of this ethic, which had been instilled in him from his childhood years, working with Malcolm Allison and Noel Cantwell, that fitted well with Greenwood's principles, and so made what they accomplished together possible.

However, this position, while founded on a conviction that one can improve, grows from an equally powerful but nagging sense that one is not good enough; as detailed in *Young Bobby* the latter feeling was something Moore carried with him, certainly for most of his early life and career. But if you think you are good enough, where might the incentive or belief that you can become better come from?

Bobby and Greenwood reached the upper echelons of their ambitions via hard work to overcome the deficiencies they understood themselves to have. Indeed, how does one become stronger unless one can honestly assess and so address one's weaknesses? Confidence is built on the bedrock of self-doubt; the lack of confidence is the engine of the necessary endeavour it takes to improve. Naked egocentric arrogance, which comes with the feeling one is supremely assured of one's abilities, leaves us with, at best, stasis, or at worst a gradual erosion of skill etc. and ultimately the fall into the pit of despair.

It was the 'suite' of attitudes and knowledge about their insufficiencies that locked manager and skipper together. This is what they used to drive themselves to strive for the perfection they both to some extent realised.

At almost every stage of Bobby's career Greenwood was a major influence on him. The older man represented a well of knowledge to match the young man's thirst for understanding. Moore founded his play on Greenwood's contention that the means to produce quality football was players building those 'good habits' he extolled. Primary to this was the mastery of the basics of the game. What he wanted to present were players who could do things correctly, but without thinking about it; he was building instinctive play in much the same way as traditional judo was taught in Japan (the habituation of good habits). He told his players, 'You must leave the ball playable,' meaning that when a pass to a team-mate was made, it had to be at the correct pace and angle so that it could be played off first time by the player collecting the ball.

Moore was taking a leaf out of Greenwood's book by not cajoling his team-mates. Ron almost never bollocked players for doing something that wasn't partly or wholly pulled off. What he did demand was a firm grasp of the underlying principles. For instance, he saw the worth of the near-post cross – calling it 'the soft underbelly of opposing defences'. It was rehearsed thousands of times in training and became a tactic that brought the Hammers innumerable goals from the early 1960s on. But to get it right, you had to take the chance of getting it wrong.

Greenwood, for Moore, was however less the affable idol than Malcolm Allison had been for him and more like a detached Sensei. While affection for Allison caused Moore to value Malcolm for the rest of his life, once Greenwood had taught him all he could, there was little to keep Moore invested in any meaningful association with his manager.

This seems more than a tad instrumental, even somewhat ruthless, but the relationship was symbiotic in that respect; Greenwood's reputation, skills and knowledge were enhanced by his association with Moore. That said, any affiliation survives to the extent that the parties concerned benefit from it – pure altruism does not exist in human connection, perhaps with the exception parent-child relationships, even those are debatable, but in the main, all relationships are transactional

Ron and Bobby never developed the close affinity that existed between Moore and Allison. Greenwood certainly grew to admire Moore, and Bobby respected Ron well enough, but Greenwood, in the first stage of his managerial career, sometimes treated players like a caring but sometimes edgy uncle might respond to errant nephews. He fell short of a curmudgeonly teacher, but he was never close to 'the good bloke' or adored big brother Allison might have been ultimately to many players.[32] One can't envisage Bobby and Ron sharing a beer together in anything but a rather self-conscious manner or even having similar senses of humour.

In 1960, as assistant manager at Arsenal, Greenwood had been keen to make Moore a Gunner. Ron made a point of talking to Moore a fair bit during that period, causing Bobby to feel the coach wanted him at Highbury, although Ron was too straight-laced to say that in so many words. Moore's impression was strengthened when one of the Arsenal youngsters in the under-23 squad told him he'd be liked at Highbury. Bobby's feelings were affirmed by one of Greenwood's favoured journalists, the estimable Ian Wooldridge. When chatting to the young Hammer the *Mail* man pointed out the advantages of raising his colours in North London, which were manifold, including the apparent luck that comes with pulling on the shirt.

It was after George Swindin had left football, at his garage in Corby, Northamptonshire, that he told me Greenwood had tried to persuade him to sign Moore. The Yorkshireman had made enquiries but Ted Fenton wanted a swap deal that would have brought Jimmy Bloomfield to Upton Park, sending Moore and Mike Grice to Highbury. For George that was never going to happen. Swindin, at that time, was less than convinced about Bobby and had next to 'no clue' what Grice could bring to the table as a Gunner. Later Bobby was to admit that if the opportunity had arisen, he would have jumped at a move to Highbury, or White Hart Lane for that matter (double-winning Spurs manager Bill Nicholson was always a great admirer). Well, of course he would, these were London's big clubs. As Bobby was to speculate, almost without doubt, about approaches by both and probably other clubs would have been made to the Upton Park board, but the money could never have been right.

Bobby moving away from Upton Park had been made more unlikely when Greenwood pitched his wigwam in the easterly realms of the capital, and by the

---

32   Allison was however a bit 'marmite' – I have talked to as many who had less than a liking for the man as I have those who idolised him.

end of 1961 the chance of him being transferred to a top-flight rival became more remote than meeting Jacob Rees-Mogg on a Jeremy Corbyn Appreciation Society beano.

West Ham having awarded Ted Fenton the order of the boot, and Greenwood letting Bobby know that the opportunity to work with him and construct a team around him were his main motivations to head down to the banks of the Thames (no pressure there then!) effectively tied Moore to Upton Park for the foreseeable future. For all that, likely to Bobby the latter statement of intention sounded just a little resonant of a key turning in a lock. It certainly was putting a lot of weight on the young man's shoulders. Why should Moore take any responsibility for what Ron decided? But I suppose this was meant to be flattering.

Most writers relate to Moore needing assurance from Greenwood about his future at Upton Park, given Fenton's apparent reticence about him. But Ron had consistently pushed for the inclusion of Moore in both his England youth and under-23 teams, so Bobby knew Greenwood rated him. Given this the new manager laying on the line his intentions with regard to Moore and West Ham sounds more like an ultimatum; an 'I did this because of you' vibe. Yes, for a moment that might be gratifying, perhaps ingratiating, but that sort of petition also lays the seeds for resentment, any ambitions, hopes or dreams of a move to bigger more successful clubs being unceremoniously and completely deflated because of Ron's ambitions. Think of it, 'I wrote this book for you, that was the only reason, so now you have to read it, every word, and not look at another book, like it or not.' How might that feel? Now times that by about 10,000. From my teenage years I sensed the antipathy growing over time between Greenwood and Moore. Later, Tina Moore in her 2005 book was to confirm my instincts, specifically in terms of Ron's feelings towards Bobby.

Cracks appearing

After Bobby's passing, Greenwood was to reflect that he knew Moore as a footballer but never as a person, and how he had grown to think that was perhaps appropriate for a relationship between a player and a manager. This implies that Bobby was two separate people. But we are all different people at different times, places, and situations. I am different with my son than I am working as a youth worker with other people's children or with other professionals in my field or students. However, there are aspects of my personality that persist in whatever role I find myself playing – I am only one person. I think Ron was similar in this respect; his attitudes and behaviour were noticeably consistent in most of his doings. That was not entirely the case with Moore.

For sure, there were traits of Bob's personality that were emphasised in his professional persona. For instance, on and off the field of play he was driven to be precise, and to make every effort to impose order, and sometimes uniformity, on his environment. Even as captain of England, he would use one pair of tie-ups for his socks that often lasted him for seasons, while others would grab a new pair for every match. He would faithfully tuck them in his boots after each game, take them home and wash them. Bobby folded his handkerchiefs and his underpants. Before a game he liked to go into the dressing room at least half an hour before the kick-off. He would take a minimum of 15 minutes to get changed after which he would try to relax for the last quarter of an hour before running out on the pitch. At half-time it was usual for players to be served tea with lemon, but Bobby didn't have anything to drink, ever. He would never touch a door jam on the way out of the dressing room, or put his shorts on until the rest of the team had put theirs on. On occasion Martin Peters tested him on this habit, taking his shorts off just as Bobby had put his on. Bobby took his shorts off and didn't put them back on until Peters had got back into his. However, away from the field of play, Moore was often downright rebellious and anti-authoritarian in his dealings with his manager and employers, and could be mischievous and chaotic in his social life. Unlike Greenwood, who was anything but unpredictable in his social dealings, relatively this made Bobby seem even more erratic, so few might have felt totally at ease in his company.

Greenwood and Moore's relationship was to become less than straightforward as time went on. Bobby always admired Ron's football knowledge, and there was a period when he became something of a palaestra in Moore's eyes. However, when Bobby grew to be a gargantuan figure, not only in the game but sport in general and beyond, something of a national treasure, Greenwood seemed to fade in the England captain's estimation, which is probably natural, healthy and to be expected. Like when your kid grows up, you, as a parent, are not adored as you were before they reached teenage.

At the same time, elements of Ron's behaviour and attitude betrayed a response somewhere between resentment and envy. It's hard to say what this was exactly about; perhaps it is often a consequence of that mixture of emotion, resentment, ideas about 'justice' and so on. However, I sometimes wonder, at least in part, although probably not totally consciously, if Ron wanted Bobby to be the player and the man Greenwood might have wanted to be, or feel he should have been if the fates had been kinder. But Moore strayed quite a long way from Ron's values off the park, and perhaps didn't always give him the level of credit or regard he might have thought he deserved.

As Tina rightly has it, no one knew Bobby better than her. She has told how she detected hints of jealousy or resentment towards Moore from Greenwood. Ron likely, and perhaps understandably, believed he had made Moore the player Bobby had become, but maybe felt he hadn't got the recognition he deserved for this as Bobby's charisma was magnified, seemingly outgrowing West Ham[33]. A strong example of this was provided by Tina recalling Bobby's fight with testicular cancer two years before his appearance in the World Cup Final. Greenwood visited his stricken skipper in hospital just after crucial surgery, and told him, 'You're not to worry, Bobby. The team's playing fine and Martin Peters is doing very well in your place.'

Tina was righteously hurt, shocked, and angered by this statement, insinuating as it did that West Ham were doing well enough without the man most central to anything they had achieved during Ron's tenure to that point. It implied, with Moore being tremendously vulnerable at that time, staring at the potential of his demise, that he was expendable. The declaration was even more unfeeling given that Tina was seven months pregnant.

Bobby's then wife saw what Greenwood had said had an impact on her husband. His insipid smile of acknowledgement, together with a glassy stare, betrayed anguish, distress, and gloom. Greenwood must have known what a sensitive issue it was. Ron's apparent total lack of empathy, or even consideration, was staggering at a point when Moore's means of making a living, his feelings about himself as a man, his very life, were in the balance. This was more than upsetting.

Greenwood could have told Moore he was missed, and that he needed to get well because the club relied on him, but he chose, although probably unconsciously (he wasn't a nasty man) to crush more than bolster West Ham's greatest ever player.

Tina, seeing Ron, despite lacking any tangible warmth, as a good and highly moral person, a generous and kindly man, gave him the benefit of the doubt. She chose to see what he did as just poor judgement, a result of not understanding human sentiments and therefore not a deliberate act of malice. Ron's wife, Lucy, had told Tina on their first meeting that Greenwood lived and breathed football, so Tina took the remarks as those of someone who put the game before everything else, perhaps momentarily losing his grip on the skills of basic compassion as a consequence. However, it is impossible not to see some of Ron's more general feelings being exposed in this situation when considered alongside other circumstances.

Perhaps Bobby was never to shake that moment off? On the training ground Greenwood often asked players to repeatedly rehearse aspects of the game, such as

---

33   By the 1964/65 season the fan mail sent to Upton Park was sorted in three piles; one for Moore, another for Byrne and a third somewhat more modest heap for everyone else.

one touch passing and so on. Occasionally, Ron would take part in these sessions. One such time was during an exercise in volleying. Greenwood stepped up looking to execute a point of technique, but what he wanted to do exceeded his talent for doing it. When this became evident Moore intervened, executing the volley perfectly on the first attempt. As you might expect, such demonstrations had an impact both on Bobby's playing colleagues and their manager.

A long road of acrimony between the two men lay ahead, not least regular – and bitter – pay disputes that, often by Bobby's actions and demands, implicated the whole team. But as Tina puts forward in her 2005 book (one of the most informative and intimate with Bobby at the centre) the real war between Greenwood and Moore was about control. This might be understood as Bobby picking up and continuing the crusade started by Allison, the attrition arising out of the awareness about how West Ham, pretty much like all top clubs up to and including Moore's playing career, exploited player talent. Greenwood, like Ted Fenton before him, served that exploitation as managers in most industries do. As Malcolm Allison had tormented Ted with his resistance, so Bobby carried on the struggle with Ron. This wasn't all about money; principles were at stake and the two men saw the moral situation diametrically differently.

Phil Woosnam, the captain Greenwood had inherited from Fenton, made a habit of meeting the manager in his office, exploring ideas and strategy, but Moore wasn't one for that type of formality or hierarchy. It was usual for Moore to implicate his team-mates in his thinking and strategy, and avoid indulging in a private *tête-à-tête* with non-playing staff. This was something his manager was never quite comfortable with. At the same time, I doubt Bobby wanted to compromise on his game, and as such kept Greenwood's counsel at arm's length from the vicissitudes of personal, formal managerial instruction. One-to-one training ground chats were Moore's way of dealing with Greenwood, but they were more likely to be technical debates than pow-wows. This diplomacy was resonant of Noel Cantwell's way of managing (manipulating) Fenton.

When Ron addressed the squad, Bobby, for the most part, kept schtum, leaving any comment to body language and demeanour. Allison had managed to ignore or override much of what Fenton had to say about how West Ham might train or play, but Big Mal's tactics in this respect were pretty much openly dismissive and attritional. Moore's attitude, characteristically of him, was more nuanced and 'subterranean' – to some extent this took advantage of Ron's insecurities that Bobby would have well understood. Cryptic silence, nor far from passive aggression, was a sharper, more unsettling weapon for Greenwood to counter than open verbalisations of disagreement.

After his first few years at Upton Park Ron felt Moore became progressively distant from him and perhaps the club generally. While ostensibly this was an off-field situation, anyone consistently supporting the Irons throughout the 1960s might have sensed that the atmosphere between captain and manager was frosty.

For Ron, Bobby could and did close himself off, although the perception of many was that distancing himself from others was characteristic of Greenwood. For all this, the manager was to argue that while his captain's 'cold detachment' was an advantage in the heat of the game, and perhaps a protection against media and public intrusion, it was, for Ron, an attitude which made his life and management role at the Boleyn Ground more difficult. As Tina put it, 'When you were on the icy side of Bobby – on the outside and not able to get in – it was horrible.'

Although it's hard not to suspect that Greenwood's feelings toward Moore included some measure of projection, he was left with the impression that Bobby was disregarding him in front of other players, or at least acting as if he was doing that. Moore got to Ron by looking blank, distracted, or bored when Greenwood was addressing his team, seemingly making a point that he had heard it all before and knew it all. Ron felt he was asking, 'Who needs a manager?' Greenwood was anxious about the example this set the other players, and to be fair, the attitude did rub off on other team members. A typical case of poor classroom management or the start of 'losing the dressing room', but Ron found it humiliating. He was to recall, 'I even wanted to sack him at one point and our relationship became unhappy and strained. There was an icy corridor between us. He was very aloof, locked in a world of his own. He even started to give the impression that he was ignoring me at team-talks. He would glance around with a blasé look on his face, eyes glazed in a way that suggested he had nothing to learn. It was impossible to get close to him. There was a big corner of himself that would not or could not give. It hurt that he could be so cold to someone who cared about him.'

More than a frisson of paranoia in all this can be sensed, but as one player told me, 'Bobby had a way of grinding Ron down.' This wasn't too far from the way he would pressurise an adversary on the field, by force of personality and apparent dismissal; he could break an opponent's focus and form. I'm not altogether sure he was purposely doing this, or if it was just something automatic or innate in his character, a learned response to someone he saw as being in authority or having control over him, so seemingly to be an opponent.

I have seen this type of performance in many classrooms with adult learners, grown men and women 'acting out', putting in a shift to encourage a perception of themselves as disinterested or simply dismissive. It is fascinating as typically the attention they are giving via the exaggerated strop often appears to be more committed than those doing their best to feign engagement. That said, it always seems very hard work but presents a definite critical engagement. Understood in that way such behaviour is at once self-defeating, but also a path, albeit and contorted one, to learning.

Moore certainly had relatively radical ideas about, and resistance to, the way football was organised. He told Jeff Powell in 1993's *Bobby Moore*, 'For a century football was just about the only business which denied a craftsman the freedom and liberty to work for whoever he wanted. Whatever opportunity came my way, West Ham said "no", that was the end of that.'

Here you can feel a hint of what Greenwood was up against, and perhaps you can start to understand why West Ham, and all the other big clubs, turned their back on Bobby after he retired from playing. Moore saw the reality of his industry, and he was solidly on the side those who, in his experience and view, had been exploited by the bourgeoise that dominate the business of football – the 'craftsmen', the artisans and the artists who populate the pitch and create the spectacle of passion; those who weave the sentiment, the commodity peddled by the parasitical corporations, the 'mega-pimps' who hold financial sway over the 'beautiful game'.

Eventually, Ron called Moore to his office to tell him not to give the impression that he was not listening. He said, 'You may be kidding some of the players, but it doesn't wash with me. Whenever I ask for something to be done on the field, you're the first to do it. I know you're listening to every word. So why the act?' Perhaps predictably Bobby didn't come back at his manager. I mean, would anyone who knew Moore, or even just like me, watched him at work for years, have expected an open response, giving his hand away to just stoke an argument? No, Moore kept his powder dry, of course he did. Unsurprisingly he bemused, hurt, and frustrated his manager all the more; he seemed to take no notice of being asked not to look like he was taking no notice. That's a ripe example of the delivery of an existential crisis.

Greenwood ultimately found it impossible to get close to Bobby, just as Moore found Ron to be someone who disallowed anything but basic familiarity, although I'm not sure he would have wanted to be in any intimate proximity to his manager (whoever they might have been). Both men believed there were parts of the other person that would not or could not be shown or trusted to others.

However, there was something to this being about football in the two or three decades after the war. Boys coming to clubs at ten, 11 and 12 years of age, ten or 15 years later, became pretty much institutionalised, with the club not only employing them, but making up almost their entire social circle, housing them, providing transport and so on. It's probably not surprising that some of the behaviour of players in their 20s and 30s appeared little more than teenage pique. At the same time, men like Greenwood, while having lives totally immersed in football, had seen service in the military, not only travelling widely, but having to spend appreciable periods of time in different cultural contexts, being obliged to get along with people from other backgrounds and circumstances. Most had been involved in industry unrelated to football, miners, craftsmen or factory work. Thus, their patience for grown men sulking, and/or acting out, trapped in an adolescent time warp, was limited.

One incident maybe sums up how this type of situation played out. At the bar of a transatlantic jumbo jet flight, having been pretty much wiped out by Newcastle, West Ham were travelling to a friendly game in New York, an encounter with Pelé and his club Santos. Moore, Jimmy Greaves and Freddie Harrison, a mate of theirs, who Bobby went into the leather coat business with, went to the bar soon after take-off. Half an hour or so into the flight Ron joined them. Not being a great lover of drink, he ordered a Coke and started chatting with the trio. As they nattered, Greenwood noticed that they were working together to surreptitiously lace his drink. Ron didn't let on, seeing it as nothing to make too much fuss about, allowing the young men some slack. He understood they weren't altogether mature, not really adults in a meaningful sense, being prone to 'japes', silly pranks, a childlike ambition to 'ave a larf'. This being the case, it is predictable the boy/men players would see Ron as something between a vicar, a father figure, and a schoolteacher. Equally predictably Ron was pulled into this psychological vortex, to a greater or lesser extent, as the psychoanalyst might have it, he responded to the projection/transference by, albeit unconsciously, playing that role.

To be fair, the rancour between Moore and Greenwood wasn't totally without cause and could be justified in both directions. Like Bobby, Ron often failed to help himself in the relationship. For instance, after Moore was named, at the age of 23, the youngest ever Football Writers' Association Footballer of the Year, Greenwood prevented anyone from West Ham attending the Café Royal event, saying it was too close to the FA Cup Final. This, after a trail of growing acrimony, left Bobby wounded and upset, not to mention feeling he had every reason to be. His relationship with his manager was from then on irreparable. If you look at the few images that exist of Moore and Greenwood immediately post the 1964 final, you might be able to detect hints of the consequences on Moore's face and some of his actions. At one point Bobby enacts what looks a bit like an invitation to Ron to celebrate with the rest of the team, but it is forced, with signs of aggressive piss-taking. Greenwood resists in quite a truculent manner, seemingly seeing it below his dignity or simply inappropriate. Bobby would have easily predicted this response. It looks an awkward and uncomfortable moment for Ron, but Bob's expression and demeanour betrays something quite different – something 'dark'.

Both men started out presenting a protective front, but ultimately, they grew to not especially like each other. Not for a minute do I believe, and there is no evidence to suggest, that either man stopped respecting the other as player and coach respectively. Outside of Malcolm Allison, every indication has it that Moore rated Greenwood as the most knowledgeable and able coaches he was to work with, pipping Walter Winterbottom but way ahead of Alf Ramsey.

For Ron, Moore became imprisoned in an image of himself, while Bobby appeared sometimes to resent Greenwood's apparent refusal to see him as an equal, or perhaps something 'better' than that. The feeling at a distance was that Moore could do without Ron, but for Greenwood, Bobby was not expendable. There is some truth in both these potential perspectives – one-way need is corrosive of any relationship.

Greenwood remembered the boy he had first met, exuding interest and resolve, and how they shared their passion for football. He had known the 'nice' Bobby and given him his first chance with the England youth and under-23 teams. He was to recommend Bobby to be given his first full cap, convincing Walter Winterbottom to take Moore to the 1962 World Cup. It had been Greenwood who had continued to cultivate what Allison had started with Moore, his understanding of the game and attitude to it. Ron had worked with Bobby to develop the specialised defensive role they fabricated together. Greenwood's belief in Moore, rejecting any criticism of him, was seemingly unshakable. Even in home life he would not have a word uttered against his skipper. Ron probably never got over Bobby's cold-shoulder treatment, because it had been Ron who cared about Bobby. He saw himself as helping the Barking boy, perhaps more than anyone else. As far as one can tell, Moore had no personal feelings about Greenwood after he moved to Fulham, positive or negative, but continued to regard him as a great thinker about the game.

Like all perspectives, this view isn't entirely accurate. While they had similarities and commonalities in terms of demeanour and attitude, we are looking at two very different personalities. To his credit, Ron was to see the rift that existed between himself and Bobby as being as much his own fault as Moore's, and in that he likely wasn't too far from right. It's often a hard truth that, for the most part, the quality and direction of our associations are always partly of our own making. It takes two to tango and at least that number to create an atmosphere in a room.

Both Moore and Greenwood, at points in their careers, adopted or defended themselves behind a veneer of what some understood to be arrogance, or it could be seen as simple pride, that hid something of an 'imposter syndrome' and the shadow of an inferiority complex. They both had 'luggage' that might incline them to question their own success and camouflage their deficiencies.

Time blunted the edges of each man's haughtiness; that carapace isn't so necessary as we grow more secure in our achievements and feel less uncomfortable with our limitations. One could wish they might have had the opportunity to know each other as older men. I think they would have got a lot from that, along with quite a few smiles.

However, while they were at Upton Park together Ron was preoccupied initially with demonstrating he was up to the job, while forwarding the integrity of the wider game. Like Moore, Greenwood was basically an introvert. Football was, to some extent, a means to hide from life for both men, as it has been for many professional players; that's part of the necessary drive sometimes. Indeed, much the same might be said of us, the spectators, supporters, and fans; football is the great distraction, offering a 'little life' within the vale of tribulations everyday existence can seem. The devotion and passion are, as often mooted by the uninitiated, out of proportion, but that is part of the draw. The more we need the game as compensation and/or diversion the bigger it gets on our horizon. It is that lover we can learn to hate, but are repeatedly and inexplicably attracted back to, giving it so much, while, for the most part, getting scant reciprocation other than frustration and the attendant angst, which of course magnifies the occasional and momentary orgasm of glory and concomitant reward for and justification of our devotion.

Greenwood had done much to assist Moore in disciplining his game and whatever the eventual issues in their relationship, these were probably as good as resolved, if not forgotten, by the time Bobby hung up his boots; he never failed to recognise that Ron had been instrumental in the mid and final stages of his development as a player.

As Moore started to play on the right side of England's defence, despite always donning the number six shirt for club matches, he had apprehensions about retaining his international place after the 1962 World Cup. But Winterbottom, supported by the counsel of Greenwood, kept faith with Moore as he prepared to leave his role as his country's manager. It was Ron's work with Bobby at Upton Park that prepared the player for the next stage of his journey into history, toward immortality. As such, in football terms, the names 'Greenwood' and 'Moore' will righteously, into eternity, always be inextricably conjoined.

Call me Ron

Throughout the chronicles of football, it's usual for players to moan about managers and to be wary of new, incoming bosses, who almost always will be looking to make their mark and/or 'turn things round'. Habits and routines are questioned and threatened as authority and personality is imposed. However, in his first few years at West Ham, there were relatively few complaints about Ron Greenwood. From the off he insisted that all the players called him Ron, not 'Gaffer' or 'Boss'. This might seem relatively insignificant, but it cultivated mutuality and some prospect of openness between the manager and player, the basis of trust. But it also set up a notion that the manager was 'one of the lads' which, when you carry the designate 'manager' and are changed with negotiating the lads' wages, depending how you look at it, is either a fallacy or a lie. Greenwood wasn't 'one of the lads', he was the managerial representative of the board and the owners. A veneer of 'mateyness' applied in an authority role fosters a feeling one is being subjected to clandestine manipulation; it wrong-foots the subordinate as they are made unsure where they stand. This propagates suspicion that erodes respect and trust.

Although his lack of 'man-management' skills have repeatedly been pointed out by former players, more than a few of whom saw him as dour, emotionally repressed, and inward-looking, Greenwood introduced different footballing vernacular to West Ham. He had a remarkable capacity, if listened to, to make things sound transparently obvious, stuff that often caused players to feel they knew or understood for themselves, but had just not been able or had the opportunity to articulate. As defender Jack Burkett had it, 'Ron opened our eyes.' That said, not everyone had the want or capacity to fully grasp Greenwood's vision. Perhaps that explains something about why West Ham never quite got to where he might have wanted the club to go.

In the mid-1960s Moore argued that 'footballers will no longer be happy to be treated like schoolboys by their clubs or anyone else'. Making the point, he went on, 'I've heard stories from older men … Like the two First Division men sent home from a continental tour in disgrace – because they were 35 minutes late back at their hotel. Or the player who was disciplined because he left the team party at a cinema half an hour before the end of the picture to get a cup of tea.'

This consciousness, that players were central to the industry and, as professionals, should be allowed to cultivate their own judgement, both as part of the team on the park and as adults off the pitch, was perhaps the foundation for acrimony between Moore and Greenwood. It was solidified in the summer of 1962. Before leaving for South America and the World Cup, Moore was in protracted and pretty discordant negotiations about a new contract with West Ham. This would be something that would become an annual battle between Bobby, Greenwood, and the club's board for the rest of Bobby's time at the Boleyn Ground.

Early in Moore's senior career, placing himself at variance with the traditions of player/management relations at Upton Park and football more generally, might have caused him to be seen as something of an upstart among the higher echelons of the club's hierarchy. What Greenwood would come to see as Moore's truculent stubbornness when it came to wage demands reached its zenith in 1966, threatening to rob history of his appearance in his second World Cup, but that's another story.

The road to becoming a serial negotiator had involved a learning curve. Bobby remembered the first time he went on tour with the West Ham senior team. He was on holiday in the south of France when he received an instruction to fly home around midday to join the party before they left for Austria. He was told to report to the BEA[34] office in Nice to collect his ticket. In the rush Moore forgot to take any French currency, so Bobby decided to try to find the BEA office on foot, getting increasingly anxious that he might miss a big opportunity. Carrying two suitcases, sweating in 90 degrees of heat, he desperately attempted to ask people how to get to the 'Promenade des Anglais'.

Eventually he caught his flight, only just in time, but the subsequent taxi from the airport reached the Boleyn Ground 20 minutes late. The party, including the players, manager, and directors, were waiting for Bobby, the youngest recruit to the tour. As he feared, no one was entirely pleased.

When the party arrived in Vienna they found that instead of staying in a city hotel, they had been booked in to what appeared to be a convalescent home, 25 miles out in the sticks. The Hammers seemed to be the only healthy people in the place; everyone else was rolling around in wheelchairs or toddling along with the aid of sticks.

Malcolm Allison, as club captain, called the players together and it was decided that the place was unacceptable. It was agreed to demand a meeting with the manager to press for alternative accommodation to be arranged. The threat was that if this didn't happen the players would withdraw their labour, and fly immediately back to London. Bobby attended the meeting feeling nervous. Having been seen as a pain in the arse before even getting off the ground, he was thinking that it was only his first tour with the seniors and that he shouldn't be taking part in any talk of strikes. However, things didn't go as planned and the team ended up staying

---

34   British European Airways – the company ceased to exist as a separate legal entity on 1 April 1974 when the merger with BOAC to form British Airways took effect.

with the oldies. The resultant 'take it or leave it' attitude humbled the players. Allison had been effectively taken down a peg or three, but Moore was hurt by his acharya's humiliation. He promised himself that would never happen to him.

The limit of the maximum wage in football had been £20 a week before 1961, but as a result of the campaign, ironically led by Greenwood's former team-mate at Fulham, Jimmy Hill, and the Professional Footballers' Association, by the time Ron got his plates under the Cain and Able at Upton Park, those days were done. The new manager would increasingly find himself embroiled in contrafactual poker games with individual players. But most playing staff had no cultural reference points in such dealings, so effectively continued to be subjected to the whip hand of their clubs. The Vienna affair epitomised this culture and mentality.

Moore, though, had a powerful role model in resisting this kind of domination. Following Allison's example, he became a pioneer of resisting the contractual ultimatums and grew to be a persistent thorn in his manager's side in this respect. Thus, the early 1960s was a time of dramatic change in football, with Moore in the first wave of that transformation. In the parabolic words of John Motson, 'The unexpected is always likely to happen.'

Very much so, I fear.

11

LIMA LIONS

At the conclusion of the 1961/62 season, Ron Greenwood 's first full term in control at Upton Park, West Ham maintained a position in the top half of the table by playing positive, intelligent football. Most of the younger first-teamers were looking forward to the sunshine and experience of the club's summer tour of southern Africa (Southern Rhodesia – that would become Zimbabwe; Nyasaland, now Malawi, and Ghana). Those with wives and families probably felt they could do without the busman's holiday, but at 21-year-old Bobby was both interested in and excited about the prospect.

It was on the morning of 7 May 1962 that Bobby made his way to Upton Park to pick up the kit he would need for the tour. As he walked into the dressing room area, Martin Peters told him that Greenwood wanted to see him in his office. 'What's it about?' Bobby asked. Peters replied, 'You're being transferred to Arbroath.'

Being summoned by authority naturally incites some anxiety in most of us, so Moore trotted along telling himself he was probably going to get an update on the post-season tour. He knocked on the office door and Ron called, 'Come in.' Bobby stood in front of his manager who was apparently engrossed in writing a letter. There was a silence before Bobby asked, 'You wanted to see me?' Greenwood didn't reply immediately, his eyes fixed on the apparent quite serious missive. As he continued writing he uttered, in somewhat matter-of-fact way, but with a hint of harshness,

'You won't be coming on the tour with us.'

Bobby's expression didn't change, but his face flushed red. What had he done wrong? What had Greenwood found out? Bobby could be a bit of a scamp in his spare time, and the previous weekend had been particularly raucous, including end-of-season celebrations with Malcolm Allison's Romford entourage[35], something of Moore's lifestyle choices that Ron would grow to be more than frustrated with over the coming years.

The silence returned. Bobby didn't know what to say. The tension had become thick in the stuffy office when Greenwood put his pen down, looked sternly at the

---

35   Allison's Romford side had finished mid-table in the Premier Division of the Southern League that season.

young player in front of him and announced, 'Yes … You are going to Chile with England. The World Cup.'

Bobby's first thought was about the prospect of playing alongside one of the footballers in the England team he had come to admire most, 'the Pass Master' Johnny Haynes. However, while Greenwood read his expression as a mixture of astonishment and pleasure, Moore wasn't shocked at the news. He was pleased, but he had been emotionally thrown by his manager – what was that about? He stood and stared at Greenwood until Ron, who had remained expressionless, said, 'Well you'd better be getting off.' Moore exited the office, only turning briefly to say 'thank you'. Ron just nodded, with the suggestion of a smile.

While Ron was to always feel that his own joy at his player's selection was at least as great as Bobby's, on the way home Moore felt a bit peeved. In his 1984 autobiography Greenwood noted that a 'flush of anger' had crossed Bobby's face in a reaction to his 'bad news/good news' manner of telling Moore the situation, and it was the case that the manager had made his player squirm. That moment of suggested punishment for an unknown misdemeanour had pricked the boil of self-doubt that was a constant in Moore's head and heart. It felt mean, and although Bobby moved on, he was never to forget that episode and it seems neither did Greenwood. Perhaps it was Ron's way to get back at Moore for his growing if subtle insolence with respect to the manager's authority, retaliation for some of the sniggering that went on when his terminology sounded a bit poncey for East London sensitivities. Whatever, the moment became another milestone on the road of the Greenwood-Moore relationship as it went downhill.

One of the first people to congratulate Bobby on his selection was his team-mate Malcolm Musgrove. It must have been hard for Malcolm as Bobby was a late choice to make up the 22-strong England World Cup squad, while Musgrove had been selected for the original squad of 28 but was one of the six dropped for the trip to South America.

By the start of the afternoon Bobby had been to the Hospital for Tropical Diseases at St Pancras, along with Jimmy Greaves and Maurice Norman,[36] getting their yellow fever jabs.[37] Then they went together to Roehampton, where England trained on the then Bank of England sports ground.

Walter Winterbottom had wanted to take at least one young player to Chile to blood them into the senior side and further their education of international football.

---

36   Jimmy Greaves once said of Norman, 'If Mo and King Kong went up a dark alley to sort an argument, only one would emerge, and it wouldn't be the fucking monkey.'
37   Moore had travelled previously, so he was already inoculated for several diseases, other players who needed a plethora of jabs became quite ill. Ron Flowers for instance wondered if 'I'd ever be fit enough to play again'

His first inclination was to pull Moore's fellow Hammer Joe Kirkup into the squad. Prior to the 1962 World Cup, Walter, who although being more Earl Grey than Ron's PG Tips, valued Greenwood's insight and told his acolyte that England had problems with cover at wing-half. The England manager believed this would be an issue, especially if his side managed to advance beyond the group stages. Winterbottom thought his players capable of getting out of their group, given their good performance in qualifying. England had remained undefeated home and away to both Portugal and Luxembourg, finishing top of their group. On hearing about worthy Walter's worry, Ron immediately asked, 'Why not take Bobby Moore?' The Oldham overlord managed to sell that advice to selectors[38] who gave Moore the nod by a whisker.

The two managers had often talked about Bobby, so the strong recommendation didn't surprise Winterbottom, although very little did. He was the kind of person to impose composure during a Donald Trump visit to a LGBTQIA+ socialist nudist camp leapfrog tournament. Nevertheless, Walter wasn't without reservations. It was a punt to take an uncapped player.

However, Bobby was adaptable and, at a push, could cover several positions. The young Hammer had been sound in a respectable First Division side and at Highbury, the evening before the 1961/62 FA Cup Final, his performance had been solid in what was the traditional England v Young England game. Bobby had been pleased with his form against the senior XI in a match that had been something of a try-out for the World Cup squad. For all that, after the Highbury match, Moore heard nothing, and had started to resign himself that he was going to be with West Ham in Africa rather than on his way to Chile with England.

Unbeknown to Moore, post-Highbury, Winterbottom had been impressed by Bobby's showing and probably a bit relieved, given England's half-back situation as the World Cup finals approached, but he needed the assurance that Ron was to give him about Bobby's temperament and attitude. Greenwood told Winterbottom that Moore would not be intimidated if required to step in at short notice. Trusting Greenwood's word and judgement, Walter decided to include Bobby in his squad. It was quite a leap of faith on Winterbottom's part, given that Moore had that far not even broken into a senior national squad. He believed Ron's parting assessment that Moore wouldn't let him down.

Few of the England side were surprised that Bobby had been drafted into the squad. Johnny Haynes had it that 'everybody had been talking about him for a good few years' and that even as a kid it had been common knowledge that he had international potential.

---

38   The England team was still chosen by the FA's section panel. This would continue until Alf Ramsey stuck a decree nisi up their collective jacksie.

So it was that just after Winterbottom got back to London from Vienna, after watching Austria play Bulgaria[39] (England would meet the latter side in their qualifying group in Chile – the Bulgarians were completely outclassed, losing 2-0, although the hosts didn't turn the gas on until the final 20 minutes of the game) in the Praterstadion, he let the world know that Moore was last addition to the World Cup squad. He said Bobby had been playing particularly well since his appearance at Aberdeen against the young Scots, and although Moore was still of an age to continue turning out for the under-23s, he had been selected for the South American adventure as a cover for Ron Flowers, England's established left-half.

However, contrary to the thoughts of Haynes, Bobby's inclusion caused few players to suspect 'southern bias' on the part of the selectors, while writer, with England's typical preparation for World Cup in mind, complained about Moore's selection on the eve of the tournament, bewailing the lack of Arsenal and Wolverhampton Wanderers[40] players in the squad, and the FA's regularly, following a disappointing result, to effectively admit 'to the bankruptcy of planning by giving new caps' by way of statements about the debutants 'having played as well as one could have expected'.

Although prejudiced and jaundiced, these conclusions did hold some water, and Winterbottom, despite Greenwood's assurances, at Schwechat, en route to Heathrow, was still of two minds. It was there he bumped into Malcolm Allison, who had also attended the game in Vienna. Malcolm, ever opinionated and straight-talking, told Water, 'Take him [Moore] with you, and play him against Peru. If he fucks up, then you know what to do. But he won't, and he's a better bet than your other options.'

For all this, being summoned to England's cause was not entirely unexpected for Moore. He had done well at under-23 level for a good while under the stewardship of Greenwood, and Ron had kept Winterbottom appraised of this, as the England manager kept a watching brief on the development of all the younger players with international potential.

Most of the England squad stayed in London the night before the journey out to South America. Peter Swan woke up with flu-type symptoms and feeling lousy.

---

39   Austria had withdrawn from the World Cup during the qualifying games due to financial problems.

40   This was a bit counterintuitive as the league champions were Ipswich, followed by Burnley and Spurs. Arsenal had finished in a mediocre tenth place in the First Division, a point behind eighth-placed West Ham, while Wolves had ended up in 18th, just four points clear of relegated Cardiff. But Arsenal and Wolves were considered to be 'big clubs', the Bentley and Rolls-Royce of English football. For England to be making for foreign shores lacking representation from those brigades was unthinkable for the traditionalists of the 'respect-able' press, especially when one of the 'interlopers' hailed from West Ham, a club thought to be 'unfashion-able', a euphemism for 'plebian' (scum).

A doctor was summonsed and diagnosed tonsillitis. For a few hours it looked like the Sheffield Wednesday centre-half might be dropped, but not wanting to miss out on playing in the tournament, Peter put on a brave face and convinced Winterbottom he'd be fine. The decision was made to medicate and hope for a swift recovery. The former Royal Signals PTI was thus drugged up for most of the outward journey from England.

'Somebody Up There Cares'

Just ten days after a 3-1 win against Switzerland at Wembley, on 17 May 1962, Bobby Moore, along with the rest of the 22-man England squad, were preparing to fly BOAC[41], on their big jet service to Lima. The state-owned airline's motto was 'Somebody Up There Cares', which was just as well because the lads were bound, via New York and Kingston, for South America – a journey, in all, of 17 hours. The flight was tiring and seemingly never-ending. Most of the players had never made a journey like it, although by now Moore was a seasoned global traveller.

It was during the journey that Winterbottom thought about Allison's advice and giving Moore his first cap. It has been claimed that at that point he had thought about Bobby's potential for becoming the cornerstone of the side. This is probably a contention made in retrospect; it was way too early for a man like Winterbottom to give too much credibility to that kind of scenario. He would have had the germ of informed hope for Moore, as did others immersed in the game; Arthur Rowe for instance, one of the most powerful footballing minds of the postwar period. According to him, 'Moore had to be in the England team. He was one of the few in England who had realised or understood that the modern game was about quick movement and accurate, intelligent passing; working thoughtfully. The thump-it-and-hope days had been gone for decades; it was primitive. But this was a far cry from heralding Bobby as pivotal to his country's future. Until the meeting with Allison, Winterbottom's intentions as far as Moore was concerned were not much more than giving a young, promising player experience of being with the national squad at a major championship.

Prior to England touching down in Chile, a friendly had been arranged against Peru in Lima. The media had criticised this move, arguing that the meaningless encounter risked injuries and/or a morale-damaging defeat. However, Winterbottom saw it as a useful test against South American opposition given that his side were due to meet Argentina in their qualifying group.

Several of the players saw England as having a good chance of winning the World Cup. The team was perhaps the strongest to have left Britain's shores for

---

41   British Overseas Airways Corporation, which would ultimately become subsumed by British Airways.

a competitive tournament since the Second World War. Winterbottom was also optimistic, but he was also a pragmatist. His feeling was that if the squad played well the semi-finals were a realistic expectation. From that point, for Walter, the fates took charge. The draw, injuries, and what team had the most energy-sapping opposition on the way to the last four, were all factors that would rule destiny. Nevertheless, he felt England were capable of getting to the final.

While Bobby was on England duty his fiancé, Tina, started to organise their wedding with the help of her mum Betty. Tina had managed to save up about £100 and spent the lot on her wedding dress and accessories. Winterbottom also had decisions to make about his resources. Swan, England's first-choice centre-half, was still suffering with tonsillitis. The obvious choice in his absence was Spurs man Maurice Norman, who had been backup in the 1958 tournament for Billy Wright. Swan had endured a deal of kidding that London-based players would be selected ahead of him. Players and supporters from or playing outside the capital had long had it there was a greater chance of being selected for England if you were with a southern club. The Yorkshireman mostly went along with such jibes in good humour, but he was to confess that at the back of his mind he suspected Norman might get the nod at his expense.

While Winterbottom was ultimately at the mercy of the selection panel at that time, he was well aware any decision he made about who he should advise to be included in the team couldn't be based on that sort nonsense or what had happened in Sweden four years previously; that was really a different world to South America in the early 1960s. There was also history to consider. Five of the England men who would face Peru in Lima had been in the 1959 side that had been smacked severely by *La Blanquirroja*'[42] – Jimmy Armfield, Ron Flowers, Johnny Haynes, Bobby Charlton, and Jimmy Greaves (the latter had made his international debut in that encounter).

The tragedy of Munich four years earlier was still fresh in the minds of all those in football. The plane crash had obliterated the Manchester United side, robbed England of some of her most illustrious players, and more importantly stolen young men from their families. In order to avoid any replication of the disaster the FA had made it practically custom and practice to split flying footballers between two planes. The first cohort of the England team disembarked 24 hours before their team-mates touched down. Winterbottom had arranged things so the side to play Peru would be on the second plane, maximising their time together.

Most people believed that Moore – including the player himself – was being taken to the World Cup for the experience, to get a feel of the tournament with

---

42   'The White and Red' is one of the nicknames of the Peruvian national team.

1966 in mind. That was the kind of thing Winterbottom would have looked to do. He was a thinker in the same vein as Greenwood and Alf Ramsey; like them he was very conscious of getting the small things right. However, when Bobby found himself designated to the second flight his hopes rose. As it was, at the last moment, Walter moved him to the earlier flight. Bobby took it that the initial arrangement had been an error, and wasn't too disappointed.

However, Winterbottom, could have juggled things around and brought in Sunderland's Stan Anderson, as Bobby Robson wasn't fully fit. Both players were much more experienced than Moore and had previously been tried in the England number four shirt. Jimmy Armfield was among several who expressed their doubts that Moore was ready, but Winterbottom, with Allison's advice buzzing round his head, unexpectedly turned to the 21-year-old. It had been in his thinking that Moore was the best choice, and when his captain Haynes told him he was of the same mind the die was cast and the future kickstarted.

Joe Kirkup was to have it that Bobby's defending style was built around interceptions; Joe reckoned that only about one in five of Moore's interventions as a defender were tackles, although when he made a tackle, it was generally a positive one. Allison had pointed out to Winterbottom that this characteristic kept Moore on his feet, facing forward, which worked to enhance Bob's capacity to aid both defence and offence as required. Likely it was the latter that sealed his selection. Thus, only a couple of months after what was to be his final under-23 outing, Moore found himself with the prospect of being a fully fledged international, having celebrated his 21st birthday just 38 days earlier.

Having convinced himself that the trip to South America was going to be more about being with the squad than playing any participatory part himself, for Bobby it was a massive buzz when he was picked to make his England debut. He was drafted into the team in his former station as a defensive wing-half.

I've been over Winterbottom's options again and again, and I do believe West Ham's long-serving secretary and former player, Eddie Chapman, might have had it right when he told me he understood, motivated by Greenwood, that it had been in Winterbottom's head all along to play Moore in Peru, to see how he reacted and give himself more options when the side got to Chile. Arthur Rowe, who Winterbottom knew well, put it more strongly, 'Bobby was always going to play in 1962 against Hungary and Argentina, and when it came to playing Brazil, what reason would there be to play someone else?'

That said, Winterbottom built his decisions rather than simply made them. His choice to draft Moore into the side for the game against Peru was the result of taking on the insights of Greenwood, and Haynes, but Allison was the man who knew Bobby best at that point, since the Barking boy's childhood and it was Malcolm's assessment that tipped the balance for Winterbottom.

The Lima match became something more than just a warm-up for Bryan Douglas. Along with Maurice Norman and Bobby, he was alerted that a decent showing against Peru would put him in a good place to be included in England's opening game in the World Cup.

Los Incas[43]

On the muggy Sunday afternoon of 20 May 1962, at 3.45pm local time (9.45pm BST) a crowd of 32,565 filled the Estadio Nacional Coloso de José Díaz in Jesus Maria, Lima, to watch England's final preparation match for the 1962 World Cup finals.

Flowers opened the scoring with a 15th-minute penalty (so becoming the fourth player, after Alf Ramsey, Tom Finney, and Bobby Charlton, to score three goals from the penalty spot for England) but Greaves's first-half hat-trick – scoring on 25, 39, and 41 minutes – provided the highlight of the game. That was the 57th England tryptic and the 20th in the postwar era.

In the 1962 Bukta away kit – red v-necked short-sleeved continental jerseys, red shorts, red socks – Moore, Norman and Flowers made up a solid-looking half-back line. Debutant centre-halves Moore and Norman were seldom tested. Although Montalvo and Zegarra promised to have the potential to be a sharp Peruvian strike force, the home side was almost completely shut out. Nevertheless, they did have a chance to get back in the game six minutes after the break but Ron Springett foiled Óscar Montalvo's penalty to become the first England goalkeeper to make two penalty saves.

England were held in the second half, but only thanks to a fine performance by Bazan, the Peruvian goalkeeper. The win was England's first on South American soil since beating Chile 2-1 in 1953. Another first came about in the last minute of the match when Grimaldo found himself the first player to be sent off against England. His sin was swearing at and arguing with the referee, Edwin Hieger. The home manager, José Gomes Nogueira, was seemingly also sent off retrospectively (his remonstrations apparently also unacceptable to Hieger), although there is no record of this action.

Hieger

How did Hieger, an Austrian, know that Grimaldo was swearing at him? Yes, he might have had a command of Spanish cussing, and Spanish is Peru's official

---

43   The other nickname for the Peruvian national team.

language, but it is a multilingual country, with about 72 often very different languages and dialects, some of which are used nearly as much as Spanish. However, Edwin, listed by FIFA as an official from Peru from 1959 until 1973, had a bit of a back story. He did start his refereeing career in his native country, but emigrated to Peru where he became a professional referee. He took charge of many distinguished games in South America, as well as matches at the 1968 Olympics as a Peruvian, although his involvement with the Copa América was as an Austrian.

The 1957 South American Championship was officiated by non-South Americans. One of them was Hieger. His last game during that competition, Uruguay v Chile, ended before the break when members of the crowd entered the field.

Edwin was present at the 1958 World Cup in Sweden. He told a journalist how he had witnessed a representative of a sporting footwear company, either Adidas or Puma, making a Brazilian player take off his boots and put on another brand.

Hieger had also been the official in the middle at the last meeting between England and Peru in 1959 at the same venue, where and when the visitors had been trampled, losing 4-1.

Apropos of not much, one Hanny Hieger (neé Spiegl) had told something of her life story on the Austrian radio. This included her getting out of Austria after the Anschluss (the Nazi takeover of the country) and moving to South America, marrying there, and coming back to Vienna. Perhaps Edwin was that man she married?

'Walt's wonders'

Winterbottom was pleased with the way England had defended and was satisfied with Moore's role in the game, to the extent that he let him know he would be getting his second cap in Chile. Bobby didn't show much emotion, not quite taking in the gravity of his effective promotion, but he was excited enough to find sleep more difficult than usual – jet lag notwithstanding. After his teenage years, Moore was a notoriously bad sleeper. He would often stay up after midnight and rise at the crack of dawn. Early mornings on Saturdays before games his routine included taking a long walk. When in foreign cities, those who might accompany him on these strolls would often feel lost, but as on the pitch, Bobby would have an idea of exactly where he was and be able to navigate back to the hotel with ease

It was Greaves's performance that dominated most people's view of the game in Lima. It was crucial for England's chances in Chile that the Tottenham man might express the genius he was capable of. The result buoyed the squad, and with

Moore looking unfazed and in control, able to impose himself with an authority beyond his years, expectations back home were rising. The two youngsters from East London looked to be ready to be pivotal in whatever England might achieve in 1962.

Bobby, even after the Peru game, took his place to only be on loan, believing the more experienced and established Bobby Robson would come back into the frame. He estimated it would be quite something for Winterbottom to change what had been, for quite a few matches, a successful England line-up. Consistency would make sense, certainly for the team's first World Cup game in Chile. For all this, the Lima encounter was just about the most important test of Bobby's lifetime that far. He was to later say, 'Greavsie was outstanding against Peru, and he could easily have had half a dozen goals. He was always my favourite English footballer...it was a thrill to play with him. I was glad to get a chance and I think I did OK.'

The scoreline did indeed flatter the Peruvians. A Greaves shot had only been thwarted by a post and Johnny Haynes hit the crossbar.

Moore, the youngest player on the field, made a confident and practically faultless debut. Belying his inexperience at the very top level, he looked every inch a solid and capable wing-half. The lad done good, and had high hopes for the coming tournament. Bobby would miss just ten internationals over the next ten years.

Peru 0 England 4
Sunday, 20 May 1962
Friendly
Estadio Nacional
Attendance: 32,565
Referee: Erwin Hieger (Austria)

Peru: Bazán, Fleming, Donayre, Guzmán, de le Vega (Arguedas; time of substitution unknown), Grimaldo, Zegarra (Mosquero 43), Nieri, Lobaton, Zevallos, Montalvo.
England: Springett, Armfield, Wilson, Moore, Norman, Flowers, Douglas, Greaves, Hitchens, Haynes, Charlton.

In Lima the team seemed to have clicked into an easy rhythm. Although some of the players were disappointed that fewer than 33,000 spectators turned up[44], it was generally agreed it was not a difficult match for England to win.

---

44   Three years earlier more than 50,000 had turned up for the game

The ball was moved fast and accurately, chances crafted, and a good proportion of them were taken. Frankly though, the Peruvians were a moderate side, although they were likely made to look poorer than they actually were by the quality of England's play. Greaves had scored his hat-trick in his best and most audacious style and the team's morale got an invaluable boost.

A constant source of amusement for the players was that throughout England's time in South America, an FA selector of advancing years insisted on calling Bobby 'Ron', taking him (presumably) to be Ron Flowers. Very much a 'Trigger/Rodney' (Dave) vibe[45].

Following the match the England squad attended a reception at the Lima Cricket club as the guests of British expats[46]. The event was well lubricated, and some of the hosts struggled to understand the assortment of accents the players brought to the event. Bobby and Jimmy Greaves conspired to make that challenge even more interesting by grotesquely exaggerating their (in actuality) quite gentle, Essex borderland softened cockney inflections, littering conversation with a mixture of East End patois, the odd bit of Polari and rhyming slang, some of the latter conceived by them that very evening. To the hosts it might have sounded a tad like 'Nadsat' from *A Clockwork Orange*. Within the resulting maelstrom, before the squad departed the event, with both lads introducing each other as 'Ron' or 'the two Rons', they managed to pick up an assortment of libations to continue frivolities post-event elsewhere.

The pair decided to take a look around Lima before returning to the team hotel. Ultimately, they stumbled across a gaff called El Cordano, which was just across the road from the Presidential Palace.

Leafing through the phrasebook they had picked up at the hotel, Greaves and Moore attempted to order at the wonderfully antiquated bar. After stuttering an incomprehensible series of words, the bloke behind the bar introduced himself as 'Kipper' and let them know that he was from Plaistow, East London, and that he was a great admirer of both men. He was a dyed-in-the-wool Hammer from birth. The players asked Kipper what he'd recommend and on his say so they sat down to *tacu tacu* (pan-fried rice and beans) and *butifarra* (French bread stuffed with country ham) with a bottle of Pisco[47], which at just under 50 per cent proof, got the two East Enders pretty merry, fairly swiftly (or three-parts 'Piscoed')

---

45   Only Fool and Horses
46   The land on which the Estadio Nacional Coloso de José Díaz, Jesus Maria, Lima was built was gifted by the British community in Lima in 1921.
47   This is colourless or yellowish-to-amber brandy produced in winemaking regions of Chile.

Into the small hours, Jimmy thought a sing-song might be in order, and with the help of Kipper[48], the locals were tutored in such cockney cultural favourites as 'Down at the Old Bull and Bush', 'The Woodpecker's Hole', 'Daisy Bell' and 'My Old Man's a Dustman'. Motivated by Bobby, 'Let's Twist Again' was thrown in for good measure. The 'turn' was completed, predictably, with 'Bubbles' and 'God Save the Queen', at which point Greaves went round with the hat, which had been borrowed by Kipper. He got about 150 sol, around £3 at the time, which was passed to Kipper as a tip. However, the lasting memory for Bobby and Jimmy was when, as they left El Cordono in the small hours, one of the patrons approached Greavsie and asked, '¿Me puede dar su autografía, señor Haynes?'

---

48   This character had been in the army with my dad, before finding work firstly in Mexico and then Peru. Thereafter he wandered around the Caribbean for several years, marrying a woman 20 years his senior, 'Lilly', of Arawak (Taino) decent. He was known by multiple pseudonyms including Johnny Lynch, Terry Tealeaf and Silvester Brownlow, but because of his 'chatty' disposition he was universally referred to as 'Kipper'. He was back in Plaistow by the early 1970s where he was gainfully employed as a potman in the Abby Arms pub, before getting into snow clearing. In the satirical words of my grandfather, 'nice regular work'.

12
PAIS DE LOS POETAS[49]

The day after the game in Lima, England moved on to Chile, via Brazil. Chile has been affectionately known by its inhabitants as the 'country of poets' because two of its most well-known and beloved literary figures were poets, who both won the Nobel Prize in Literature.

From Santiago airport, it was a 90-minute drive inland to get to the mining city of Rancagua, the capital of the Cachapoal Province and of the O'Higgins Region, where England would play their group games. It's located 54 miles south of the national capital of Santiago, approximately in the middle of the strip of a country that is Chile.

Now a much smarter place than it was 60 years ago, and a popular ski resort, in 1962 Rancagua was historically a farming region, but had latterly had a strong association with copper mining. It was a typical Chilean city, with pockets of affluence, but also considerable areas where poverty was rife. The population, about 140,000, was around the same as Norwich and not much larger than the Hammers' home borough of West Ham, but lacking its glamour and elan(!).

The English lads dubbed their host metropolis, with a nod to New York, being 'the city that never sleeps', as 'the city where the hardware store stays open to half-five on Wednesdays'. The central square, known as the Plaza de los Heroes, was dominated by a striking cathedral, flanked by impressive bell towers. If you are familiar with Clint Eastwood spaghetti westerns, you'd have an idea of the look of Rancagua Cathedral in the early 1960s.

The surrounding buildings were of the old Spanish colonial style, giving the impression of a city that had once been prosperous, but the area's vineyards, producing fine wine, gave Rancagua some optimism for the future. However, the further you got from the centre, with its nice offices and charming shops, grey, concrete, monotonous housing apartments, draped with the inhabitants' washing, took over. Apparently, every day was washing day.

The England party was struck that everything felt old, decrepit, and weary. Streets were piled with litter and the residents gave the impression of being suppressed, empty of spirit and drained of cheerfulness. These people were poor, and such were the price of match tickets few of those who lived in the city would have taken in any of the group games the municipality was hosting.

---

49   'Land of the Poets'.

Like most of the England players, for Bobby, Chile was unseen, unknown, unexplained, and unpredictable. He had by then travelled more than most young men his age, but the South American experience was something of a cultural shock, and Coya, where the squad would be based during the group stages, felt like the end of the earth. On the very first morning in the camp, Blackburn Rovers winger Bryan Douglas confessed, 'I feel homesick already.' Likely jet lag would have had an impact on the group's general mood early on; it can take some a week or more to acclimatise after a long trip across time zones.

Met by massively foreign terrain, a culture he was totally unfamiliar with, and lifestyles unlike anything he had previously encountered, Bobby began to feel much the same way as his team-mate, as did many of his travelling companions. The road signs and advertising hoardings were mysteries, and everything from the local tipple to fruit and vegetables offered unfamiliar tastes and smells. This fostered a moroseness that was to fester in a relatively long wait for the first game. For Bobby Charlton, together with the lack of competitive focus, the situation conspired to produce lack of the unity necessary in high level-football.

Outside of Coya the police and army were everywhere, something that was particularly alien to the younger players. Even though at first largely confined to their remote training camp, the unfamiliarity of the music they heard, the sounds of nature, and the mountainous atmosphere made the experience quite overawing for some. This was a time before mass overseas travel, and the internet, for most of the players television had been something that had only come into their lives a few years previously, and then only, for the most part, grainy black and white. Yes, there was cinema, but for most, movies were set in contexts quite familiar to young men in their 20s and 30s.

After a few days the squad were meeting people whose lives were totally different to theirs. The experience of young men from East London, the north-east, and Liverpool, despite the presence of the great ports of the former centre of the British Empire, would never have, in the normal course of things, intersected with those they were surrounded by in Chile. But Bobby and others also felt a sense of adventure. There was a unique thrill in the unreality of being at the world's greatest football tournament, which added to the heady mix of the whole experience.

On the rare occasions some of the players were allowed to go shopping, they were inundated by raggedy people doing their best to peddle a range of worthless tat. It was a challenge to hold these hawkers off, while being constantly wary of pickpockets they had been warned of. The chasm between the well-to-do and the poor was painful. On one occasion, when the squad were on their way back from an extravagant reception at the grand home of the local mayor, where it seemed no expense had been spared on food and drink, it was difficult to think what would have been made of such sumptuous fare by those living in the shacks and slums that surrounded the town centre, including the children playing on the unpaved roads.

However, somehow the party needed to keep their minds on playing. The group England had been drawn to contest, while not looking a cakewalk, was by no means in 'the group of death' category. The more experienced players felt they knew a lot about Hungary, having played them as recently as 1960, and it was understood that they were no longer the wonder team of 1953. While some fancied Argentina to win the tournament, they weren't seen as strong as other South American sides. Bulgaria were unknown in senior international football and had been surprise qualifiers, having won a play-off match with France. So, it's fair to say England had some confidence of finding their way into the quarter-finals.

England on a high

Coya was a tiny hamlet located in the foothills of the Andes, right at the confluence of the Coya and Cachapoal rivers, amid the trees on either side of the water. It was about an hour's bus drive from Rancagua, 20 miles up a dusty, bumpy bullock track. The alternative and the England party's usual transport down, to and back from the stadium where they played their group games was a rickety single railway track. The carriage seemed to be a converted bus that creaked and shook as the track wound its way round the mountainside. For their initial railway trip up into the hills to the camp the train had been wreathed with union flags. On arrival a little crowd greeted them as a local band played a charmingly distorted version of 'God Save the Queen' which was followed, in odd juxtaposition, by an extended and macabrely extended, painfully slow tempo rendition of 'Happy Talk' (from the movie *South Pacific*).

When England finally reached their base, they hadn't eaten for around 14 hours. The coach taking them round the quite extensive training camp made glacial progress. Bobby and Jimmy Greaves were among the last to be dropped off at what would be their home for the next couple of weeks or so. All the squad were ravenous, but everyone was obliged to wait a seemingly interminable time before even being able to get off the coach. So the grumbling that was to be a feature of the group experience started; the noise of the ancient bus's engine seemed in danger of being drowned out by that of rumbling stomachs.

The venue was to be the source of some discord within the squad. To most of the party a copper mine, with wooden huts for rent, dozens of miles from the nearest sizeable town, didn't feel like an ideal location to prepare for the World Cup finals. Bobby Robson said it was 'spartan'. Sardonically, Jimmy Greaves recalled, 'A five-star holiday resort, this was not.' One of Jimmy's enduring memories was of Burnley winger John Connelly perched on a cornerstone on the training pitch, staring into the distance for hours. For the Tottenham striker it was 'Butlin's with an emphasis on "but"'.

Walter Winterbottom had visited Rancagua the previous spring and reported back that the climate in Chile during May and June would be cool and entirely tolerable. It was the Chilean winter then. He also checked Coya's facilities, referred to as a small resort village in the mountains. Walter had looked at other potential training camps, and on paper Coya came across as an Andean nirvana, set amid snow-capped peaks, beneath clear blue skies. Methodical by nature, Walter brought back coloured slides of both Coya and Rancagua, investigated the food and water situation, really leaving no stone unturned (and the place was full of stones), even down to making sure that an there was an efficient supply of English newspapers during the championship and ultra (relatively) fast mail deliveries and collections.

In June, rain was always expected in Central Chile, so it was taken that the English would be very much at home. As early spring was, well, springing during Winterbottom's South America trip he had stopped over in Buenos Aires and Montevideo, tasking himself to take a protracted gander at Argentinian club football, as well as the national side. At two subsequent Lilleshall training sessions he was able to feed back his findings to his players. This was also an opportunity to study both the Brazilians, the tournament favourites and potential quarter-final opponents, and the Hungarians on film.

Up in the air

Close up and personal, Coya was to prove less than ideal. At nearly 800m above sea level the altitude, some 200m higher than Rancagua's, might not have been entirely helpful for the players. To say that England's training camp was situated in a remote spot is an understatement akin to saying that Arsenal are sometimes fortunate. It was about as isolated as you might imagine, in the midst of the foothills of the highest mountain range on the planet outside of Asia. As lonely as a trophy in the Tottenham Hotspur trophy cabinet over the last generation or four.

Coya isn't, for example, Mexico City at an altitude of 2,240m, but that mountainous area in Chile is dozens of times higher than Barking at 9m above sea level and to say that would have no impact is perhaps a bigger jump than saying it might. For every 300m of elevation increase over 3,000m above sea level, the maximum rate the body can use oxygen drops by 1.9 per cent. Additionally, time to exhaustion at a constant speed is decreased by 4.4 per cent per 300m. Those coming from sea level may start feeling the effects – lightheadedness, pounding heart, stomach upsets, dehydration, and compromised performance, to name a few resultant maladies.

However, these figures relate to relatively 'normal' activity. The impact of altitude on athletic performance can be observed at elevations as low as 600m above sea level. Of course, they are usually less severe than at higher altitudes, but likely any high-level athletic performance will begin to induce some level of the physical effects detailed above, which can have consequences for psychological well-being.

Any significant move to higher altitude means you are living in reduced air pressure; the higher you go, the more oxygen molecules will spread out. Thus, every breath has less oxygen compared to sea level. That means each breath will deliver less oxygen to your muscles. During training at higher altitudes athletes feel like they're putting in more effort to perform as well as they might closer to sea level. The increased rate of perceived exertion is caused by altitude-induced hypoxia, which is a decrease in the amount of oxygen being delivered to the muscles to burn fuel and create energy.

While living at higher altitudes and getting used to breathing thinner air can enhance athletic performance in competitions at lower altitude, before the benefits overcome the drawbacks one needs to spend 300 to 400 hours at altitude – that works out to a period of at least 20 days. Your body can and does begin to adapt to the new altitude in less time, about ten to 14 days, but those timings are optimal, and what might be thought of as an absolute minimum for acclimatisation to kick in. Physiological adaptations to higher altitude nearly plateau after a two-week acclimatisation.

When you first arrive at altitude, the body senses the reduced pressure. The kidneys will respond by communicating with the bone marrow to begin to produce more red blood cells to be able to carry more oxygen. Because the body is making more red blood cells, it also increases the volume of plasma – the non-cell part of the blood – so the blood doesn't get too thick. The body must work harder to do the most basic things: even walking, digesting food, and thinking straight.

England arrived in Coya ten days before their first-round games against sides who had been in the area or at similar altitudes for much longer. Moore was to suggest that English footballers were just not used to 'mountain life' – there is more to this than he likely knew at the time. Because Coya had lower atmospheric pressure than the lower altitudes the players were used to, their blood oxygen levels would have tended to be lower. This will often swiftly affect mood and make people unused to living at these altitudes more susceptible to agitation and depression.

Certainly, throughout all the group games, England looked lethargic compared to their form in Europe and well below par relative to their previous run of good performances. The concentration of strikers like Jimmy Greaves and Johnny Haynes seemed uncharacteristically blunt, while for almost the whole trip, a mist of disgruntlement pertained throughout the camp. Greaves had moved from Milan to Tottenham just before Christmas in a welter of publicity, and in the English game he had recaptured the form he had lost while playing in Italy, but he seemed to have lost something crossing the Atlantic.

It probably doesn't need to be said that the knowledge we now have about the impact of altitude on elite athletic performance is much more advanced than it was in 1962, but six years later it became the focus of attention and subsequent research in the light of performances at the Olympics in Mexico. However, it is more than doubtful that any questions were asked at Lancaster Gate about altitude training prior to the World Cup in Chile. Indeed, the prime reason England found themselves in Coya so close to the start of the tournament was a consequence of relative penny-pinching.

Down in the dump

At the previous World Cup in Sweden, with the austerity of wartime still fresh in the national memory, England were frequently criticised on two counts. Firstly that the team delayed their departure for the finals until the very last moment, leaving the UK on a Thursday with a first match against Russia coming up the following Sunday. Secondly, that the players were accommodated in a luxurious city-centre hotel. There were pointed references in the press to the tranquillity of Brazil's country headquarters, Russia's grand isolation and so on.

Whatever Brazil and Russia had in 1958, England had a bit too much of in 1962. Isolation trumped tranquillity. One plus was that there was little intrusion from English journalists, who were disinclined to make the protracted and dusty journey from the city, seemingly seeing the trek up into the Andes as a safari too far. After one or two visits to Winterbottom's eyrie the British hacks were satisfied to view things from afar in their Santiago headquarters.

The relationship of the English team and the media of the day was not the best. On two occasions, Winterbottom and Haynes let the ravenous regiment of reporters know that they believed the press corps preferred the team to lose, as it gave them more to write about. Having originally made sure British newspapers would be on hand, during the tournament Walter banned them from the training camp so none of his players got to see what he saw as all too often jaundiced reports of their games.

In the light of the criticism in 1958, Winterbottom and the FA had accepted an offer from the American-owned Braden Copper Company to stay, free of charge, in Coya, at the company village there. The 'resort' was used as a rest and recreation centre for their executives from the company's various settlements, although some made a home for themselves and their families there. The centre of Braden's operation was the El Teniente mine, at that time the world's largest underground copper mine, 50 miles up in the Andes from Rancagua.

The squad occupied three large bungalow/chalet complexes. The party had to cross a bridge over a ravine to get to the canteen, which served plain but decent enough food, which they ate in a room leading off from the mining workers' dining area.

The player accommodation was sparse. Each room had camp beds and an ensuite, albeit basic, bathroom. Facilities were, to say the least, comparatively down at heel, a world away from even the most rudimentary hotels the players had stayed in on previous England trips or away games with their clubs. According to Peter Swan, it was 'like a Boy Scouts' camp instead of a base for the World Cup finals'. Several players complained about the standard of their lodgings. Their comments such as 'I'm not sleeping in that' were repeated from the start and soon the constant moaning became toxic.

The England party were provided with 'British-style' cooking, overseen by Bertha Lewis, a nice, grey-haired, maternal, English woman, who attended to the squad as if she were indeed their mother. She had a catchphrase, randomly hollered, apropos of nothing, followed by a deep, hearty laugh, 'IF YOU CAN'T BEAT 'EM, JOIN 'EM!!' Over time and several times every meal, this mantra ground on more than few nerves. But the menu was wholesome, if more akin more to school dinners than anything too 'entertaining' or exotic.

A storage shed had been converted into a gymnasium, or perhaps it had been a gymnasium in a previous incarnation that had become used for storage; it was hard to say. Some 200 yards from where the players were billeted was the main road into the complex on which large lorries continuously went backwards and forwards, banging and squeaking under the heft of their burdens.

The resort was the home to a forest of massive cactuses, five or six feet in height; few of the party had previously seen a cactus protruding more than a few inches out of a dinky pot. These bastards had wicked spines on the leaves, some of which were three or four of inches in length and terminated as sharp and tough as the business end of a Spartan's javelin. They soon began to be known as the 'triffids'[50], and some with distinctive anthropoid looks were given names such as Harold (after prime minister Macmillan), Graham (Doggart, given the plant's supposed resemblance to the chair of the FA) and Bertha. Beyond the mine the terrain swept abruptly upwards to the daunting Andes.

During their downtime there was little for the players to do. Their accommodation didn't boast a television, and really there was nowhere to go outside the small, rather dowdy 'Hi-de-hi' holiday village type venue. The camp was more remote than secluded, more lonely than private, more dead than peaceful. There was of course a training pitch, several tennis courts, a games room with a sad-looking, battered ping-pong table, a heavily worn snooker table and a shabby, antiquated bowling alley, where playing was heavy work because you had to set up the variously sized skittles yourself after each bowl and deal with a bizarre range of bowling balls, varying wildly in size, weight and even profile (one was close to a rugby ball in shape).

An on-site cinema at first seemed like a bit of a godsend, but it showed mostly awful Spanish language films with no subtitles, although very occasionally an American film was on offer. When a Brigitte Bardot movie was shown one evening, although it was in French with Spanish subtitles, for the first and the only time all the England party were in the audience, pretty much collectively entranced. Many of the films included sugary, twee love scenes, which were invariably accompanied by heckles of, 'IF YOU CAN'T BEAT 'EM, JOIN 'EM!!'

However, a country club a few miles away on the other side of the valley offered a tatty but useable nine-hole golf course that was regularly visited by members of the squad. Jimmy Armfield was playing a round with Ray Wilson when a young lad asked if could act as caddy. The players agreed, but before they got halfway the boy was exhausted. Jimmy was obliged to carry the caddy back to the club house while Wilson dragged the two bags of clubs.

George Robledo[51], the former Newcastle United inside-forward who was Chilean-born and played for Chile in the 1950 World Cup in Brazil, was the

---

50   The Day of the Triffids is a 1951 post-apocalyptic novel authored by John Wyndham. After most people in the world are blinded by an apparent meteor shower, an aggressive species of plant starts killing people. The story was made into a feature film of the same name in 1962, after three a radio drama series in 1957 (there were two more subsequently in 1968 and 2001) and two TV series, in 1981 and 2009. It was nominated for the International Fantasy Award in 1952, after which Percy Thrower's mail bag doubled in weight (no, Google him yourself!).

51   Robledo was the first non-British-registered foreign player to become a top scorer in England. He was born in Iquique, Chile, to a Chilean father and an English mother. He emigrated with his family to Brampton, Yorkshire, in 1932, at the age of five, due to the instability in Chile at the time. After his death in 1989 the shirt George wore when he scored the goal against Arsenal in the 1952 FA Cup Final was auctioned for £7,500 – an impression of the goal drawn by John Lennon was included in the artwork of his album 'Walls and Bridges'.

squad's interpreter and guide. He was living in Rancagua at the time and worked for the Braden Copper Company in their public relations department. He and his brother had acted as consultants to the FA for the World Cup trip, and it was he who had sourced and recommended the mining complex as a base. When questioned about this George was to tell some horror stories about the hotels in Rancagua, so things could have been worse (maybe).

George was serious and unsmiling, but desperately anxious that, to the best of his means, the team should have everything they needed. George knew a lot about South American football, and as was Bobby's wont, he took every opportunity to question Robledo about both the Argentinians and the Brazilians. The local man was intrigued by the curious youngster and asked him about his motivation for playing the game. Bobby's answer was typically thoughtful, but more abstract than George had expected. 'I'm fascinated by the patterns,' was Moore's reply. Robledo asked him to elaborate, and was told, 'I've always been interested in the shapes that come out of playing, and being able sometimes to make them; pulling what at first looks like a mess into order … something that works towards something else – a plan on the move.'

For all Robledo's efforts, from their first day in the camp some players were complaining of feeling fed up to the point of tears. Johnny Haynes recalled that 'boredom became a problem'. Another party member flippantly (probably) advised, close to the first group game, 'Don't score today lads, let's go home at the first opportunity.'

When they weren't training, time weighed heavy on the players; reading, playing heading tennis, telling each other stories, endless games of cards (a few packs of cards were the only leisure option the party had brought with them from England) and an occasional sing-song filled the empty hours. The nearest bar was two miles away. The jaded golf course was a limited distraction, while walking around the foothills had its limits. A constant diet of pranks irritated as many as they amused.

In an effort to brighten things up Winterbottom organised games of bingo. Liverpool's Roger Hunt proved to be the party's unofficial champion. In the first week the most common pastime was constantly writing letters home. Jimmy Greaves even posted a letter to Bobby, who returned a postcard that depicted practically the same view of the Andes they had from the camp. It was worked out that the squad spent about 25 shillings[52] on postage. That was quite a lot of dough at a time when you got about ten times more 'postage bang' for your quid

---

52   Close to £35 today. The average weekly earnings of adult male around that time were just over £15.12s. The standard rate of unemployment benefit was the same. The rate of unemployment was 5.5 per cent; at the time of writing it's about 3.8 per cent.

than you get today, when it costs you a cockle to send your aunt Fanny on the Isle of Wight the photo of her doing 'Knees up Muvva Brown' with the Green Cross Man and the bloke who had come to read the gas metre at the uncle Jasper's funeral.

A highlight of the first week was when Johnny Haynes ran up to a group of players yelling that a giant spider had crawled out from under his bed. It was a convincing performance, but all assumed it was a wind-up. Nevertheless, the group followed John back into his billet and, sure enough, squatting broodily in a corner of the room, was a giant representative of the local arachnoid community. The beast was about six inches in diameter and looked ominously unpredictable, not to mention decidedly unfriendly. When everyone was in the room the monster decided to shift, just as Bobby made a move to bend down to pick it up. The noble Lions collectively shat themselves as they rapidly evacuated the area. Ultimately, a member of the local staff, allegedly a Mapuche[53] spider rustler, lassoed and hog-tied the beast.

Much the same press leeches who had been critical of the choice of the luxury hotel where the England team had stayed in Gothenburg during the 1958 tournament portrayed the 1962 base, mostly from a distance, as ideal and, on the positive side, it was true that a few of the players were fine with the situation, especially those who had experience of national service. The latter quite enjoyed the chance to 'get away from it all', not least the ceaseless phone calls, people asking for tickets, and so on. For Bobby Charlton, the days 'passed by easily enough'. He was to tell how he was simply grateful for his good fortune to have been selected to go to a World Cup (although his Mrs back home in Blighty was pregnant with their first daughter). Ray Wilson, a former railwayman and one of the older members of the party, had a love of the countryside – the previous summer he had walked the length of the Pennines, and was elated by breathing the bracing air of the moors. Ray, a man of few words, was pretty much at home in the camp, enveloped by nature as it was.

England's quarters were certainly away from any chance of snooping and the place did offer fresh clean mountain breezes. However, there's 'getting away from it all' and then there is being 'kept away from anything'. The experience of most of the players was that they had been dropped in a place that was geographically, physiologically, and socially detrimental for them. Probably unbeknown to anyone, it was likely a factor that would have negatively impacted on their chances of advancing too far in the tournament. For blokes like Greaves and Moore, Coya was a shit hole. As Bobby was to reflect, the sad little golf course likely saved the sanity of some, preventing them from 'going slightly bonkers over Chile snooker'.

---

53   An indigenous inhabitant of south-central Chile

On the face of things, Coya, with its a swimming pool and gardens, practice pitch, hospital (really a sort of first-aid post), cinema, largely English-speaking community, golf course, and bowling alley, fitted the bill, but in reality it saw England's morale dissipate into the mountain mist. Certainly, I think if I'd been there, after a few days I'd be yelling, (as Patrick McGoohan in *The Prisoner*) 'I'm not a number, I'm a free man!' (Bobby was 'Number 6' of course…'be seeing you').

Coya had apparently also been favoured by Germany's Sepp Herberger; well, that was the rumour, but Herberger was one of the shrewdest of international team managers. I'm not sure the likes of Winterbottom's eventual successor, Alf Ramsey, would have taken Sepp's messages altogether at face value, Alf being less than averse to a bit of double-bluffing himself. As it was, the draw took Germany to Santiago, so England had a clear field (or mountainside) with regard to Coya. Retrospectively, one might not be blamed for concluding that the German had laid a 'cunning plan' that Winterbottom breezed into like a monkey at a banana-sampling fest.

That aside, the whole setup reeked of a penny-pinching exercise. The copper company laid on almost everything gratis, including the food and rather batted golf clubs, loaned by the company employees.

A few days into their time in Coya with most of the players bored out of their noggins, a cloud of irritability spread throughout their number. When it rained most of the squad resorted to endless games of cards. As the days went by the description of Coya as a 'prison camp' became something of a meme. The group badly needed the boost of meaningful action. The players were however to carry over their growing melancholy into their match play.

In the England camp, associated as it was with a working mine, alcohol was nowhere to be found. One evening Winterbottom, in an effort to alleviate the crushing tedium being suffered by his players, allowed them a visit to the only bar within a ten-mile radius. As they got on the bus, thirsty for a taste of freedom, Jimmy Adamson, Walter's informal number two, told the squad, with serious Lancastrian intonation, to restrict themselves to just couple of drinks, to remember they were at a World Cup (not sure how they might have forgotten that), and as such, representing their country. He asked them to be 'ambassadors for England'. Some hours later, as the party clambered back on the bus, Greaves was standing at the front, next to the driver, leading a sing-song, including a few risqué numbers encompassing some fruity lyrics. Jimmy was obviously a pissed ambassador, which, football wise, has historically been a fairly accurate representation of the country.

For players who failed to get a game the monotony would be worsened, exacerbated by a feeling of 'What am I doing here?' Even among those who didn't voice such feelings, they were symptomatic of the mood of the majority of the squad. This might have been intensified by their manager's disposition and experience. Winterbottom often seemed to be out of touch with the anxieties and concerns of the players. He hadn't had a grounding in the professional game at the chalk-face of a club. As such, he had little routine comprehension of day-to-day player issues. Thus his skills in handling the problems, big or small, that got in the way of young men performing to their potential, were limited. The England party were suffering from a fragile sense of solidarity and purpose; this was particularly the case with some fringe players.

However, it was what it was, and the squad needed to do what they could to prepare to meet their first-round opponents: Hungary, Argentina, and Bulgaria. To fill time, the players undertook more training than was necessary, or probably wise, even in 'normal' circumstances. Overtraining is a curse of top athletes. It would have been risky if not disastrous, in terms of reaching peak performance, after the tiredness induced by a long European season, jet lag (known in sporting, business and other arenas as possibly amounting to desynchronosis or circadian dysrhythmia) together with the potential impact of altitude.

Greaves and Moore had been room-mates from the start of Bobby's international career at youth level. Jimmy recalled how Moore would lay out his clothes in lines and place his watch 'just so' on the bedside cabinet. He found Bobby's penchant for order, which has been regularly commented on as both amusing and somewhat mesmerising, but it's not an unusual trait of genius. Charlie Watts, the late, great Rolling Stones drummer, had a similar set of propensities, and for the Stones he took on a similar leadership role to that Moore adopted on the pitch. Like Bobby, Charlie also had a taste for top-notch, smart clobber. Greaves talked about their stay in Chile together, 'When we got to Rancagua, we had to go up into the mountains to do the pre-World Cup training. We were in this shack somewhere in the Andes. We were in this room together – with a corrugated iron roof! We'd sit there at night listening to the rain. We didn't see ourselves getting home.'

The players were staying in what were called 'chalets', but they were little more than wooden huts.[54] But, as Jim explained, the situation did much to enhance the friendship of the young East Londoners, 'We made a solid bond, we had to talk each other through. We were both very young; we were lonely – all the team

---

54   Initially three players were assigned to each room, but given there was some 'voids' a few ended up sharing with just one other team-mate. Not everyone stayed where they were originally roomed.

was. But Bobby made himself at home by ordering and straightening everything in the room. Just for an experiment I would move bits and pieces around when he wasn't there. The next time I was in the room everything would be back in exactly the same place I moved them from! It was fascinating really.'

Even in the remote situation, Moore always looked impeccable, but on this trip he wasn't alone in that respect. Gerry Hitchens, who had been playing in Italy the previous season, had turned a few heads lugging a huge trunk with him from London. It turned out it was packed with 19 immaculately tailored Italian suits. Unfortunately, for the duration of their stay, the players hardly had the occasion to be dressed in much more than tracksuits and shorts, so the stylish whistles hardly saw the light of a South American day.

On the subject of all things sartorial, each member of the squad was issued with a suit, and rather nasty bri-nylon shirts. These 'sweat vests' in the South American environment crackled with every movement. England ties, metal lapel badges, tracksuits, training shorts and socks were given to each player as well as and two pairs of Adidas football boots, one pair with removable studs and the other with rubber moulded studs (keepers were given only one pair). Requirements above and beyond this kit had to be bought out of players' own pockets. It was as well the goalkeepers had packed their own gloves, caps, and training jerseys, although Ron Springett found a very handy pair of welding gloves, seemingly made for Godzilla, should a spare pair of turtles have been needed.

Moore and Greaves were among those who gave up a lot of their time helping the keepers with practice. When they expressed their gratitude for this, Jimmy said, 'Well, we might as well come out and help … there's bugger all else to do round here.'

In retrospect England were always going to be up against it in Chile. While they had some accomplished players, in terms of a creative spark, the team's collective head was not at the tournament. They were not in a good place in several senses.

After what seemed like months to most of the players, the day of the opening ceremony arrived. They all climbed aboard Chile's prequel to Thomas the Tank Engine, and headed down to Rancagua. The single-track railway from their training camp was a journey, on a good day, of about an hour.

On a grey afternoon the four squads in England's group stood to attention in the town square as the local brass band played each country's national anthem. They made the Leytonstone Silver Band, a regular for the pre-match entertainment at the Boleyn Ground, sound like the best the Coldstream Guards might offer. The short and very round mayor gave a speech that none of the players present appeared to understand, then everyone clambered back on the train and returned to Coya. For Greaves it was 'an exercise in pointlessness … the best of it was it got us out of "Stalag 17"[55] for a bit'.

Before their first match most of the England party attended the opening group game, Argentina v Bulgaria. The South Americans were one of the favourites to win the competition, but they weren't convincing. Indeed, the match was a frightening, violent spectacle, and not an appetising prospect for what was to come. The Argentine outside-right, Héctor Facundo, scored the first goal of the tournament, a fast long-range cross shot after just four minutes. To the amazement of Winterbottom's men, the Argentinians decided that was good enough for them. They promptly adopted a ruthlessly defensive strategy for the rest of the game.

The Bulgarians were just emerging in international football and had brought a young team to give the players experience, with later championships in mind. They must have been astonished by the treatment they got from their first opponents.

Bobby noted that the Argentinians were skilful with the ball and their system of play, with the half-back Federico Sacchi being the intersection in midfield for most of their movement from defence into attack. However, they looked a bit slow and used, what Moore felt to be, an unwarranted number of passes to advance.

After the game most of the England squad felt confident that they had the beating of both sides. Answering the predictable questions from Moore, George Robledo told him, 'The *Criollos* [Argentina] will not be your problem, it's *Los Húngaros* [the Hungarians] you need to be ready for.'

---

55   A reference to the film of the same name about a German prisoner of war camp that stared William Holden, who won an Oscar for his performance.

13

MEETING THE MIGHTY MAGYARS

Of the four group venues none was more remote than Rancagua, but the stadium where England's games were to be played was still a bit of a surprise for the players. Jimmy Armfield, not a man prone to exaggeration, later described the venue as being equivalent to 'a decent Conference ground'. Rancagua did leave a lot to be desired; today it would probably not be deemed fit for a Championship training pitch. It was owned by the copper company – the firm had built its new single covered stand and dressing rooms.

Set in the Valle de las Flores ('Valley of the Flowers') with the towering Andes in the background, the stadium was picturesque. Surrounding its running track were clouds of geraniums, and the entrance to the arena was through a series of flower beds. Even though it hadn't rained for weeks the pitch was fresh and green.

Prior to the meeting with Hungary, Winterbottom went through a film of the last game England had played against them in May 1960, a 2-0 home victory in Budapest. During the seminar following the film, Moore was involved in a discussion about the Hungarians' capacity to not only absorb hard play, but avoid retaliation in the face of pettiness or rough tactics. They were able to retain their dignity, refusing to lose focus. Subsequently a practice match was organised, with one side adopting the Hungarian style and formation.

In the spring of 1962, it's almost certainly true to say that few felt Moore was not going to be an automatic choice for the first of the group games, or probably any of the matches England would be tasked to fight out in Rancagua. But following Bobby Robson injuring an ankle while training, putting him out of action for several days, maybe Moore thought his chances of playing in the tournament had improved, although in terms of the credentials of experience he was at the end of a queue. However, the West Ham lad maintained his place in the starting XI. As he recalled much later, 'Walter was pleased with the defensive performance [against Peru].'

Galloping Trots

The side that faced Hungary was the same one that had beaten Peru. Peter Swan continued to be sidelined; he had appeared to be OK by the time the squad had got to Coya, but following his recovery from tonsillitis, he picked up a dose of dysentery. He suffered agonising and relentless sickness and diarrhoea. No matter what he ate, it was out almost as soon as it went in. He was shut up in his hut at Coya for the best part of three days, being looked after by the Sheffield United goalkeeper Alan Hodgkinson.

Bobby Robson and Don Howe decided to visit Peter. They banged on the door of his room but no reply came, so they went in. The bed clothes were rumpled but there was no sign of Swan. They found him sitting on the bog, doubled up. When the visitors asked how he was, he replied, weakly, 'I'm at death's door! I'll tell you something else too, my wife's just written to me, and she thinks I'm having a whale of a time!'

Just before Swan had been laid low the squad had been invited to a local concert in a village hall near the camp. No one in the English party could understand a word of the concert, but they could appreciate the beauty of a girl member of a troop of flamenco dancers. As she sang a folk song, she was swinging an exotic scarf round her head. At one point she stepped off the stage to invite one of the English guests to join in the routine. No one was too keen to take up the invite; many of the younger players, like Bobby, were inhibited in front of their team-mates, not wanting to look foolish. However, Peter was up in a heartbeat, gyrating around the stage with a huge smile on his face, swinging the scarf round his head.

Without his knowledge, someone took photographs of Swan's cavorting and, amazingly swiftly in those pre-internet days, they appeared in a Sheffield newspaper. Unfortunately Peter's wife, Norma, saw the pictures and wasn't best pleased to see him twirling with a nubile Latin beauty. It was easy to see the frolics as the result of alcohol, but everyone was on the Coca-Cola that had been shipped out with the squad as the FA were strict about not allowing the players easy access booze during the tournament.

Norma was about to give birth. Peter had managed to phone her to let her know he was under the weather, but not wanting to worry her, didn't let on quite how much he was suffering. While phoning out from the camp was possible by arrangement, getting through from Coya to England was a trial, so Norma sent her pot and pan a letter, writing, 'Here I am at home, having your baby, and you're out there enjoying yourself with a beautiful Chilean lady.' On his sick bed (or rather lav) Peter showed his team-mates the missive. What she didn't know was that by then he was confined to his bed and the khazi, unable to leave his room for fear of shitting himself.

Ultimately, Swan was hospitalised and placed in the hands of local medics. There was no team doctor with the England party and any medical matters were left to trainer Harold Shepherdson who, at breakfast each day, distributed medication, such as the diarrhoea and dysentery tablets. The latter were close to table tennis ball-sized sulphur pills, akin to orbs of salt. As he dispersed the dreadnaught scale medication, Shepherdson's – 'Shep' as he was known to the players – incantation of 'eat it, eat it, eat it' was testament that the mass of the rotund dimensions of each of the tablets was not much short of those passed on to Moses on Mount Sinai.

Given Swan's condition it was taken Shep's acerbic gobstoppers were acquired on the cheap by the FA, possibly leftovers from the Chindits that had gone off in the years since the Burmese campaign of the Second World War. However, Swan was paying for dodging the 'Chile-itus' precautions, having deployed them as ammunition to deter the Great Kiskadees that gathered from sunrise on the roofs of the players' accommodation – crapping all over the place and their high-pitched, shrieking call making sleep impossible – was for the better part of a ten days unable to consume anything but fluids. He lost around three stone, and was on a glucose drip for a week. Dehydration had set in and he was told that without drip he would have been in serious trouble. The hospital was basic, nothing close to its equivalents in Britain. Placed in a room by himself it was a lonely and tedious experience. Fortunately for most of the time he slept.

Swan's plight was to motivate the FA to take their own medical staff on future overseas trips. Come 1970, Ramsey even took the England squad's food with him. But even that didn't work. Gordon Banks getting the shits was probably the reason England didn't make the final that year, but that's another story.

Prelude

Maurice Norman stepped into Swan's estimable boots, partnering Ron Flowers in defence. Peter Springett was in goal and Jimmy Armfield and Ray Wilson were the full backs. Moore, as the replacement for Bobby Robson, linked with Haynes in midfield, while Bryan Douglas, Jimmy Greaves, Gerry Hitchens, and Bobby Charlton were the forwards.

Robson had recovered from his knock picked up in Peru by the time he got to Coya. However, the England party hadn't been in Chile long when Winterbottom received an invitation from the local equivalent to a pub side to take part in a friendly match on the camp's practice ground, which was comparatively decent. Walter put the idea of taking on this crew to his players and, already being bored stiff, they were up for it. So rather than picking a team he asked for volunteers. Robson, thinking it'd be a chance of some match practice, put his hand up.

Predictably perhaps, one of the local boys caught Robson with a tackle that caused him to fall awkwardly. His foot blew up like a beachball and a subsequent X-ray revealed that an ankle bone had been chipped. Although Robson healed quickly, and would be over the injury after England's group games, it was clear that his fitness would not be up to the level of other squad members who could cover his position, such as Moore.

Before the game against Hungary, the England party were invited to attend a reception at the British Consulate in Rancagua. For many of the FA officials accompanying the squad – there were approximately an equal number of these functionaries as there were players – such bashes appeared to be the best part of the experience. The players wore their England suits and the noisy bri-nylon shirts and went with the flow, replete with polite chit-chat with consulate staff, representatives of UK and local dignitaries, the great and the good. There was a recognition that they were representing their country, and the importance of appropriate conduct, although a few of the FA bureaucrats were a bit too thirsty for the local grape. Thus fuelled, one or two, rather too enthusiastically, set about denouncing seemingly all incarnations of football except the English offer. Even the older English players found this embarrassing, but such chauvinistic views remained endemic in the FA, even contrary to the obvious evidence it was inane shite.

Unfortunately, England's footballing performances had to share the headlines with their off-field activities. The only English-speaking people in the vicinity of their training base were mainly American mining engineers. Members of this hardy community asked some of Winterbottom's boys to a cocktail party. According to Moore it was a relatively brief, mannered, and civil event. However, the next morning the local papers were naming the soiree 'an orgy'. One headline had it 'ENGLISH PLAYERS IN DRUNKEN BRAWL'.

A regiment of international journalists appeared from nowhere in the hope of recording more alcohol-charged antics. I have been told that one of the more gobby Americans (there's me thinking the foundational definition of a Yank is to be vainglorious verbose) had been served a Kirby kiss by one of the band of the sons of Canute with the England party, but gossip and rumour are nearly always productive of fantasy. The Greaves and Moore partnership would be subjected to the same in the future, being implicated in the unthinkable and unjust accusation of carousing – they would never do that, not ever; they were saints with cockney accents!

On the field of play the first week of the tournament was to look a bit like an exhibition of anger. Violent outbursts resulted in a series of significant injuries for all the teams concerned. Argentina had set about Bulgaria like a gang of thugs intent on brutal ambush. The eastern Europeans limped from the field pocked with stud marks. For a couple of their number, centre-forward Hristo Iliev and outside-right Toro Diev, the tournament was over.

The South Americans' coach, Juan Carlos Lorenzo, was to generate a bit of form in the dirty bastard stakes. This was the same man who managed Argentina in the 1966 World Cup – the side Alf Ramsey publicly castigated for their savagery after the quarter-final on the evening of 23 July that year. Lorenzo was also in charge of the Lazio team that post-match attacked the Arsenal team outside a restaurant in 1970 (hard to not understand that though). In 1974 he was the manager of Atlético Madrid when three of their players were sent off against Celtic.[56]

Thus, England met the Hungarians in a tense and aggressive atmosphere. England's opponents had trained in a diligent but measured manner for ten days and looked fit. In truth, they were just an echo of the side that had twice well beaten England during the previous decade, but the team had qualified with ease from Group 4, leaving the Dutch and East Germans in their wake.

Hungary had contested the World Cup Final in 1954 (the outcome had been a narrow defeat at the hands of the West Germans) but the Hungarians had lost key players in the aftermath of their country's 1956 uprising against Soviet domination. By 1962 Ferenc Puskás was playing for Spain for instance, having made that country his home after the Red Army descended on Budapest.

The English, although not in the best of spirits, were feeling confident enough. Knowing that Hungary had been knocked out of the 1958 tournament by Wales and Sweden in the group stages, gave Winterbottom's side a favourable precedent, but Hungary probably remained, at that point, a superior side to England.

The first hurdle

Bobby was tasked by the 49-year-old Winterbottom to mark the long-legged Hungarian inside-forward Lajos Tichy, understood to be the Magyars' most prolific goalscorer in recorded history, with over 1,912 goals scored in around 1,300 matches. His 201 goals scored during a single 85-match season was another record. He also hit 51 goals in 72 internationals for Hungary, including four in the 1958 World Cup. So, no pressure, Bobby!

On the day of the game England took the train into the city. Johnny Haynes was to tell how it was 'a bit hairy coming down that mountain for matches'. Under surly skies and steady mizzle, the train creaked and cranked down the mountainsides. Much to the puzzlement of some of the England boys, who had

---

56   Forever known as 'the game of shame'. The Argentina defender Diaz was sent off for a wild assault on Jimmy Johnstone in the Parkhead clash, and was banned for the final against Bayern Munich – which Atlético lost after a replay. Four decades later, Diaz confessed, 'I cursed myself for years about the tackles, but I can't change anything. I meant no malice, I did it for the team, but it stopped me playing in the final … I got a three-match ban. We knew we'd acted poorly but we still got a draw at Celtic Park.' At the same time Lisbon Lions skipper Billy McNeill said, 'Real [Madrid] were the aristocrats of Europe, Atlético the scum. Forty years on, just mentioning them fills me with revulsion.'

an idyllic idea of 'sunny' South America, the day was damp and cold, akin to an East London winter afternoon. So much so that the displays of traditional dancing – which took place before every game – felt somewhat out of place.

The fine rain and wet surface threw most of the English as they failed to get an early 'feel' of the ball.

England 1 Hungary 2
Thursday, 31 May 1962
World Cup Group 4
Estadio Braden Copper Co.
Attendance: 7,938
Referee: Leo Horn (Netherlands)

England: Springett, Armfield, Wilson, Moore, Norman, Flowers, Douglas, Greaves, Hitchens, Haynes, Charlton.
Hungary: Grosics, Mátrai, Mészöly, Sárosi, Solymosi, Sipos, Sándor, Rákosi, Albert, Tichy, Fenyvesi.

Although not the 'Mighty Magyars' of the 1950s, Hungary were still a more than respectable side. The team's defensive line-up had changed during the course of their disappointing South American tour of the previous autumn. Twenty-year-old Kálmán Mészöly, 'the blond rock', played at centre-half, a slot he had made his own. Ferenc Sipos had switched to left-half to make room for Mészöly, while 37-times capped Antal Kotasz was the player who made way and didn't make the final squad. Utility forward Gyula Rákosi, who would be part of the Ferencvárosi TC side that won the 1964/65 Inter-Cities Fairs Cup, was at inside-right instead of the 1960 Olympic bronze medal-winning János Göröcs.

Hungary were at full-strength against the team who had so comprehensively overcome Peru in Lima 11 days previously. But with Bobby Moore and Maurice Norman appearing in just their second full international game, the eastern Europeans might have fancied their chances.

For some critics, this was to be the best match that would be played in the Rancagua group, but the atmosphere was, on a dull day, with the stadium barely a third full, something not much better than dead. A pleasant breeze filtered a suggestion of relatively chilly humidity, and the Bermuda grass pitch looked in good nick, so conditions, initially would have felt not unfamiliar for a European player.

Legendary commentator Kenneth Wolstenholme, who to me, always gave the impression of hiding that he was pissed off (perhaps Richard Dimbleby had beaten him to the job he had really wanted?), led delayed coverage by the BBC. Even from what remains of this and other tatty footage of the match, you can discern that the Hungarians were clearly conscious of the expectations of their famous plum v-necked red jerseys, with white shorts and red socks, and although their recent pre-Chile performances had been wanting, the quality of their early attacks, and energetic approach generally, was impressive.

England, in their 1959 Bukta home kit – white v-necked short-sleeved continental jerseys, blue shorts, white socks with red, white and blue tops – looked lethargic from the get-go. Their kick-off was indicative of the lacklustre spell that seemed to have been laid on the lads from Albion. Haynes, almost absentmindedly, sent a floppy short pass in the direction of Hitchens, but the ball hit the Inter striker on the back of his calves and rolled straight to a Hungarian attacker. It could have given Lajos Baróti's men a dream start as Moore totally missed his tackle, but the defence recovered putting the ball away for a Hungarian throw.

Tichy scored the first goal for the Hungarians in the 16th minute. Sándor Mátrai's centre from deep in his own half was acrobatically latched on to by the big and powerful inside-forward, who stretched to flick the ball over his head, back towards the centre circle. The man who was known in his country as 'the Nation's Bomber' proceeded to play a one-two before setting off again towards the English goal. Galloping forward, he powered on unopposed until about 30 yards out. Tichy, who would spend nearly two decades with Budapest Honvéd, rounded Moore, totally wrong-footing him with a smooth body swerve – the elaborate sidestep making the young Hammer look flat-footed – before thumping a deceptively crafted left-footed effort from 20-yards out that defeated the leaping Springett.

Not having appeared to be a threat, Tichy had wandered outside the box, seeming well covered by Moore, and there were other defenders closing down space in front of the keeper. However, the Hungarian abruptly fashioned the sort of inspiration that had blasted apart England's complacent world view at Wembley nine years previously. He had barely altered his stride when he released the powerfully elegant shot.

For all that, in the canon of goalkeeper shot saving, Tichy's effort probably would have been logged in the 'harmless-looking' section. Given that Springett had positioned himself well enough, having clear sight of the charging Hungarian, letting in what was a predictable drive, was disappointing. 'Dubonet Springo'[57]

---

57   Springett's England colleagues mostly drank beer, but his tipple of choice was Dubonet and lemonade, thus his nickname.

had seemingly been bewildered by the flight of what looked like the type of shot he might have been expected to deal with most Saturday afternoons. Tichy had put some pace on the ball, but it looked as though the Wednesday stopper had tried to punch it over the bar when he might have caught it. That said, the ball did appear to pick up speed in the air, leaving Springett to soul-search.

Tichy, having been allowed to drift through the inside-left position, had caused the English defence to fall back comfortably in front of him. But the shot had been sudden, straight, and fast, going above the head of Springett.

England were more up for it after going a goal down. Armfield made a penetrating run on the overlap down the right and, as Charlton broke free on the left, he crossed into the heart of the opposition box. Gyula Grosics was downed and dazed in the resultant collision with Hitchens, but the Hungarians cleared their lines.

England continued to pressurise, as they would for much of the match, but the predictable English tactic of the high ball was never going to foil Mészöly. He would be the future rock of the Hungarian defence. The 1962 meeting with England acted as his fanfare on the world stage. He was almost faultless and dominant aerially.

A decent forward movement through Douglas and Haynes led to Charlton screwing his shot into the side-netting. Moore almost scored with a magnificent strike from 30 yards but Grosics desperately turned his thunderbolt over the bar. These efforts notwithstanding, there was little from England to spark the necessary inspiration. The forwards habituated moving the ball way too sluggishly, so posing no threat to create anxiety in their opponents quick-covering defence.

Károly Sándor, Hungary's right-winger, almost scored a second goal in the 44th minute, but Springett, looking a tad distracted, had invited the danger. He only half-collected a free kick taken by Tichy, although he recovered well from his own error. Flórián Albert, later the leading scorer in the group, was also to miss a chance from six yards out.

Haynes, getting increasingly irritated by his side's incapacity to shape into the necessary silky passing game, hollered for more endeavour. His entreaties were answered when England managed to draw level.

England rallied enough to stage a hard-worked fightback. The first third of the second half had not yet ticked by when Hitchens rose above the Hungarian rearguard to meet a Douglas cross from the right. The former coal miner challenged the seemingly ageless Grosics, and the ball fell from the arms of the 36-year-old for Greaves, maybe four to five metres from the goal line. Like the predator he was, Jimmy was on it with a goalbound volley. Full-back Ferenc Sipos, standing on the goal line, stopped the shot with his arm, the consequence of which was Flowers, the left half-back, pulling England back into the game in the 58th minute, converting the penalty.

The 'Edlington Edson' had been taking his country's spot-kicks for the previous two years – it was his fifth conversion, which made him England's highest scorer from 12 yards. However, his side had been fortunate to benefit from the referee missing Grosics being obstructed by an English forward moments before the penalty was awarded.

The equaliser seemed to motivate England as they gave themselves over to more attacking football, and although it was less than best organised, they continued on the offensive until the last kick of the game.

After an hour of hard and intensive play, England may have subconsciously relaxed, but they continued to appear languid going forward. Nevertheless, there looked to be the potential to hold on to the draw until an error by Flowers opened the door. The ball ran loose towards the defence through Hungary's inside-left position and Albert chased it. Few would have given him a chance to get to the ball, which should really have been left to safely run to Springett, but Flowers looked to clear it only to suddenly slip on the wet turf. The blacksmith's son from Hercegszántó picked up possession left of the penalty area, controlled it, accelerated past the floundering Flowers, beat Springett in the race for the ball and was past him.

Meanwhile, Ray Wilson sprinted across from left-back to cover the post, but with Sandor coming up in support through the centre, the tenacious Terrier was caught between Albert and Sándor. The player who would be known in Hungary as 'The Emperor' brought the ball back on to his right foot to judiciously squeeze a shallow shot between the post and Wilson, inserting it into the vacant rigging for what would be the winning goal.

Baróti – who would lead his side to the gold medal at the 1964 Olympics in Tokyo – stalked the touchline in the final minutes, at one point being warned by the referee for encroaching on the pitch. But you didn't need to get too close to the play to see that neither team had shown the quality required for tournament winning potential. Sadly, the result had been decided on a basic mistake that left Bobby to wonder if the FA selector who had thought his name was 'Ron' might have taken him to be the one who had slipped up.

Drawing off a few positives, it's fair to say that the full-backs, Armfield and Wilson, were notable, and the new internationals Norman and Moore played with commitment, and although Bobby had made one or two errors he had done perhaps the better side of OK. His showing was not the worst in what was a substandard England performance. Overall, he had coped well enough, although he was unable to connect much with Haynes, but he had got that shot at goal, and if he had been faced with a lesser keeper than the legendary Guyala Groscis he would probably have scored. The man known as *A Fekete Párduc*[58] demonstrated he still had it in him to tip a good effort over the bar with aplomb.

The English forwards could not match the quality of their team-mates in defence. Inside-forward Haynes, captaining the team for the 18th time, was unable to find a hint of accuracy and was too easily dispossessed. He appeared to be drained of his usual skill level, which seemed to have a detrimental effect on his attitude. Outside-right Bryan Douglas also looked to have been deserted in terms of form, while Greaves, plying his trade at inside-right, made little contribution at all. Hitchens, England's centre-forward, was thus isolated, lacking any semblance of the type of service he might have justifiably expected from his esteemed fellow forwards. He was made to appear slow and awkward, and ultimately was to pay the price for the whole of the strike force when he was dropped for the next game. Only Bobby Charlton at outside-left demonstrated the kind of passion, fight, or usual standard of play that Winterbottom might have hoped for.

While the game had been discouraging from an England point of view, the achievement of the Hungarians could not be diminished. Winterbottom was to later confess that they were the better team on the day and admit that there were no excuses, saying, 'England did not have the skill and speed to combat a blanket defence.'

So the critical first game was lost. There could be no complaints. England probably were unable to point to more than half a dozen decent scoring chances. They had failed their first World Cup test, beaten by a better team, being unable to fully respond to their opponents' fluidity and well-drilled, solid rearguard, that at crucial moments knocked on the door of their momentous best.

England returned to their gloomy training camp, in the damp foothills that surrounded Coya, less than happy. The mood on the chugging train taking them back up to their dismal quarters was subdued. This time there was no band to greet them and the flags on the train were dishevelled and flaccid from the precipitation.

It was to be pointed out that the pitch had not favoured Walter's troops; the grass had been longer than the England players were used to (very 'leaves on the line'). Partly as a consequence, although some players had changed boots at half-time, it was likely that most of the Englishmen had the wrong studs fitted for what was a wet and slippery pitch. The playing surface had been covered with plastic sheeting to mitigate the effect of the pre-match downpours, but this protection appeared to have been of very little effect. The damp atmosphere that had at first seemed

---

58   'The Black Panther'.

home from home for England made the top of the field soft, while it remained firm underneath. This had a particularly detrimental impact on the forwards, who appeared to spend most of the first half skidding about. Springett was constantly hampered by the sloppy, mud-soaked ball. However, English complaining about the inclement weather might have felt a tad rich; after all, the side's keeper was born in Fulham, not exactly Southern California.

Johnny Haynes, although he had it that his team had bettered Hungary for most of the match, was to admit, 'We didn't get it together … it didn't help that only about 3,000 people showed up. I'd played in front of bigger crowds as a boy in Fulham's reserves.' Some harsh critics might have thought the Cottagers' reserve side might have fared no worse that day.

Defeat and dejection

It's never a bad idea to win the opening match of any tournament. Failing that, you try to make sure you win the next one. There were those who suggested that England's first game was more a case of Winterbottom's team losing than Hungary winning, and there was something to that. England were unable to prise anything that resembled rhythm out of their play and overall made themselves too often an easy target. The form they had shown 13 months earlier in the 9-3 slaughter of Scotland appeared to have gone right down the allegorical plughole.

After the game, according to the legendary football writer Brian Glanville, Haynes scolded a journalist when saying, 'You want us to lose,' and this reflected the downhearted mood of the whole team. Haynes argued that the Hungarians hadn't expected to beat England, and along with the whole team, he was choked about losing.

Matters seemed to be made worse when the word from the Hungarian camp confirmed the England captain's contention – that they hadn't envisaged winning. The local critics hailed the game as a great one, but like some of his colleagues, Bobby was particularly unhappy about the way the goals were conceded.

After going ahead early on, the Hungarians seemed just as content as Argentina had against Bulgaria the day before to give themselves over entirely to defence, and play that way for more than an hour if necessary. It became obvious that all the teams in England's group wanted to win, but at the same time they seemed scared to lose, which impacted on the games as spectacles.

The Hungarians had successfully put defence first, relying on counterattacks whenever they had the chance to threaten. Breaking this down was very hard labour for England, but after levelling the match they let their guard down.

For Haynes, there had been nothing between the teams before the first goal, but in the dying minutes of the encounter England had been faced with 11 defenders as the plum-shirted Hungarians packed their penalty area. Haynes and co. had fallen into the trap of running with the ball and trying to dribble it through the impassable wall. This point of criticism was easily made, but it is a huge ask to do anything else when strikers are unable to break free from defenders and make themselves available for a pass, especially when your forwards are forebodingly outnumbered by a team intent on parking the bus and little else.

Greaves, who had been conspicuously under par, retrospectively saw his fellow East Londoner as part of England's disappointing start, commenting, 'With Bobby Moore, Mo Norman and Gerry Hitchens replacing Bobby Robson, Peter Swan and Bobby Smith we were unable to find our usual rhythm.'

Just about every team England played were intimidated by Smith, a dreadnought of a player who caused problems for defenders. He'd had a good season with Spurs and had looked good at the England training camps. It was significant that many of the players from other teams were asking about him. Peacock and Hitchens, the available centre-forwards were good, strong attackers, but they were seen by many as less effective than Smith.

What – being generous – Jimmy had probably grasped was that the younger players would have needed to mature sharpish if England were to avoid a humiliating exit from the competition. However, most of the team had looked conspicuously out of sorts. But whatever stance one might have taken on the game, it had been hard work for England. Haynes and his team had looked uninspired and jaded. Their camp had been an isolating experience; most of the squad had wanted to be anywhere else than that increasingly claustrophobic corner of the known universe.

For sure, perhaps Hungary might have shown themselves to be over-committed to the counterattack, but that takes skill, and from any angle, they were the more organised and so purposeful side. Their tidy football, with accurate passing, meant that England were, for the most part, on the back foot and had to do the most of the work. But Bobby was correct in seeing that the match was swayed by the strong Hungarian defence. Baróti's men had also proved that pre-finals form (they had lost by five goals to host country Chile a few months before) could not be taken as decisive, and that in the World Cup there is no such thing as a less-than-formidable team. Hungary would conclude their group matches having played a better standard of football than any other team in their pool.

The subsequent postmortem included some soul-searching in the England ranks, and predictably the press were ready to be hypercritical. The team had for long periods in the early part of the game been on the defensive, as their opponents broke down their attacks and came at them from that foundation. Only Armfield impressed. There was focus on how Haynes had been made all but ineffectual,

Baróti having called on the lively Gyula Rákosi, tasking him with suffocating the Fulham legend. While this took up most of Ferencvárosi midfielder's time, more tellingly perhaps it effectively cut off the supply lines to England's forwards. The defence had performed satisfactorily, but given the result not adequately enough.

Springett was to be the main scapegoat, sadly not totally unjustifiably given his misjudgment of what was a long-range shot that gave Hungary the lead. That blow was costly, and while England had shown glimpses of potential, they were vulnerable from that point on.

Baróti would ultimately head into the quarter-finals with the sure knowledge that Hungary had done football more credit in Rancagua than the other three nations in their group. They beat Bulgaria handsomely and while only drawing against the dull, even primitive Argentinians, the Hungarian manager had rested his best forwards for that game. Like England and Argentina, Hungary depended heavily on a powerful defence; but unlike those sides, the eastern Europeans had proved themselves capable of speedy counterattacks.

The Hungarians had looked more of a team; they had rhythm, and were sensibly economical. The young Mészöly showed outstanding promise, and continued to shine in his next game, the 6-1 annihilation of Bulgaria. The England squad watching that match found little about the Hungarians that was short of perfect, getting the scant consolation that they had fallen to a fine side.

What television recording of the match is still about today, shows Moore, playing on the right of midfield. He looked industrious, with the number 16 on his back, persistently working to get in the mix, darting to take throw-ins and corners. When watching these images what stands out is how upright Bobby looks, rigid in fact, relative to his later self, although he would always have, comparatively, a very erect bodily stance. Noticeably, and a bit uncharacteristically, he was chasing the game more than directing it as he had done at other international levels and with West Ham. What really comes home is how right Ron Greenwood was feeling that Moore was better placed in defence than midfield. That said, while Moore was always to be happier with play coming at him, he did a solid enough job. Jimmy Armfield was to recognise that the game was never going to be easy for Bobby, but the Blackpool man did see that the young Hammer never once looked flustered or out of his depth.

England were, so early in the tournament, in trouble. They went into the next game against possibly the most exacting of their group opponents needing a win, and Bobby's name was on the team sheet to face the Argentinians – the nation whose team, back in 1951, when his dad took him for his first visit to Wembley, had first set the compass of his imagination on playing for his country.

14
FÚTBOL CRIOLLO

The expression *Fútbol Criollo*[59] refers to the classic bravura of Argentinian football. The 'gaucho game' puts an emphasis on individualism and free movement. When British immigrants imported football to Argentina, the nascent clubs followed a policy of exclusion of the local creole community. Consequently, the indigenous population developed their own style, which placed strong focus on technique and movement, something quite different from the more physical and tactically inflexible British style. The creole players evolved a local footballing vocabulary, as poet Eduardo Galeano explained, 'Football players created their own language in that tiny space where they chose to retain and possess the ball rather than kick it, as if their feet were hands braiding the leather.'

The game that originally evolved was similar to a mid-19th century Scottish style, which blossomed out of close ball play around school cloisters, while the organised English game grew out of the vast playing fields of the public schools, making for the original expansive forms of play.

Walter Winterbottom was aware of this *autochthon*[60] approach, but perhaps believing his players could do no worse than what they did in their first World Cup trial, he made just the one change to his side to face the South Americans, bringing in Alan Peacock for Gerry Hitchens, pitting Yorkshire grit against the belligerence and guile of the *villa de emergencia*[61]. No one outside of the England camp gave the Lions much of a chance. Injuries and relatively inexperienced replacements were the basis of the doubts.

In the 1958 World Cup Argentina had been humiliated by the 6-1 defeat handed to them by Czechoslovakia. This time round they were looking to be quicker and tougher, as they had demonstrated to extremes in their match with Bulgaria.

En route to their game with Argentina, the rickety locomotive that transported the England party from the mountains to Rancagua came to a sudden and unscheduled stop somewhere between the mountains and the city. A goods train

---

59   'Creole Football' what 'soccer' was called by Latin Americas shortly after the introduction of the game by the British.
60   Original or indigenous.
61   A nickname for Argentinian football team – Also known as villa miseria – the name given to shanty towns or slums found in Argentina, mostly around the largest urban settlements.

ahead was said to have caused the situation. They arrived at the stadium just 40 minutes before the kick-off.

As the group came within a few miles of the ground they could hear the crowd chanting, louder and louder by the minute, 'AR-GEN-TINA, AR-GEN-TINA!' Clearly many had tangoed their way from 'the land of silver' to support their boys on that hot afternoon.

England seemed somewhat rejuvenated for this match, maybe at last having become more acclimatised to their environment. Relative to the game against Hungary, a healthier attendance and sunshine made this a more appealing event for all concerned.

Winterbottom had told his players that they would need to be both resilient and robust in the face of any intimidation, but thankfully, Argentina were better behaved than they had been against Bulgaria. Perhaps, at least in part, this was out of respect for Winterbottom. Some of their number had attended a course at Lilleshall, where Walter had been directing the coaching. But maybe the fear of expulsion from the competition might also have been a bit of a straightener for those with leanings towards a *barra brava*[62] instinct. A decent referee, ready to put a stop to too much shit early on, was likely also a factor moderating the South Americans' attitude. That said, I doubt they had come across men like Alan Peacock, Ron Flowers, and Maurice Norman much before. Most people on the sunny side of sane would think twice before looking to try it out on any of those 'solid' individuals, drawn from the resolute stock of English working people, the children of a postwar, truly martial generation.

But England's opponents were who they were. Before the game was very old one of their number tapped Jimmy Armfield on the shoulder, when he turned round the bloke spat in his face. There was a fair bit of that sort of bollocks.

Bobby Moore was facing the talented José Sanfilippo. In 1963 he moved to Boca Juniors, but the following year he was dismissed from the club following a disciplinary incident in a match against his former club, San Lorenzo. He joined one of the leading Uruguayan sides, Nacional. Bobby did a good job on *El Nene* ('The Baby') for most of the game, practically blotting out the man who, at that time, was thought to be among the most talented ball players in the world, and who would become the fifth-highest scorer in Argentinian football up to the time of writing.

The press were confounded at the selection of Peacock at centre-forward and that he had been preferred to Hitchens. Winterbottom's thinking was that Peacock was

---

62   'Fierce gang' – the name of organised supporters' groups of football teams in Latin America, analogous to British hooligans, provoking violence against rival fans and the police.

that bit taller than Internazionale's 16-goal top scorer in what had been Hitchens' first season with the Italian side. He also reckoned Peacock was stronger than Hitchens, so more likely to endure the expected assault from Rubén Navarro. Overall, the Middlesbrough man was to prove any fears about his inclusion to be unfounded. The 24-year-old had been grafting in the Second Division, and while his pace and skill were conspicuously short of what might be considered international class, the tough Tyke wasn't one for being fucked with, and had distinguished himself in training. He was also recognised as an outstanding header of the ball.

Weeks before, and during the tournament, Argentina had been a country in the midst of revolution and political upheaval. Given this, it had been quite a feat to get a team together for Chile. The players likely had so much more on their minds than the England game, football being very much a secondary consideration to the safety of their families. Lorenzo also had to deal with an injury list half a dozen long following their tumultuous encounter with the Bulgarians, but chose to make just four changes.

The president of FIFA, Sir Stanley Rous, was in attendance for the game, along with Raimundo Saporta, the treasurer of Real Madrid no less. Senor Saporta was reportedly hoping for encouragement to sign Sanfilippo for the then substantial fee of $600,000 – at that time about £750,000. The equivalent today would be about ten times that amount – but for a player of Sanfilippo's standard you'd be looking at about £95,000,000 nowadays.

By that point, the third playing day of the finals, something of a pattern was emerging in terms of the character of the tournament. Games continued to be contested on the basis of tough, obdurate defences, served with dollops of yobbish-hooliganism. Speaking of which, you might note Antonio Rattín in the Argentina line-up, the man who would captain the side England were to defeat four years later. He was sent off in that game, for ever to be known as the inspiration for Alf Ramsey's accusation that he and his side acted like 'animals'.

England 3 Argentina 1
Saturday, 2 June 1962
World Group 4
Estadio Braden Copper Co.
Attendance: 9,794
Referee: Nikolai Latyschev (Soviet Union)

England: Springett, Armfield, Wilson, Moore, Norman, Flowers, Douglas,

Greaves, Peacock, Haynes, Charlton.

Argentina: Roma, Cap, Marzolini, Navarro, Sacchi, Páez, Rattín, Oleniak, Sosa, Rubén Sanfilippo, Belén.

England went into their second game of the 1962 tournament having had the advantage of observing their opponents' tactics against Bulgaria. Bobby, many years later, had it that immediately after the defeat to Hungary, 'The manager and the players agreed that England weren't going to fall into that trap [responding to intimidation]. We knew we had to win and that would mean upping the team's performance.' The task would thus be not to retaliate and break rhythm, but hold the line both in terms of the side's shape and temperament.

This memory was confirmed by Walter Winterbottom's assessment at the time; England were no longer 'playing back lethargically' but were 'biting in'. Thinking of a possible quarter-final against Brazil or Czechoslovakia, he grasped that too much of his side's forward play was premised on spirit and fight, burning up energy way beyond their opponents' expenditure; the players were not blending as well as they might, lacking the collective intelligence needed to claim a semi-final place.

However, even though the comparatively impoverished state of Argentinian football at that time had been made evident, England's opposition were never going to be less than a challenge for any team.

In their all-white strip, England looked elegant as they began to shape some meaningful play. The sides faced each other on the Queen's birthday (gawd bless er!) in an atmosphere of discernible tension from the start. A defeat for England would have led to almost inevitable elimination, while a win or draw for Argentina would probably translate to their passport to the last eight. So, as the rather austere-looking military band that had 'entertained' the crowd for some time before the players took to the pitch painfully churned out 'Oíd, mortales, el grito sagrado: ¡Libertad! ¡Libertad! ¡Libertad!' ('Hear, mortals, the sacred cry: Freedom! Freedom! Freedom!'…catchy title eh?) followed by a distorted dirge-like rendition of 'God Save the Queen', everyone involved knew only too well what was at stake.

The match was still young when England pulled off a sweet movement of first-time passing involving Ray Wilson, Johnny Haynes, Bryan Douglas, and Alan Peacock. The latter's drive went close to opening the scoring. Armfield, likely more intending a cross than a shot from the wing, rattled a post. However, during the opening minutes Argentina appeared confident enough in their dark blue jerseys, black shorts, and pale blue socks

Once more, Flowers gave England a start with a 17th-minute penalty (if only that ability had carried over into the later decades of the century). Peacock, now imposing himself on the encounter, was dodging the ruthless attention of the Argentine captain Rubén Navarro, and probably thought he had got his international career off to a scoring start when he rose above the opposing defence to head a Bobby Charlton cross strongly toward Antonio Roma's goal, but it struck the underside of the bar. Although it seemed clear that the ball had crossed the line, centre-half Navarro, on the goal line, pushed the ball out with his hand. Reliable Ron ruthlessly converted superbly for the third successive match with a shot that cannoned into the top of the net. For the first time, England had scored from four penalties in a single season. This first critical goal of the match spread a wave of confidence throughout the side.

Despite their opponents' early goal, Argentinian heads didn't go down. They clearly had fight left in them, but thereafter the cracks began to appear. They slowed significantly while arguing among themselves, and it wasn't long before Peacock, yet again breaking free of the fierce company of Navarro, once more thought he had scored on his international debut. His head connected with another superb Charlton centre, but this time his effort went wide of the goal.

England seemed invigorated, not looking at all like the side defeated just 48 hours earlier. The team that had been so short of imagination was transformed as Haynes showed himself to be a commanding presence in midfield. They appeared to hit form in unison and only Greaves looked less than happy, being unable to lose his marker. Whatever the effects of being dropped into the mountains from sea level might have been, they seemed to be abating.

The goal had provided an impetus for England, a momentum they were able to maintain throughout the game. Peacock consistently got by Navarro, pretty much to torture level, as England started to move slickly. That said, they didn't manage another shot until six minutes from the break, although the good news was it was Greaves who had threatened.

For all this, Argentina at no time looked as if they could be taken for granted and they gave the impression they might spark at any moment. Certainly Maurice Norman was being consistently tested by the strong centre-forward Rubén Sosa.

In the 42nd minute Charlton scored with the kind of right-footed piledriver that had first brought him international attention four years earlier. After collecting a long pass from around the halfway line, persuading the attendant defenders to think he was looking to go around the full-back, the United man's low shot to the far post lodged the ball firmly into the corner of the net to put England two up.

Argentina responded with vim and courage after the interval, forcing a trio of corners in a couple of minutes. But unable to sustain the pressure in the face of a sturdy and well-tuned England defence, they failed to make any advantage pay. Their cause was not helped when left-winger Raúl Belén was all but taken out of the game with stomach trouble.

Twenty minutes into the second half Greaves claimed his country's third goal, slotting a loose ball carefully past Roma after a lightning-fast Douglas cross had been parried by the keeper. With Roma still on the ground, Jimmy, the master poacher, became the youngest England goalscorer at a World Cup, aged 22 years and 102 days – taking a year off the record set by West Bromwich Albion's Derek 'The Tank' Kevan who in 1958 had scored against both the Soviet Union and Austria.

Although Sanfilippo was allowed an easy goal 12 minutes from time, following rare confusion in English defence, as a little clutch of British fans (yes, the clutch included a spattering of Scots, Irish and Welsh – nationalism within the UK had not at that stage reached the chauvinistic proportions we limp along with today) celebrated in the stands, England were still in the tournament. There was budding confidence in their ranks, lightening the formerly low spirits of the disheartened Lions. They had played intelligently, moving the ball swiftly, keeping their play simple, backing each other as much as possible – they were too fast and too strong for Argentina.

On the downside, toward the end of the game England had appeared to feel the pace, but following the final whistle there was a euphoric atmosphere in the English dressing room. The stars of the match had to be Winterbottom's defenders. Moore looked almost a different player from the encounter with Hungary. He seemed much more self-assured, involved in both attack and defence. The strikers also looked in better sorts, having created a string of chances in the second half. Charlton had demonstrated his class and panache, which didn't escape the notice of the local media. Enthusiastic reports in the Chilean press hailed the Ashington lad as 'justifying his title of being the world's leading player in his position'.

Years later, Winterbottom said how leading football commentator of that era, Peter Lorenzo, had told him that when Argentina failed to qualify from the group, they were frightened to go home because they had so wanted to take some good news back from Chile. That probably did much to explain their desperate behaviour at points, although they had not disgraced themselves in the second game.

The temperature of the tournament more generally continued to be at boiling point. While England played Argentina, a violent confrontation had been played out between Chile and Italy in Santiago; the game turned into something of a war. The bruising encounter would come to be emblematic of the disgraceful and often ruthless play that blemished the 1962 competition.

The meeting between the home side and the *Azzurri* would be known in the annals of football history as the 'Battle of Santiago'. That sour and bitter conflict was perhaps the final straw that caused Sir Stanley Rous, prior to the third round of the group matches, to plead with the 16 competing teams to look to the sporting spirit of their game. Rous managed to combine implied guilt with an incorrigible superiority complex, adding more than a dash of stern schoolteacher come pissed-off vicar when presenting his telling off – the qualities (and arrogance) that built an empire.

While the turmoil, recrimination and entreaty went on, English hopes and morale were lifted by their victory. It was a good result for Winterbottom's band of melancholy men. Despite some impressive form at the start of the 1960s, the players and the manager had understood that the relative quality of the English game had been eroding over the postwar years. The reversal against Hungary had dented the none-too-high confidence of the English camp, but with an opportunity to get into the quarter-finals, together with a chance to at least to put on a show and bring some brightness back to football at home, there was a sense of the potential for a new start and a shot at glory.

If the Hungarians defeated Argentina then the English would be in a good place to get into the last eight. However, whatever happened, Moore knew that qualification for the latter stages was very much in the hands of his team, although back up in the clouds in Coya no one dared talk about that too much. The mention of the possibility of getting to the final was mostly met with wry smiles and little more. So yes, while belief had peeped over the parapet of lugubriousness, it was a fragile creature, prone to scarper at the first sign of expectation.

With only Bulgaria left to play, England had two points, with four goals scored and three against. Argentina drew 0-0 with Hungary the day prior to England's group closer, so they knew that a draw by any score would put them ahead of the South Americans, and that, against the pointless Bulgarians, would not have looked a big ask.

The victory over Argentina was England's first World Cup win since 1954 (outside the qualifying competitions). Bobby was to recollect, 'John Haynes, who had had the hump from after the Hungary game, looked a bit less miserable.'

The England team that took the field against Argentina had been comparatively youthful. More than a few of the players didn't have vast senior international experience. Moore, Norman, and Peacock combined were well short of double figures in the cap count, with just seven between them. The question that buzzed around, even in the English party, was why you would field any player with so little international experience (in Peacock's case the game gave him his first cap) in a crucially important World Cup match and expect them to form an instant partnership with the likes of Jimmy Greaves? As it was, Jimmy was obliged to try and form a partnership with a new striker in ultra-swift time. That said, the Greaves-Hitchens relationship hadn't been successful either; they had almost totally failed to read each other.

Looking at the game critically, although it had been a spirited victory over Argentina, England's forwards, as a unit, did not inspire sky-high confidence. They made fewer chances than any of them might have hoped, and failed to totally capitalise on those they did create. One could not have imagined, particularly after the pre-tournament victory over Peru, that the Lions' strike force could look so limited. Haynes, Greaves and, to a lesser extent, Douglas, while showing glimpses of what might have been expected of them, had not shone in the first two group matches. Their performance and form on the fields of England had clearly not travelled well. But while England lacked experience in certain quarters, the team had enough quality and football nous to cancel out the South Americans, although Argentina were a side that, with regard to potential, were England's inferior in terms of organisation and strategy. For all that, the win surprised most involved in the tournament, particularly the Argentinians, who on their home continent might well have at least anticipated a draw.

More positively Moore, who was always to savour the most important games, had shown indications that he was beginning to link up usefully with Haynes in midfield. Although he had really done the donkey work next to the Svengali Stevenage Road, they were building an understanding, something that had been missing during the meeting with Hungary. Bobby had noted the elegant Fulham forward's awareness, how he moved and placed himself. He had been impressed by his focus and eagerness to be involved. Haynes was a model Moore was to learn from. Bobby was to say of the man he would ultimately succeed as England's captain, 'Johnny was always available, always hungry for the ball.'

Haynes, who appeared vindicated after forcefully telling the press following the game with Hungary that they had been too quick to write off England's chances, had seen the chemistry between himself and Bobby as the key to the performance against the South Americans. Walking off the pitch after the final whistle he had said, 'Keep it like that Bobby, and we'll be all right. Holding the centre and pushing it forward will do the trick … you can't beat people that won't let you win.'

Johnny was always to have it that England could have won the 1962 tournament, arguing that in Chile he didn't see any team that was unbeatable, and that it was only self-inflicted mistakes that got in England's way. Moore admired that perspective, 'If you get it right, you can't go wrong.'

15
LIONS V LAVOVETE[63]

Following the game with Argentina, England's long injury list was added to when Alan Hodgkinson was wounded in the most bizarre circumstances. During a practice match he trod on a pad-like leaf from one of the big cactuses growing around the England training camp. A spike went straight through the sole of his boot and into the big toe of his right foot. The pain was excruciating, to the point that the Sheffield United keeper almost passed out. After Harold Shepherdson removed the spike, Ron Springett and Bobby Moore helped the wounded Hodgkinson to the dressing room, where the injury was cleaned and dressed.

Later Hodgkinson was informed by an FA official that no replacement boots had been brought, but the boot the spike had pieced seemed to be in good enough repair to wear again. As other players were to remark, that demonstrated the measure of concern for the players, a boot being considered more important than a goalkeeper's foot. That aside, England were not only out of spare boots, they were down to one keeper. If anything happened to Springett it'd be Moore in goal. A somewhat embarrassing predicament at a World Cup.

England knew very little about the team they would face in their final group game, other than they were taken to be underdogs of the four sides playing in Rancagua. The match would be the first between England and Bulgaria in a full international.

What was known was that against the Bulgarians, Hungary had scored with their very first attack and were so inspired that they were four up in 12 minutes, eventually winning 6-1. On the other hand, Argentina, proud and desperately anxious to qualify, held Hungary, that match finishing goalless.

As a result of having to play all the group games in the same stadium, by the time England faced Bulgaria they knew what was required of them. Hungary topped the group with five points and Argentina were trailing with three points, while England were a point behind the gauchos with a better goal average, so a draw would qualify Winterbottom's lads in second place. Bulgaria needed to earn a point if they were to be able to return home with minimal shame, avoiding a record of three defeats, rather than going all out for a famous victory over the English.

There was a lot at stake for England, although no one in the squad doubted

---

63   The Bulgarian national football team, like England, have the nickname, the 'Lions'

the team's abilities compared with the Bulgarians. The manager's strategy was premised on scoring a quick opening goal, but as the old military saying goes, 'When the battle starts, forget the battle plan.'

There was a school of thought that had it that the selectors should have rested key players before a likely quarter-final, but Walter was reluctant to take the chance, persuading the selection committee to go with his judgement. He might have been tempted (and wise) to have called upon some of his reserves, but at that time English football culture was not disposed to rest or rotate players.

Elsewhere in the tournament, teams marching towards the last eight were busy shuffling their various packs. Czechoslovakia were still keeping FC Baník Ostrava's Tomáš Pospíchal in reserve, the man credited with saying, ' Fotbal nemá logiku' ('Football has no logic'), while the Soviet Union had held back Aleksei Mamykin (who once had it that football 'was the triumph of the human potential for reason over humanity's propensity for disorder') for the match against Uruguay, which paid off as he scored in that game, having also earlier in 1962 registered a hat-trick in a friendly with *La Celeste*[64]. Hungary had used Rakosi rather than Gorocs to shadow Haynes, but they had rested Sandor, Albert and Fenyvesi for the game with Argentina. Sepp Herberger had also made switches and changes when West German qualification was certain. It seemed only England had no time or inclination for bold experiments.

Bulgaria 0 England 0
Thursday, 7 June 1962
World Cup Group 4
Estadio Braden Copper Co.
Attendance: 5,700
Referee: Antoine Blavier (Belgium)

Bulgaria: Naydenov, Zhechev, I. Dimitrov, Velichkov, D. Kostov, Kovachev, A. Kostov, Dimov, Asparuhov, Kolev, Dermendzhiev.
England: Springett, Armfield, Wilson, Moore, Norman, Flowers, Douglas, Greaves, Peacock, Haynes, Charlton.

It was a cloudy day, with a sort of hollow atmosphere, a consequence of the sparse attendance; the 5,700 who turned up for the encounter were lost in the expanse of the stadium. This, together with uninspired play, gave the event the aura of a half-dream.

---

64   'The Sky Blue', the nickname of the Uruguay national team.

In the first half England, wearing the 1962 Bukta away kit – red v-necked short-sleeved continental jerseys, red shorts, and red socks – made some attempts to attack, but pretty much failed miserably. Once again the forwards performed far below their pre-tournament form. Haynes, Greaves, and Douglas (the latter had the excuse of a leg injury) were without inspiration and thus ineffective; Haynes was woefully lacking. The Bulgarians, in their white jerseys, white shorts, white socks, did little to motivate much more of a response.

Again, Greaves had early chances, but uncharacteristically he vacillated and so couldn't make the best of his opportunities. Throughout the group games he had shown brief indications of his genius, but there was too little of his well-known and lethal first-time shooting in the box.

It was painfully obvious that England were fixated on the need not to lose. Both sides exhibited clear signs of nervousness that some, including one or two of the English players, saw as cowardly and so pathetic. However that situation appeared to have a tranquillising effect. With the Bulgarians resorting to a full retreat into defence for practically the whole game, the contest degenerated into a tedious shit-show.

Cries of 'Malo, malo!' ('Terrible, terrible') pursued the teams as they left the pitch at half-time, but the more 'colourful' condemnation emanated from the area where the small troop of England fans who had congregated in one corner of the ground. North v south or derby situations in the context of British football can fabricate enough abuse to register 11 on the Richter scale of scorn, but when those of the Anglo-Saxon persuasion coalesce in a contempt fest the fallout goes off the excoriation gauge.

With a quarter of an hour to go England came within inches of conceding a breakaway goal. Their opponents' most significant player, winger Ivan Kolev, who was similar in style to the Italian striker Gianfranco Zola in his 1990s pomp, broke free to drive a succulent cross from the left that beat everyone. Aleksandar Kostov appeared perfectly set to score but somehow managed to miss an open goal, his header finding its way just wide of the far post. It was to be the best opportunity of the match.

Earlier, Georgi Sokolov missed a half opportunity to score. Had either he or Kostov given the Bulgarians a win it would have been hard to imagine the consequences for Winterbottom and his players. Banishment from a World Cup in such circumstances would have been the least of it, and unforgivable.

The anguish this situation engendered in Bobby Charlton festered for years. Moore was to understand the feelings of his team-mate, saying, 'We would have a dozen passes at our end and then try to hit the ball up to our one forward. He was bound to lose it. So, then England passed the ball between themselves, while the Bulgarians decided not to come and get the ball.'

This 'Groundhog Day' vibe continued seemingly interminably. In retrospect, Bobby was to wonder how the eastern Europeans had managed to defeat France in the pre-Chile qualifying matches to make what was their first appearance in the final tournament.

Ultimately, everyone was relieved to hear the final whistle. Both teams left the pitch to the accompaniment of a chorus of boos from the modest huddle of spectators, many of them Argentinians who had come along to gee up the Bulgarians to put their team into the quarter-finals. They probably deserved to get their money back for putting up with what was really a non-event.

Postmortem

So, the door had been opened for England to go through to the last eight to meet the 1958 World Cup winners and tournament favourites Brazil, who had finished atop Group C in Viña del Mar. However, their performance against Bulgaria would not have raised any hopes for England getting into the semi-finals; it was dismal. The side had to qualify of course, and a draw ensured they kept a better goal average than Argentina, but there is always a cost to acting in soulless ways.

If we stain our endeavours with a purposeful deficit of distinction it drains us of the means to excel; mediocrity is an insufficient sire of success. While there was encouragement in getting out of the group, the prospect of heading to Viña del Mar with the elimination of the world champions in mind, following the farce enacted with Bulgaria, would have not convinced the neutral spectator of giving England as much chance as a jellied eel at an orthodox cockney wedding.

Another consequence of FIFA having only four playing centres was that the distances involved left no time for play-offs and replays. As a result, the mood had been set by the organising committee's decision that goal average should count in the first phase; if teams were level after this calculation their fate would be settled by drawing lots. England's debacle acted out with Bulgaria showed Moore to be correct when later he pointed out that FIFA had created a situation that caused teams to become risk-averse and the subsequent tension invited much of the acrimony that seemed to reign throughout the group phase.

Drawing off the positives you could have taken England's performance as a tactical victory. More realistically, with Bulgaria having lost both their games, so having only a consolation point to fight for, it was an exceptionally insipid performance by both teams with no one coming out with much credit. Moore was to complain that the Bulgarians had camped nine players in their own half. England had made some attempt to make a game of it, and Greaves missed a couple of opportunities, but they eventually realised their opponents were just waiting for them to make a mistake, hoping they might capitalise on any such error. This caused England to move into a lower gear, cautiously passing the ball around in their own half and bashing it up the field now and then for the forwards to chase. The Bulgarians would repossess the ball and just replicate the same impoverished tactics.

Bulgaria, adopting a sort of hybrid strategy that latched tedium to a siege mentality, resulted in a deathlock of negativity, that embraced allowing a limit of just two players at the most to enter the England half at any given time, including for corners and probably meteor strikes.

Most of the England players looked tired, but, for Bobby, it was just a monotonous circus of lethargy that left something of a bad taste in the mouth. The Argentinians in the crowd were willing the Bulgarians on. This would have been a very odd cultural affiliation of interests at any juncture, but the more so given their team's recent blisteringly brutal butchering of the Bulgars. They were about the most animated group in the stadium. Despite their enthused defection to all things of the 'Land of the Roses', their chosen side managed to produce just a flicker of attacking intention. Sadly, their timid opponents were little better.

The contest had been sterile. Without the urgency of needing to win England settled for compromise as the ball shuttled around the midfield area creating a narcoleptic spectacle (if such a contradiction in terms might be imagined). The goalkeepers did nothing. If it had been an animal a goal attempt from either team would have been an endangered species.

What scintilla of consolation managed to seep out of the tedium was reserved for Bulgaria. This was their departure from the tournament and, giving them the benefit of the doubt, at times they did make the effort to put on something of a show, albeit akin to the dragging, ossification of trench warfare, avoiding a group whitewash, a point and against mighty England no less!

Bobby Charlton, unhappy that his side failed to make the game a contest, had throughout the latter stages entered into an unseemly row with his captain. Johnny Haynes, who had been pleased with the draw that took England through to the quarter-finals, couldn't see the problem. The spat continued as the teams departed the pitch, uncharacteristically Charlton noisily remonstrating with Haynes about the skipper celebrating the draw.

'How can you say that was a good performance?' demanded Charlton, complaining loudly that while others had been disinclined to work on the Bulgarians, he had been grafting his arse off. He thought the attitude his side had adopted was disgraceful and hazardous.

Haynes didn't see the issue because his side were in the last eight and it was job done. But Charlton was having none of it, 'Yes, but we're talking about bloody Bulgaria … and what kind of a disaster would it have been if they sneaked a goal? What would the press have made of that?'

The protests echoed above the derision of the few spectators still awake or physically present in the stadium. Like most of the players, including Moore, Charlton was to see the match as among the worst he had ever played in, and that it was not what football should be about. Moore was to tell me, 'Bobby Charlton wasn't happy and he let everyone know it. While John never said it was a great performance, he was pleased we were through. Bobby was angry as he thought he and a few others had put a lot of work in, perhaps while some hadn't done so much … At the same time, John didn't seem to understand where Bobby was coming from; he was saying, "Bloody hell, we're in the quarter-finals!"

'Bobby and John were always friendly, I never saw them fall out before or after … But I think it was about being held by Bulgaria, and Bobby's feeling that if we had let a goal in it would have been terrible, and we'd be torn apart by the newspapers … and that nearly happened; a header directly in front of our goal. It went wide but it could just as easily have gone in. So to be fair, Bobby had a point…but [smiling] so did we!

'It was an awful game, The most boring I can remember playing in for England. Bobby Charlton and others thought the same … The lads were more nervous than any team I can remember playing in. There was a lot in getting a result, but we did think we were better than the Bulgarians. There was nothing said about playing for a draw, in fact the talk was about getting a quick goal to give us a cushion. That didn't happen though. Straight away the Bulgarians shut up shop, with eight or nine men behind the ball and that's how they stayed.

'We never got the goal, so that made everyone more nervous and because of that not keen to go forward, which would mean we'd be inviting possible counterattacks. So the team, practically as a whole unit, fell further and further back.'

As a draw was enough to reach the quarter-finals, together with the fiasco of the performance there was gossip that the two European teams had conspired to prevent Argentina from qualifying. It was also said the game was an act of revenge for the South Americans roughing up the Bulgarians in the opening group match.

It has to be doubted if England had consciously or deliberately gone for the draw. If that had been the case, resting both Greaves and Haynes would probably not have altered the result, and at the same time creating a chance they might have been a bit sharper for the next challenge. Retrospective wisdom is a great thing, but in the last analysis, all the suggestions of off-field skulduggery were not characteristic of Winterbottom.

The match was indeed a spiritless affair, without any distinction whatsoever, but of course England's priority would have been to qualify. At the same time, there was prestige for Georgi Pachedzhiev[65] and his boys pulling off a draw with England in their first appearance in the World Cup finals. Added to that, and taking a step back, there was not much to encourage the English to take any unnecessary risks, keeping in mind the possibility of injury, energy expenditure or of conceding goals.

The Chilean press cited the game as the 'worst of the series'. It hinted at what football would look like if no one was prepared to make a mistake, so creating situations wherein the ball hardly takes a holiday out of the midfield area and goalkeepers stand untested. As Greaves had it afterwards, 'There are some good players here, playing some rubbish, and they're afraid to hold on.' Years later he summed up the match by saying, 'If ever something that didn't happen, happened then that game was it.'

The result had become predictable as soon as the match fell into its stolid pattern; a procession of sorts, with the mutual intention of staying safe. Why do we call such games 'a goalless draw'? If a game is goalless how can it be anything else but a draw? It's the same with a 'one-all draw' – you can't have a one- or two-all win or loss!

The final table was:

	P	W	D	L	F	A	Pts
HUNGARY	3	2	1	0	8	2	5
ENGLAND	3	1	1	1	4	3	3
Argentina	3	1	1	1	2	3	3
Bulgaria	3	0	1	2	1	7	1

On the train ride back to their training camp some players were in the mood of self-congratulation; needless to say, Charlton was not one of them. Moore too was subdued. The meeting with Bulgaria might be taken as key to England's World Cup showing. Winterbottom's team couldn't quite make their collective mind up whether to go for an early goal and shut up shop, go boldly for a convincing win or cold-bloodedly adopt defensive tactics and hold out for a draw. The consequence of that indecision was a mess, with England, by the end, a bag of nerves.

That said, no England team had ever done better. Only one, in 1954, had

---

65   The first Bulgarian manager to take the national side to a World Cup Finals tournament as a player had been with the successful Levski Sofia, and had been the top scorer in their League in 1939 with fourteen goals.

done as well. Predictably, this did not satisfy the critics. Johnny Haynes was likely correct when he argued, 'Football writers live in a world of black and white. The England team is either brilliant or bad and as far as the journalists are concerned, the quality of the opposition or the luck of the game does not exist.'

Even now, and more then, England are pretty much expected to win every match simply because England ought to win every match. This is of course fantasy and as naive as the critic who announced to the world that England would beat Hungary 3-0.

The squad had initially got the newspapers from home, but this kind of writing caused a very deep and real resentment among the players, hence Winterbottom swiftly banning the papers from entering the camp.

The lesson for Moore in all this was he didn't want to play football in such a way, because ultimately nothing good could come from it. Going through the motions was never going to be his way as it was clear that his mentors, the likes of Ron Greenwood and Malcolm Allison, were correct in their guiding belief that success has to be cultivated from something of beauty, and as such it can't be attained by ugliness. Yes, you may get a result, even win the odd grudging accolade via churning, brutish, obduracy, but greatness is the progeny of the exquisite – not Vinny Jones or Conor McGregor, but Muhammad Ali, Pelé, Real Madrid, Michelangelo, Margot Fonteyn, and Bobby Moore.

Farewell to Coya

This final group match marked the squad's departure from Coya, and for most of the party this was a relief. The people of the village had welcomed the players with extraordinary warmth. For their entire stay the camp residents and staff had been open-handed and friendly, while the hospitality of the Grant family from the USA was exceptional. Byron Grant, the copper company manager, had from the moment the squad had arrived opened his home to the players, manager, and officials.

By the start of the second decade of the 21st century the copper mine had closed, and the former camp had become a working museum with the predictable gift shop and cafeteria. There were plans to open a garden centre too, likely with the ubiquitous greeting cards and scented candles. Down in the city the hawkers and pickpockets continued to proliferate and ply their respective, if perhaps related trades.

On the final night of England's stay in Coya, the Grant family entertained the whole party with a farewell dinner that according to Jimmy Armfield was 'fit for a king'. This event produced the best memory of their stay in the mountains – Peter Swan dancing the *cueca*, a Chilean national dance, in a raincoat and big snow boots he had found in his room, provoking great hilarity and approval.

16

THERE'S AN AWFUL LOT OF FUTEBOL IN BRAZIL

Esquadrão de Ouro[66]

In the 1962 World Cup in Chile all four quarter-finals kicked off at the same time, and for the final time in that tournament the British (not English) flag flew during the usual ceremonies of anthems and salutes. It wasn't until the 1990s that the Union Jack Flag was completely replaced by the St George's Cross by England fans. Before this, the Union Jack and the Three Lions were the symbols used to represent England's football team. It seems up to that point, before the rise of political nationalist movements in Scotland and Wales, that British and English identities were a lot more interchangeable than they are now.

The England squad, as a group, believed they had enough about them to beat Brazil. Bobby Robson, whose injury kept him out of all the matches in Chile, and Jimmy Adamson had watched the Brazilians play a couple of times and had given Walter Winterbottom and the rest of the players full reports on what they saw as strengths and weaknesses of the 'Samba Boys'.

Adamson, the Burnley skipper, had travelled out to Chile officially as a member of the 22-strong squad, but his main task was to help Winterbottom with the team (he was considered, semi-formally, Walter's assistant). Walter had chosen Adamson to take the role that he had asked Tottenham's Bill Nicholson to assume in Sweden four years earlier. Jimmy had been a miner in the same north-eastern town that Bobby Charlton came from, Ashington. As a wing-half in the Burnley side that won the First Division in 1960, he was voted England's Football Writers' Association Footballer of the Year in 1962, captaining the Clarets in the FA Cup Final (although it was the brilliant Tottenham side of the early 1960s that won the trophy that year).

An FA coach, Adamson had worked with Winterbottom at Lilleshall. In Chile, Walter entrusted him with the important role of reminding players of their basic strengths and the need to carry them on to the field, which he did with great authority. Prior to the meeting with Brazil, Jimmy let it be known that for him the South Americans hadn't been close to finding their best form in their group games.

---

66   'The Golden Squad'.

Several key players were probably just beyond their best years, but the whole side did not appear to have the confidence of the Brazilians of 1958. Nevertheless, the absence of Pelé notwithstanding – he was still carrying a groin injury from a group game with Czechoslovakia and would miss the rest of the tournament – Brazil still had their wondrous winger, Garrincha, 'the Little Bird'. His bowed legs, deformed from birth, presented an apparent disability but one that, counter-intuitively, enabled him to do things with a ball others could not achieve. Four years previously in Sweden, Garrincha had presented his extraordinary talents to the world, and in the group games in Chile he had shown he continued to be capable of torturing the best defences.

Brazil had the advantage of playing their quarter-final on the same pitch that they had won their qualifying group, while Bobby and England were becoming more conscious that they were being obliged to play football in a way they were not accustomed to. At that time, the English game was characterised by its comparative openness, and freedom. When a forward got by a defender there was no 'queue' of other defenders lining up behind the beaten player, just waiting to quickly pounce, within a few feet. This was the way of things against teams like Hungary and it had perplexed some of the squad, although this was one of the first tactics Alf Ramsey would introduce into England's play.

England had played more rationally against Argentina, shifting the ball swiftly, keeping things simple, backing each other up as much as possible. But it was as if they were relearning their game on the hoof, although for Moore it was familiar territory.

For the encounter with Argentina the team had made themselves faster and stronger than the South Americans. It was doubtful the same situation would pertain in the meeting with Brazil. England's meeting with the World Champions might have been understood to be a case of the masters meeting the pupils. It was probably a relief when everyone involved in the quarter-finals, without some sort of affinity to Brazil, found out that Pelé would not add to their problems.

Garrincha

Moore was to rhetorically ask, 'Is Pelé the world's greatest player?' His reply to this reflection was, 'Tell me first how greatness is measured before I answer.'

Bobby didn't believe that one could say, with much degree of certainty, that one high-performing player might be 'better' than another. He gave the example of Luis Suárez, Internazionale's inside-forward for most of the 1960s. Moore described him 'a great team general', but went on to question how one could compare him with an inside-forward whose role was more about scoring goals.

How might it be convincingly claimed that a top full-back was better at their job than a high-performing striker? He went on to point out that many people believed that Real Madrid's Alfredo Di Stéfano was the greatest all-round player of all time, but did these same champions of the *Saeta Rubia* (the 'Blond Arrow') ever see Stanley Matthews at his best? Those who did often argued that Sir Stan rated Tom Finney to be the better player (and they were probably right).

Controversially, I don't think of Pelé as the footballing god he is usually taken to be. He was outstanding in his context, but I can't hand on heart say he would have played better for West Ham than Johnny Byrne, or in the winter mud of the mid-20th century English game he would have outshone George Best. In his pomp Rodney Marsh had as good, if not better ball control and at least equal vision. Although in a completely different role, Jim Baxter was so much more robust, and probably more powerful. Then there is Garrincha. This is not doing the Santos man down, that would be idiotic, just a little bit of rational if contrarian reflection. The most imperious player I have ever seen is the former Italian captain Andrea Pirlo; he'd have done well at Upton Park, with Dellamura ice-cream being produced just a bit more than an Ernie Gregory goal kick away in Parker Street, Silvertown, and E. Pellicci, down Bethnal Green Road

While the absence of Edson Arantes do Nascimento might have been thought of as something of a bonus, there wasn't an England player who doubted that Manuel Francisco dos Santos was capable of winning a game on his own, perhaps to a greater extent than *O Rei*[67].

Bobby tried to describe Garrincha's talent and approach by positing the right-winger as a mix of Matthews and Finney in their splendour, but that really doesn't do him justice. Moore was to say that Garrincha's speed and finishing power bettered even Pelé – his feet moved like lightning, which gave his shooting extra power and made any attempt to rob him of the ball invariably a fruitless endeavour. During his playing years Garrincha was like a deity in Brazil. In 1964, when he had to undergo an operation, it was screened live on Brazilian television!

Hobbled from birth, Garrincha's legs were bowed in parallel. Hardly literate, he would leave this world prematurely, ending his days as a poverty-stricken alcoholic. However, 1962 saw him at his best.

Winterbottom came up with potential ways of managing Garrincha, but as Bobby later asked, 'How do you predict what is just unpredictable?' Wary Walter's worthy warnings about the Brazilians were all well and good, but that was like being cautioned about the potential effects of an earthquake when you were standing in the middle of one. Jimmy Greaves asked Walt, 'How do we beat 'em?'

---

67   'The King', the nickname given to Pelé during the 1958 World Cup.

Winterbottom replied, 'Well we score one more goal than them.' That was that sorted then! In truth, no one had seen anyone like Garrincha, so there was no comparator on which to base a strategy to somehow counter him.

Most of the Brazilians who England would face had been part of the side that won the final in Stockholm four years earlier; Gilmar, Djalma Santos, Zito, Nílton Santos, Garrincha, Didi, Vavá and Mário Zagallo had all played in that match, and Zózimo had been watching on from the bench in the Rasunda Stadium. The Brazilians were really a team of legends, and that kind of experience was not something England came close to matching. For all that, Johnny Haynes and his men went into their quarter-final test with a modicum of optimism. The squad made their way down to the coastal resort of Viña del Mar (at an altitude of two metres) in better spirits than they had been able to summon since arriving in Chile.

Given their overall showing in the tournament that far few gave England much of a chance to better the World Champions, who had beaten a good Spanish side and Mexico in their group, and had drawn with Czechoslovakia, who ultimately would make the final. The best hope for England was to get an early goal and hold on to that the best they might, although anyone seeing that as a viable strategy against Garrincha et.al.. would likely have been a monumental poltroon with a terminal case of naivete.

Moreira's men

Brazil were led by Aymoré Moreira, in his second stint as manager, and had been favourites to retain the World Cup. For more than a few that estimation appeared to be vindicated even before the match against England kicked off.

Moore, with Bobby Robson continuing to be unavailable, maintained his place in the team. Trying to be positive about the game, although he had never seen the Brazilians in live action, he 'thought we could put on a good show and if we could hold it together, get a result'. This attitude was an echo of Malcolm Allison's disposition, 'Never think about losing. No team is unbeatable and many losing teams, most things being equal, bring defeat upon themselves by starting out believing they can't win. Anyone running a football team needs to get away from thinking like that. You can always win, but you can't win if you make your mind up you are going to lose.'

An important competitive game against the world's best team was to be a major education for England's future captain.

Having spent more than a fortnight at Coya, the England party were generally glad to get away from what many of them had seen as their practical incarceration.

The Hotel Miramar, 8,000ft below Coya, was a move up from their last barracks. It was built on a rock overlooking the beaches of Viña del Mar, a pretty coastal resort, across the bay to the harbour of Valparaíso, where Bobby watched the pelicans swooping over the azure waters of the Pacific. It also had a bar.

England had beaten Brazil 4-2 at Wembley in 1956. A goalless game was played out in the 1958 World Cup in Gothenburg, a year later England lost 2-0 in Rio. The sides were, on paper even, so the 1962 encounter was considered by some as a decider of sorts, but to purloin the much used adage, football isn't played on paper.

For the first time during the tournament England, wearing their 1959 Bukta home jersey, ran out to play in an authentic World Cup atmosphere. The relatively diminutive but beautiful Estadio Sausalito was packed almost to capacity. The venue, originally built in 1929, had been all but destroyed by the Valdivia earthquake in 1960[68], but the swift reconstruction meant it was ready to host all the Group C games. At the time of writing it is the home ground of CD Everton, having a capacity of 22,360. The 1962 semi-final between Czechoslovakia and Yugoslavia took place there.

Not for the first time in Chile, a sizeable hoard of noisy fans gave Brazil boisterous support, maintaining a continuous cacophony from an impromptu steel band consisting of, among other things, frying pans, biscuit tins, and coffee drums. They danced sambas, let off fireworks and waved vast green and yellow flags. Good, however not a patch on a raucous rendition of 'Bubbles', but at last this was the real taste of the intoxicating atmosphere of South American football.

The smaller group of English fans did the Hokey Cokey, waved whatever came to hand, sang 'God Save the Queen', and let of a few voluminously boisterous farts ignited by the local Bohemia beer as, for the 21st and final time, Johnny Haynes took the field as England's captain.

The Brazilian captain, Mauro, was fastidious in the middle of the field when the football was checked, being convinced that it was an English ball (although it was actually Swedish in origin) somehow designed in favour of his opponents.

There was a history of Brazilians messing about with their balls. The lighter Chilean ball was something that European teams were simply not used to in 1962. The Brazilians retorted that using the heavier European ball in 1958 hadn't stopped them winning that tournament, and from their first match in the 1962 competition, for each fixture the ball had to be changed sometime after the kick-off.

---

68   The most powerful earthquake in recorded history (magnitude 9.5) struck southern Chile. The rupture zone stretched for estimates ranging from 311 miles to 621 miles along the country's coast. The greatest impact was on the city of Valdivia. Two million people were made homeless, at least 3,000 were injured, and approximately 1,655 died. The earthquake triggered a massive tsunami that raced across the Pacific. Waves wrecked coastal communities as far away as New Zealand, Japan, the Philippines and Hawaii.

The original was a Chilean ball that had a very thin covering of plastic. This wore off during play and it became patchy, which had an impact on its flight. A Swedish leather ball was substituted, which of course soaked up the moisture from the field like a rapaciously demonic Atlantic sponge, so after about an hour, such was the weight gain, no one could have scored from outside the penalty area.

When I was at school, from a time before the Beatles' first LP to around the release of the *Sticky Fingers* album by the Stones, we played with the ancient ancestors of such balls. On the for ever muddy pitches they refused to bounce and in the second half you risked a severe foot injury if you attempted anything like a shot.

England made one unanticipated change shortly before the match; Gerry Hitchens was reinstated at centre-forward, replacing Alan Peacock, who was suffering from a groin strain. The Internazionale striker only found out he was to start at lunchtime on the day of the match. Given his experience in the Italian game, Winterbottom could have hoped that Hitchens would have been better equipped to face the Brazilians than any other possible selection he might have made, although his options weren't extensive.

In the England dressing room, the manager told his team that the older Brazilians were likely to be feeling the pace of the tight schedule of games. He got that wrong. Part of their talent was to pace themselves throughout what proved to be a good encounter.

Samba lesson

Brazil 3 England 1
Sunday, 10 June 1962
World Cup quarter-final
Estadio Sausalito
Attendance: 17,736
Referee: Pierre Schwinte (France)

Brazil: Gilmar, Djalma Santos, Mauro, Zito, Zózimo, Nílton Santos, Garrincha, Didi, Vavá, Amarildo, Zagallo.
England: Springett, Armfield, Wilson, Moore, Norman, Flowers, Douglas, Greaves, Hitchens, Haynes, Charlton.

Not long after kick-off, the mournful-eyed and noble-looking Didi was off the field for three minutes being treated for an injury. On his return to the fray, his first touch sent Vavá clear away with an extended, typically precise, lobbed pass. The way Didi was performing, the man mysteriously offloaded two years previously by Real Madrid. might have raised misgivings in the head of *Los Blancos*' treasurer, Raimundo Saporta, sitting in the best seats with the FIFA dignitaries, munching on *cuchuflí* and *humitas*[69].

Garrincha gave an early warning of his potential when he brushed through the English defence, and was only stopped by a frantic Haynes tackle, but for all the grace and poise of the Brazilians the first touch of individual brilliance emanated from Bobby Charlton. He rounded Djalma Santos with a sublime dummy to centre, Greaves dashed to meet the cross but, perhaps with a rush of nerves, volleyed over the bar. England had come close to getting that valued opening goal. Shortly after that Hitchens and Douglas both missed good chances which, if they had gone in, might have made history.

Both Djalma and Nílton Santos, although in their mid-30s, still looked a world-class pair of full-backs and they held off much of the best England had to offer in terms of firepower. On the bay of Valparaíso, down at sea level, Brazil had clearly raised their game. In the first half an hour they showed something more than of a semblance of their former sublimely skilled incarnation, but that was long enough to cause their opponents concern, somewhat overshadowing the spirit and resistance Winterbottom's team had endeavoured to muster. As the contest matured most involved in British football might not have been blamed if they started to wonder where the national game might go in the future.

Garrincha was the brightest star in the Brazilian firmament in 1962. Left-back Ray Wilson was tasked with close-marking this exceptionally dynamic right-winger. Initially the Shirebrook Terrier looked apprehensive, and it was his mistake, making a headed clearance, that the lightning instincts of Garrincha looked to take advantage of. His penalty area raid was foiled at the last second by the swift reaction of Maurice Norman, who made a well-timed and executed tackle.

A courageous goal-line clearance by Armfield followed, Springett having been limited to a half-save of a Garrincha drive. Throughout the match the goalkeeper pulled off some commendable feats, but Springett's handling of the ball was not looking great. The Sheffield Wednesday man was the established and reliable guardian of the English onion bag, but his clear and continued search for form had a negative impact on the confidence of the team, with his defence feeling obliged more to protect than rely on him.

Shortly after Armfield's clearance, England were caught static while appealing for offside to Gottfried Dienst[70], the unsympathetic Swiss linesman, as Amarildo

---

69   Chilean snacks
70   Dienst was the referee of the 1966 World Cup Final and one of only four men to have refereed two

broke through on his own. Fortunately for England, he messed up his shot as Springett came in close to challenge him.

Minutes later, with a cold mist coming in off the ocean, a thundering 20-yard rocket from Greaves was touched over the bar by Gilmar. At that point some might have argued there wasn't much between the sides. Neither seemed to be in top gear, displaying nothing like critical pace or consistent accuracy. Both defences gave little away to the relatively cautious attacks they were being asked to meet. The more discerning eye, however, could see that Brazil had the classier edge and that England were putting in a heavier shift than their opponents. England were being 'felt out', pulled around, as Brazil waited for the opportunity to strike.

Amarildo, who was proving a capable understudy for Pelé, looked a high-quality player in his own right but needed treatment in the 20th minute after a tackle by Flowers. On recovery he switched position, limping to the right-wing. Flowers, indifferent to the injury he might have inflicted, banged a thumping drive just wide of an upright during Amarildo's two-minute absence.

Didi, the absolute master of the dead ball, was beginning to test Springett with his uncanny capacity to swerve his shots, while Garrincha, the voracious artist, pulled down high balls as fluently as a refined Rio de Janeiro sommelier might pour a glass of Ao Yun, Shangri La. After one such accomplishment he took off to beat three defenders effortlessly; it was left to Haynes to save the moment, clearing the ball level with a goal post

In the 31st minute 5ft 7in Garrincha got to an impeccably placed snapping corner delivered by outside-left Mário Zagallo. The Botafogo Bandido had sprinted into the centre of England's defence to head flawlessly. Big centre-half Norman was the nearest to him, but he timed his jump poorly, being a yard or so away from Garrincha, despite standing at least six inches taller. As the Brazilian's head made contact with the ball Springett was caught on his line. Later, Charlton was to name this a 'perfect goal'. Detracting from the culpability that would be heaped on the keeper, the Manchester United man said any blame was his for not keeping as closely in touch with Garrincha as he might have done. Charlton in fact was making a huge contribution to the defence in tackling back, just as Zagallo was doing for Brazil.

The smoke from the fireworks that greeted the goal draped like a ghostly vapour over the crowd for some minutes, an aroma to remind England of the wound they had sustained.

Five minutes on, Amarildo, apparently back in gear, picked up a clearance and broke through. To the hands-in-the-air despair of the Brazilian the low shot was

European Cup finals, which he did in 1961 and 1965, and one of only two (the other being the Italian Sergio Gonella) to have refereed the finals of both the European Championship and the World Cup.

suffocated by Springett. Just seconds later he tried again with a delightfully struck effort but he was once more unfortunate, the ball travelling just over the bar.

England's search for a reply was rewarded in the 38th minute. Pushing their way back into the match, a lofty, majestically executed Haynes free kick from the corner of Brazil's penalty area was met by the prowling Greaves. The six-yard box assassin nutted in a solid effort only to see it foiled by the corner of the post and crossbar. Hitchens scampered on to the loose ball and struck it past Gilmar. That was his first and only World Cup goal, and his fifth in seven international outings overall.

The joust continued, with England fighting back stoically but expending much more energy than their opponents in the doing. Just before half-time Amarildo got clean through, with only Springett to beat, but Ron just managed to deflect the shot with his boot. Brazil had upped their probing.

As the teams left the field at half-time it was fair to say Brazil had been more accurate in their distribution and shooting. They had paced themselves better and made England work harder. Some commentators argued that they had thus far failed to fully control the game, but the breakdown of the action suggests otherwise. England had expended more effort, and their exertions had kept them in the mix, but Brazil were winning on points. Their sharper individual skills and livelier imaginations could be said to have been equalled by England's more solid and sturdy collective labour, but having put in much more of a shift then their opponents they were destined to need to dig deeper into their stamina reserves.

Nevertheless, the feeling was that if they could contain Brazil for the first quarter of an hour after the break they would be in with a chance, but somewhere in Winterbottom's mind he likely knew that the South Americans were going to shift up a gear after the break.

The embryonic second half saw Wilson slice a clearance that ignited a threatening Brazilian assault down the left wing. Vavá beat Springett, but was judged offside by the French official. Springett was once more bettered, this time by a Garrincha cross, but he did well to swiftly regroup and save the ensuing header from Amarildo.

Eight minutes after the resumption of play the referee awarded a debatable free kick against Flowers on the edge of the England penalty area. A fast cross from the right had unavoidably struck Ron on the arm; there was no chance that he could have moved the limb out of the way.

The next moment was etched into the mind of Moore. He was to tell how Garrincha's free kick both veered and arched over its journey of 20 yards or so though the English wall with a mystifying trajectory. Bobby had never experienced, imagined, or would have ever believed such a kick was possible. This was the Brazilian's 'dry leaf' – a piece of magic he had performed many times, in apparently endless variations. The seemingly entranced Springett could only watch bemused as the ball bounced off his chest, teeing up Vavá to head home.

As Bobby put it, 'The ball had swerved and dipped at the same time … to be fair, Ron Springett done well to get his body behind it.'

The referee had effectively turned the game, and not for the last time had whistled his way into history. Pierre Schwinte's most famous match was probably Italy against North Korea at the 1966 World Cup. North Korea shocked the world by winning 1-0 against the *Azzurri*, who at the time had won the trophy twice. He co-wrote a book, *L' Arbitrage du Football*,[71] which is probably the best book on football refereeing written in French that I've yet to read.

At that juncture England had little option but to commit to attack and work to find an equaliser, which meant pulling on their already taxed energy tank. This, predictably, not only allowed Brazil to dictate the pace of the game but left gaps at the back, opening doors for Garrincha, the man with two left feet. He plunged into the voids and soon conjured another effort from more than 20 yards, this time a magical drive that veered furiously into the top corner of the English rigging. This was perhaps the most memorable goal of the tournament; his shot had seemed to be wide of the post, but then, as if possessed of a mind of its own, the ball dipped and swung under the bar, leaving the mystified Springett hapless, humbled, helpless and hopeless. As Moore put it with good old East London succinctness, 'It bent all over the bloody place!'

This was a phenomenal shot. The 'Little Bird' had manoeuvred himself around the inside-left position, then suddenly let go of a swinging missile, focused on the far post. Some remarked on the power of this effort, but it was more the result of how the ball was struck and its placement. He put so much hook and swerve on the shot that, in what tiny shred of a time he had to think about and assess the assault, Springett had clearly concluded it was going wide; he moved too late, but probably the only other alternative would have been to move too soon. As the ball fell, bewildered and dizzy, after hitting the top corner of the net, it fell like a stone to the turf inside Ron's goal, causing English hearts to sink. Casting his mind back to that moment, Moore remembered looking around and recognising his side had all but been broken. It was the sucker punch that was always coming.

For Bobby, it probably wasn't possible for anyone to mark Garrincha. At the same time, it seemed as if Brazil had been able to turn on their collective genius according to desire; to switch from better to brilliant at will. Reminiscing about

---

71 'Football Arbitration'

this lesson Moore commented on England's vulnerability in the face of the talented Brazilians, but he recognised their quality; in defence of England, it has to be said it is likely no other national side would have been in any less exposed.

Greaves didn't have the best of outings. In the second half in particular, he gave the impression that he wanted to avoid physical contact. Talking of which, the referee felt obliged to warn Flowers after he yet again decked Amarildo, as the Brazilians started to take control.

While the effectiveness of Didi and Amarildo had been somewhat tempered by injury, Brazil maintained the refined workings of their fast-moving defence-attack forward movement. They were able to ratchet up the pace for menacing counterattacks, while England looked increasingly wooden and bewildered, just attempting to hold back the tide, but being ground down by struggle.

In the last part of the game only Charlton looked equal to the cause, providing himself and his team with a string of chances. All through the match he had given the Brazilian right-back, Djalma Santos, a real run around. Should the Manchester Reds have been so inclined, after 1962 he might well have made his future with Barcelona or even Boca Juniors, as both clubs – and others – were hot for him. Charlton was to tell how his family circumstances were the basis for his resistance to the temptation of the seeming clandestine approach of the famous Buenos Aires club. He let their representatives know that aside from his allegiance to Manchester United, given that they were expecting a family, his wife Norma wouldn't want to make such a move. The Boca people didn't seem to see this as an issue as they were ready to arrange for the baby to be born in the British embassy, so if the couple had a boy he would be qualified to play for England. Can't think why he didn't jump at that.

England continued to fight hard to salvage the game in the last 20 minutes, but the Brazilians remained composed behind their lead, holding the ball in defence, practically relaxing, making no attempt to move it forward but simply passing it square and backwards among themselves, while their opponents emptied the last drops of their reservoir of endeavour.

Despite England wilting somewhat, this was probably the best game of the tournament thus far, but while not overtly apprehensive, they had gone into the tie probably too warily. They had shown both passion and pride, but straightforwardly they were outclassed and outthought by a team that appeared to be blessed with the full set of footballing talents, even without their most legendary player. In the last analysis Brazil had an asset that England couldn't address; little Garrincha was the critical difference between the sides.

As Brazil set out on their lap of honour following their victory, waving the Chilean flag, few doubted they would ultimately retain the World Cup.

Winterbottom had warned his side that Garrincha's free kicks were particularly deadly. Although he looked almost disabled as he walked, well, he was really, his apparent deficiencies were his advantage; he could do things because of those legs – there's an enduring social message in that – most doors that seemed closed are often half open, it's about how hard you push. At the same time, his speed of thought and movement impressed every English player. No matter how the ball got to him, he was able to control it instantaneously before darting off in the way a startled squirrel might. He was deceptively strong and balanced; his explosive, but at the same time nuanced shooting never ceased to amaze. Brazil cleared the field in front of him. The right wing, from halfway line to corner flag, was exclusively his realm

Jimmy Armfield, who was voted the best right-back in the world after the tournament, was so disappointed at being knocked out that he didn't stay on in Chile to receive his award. Even with key players missing he felt that if England had taken their chances then they could have done better. Looking back, he also believed that Winterbottom had tinkered too much with the team. However, Moore didn't think there were any excuses, beyond Brazil being the superior side and that England just had to get better, which of course, they did.

In the summer of 1962 Bobby was only the 13th Hammer to be selected for England and just the 25th Iron to represent his country in peacetime football. He was the first West Ham player to appear in a World Cup finals tournament, and he did so with some distinction. The tournament of '62 had been a university of the game for Moore, the time and place he graduated to England status. Hence it represents a crucial period and experience in his life and development, but also it was a landmark for his club. To have a young ambassador visible on the global stage was invaluable in terms of status and future of the Hammers, as it could be understood as an institution capable of producing international excellence. His performance brought a sense of belief back to East London, as well as an appetite for ambition. Young Bobby had led West Ham out of the shadows and into the limelight.

17
SUCCUMBING TO THE SAMBA

The Brazilians had finished playing a cocky but composed game. In the final minutes they predictably, if wisely, but frustratingly played with England, keeping possession, flaunting their pre-eminence. The work England put in to get attacks started was easily snuffed out. The argument that the consistent, astounding, intractable, and explosive genius of Garrincha opened the gap between the two sides was obvious, but for Moore, while the little man should be given his due, Brazil were, as a team, a considerable notch better than England.

Throughout the game the South Americans balanced their skill with solid teamwork. Their forwards fought for possession, being willing to get tackles in to win the ball. This was confirming to Moore. Early in his career Noel Cantwell, had always emphasised that possession was the key to winning football matches. Brazil did not stick to a single pattern or style of play, leaving the English defenders somewhat in disarray, not quite knowing what to expect next from their opponents. They were a side that made a habit of thinking of new and original approaches to forward play, which gave opposing defences few options in terms of strategic planning, which predictably led to confusion in the face of the samba attack.

England did miss a few opportunities and Jimmy Armfield had a good game. However, from the moment a Garrincha's shot was cleared off the line, he became more and more influential, and really, that marked the English card, but at least they had gone down fighting, so much so that some of them were brokenhearted at the end.

Armfield was distinctly unimpressed by the incessant samba rhythms, recalling, 'The only instruments are tin cans of every variety on which a hideous clattering tattoo is beaten interminably.' But what did impress him was the way in which it seemed, on occasions, the Brazilian football matched the tin-can rhythm when they were seeing out the game and showboating.

Armfield's words, written just a year later about coaching a team, could as easily have been said by Allison or Greenwood, 'It is not sufficient to field 11 men fit as men can be. They must be a team. Good coaching alone can ensure that each has a perfect understanding with the others, so that each knows, almost by instinct in the end, where to move for a pass or to close a gap, how to play not only with the ball, but off the ball.' That would fairly much sum up how the Brazilian team had worked.

Hindsight is a wonderful thing, but the truth is no one had anything in the way of foresight as an answer to Garrincha. The 'Little Bird' repeatedly twittered the apparent endless variations of his unique song. He flew up, back and forth along the left wing, leaving the English confused and beaten in his train. Explosive acceleration, coupled with baffling ball skills perplexed, confounded, and finally did for the English defence. A short-arse of the first order, contradictorily he was highly effective in the air; his bullet-like header that gave Brazil the lead was a phenomenal example of this talent. There was nothing in England's arsenal to answer or even temper his extraordinariness.

Unlike Armfield, Johnny Haynes and some others, although disappointed, Bobby wasn't distraught. In many ways the whole experience had been an excursion into wonderland for him. That, initially, England had appeared to have held Brazil, who had looked majestic in their traditional yellow jerseys, light blue shorts, white socks, felt like a bonus. But with the score at 1-1, the South Americans profited from a couple of errors by Ron Springett (who was equalling Harry Hibbs's 1935 record as being England's most-capped goalkeeper). Netting twice in a six-minute spell, Brazil put England to the sword but their keeper would ultimately and unfairly become the scapegoat, although no one could dispute that the better team had won and in so doing raised pretty much the same questions and criticisms about English football voiced by Malcolm Allison for decades.

Dog-end

The match had twice been held up by a woolly black dog running on the pitch. The second time he gave Garrincha some of his own medicine, swerving past the amused Brazilian as he tried to grab the playful mutt. Some took the animal to be the same chap who had interfered with the Brazil-Spain game, but this lad was just a bit bigger than his predecessor. The admirable canine, managing to avoid the pursuit and attentions of officials, was ultimately persuaded to leave the field by Jimmy Greaves. On the sardonic suggestion of Moore, the Spurs striker went down on all fours, to 'dog whisper'. Jimmy won the exuberant animal's trust and attention, allowing him to pick the four-legged invader up and escort him from the pitch, with the crowd cheering both dog and man. History is always a matter not only of incident, but also recognition. In the 1990s Greaves was to relate, clearly with a feel for irony, how the dog had pissed over him as he carried it off the field (hence honouring a long tradition of Spurs forwards being pissed on). Greaves reflected that Moore should have taken on the responsibility for mongrel's removal as he was more familiar with Barking. There was no change of shirts in those days, so Jimmy was obliged to endure the stink he was left with; he later reflected that at least it kept the Brazilian defenders at a distance.

Following the tournament, the hound was taken to Brazil and raffled among the Brazilian squad. Garrincha won. The media named the dog *Bi*, short for *Bicampeóes* (Two-time champions) in homage to Brazil's second World Cup triumph. But after Garrincha got the pooch back to his hometown of Pau Grande, in the state of Rio de Janeiro, the immortal pup had been christened 'Greaves' in honour of his captor and urinal.

'If'

Johnny Haynes once said to me, 'The biggest word in football is "if".' Sir Geoff Hurst has had it that 'football is a game of tomorrows'.' Sometimes I think the saddest word in life can be 'yesterday'.

So England and Bobby's Chilean adventure had concluded in defeat. Football, ultimately ends with either defeat or victory; draws just take the conclusion toward one or the other. The events of May and June 1962, now more than 60 years ago, entered history and memory, fading like the haze over the Pacific just beyond the Estadio Sausalito, melting as the snow in the Andes summer.

Two days after the game in Viña del Mar, Moore was flying home with the rest of the squad. With most of the other members of the party he watched what was left of the championship on television. There was a deal of criticism in the press about this, the feeling being that the side should have stayed in South America and seen out the tournament, as long as they stayed in a tent presumably.

When the team got back to England, retrospectively most people thought the lads hadn't done too badly, that the matches against Hungary, Argentina and Brazil had come over well on the TV. As always, there was talk of a lack of luck, and 'Johnny Foreigner' bending the rules to disadvantage the plucky English. But, of course, there was no shortage of journalists calling for the heads to roll. Football is full of know-nothings who know everything, with no responsibility and so no consequences for their blithering and shallow opinions, that really are made to self-promote rather than do any benefit to anyone else.

In the 2010 World Cup it was Wayne Rooney who, in the best traditions of Scouse sarcasm, protested, 'Nice to see your home fans booing you, that's what loyal support is.' This echoes a tradition among postwar England players, a feeling of 'you can't win'. No matter what they do, it seems sometimes a vocal majority or a small, narcissistic minority, will call it 'wrong'.

From Moore's point of view, one learns more about a team and the football culture it is set in by playing against that team than you can from merely watching them. On the other hand, professional, competitive sport must be, ultimately, doing what one can to better an opponent. Latterly however we have got into a mentality in the Premier League that 'doing OK' is a win, when it really ain't. West Ham have been susceptible to this over decades now; we celebrate finishing seventh or overcoming second-rate opposition in a third-rate European competition – that's not a bad thing in itself, but when it's taken as 'success', say in comparison to not being relegated, something has gone awry. It's like having a flat tyre and thinking that replacing it with one that is not so flat, but still flat, is as good as it gets.

If you are involved in sport purely for the aesthetics, the art, if you don't win, it doesn't matter where you finish. Although having a Vladimir Tretchikoff painting over your fireplace is never going to be as satisfying as the best of Joe Turner.[72]

To crudely paraphrase the perspective of ancient Greeks, if it is beautiful, it is perfect; it can't be beaten. What Moore and the likes of Ron Greenwood pursued was just that – the better it looks, the better it is. But that doesn't alter the reality that no one remembers, or in the long run cares about, the losers. And the fact is England were beaten by a prettier team, on the pitch, and that's the only place footballers can be beaten or win. England, in the last analysis, had no excuses about climate, food, luck, training camps or anything else off the field. They were punished for defensive errors, their lack of application in attack and imagination in midfield. They were not short of graft, but sometimes it looked like that's all they had. The only way to ultimately win is to admit this sort of stuff and learn from it so that eventually, you minimise your chances of losing.

All competitive football entails emotion and tension. The game's rewards go to those who can combine knowledge with swiftness and courage; the ugly, ignorant, and cautious are the ones who, in all but the short term, fall by the wayside. Moore, like Greenwood, expressed puzzlement that few in English football noticed the extent to which the Brazilians generally make very few defensive errors. This is because they are fast, brave, and wise. You can only score more goals against a team that makes more mistakes in defending than you. Brazilian defenders are traditionally skilful ball players and so are unafraid to play themselves out of the tightest of defensive situations. Without that kind of ability mistakes are invited. The alternative is the, at best, 50-50 option of the 'big boot away'. As previously stated in this book, fortune favours the brave, but it shines on the skilful and the courageously wise.

If we want to break wisdom down to its constituent parts, preparation might be foundational. However, some England players only really started to think about

---

72   Green Lady v The Fighting Temeraire for instance.

the World Cup when they were on the plane to South America. Jimmy Greaves for example, who performed well below par, was occupied right up to close to the start of summer with his club in the FA Cup and European Cup. He, like a few other players, had little time to think about Chile. Likewise, Haynes had been completely preoccupied with Fulham's relegation problems and their run to the FA Cup semi-final.

In the six months before the tournament, Walter Winterbottom had four days with the national team at Lilleshall and maybe, at best, ten at other venues. There had been two international matches against what might be taken as serious opposition. The Brazilians were in training for two months before going to Chile and played six international games over that period. The Chileans started their serious preparation in the middle of February, nearly four months before the first match. During the winter at Lilleshall, Winterbottom had pleaded that his players start thinking about the World Cup, how the side had to build themselves into a unit, get into the right frame of mind for the challenge. He knew that it was crucial, but under the circumstances of the English game, then as now, it was not possible.

For Peter Swan things were more straightforward than this. He felt Winterbottom made a crucial error in the build-up to the tournament. The England manager had kept a relatively settled team together for a couple of years; the group had built a good understanding, and then suddenly, Walter changed the team. Swan had it, 'Players who hadn't played for England before were brought in for important games. That seemed wrong to me after we'd been together for such a long time. I couldn't understand why he did that and I think other players felt the same.'

I'm not sure Swan was taking into account the long list of injuries Winterbottom had to deal with, but what seems obvious is that England only started devoting significant time to sorting out their game strategy, taking their opposition into consideration, after they got to Coya. They were still working it out when Bobby Robson and Jimmy Adamson were sent to watch Brazil in a group game.

Looking at England's performance against Brazil, if they had drawn any of the other quarter-finalists their play might well have won them a place in the last four. England were not disgraced, doing all that might be expected of them in the face of a better prepared, and drilled, side, with an extraordinary level of talent in their ranks. Haynes and his men chased everything, and showed more fight than they had in all the group games combined. This was by far the biggest, most prestigious game Bobby had played in, with the most to win, but paradoxically, for him, relatively and in retrospect, not much to lose. In short, both he and the England team generally rose to the occasion.

As was his habit over his entire career, Moore reflected long and hard on what he had learned from his playing experiences. After Chile he grasped England's predicament compared to very top sides in the world, all of whom were developing, but he also was beginning to have ideas of how the situation might be addressed. Moore was sure that experience, and skilful ball play were great assets in defensive strategy, but more than that, Bobby saw that *O Verde-e o Amarela*[73] echoed Malcolm Allison's vision: they were never afraid to play themselves out of the tightest of defensive situations; they used their ability, their brains, but also a conviction and attitude to approach the game in a creative and adventurous way.

Throughout the Chile World Cup the fear of failure had been the dominant factor in some poor performances, particularly in the group games. What promised to be 'a feast of football' in the end disappointed. The FA advertising the event as 'a World Cup to remember' looked more than a tad thin given some of the dreadful contests and the very fractious confrontations between European and South American sides. The sudden loss of some key England players put a dampener on the hype that abounded before the tournament started, while Winterbottom's preparations for the competition were much criticised, along with what was seen as an over-reliance on Haynes. However, there was a new dawn coming for England; the crop of young players, like Bobby Moore, Bobby Charlton and Jimmy Greaves might with hindsight be understood as the real fruit of 1962.

Having been involved in the measured, unfolding tapestry of Brazilian brilliance, Moore could not help but dwell on the committed albeit comparatively stilted performance of his own side. It cut him deeply that England were dismissed with so light a touch by players mostly from a background of poverty and yet whose maturity and stylishness exceeded anything Winterbottom's team had to offer. Moore recognised England were not good enough, but understood his nation would never simply emulate Brazil. The strength coming out of that is Brazil could never be England, so England had to do better at ***their*** game, and not take a message home that England should try to 'do a Brazil'. What England could do was be more 'economic' and 'efficient'. Once Bobby had said that while football is reliant on each team member's level of skill, the difficulty is to get a team working effectively as a unit, which conserves energy and combines skill. Players need to think and know what each other are thinking.

The Brazilians' confidence in their individual talent, and the collective skill of the team, was far in advance of what England or most other European countries might have been able to summon. In the grim hours and days that followed

---

73   'The Green and Yellow', one of the nicknames for the Brazilian team.

England's exit, Moore understood that his mentor Allison was right; if football was to rise again from the land of its birth to claim to be a world power in the game, it had to change, change dramatically, and look to become all that it might be – not merely follow an example, but to be the example.

After the elimination of his team Winterbottom fouled FA rules, allowing one or two of the side to meet the press. Armfield talked of England's exit as the most disappointing moment of his career. He had believed that if he and his team-mates could have got past Brazil, they would have brought the World Cup back with them across the Atlantic, but as John Lyall once said to me, '"If" is a dream, "have" is reality.'

'If' England had gone to South America with the team events and history robbed them of, like Jimmy Greaves, I believe they would have won the World Cup in 1962. That side would have been better than the team that won at Wembley four years later. That said, we may never have seen Bobby Moore capped had events played out more kindly for England prior to Chile.

I also believe there could have been an English European Cup-winning team in 1958, but those possibilities crashed with Manchester United's ill-fated aircraft in Munich four years before England landed in South America in 1962. United and the world had been robbed of some outstanding players, three of whom were critical to the future of the English national team: Duncan Edwards, Roger Byrne, and Tommy Taylor. Replacements Maurice Norman, Gerry Hitchens/Alan Peacock and Bobby Moore did well enough, but they stepped into key positions in an established side, while gaining their first international caps in a World Cup – hardly the preparation one might see as ideal – 'if' survived Munich.

England were a patched-up side before the loss of Bobby Robson, who had for some time combined so well with Haynes in midfield. The impact of Robson's injury was exacerbated by absence of Peter Swan, a rock-like presence at the heart of defence, who had a seemingly telepathic connection with Ron Springett. The void he left undoubtedly undermined the spine of the team. Bobby Smith was also missed, particularly his productive partnership with Greaves. The Tottenham striker failed to replicate anything like the understanding he had with the North Riding Rampager alongside Hitchens or Peacock. All in all, more than half of England's 'ideal' team coming out of the 1950s was missing in 1962 and that had the knock-on effect of degrading the other half of the side.

Greaves and Gerry Hitchens playing in Italy for the majority of the 1961/62 season had been a further source of disruption. Hitchens was unable to match the kind of quality Smith had offered, while Greaves and Haynes failed to live up to their potential in Chile.

The training camp at Coya had been a source of the comparatively low morale for most of the squad, particularly perhaps those who didn't play in the tournament. This 'mood' phenomenon was something Moore was to learn from, and the extent it can impact on any team. Reading about the feelings of the players left me wondering if it somehow became a place of mourning for what might have been – a place haunted by 'if'.

Jimmy Adamson was shocked at the level of homesickness some of the players felt. The Burnley skipper was to recognise that more attention had to be given to the overall mental disposition of future squads. He later remarked that such feelings were unavoidable sometimes but said, 'Everyone has to feel that they have a part to play,' because the non-inclusion can cause melancholy to get out of control as 'a symptom of other problems'. The latter conclusion is critical; Coya masked the deeper issues that plagued the team, the camp became a powerful projection of a more profound and foundational disgruntlement.

In the final Brazil defeated the good Czechoslovakia side. Few ever had any serious doubts where the trophy was going as soon as Brazil had crushed Chile following the win over England. Bobby was to say that he knew Brazil would go on to win the tournament, 'Stuck four past Chile in the semis and three more past Czechoslovakia in the final, always having plenty in hand to turn on the magic when they went for the kill in the second half.'

While Brazil were in a class of their own as a team, Garrincha proved to be more wizard than winger. He would be remembered as the star of the tournament. Chile's 2-1 quarter-final victory over the Soviet Union was probably the most theatrical game of the 1962 World Cup, discharging extraordinary patriotic passions, but England's meeting with Brazil produced some of the finest football of the tournament, helping to ameliorate the eventual profile of the competition as an often violent and negative example of the worst of what the game can be. Brazil and England had together provided a fast, open, attacking game, the sort of match one would reasonably hope that the World Cup might produce.

In defeat England rose to the occasion, but were so clearly surpassed by the side that brought the best out in them. Bobby said later that he would have applauded some of their moves if he hadn't been preoccupied trying to hold back the yellow and green tide.

England returned home without disgrace, although not with a great deal of pride. The big advantage they gained was knowing that they had a long way to go before they could compete with the best teams in the world. Winterbottom came away from Chile doubting if England could ever win a World Cup. Later reflecting on England's exit from the tournament he stated that Garrincha's free kick had emphasised their naivety. His players had been standing around instead of creating some movement in an attempt to confuse their opponents when Brazil altered the position of the ball so that Garrincha could get a clearer sight of goal. I'm not convinced the South Americans would have been confused by such a simple ruse, and I doubt Walter really believed that they might. He resignedly mused that this lack of movement was 'the way we've been brought up, but not the way to win World Cup matches'. That statement was however sublimely naive.

The success of the world champions emerged out of them being all they could be as a team, making a committed and combined effort. England's failure was a failure of morale, application, and method much more than a failure of ability, although the sum of difference in terms of raw talent was a factor. This said, there was no one thing that caused their loss; Brazil's victory was the result of one team, globally, playing to its cultural strengths and their opponents failing to do that. For instance, Greaves could not do what Garrincha did, but for all the talent of the little bloke from Pau Grande he couldn't do what Greaves was capable of; I saw Jimmy play many, many times and he was a truly wonderful striker in and around the box. Jimmy never found his true capabilities in Chile, Garrincha did. Multiply that by the performance of the likes of Haynes and you get the result that happened.

In short there are reasons for these situations; not understanding those reasons, they couldn't be addressed, and so England didn't do the potential of English football justice. That's a Malcolm Allison-style analysis and you can't expect anything else from me because I was brought up in the light of his work.

It's usually a mistake in any facet of life to look to replicate someone else's personality or behaviour, to try and be someone or something else (look at Boris Johnson trying to ape Winston Churchill for instance). That's true of individuals, organisations, and teams. Leicester City, in their Premier League-winning season, never tried to 'do a Liverpool' or pretend to be Manchester City. Likewise, England's success four years on from Chile was not premised on becoming 'more like Brazil'. Geoff Hurst or Martin Peters had little in common as a pair with Pelé and Garrincha.

It might surprise some, that in his early 20s, Bobby openly admitted that he had 'reservations about Pelé'. He came to this conclusion after watching a match between Brazil and Argentina. Moore told how he had discerned Argentina's game plan early on, detailing a single defender to closely shadow Pelé and stifle him. It wasn't long before this attention clearly annoyed Pelé, an emotion that built up as the game proceeded until, ultimately, the watchman left the field with what looked like a broken nose.

Apparently, Pelé eventually apologised to the injured party for his part in the wound, but Moore's instinct was that however one might measure a player's 'greatness', the ability that individual has to control their temper must be part of the assessment. Moore related how the likes of Stanley Matthews and Tom Finney coped with defenders who were often fanatically frantic to just stop them by any means necessary. He couldn't think of one occasion where either of these immortals had retaliated or got webbed up with 'incidents'.

All that said, Moore rated Pelé high enough that he and Tina were to name their Siamese cat after him – another one with a bit of a temper.

All endings are beginnings

Johnny Haynes remembered the Chile World Cup in a single word – 'crap'. But he was probably finding international football not as fulfilling as it once might have been for him. In a way he was likely responding to the way Brazil set themselves up after 1958, the 4-2-4 formation, which not unusually morphed to 4-3-3 by way of outside-left Mário Zagallo's industry. Flat defences had become *de rigueur*, which made life harder for Johnny and his ilk to switch play and make openings with lengthy through balls.

In the end, most of the England players shared their skipper's feeling of 'never been more glad to get out of a place'. The mood of the camp had failed to rise above moderate for any length of time and at points it was rock bottom. Jimmy Greaves, remembering Chile, was to say, with his tongue not so firmly in his cheek, 'When Brazil knocked us out, when Garrincha scored the third goal, we all ran over and congratulated him, or thanked him. It meant we could go home.'

The 1990 World Cup probably qualifies for the worst ever, but the 1962 tournament, carrying the blemishes of violent cynicism, might be best forgotten. All playing centres – Santiago, Arica, Viña del Mar, and Rancagua – generated ill-tempered, poor behaviour and the predictable serious injuries that were a consequence of the same. Before the first week of the tournament had been played, in excess of 40 casualties were reported. Soviet Union full-back Eduard Dubinski, Colombia captain Francisco Zuluaga, and Switzerland's inside-left Norbert Eschmann were all hospitalised with broken legs. The campaign had been over almost from the get-go for the two Bulgarians attacked by the Argentinians. Over the course of the tournament more than 50 players were hospitalised. Four players had been dismissed from the field; two of them, Italy's Mario David and Giorgio Ferrini, were disciplined by the match referee Ilford schoolmaster Ken Aston. A headline in the Santiago newspaper *Claron* bugled 'World War'.

Called to appear in front of the World Cup Organising Committee, the 16 participating managers were cautioned that continued unsporting play might mean teams being expelled from the tournament. Haynes was to complain that England weren't guilty in any respect and that he had 'never known anything like it'.

However, the World Cup in Chile was important for England as it marked the emergence of Bobby Moore into what was to be his natural habitat, the international arena. Steps taken as an all-purpose wing-half, not as the uncannily perceptive central defender he would soon become, were a big plus for England's future . This and other lessons learned in South America would project Bobby, West Ham, and England into the still young decade; this learning might be thought of as the ground out of which the Hammers FA Cup victory, their success in Europe and England's triumph of 1966 grew out of.

Somewhat surprisingly to modern perspectives some of the northern-based players flew to Manchester, via New York, where they stayed a night at the Waldorf Astoria (just as well the *Daily Mail* didn't get wind of that) on a different flight, while the players with southern clubs flew back to London from Santiago, via Lima and Miami, on the official flight. When Moore got back to London, he pre-empted the now-famed statement made by Alf Ramsey, 'I am convinced England, with home advantage, can win the World Cup in 1966.'

Justifying Bobby

Jimmy Adamson let Ron Greenwood know how committed Bobby had been, but also highlighted the few flaws he had noticed in his game. The former miner said that Bobby was a 'bad passer', inclined to be erratic under pressure. Greenwood knew his player well enough to be confident that when this assessment was passed on to Moore he would attend to it, but at the same time he also understood that the rising star was not the finished article.

Of course, much, much more was to follow. Moore had a 16-year international career, starting with his first England youth appearance in October 1957 and concluding with his inclusion in the team that faced Italy in November 1973. His 18 youth and under-23 outings and 108 full England caps broke records in their time. If things had worked out differently Moore may well have achieved a record number of under-23 appearances. At the time he was called into the World Cup squad the record was held by Maurice Setters; the tough West Bromwich Albion man appeared 16 times for the under-23s between 1958 and 1960. It's probable however that the record would have been scant compensation for Moore being overlooked in 1962.

It was Ken Jones, a top sporting journalist with *Daily Mirror* and Moore's future biographer and self-proclaimed 'friend' (by the time of that publication anyway) post Chile referred to Bobby as, 'Uncapped, pedestrian, not up to much in the air, suspect stamina', and asked 'How could England select the 21-year-old Moore for the 1962 World Cup finals?' But Moore's five caps from the South American experience, for Bobby and significant others, demonstrated that he was ready for the international stage.

Bobby Robson told how he had watched 'a studious player, not a vigorous one'. He noted that Moore didn't look to hunt down opponents and 'bury them with a tackle' but 'waited for people to come on to him' and at that point managed the danger. 'Managed' was an insightful assessment, it essentially being the ability to translate logic into action. Most tellingly, Robson felt, '[Bobby] didn't like the idea of people getting in behind him and reasoned that, if he chased strikers around the field, he would leave space for others to run into. Bobby worked out that the hole in front of you is less dangerous than the hole behind you.'

Robson also noted, '[Moore] knew when to press, when to drop off, and had a good, early pass, which he didn't spoil with over-elaboration. If the pass wasn't on, he could "cuddle" the ball and run five yards with it before playing it to someone else.'

Robson's analysis seems far more insightful than Adamson's, and you would be fair to wonder why that might be. The England manager between 1982 and 1990 saw things in the young Moore that were new to him. Maybe he also perceived something of the future in the Barking boy, but like Greenwood, he was convinced Moore needed to operate *out of* defence and not *in* midfield.

Many years on, Robson admitted that immediately post-Chile he hadn't suspected Bobby might become the giant of the game he would grow to be. He did see Moore's application and assiduousness, and recognised him as a 'nice, earnest young man' who was 'very respectful, very polite and trained well. He was the guy you wanted your daughter or sister to marry.' But by the time Moore returned from Chile he already had a bride waiting for him.

However, in his 2005 autobiography *Farewell but not Goodbye*, Robson wrote of Moore, 'He was always going to be a left-half because he didn't quite have the ability to play midfield. His qualities were anticipation, reading the game, judgement and a firm, clean tackle. He could breast the ball down rather than head it into nowhere – which you see a lot of centre-halves do. He was a thoughtful player, even at 19, and polished all those little skills while learning to concentrate hard on the specific disciplines of defending – hence his exceptionally low error ratio. The one he made against Poland in 1973 in World Cup qualifying stands out precisely because he made so few. Bobby Moore made fewer mistakes than any defender I've seen in my life.'

If Winterbottom had been less far-sighted, if he hadn't effectively taken a gamble on Bobby, if Moore had never experienced the rite of passage of a World Cup, including the education of dealing with the Hungarians and tasting the awesome power of the Brazilians, he would have returned to East London from West Ham's tour of southern Africa much the same has he left. The Hammers would have been less for that, lacking the wisdom of epiphany that he gained in Chile. The Irons' march to Wembley in 1964 and their conquest of Europe a year later would have been less likely, and without that 21-year-old, tutored under South American skies, come the 1966 World Cup it's unlikely that the Bobby Moore the tournament saw would have been as rounded or as ready as he was. That being the case, England would have been a lesser force for that.

Winterbottom's retreat

England's manager was probably the individual most distraught by the showing in Chile. Walter had known that the defeat by Brazil was the end of his last chance of leading England to World Cup victory. While there were no mass calls for his dismissal (that wasn't how things were done then) he understood he had taken the team as far as he could and thus a fresh approach was needed. It was common knowledge that Walter had for some time seen Jimmy Adamson as his preferred choice to eventually take his place. The Burnley man had the backing of Bobby Charlton, who was impressed by and valued Adamson's plain, common-sense attitude, and advice. For instance, Jim had once told his fellow Ashingdonian 'What you can never forget, and if you do, you let down both yourself and your team, is that generally speaking, if you are an influential player and you play badly, if you don't give it all you have, everybody else will follow suit and play badly.' Charlton was to base his attitude to his game on that advice.

As such, Charlton was in no doubt that Adamson would have been an excellent choice to take over. He would comment, taking a not-too-subtle dig at Winterbottom between the lines, 'He would surely have brought valuable insights and strength to the challenge presented by the departure of Walter Winterbottom. Unlike Walter, and this for the record is something that does not have to be couched in diplomatic terms, he would have been quite specific about his requirements of individual players and his requests would have been made in the specific language of professionals.'

Charlton's remarks were, of course, made with the benefit of hindsight. At the same time, while Adamson was not Winterbottom, he hardly represented a 'new broom'. From Charlton's quote (above) alone it's obvious that Jimmy was 'old school'.

It feels strange when I read books by seasoned football writers that no one then had any inkling Walter was going to submit his resignation two months after the 1962 World Cup – remarking, in one way or another, that his departure was a shock to the football world. In actuality, well before the 1962 tournament, Winterbottom had announced his intention to resign. His hope was to succeed Sir Stanley Rous as FIFA secretary, but this never happened. He failed to win enough of the votes of the ruling elite of the game. It was something of a surprise though that Adamson turned down the offer of replacing Winterbottom, leaving the door open for Alf Ramsey to take the reins.

18

TRANSITION

A couple of weeks after Bobby Moore got back from the World Cup in Chile, on 30 June 1962, he and Tina Dean got married at St Clement's Church in Ilford (the CofE place to be in IG3!). The bride wore an Alexandrine tiara[74], while the groom looked sharp in a dark blue mohair whistle and white dickie. By the mid-1960s the players in Bobby's social circle were getting their shirts tailor-made, and cleaned by a specialist Chinese laundry, run by a bloke known as 'Hong Kong Harry', who first saw light of day in Silver Town, E16, had never been further east than Southend, and swore like 'ow's yer father'.

The year was a big one for Bobby and Tina. Bobby turned 21 in April, made his England debut in May, and got married in June.

When Tina got to the church, having factored in the obligatory slight and symbolic unpunctuality, she was astonished at and excited by the size of the throng of well-wishers.

Perhaps predictably, the press were outside the church in force, denoting Moore's rising fame. The photo opportunity of the day was the couple posed under an archway of football boots held aloft by Moore's fellow Hammers. Apparently, they were supposed to be arranged left/right either side of the happy couple, but without Bobby to organise, and the libations flowing liberally prior to the nuptials, that good intention got lost in interpretation.

By that time Tina was friends with most of the players. In later years she was also something of a mother figure to some the younger ones. They would talk to her for ages in Moore's sports shop, opposite the Boleyn pub, at the Barking Road end of Green Street, which in due course she ran for Bobby. Sometimes he would invite her to join him and some of the players for a drink after training or a reserve game. They enjoyed her company and considered her to be one of them – she was practically an honorary lad.

On exiting the passageway of boots, the crowd regaled the pair with England and West Ham banners, scarves as well as the usual blue (and some claret and blue) garters and black cats (not actually 'real' black cats – that would have been macabre).

---

74   One of the perks of being a royal princess is that you often receive your very first tiara on your 18th birthday. Some of them are modest and delicate, others historic family pieces. On her 18th birthday, Margrethe II of Denmark's parents gave her a diamond drop tiara, which originally belonged to her grandmother, Queen Alexandrine. The name stuck from then on.

The reception was held at the Valentine pub, Gants Hill, an old mock Tudor gaff built in the 1930s. In recent years there has been an ongoing battle to save the place from demolition.

The couple romantically opened the dancing with 'Blue Moon', the song they had danced to on their first meeting, just before Tina's 16th birthday. Less romantic was her overhearing Malcolm Allison telling Bobby he'd booked the Astor Club[75] for later that evening. Her heart sank; how could Bobby go out on the piss on their wedding night. It turned out that Big Mal was kidding, or was he?

The social side of proceedings done, the newlyweds headed off for their honeymoon in Majorca. They were chauffeured to the airport by Johnny Byrne, one of the hard-partying and drinking crew that made up Bobby's carousing entourage. It was a hair-raising journey, in the days before seat-belts and breathalysers. Bobby and Tina were slung around in the back seat as Budgie 'floored it' the entire trip from West Essex to Heathrow.

On surviving Byrne's driving, the somewhat shell-shocked couple tottered into the Skyline Hotel to rest up before the following day's flight.

Having got to Spain the newlyweds picked up some company. Contrary to tradition, best man Noel Cantwell, together with Malcolm Allison and their respective other halves, rocked up during the couple's first week of marriage. West Ham striker Alan Sealey and his partner Janis (one-time Dagenham Carnival Queen, who would become Alan's first wife) also turned up, as did Denis Law and his wife-to-be Diana, they were married in December 1962.

Malcolm had become something of a Falstaff to Bob's Prince Hal for some time, leading a posse of revellers around the West End night spots, energetically imbibing the golden liquids (lager and champagne), although it was quite the surprise that he was in tow to Spain.

Predictably the fountains of booze gushed. However, when it was clearly high time for the new Mr and Mrs Moore to make tracks to their designated love nest, Bobby wasn't too keen to end the party and ultimately a bull'n cow

---

75   The Astor Club was a nightclub which operated in Mayfair, London from the 1930s to the late 1970s. The haunt of royals and car dealers, gangsters and landed aristocrats, it was a fixture in London nightlife. The peak and most notorious years of the Astor were between 1950 and 1970. It was one of the most prestigious of several 'hostess clubs' which flourished from the end of the Second World War in 1945 and the opening of the 1960s and 1970s discothèques. Such watering holes had almost all disappeared by the 1980s, when discos and nightclubs culturally merged, a situation which led up to the present-day London night-time economy. The Astor flourished even during the dangerous times London experienced during the Second World War, including the Blitz of 1940–1941 and the V-1 and V-2 rocket attacks of 1944–1945. The venue was owned by Bertie Green, a businessman and manager of show business performers. Green was variously described 'a greedy bastard' and 'a no-good greedy bastard'. He had a reputation for villainy, in particular signing artists/entertainers with the sole intention of doing nothing and then suing them. In his favour he was a big Hammers supporter.

betwixt the nuptial pair ensured, culminating with Bobby upchucking in their apartment and Tina crying in the arms of Maggie Cantwell.

It was during the wedding reception that Noel Cantwell had advised Tina that she might need to acclimatise to being a 'football widow', as it was clear to him that Moore was going to become much more in demand, and so would be obliged to give the majority of his time to the game. Noel went on to predict that Bobby would be England's captain. That prophecy having been fulfilled the friends would ultimately meet as rival skippers when Noel led out Ireland. On that day, Sunday, 24 May 1964, at Dalymount Park, Dublin, Cantwell quipped, 'Bobby was best man.' England won 3-1 with Iron of Irish heritage Johnny Byrne, scoring in the 22nd minute.

Cantwell's forecast about the growing demand football would make on Bobby was seen to be accurate a bit sooner when Bobby was chosen for the England side to play on Wednesday, 3 October 1962 at Hillsborough in the first leg of a UEFA European Nations' Cup – as the current European Championship was known then – preliminary qualifying round tie.

It was after the World Cup in Chile that Bobby started on the road to celebrity. By the end of 1962, Alf Ramsey had made it clear that he saw Bobby as central to the future on the England team. Tina had to wrestle with her feelings about Bobby's increasing fame; she was thrilled for him, but trepidatious about how it seemed everybody wanted a piece of him. Before they got married, they had been as close as one might expect an ordinary courting couple to be. The sudden change, epitomised by the hordes of press at their wedding, as well as a great crowd of people, many of whom she understood to be well-wishers, but there was also a phalanx of the curious and plain nosey. While that was mostly a positive experience for her, the imposition of the public gaze was also more than a bit of a surprise.

Tina had become accustomed to having Bobby to herself most of the time and, somewhere in her heart and head, that was how she hoped it would continue. She quickly grasped that wasn't going to be the case, and she was going to be obliged to share her husband with the world, including the sycophants and parasites, who weren't slow to attach themselves to Moore. When the couple were repeatedly accosted while shopping or interrupted while out having a hoped-for quiet meal, Tina was sometimes quite taken aback.

The new Mrs Moore was not at all practiced at household chores, and she never pretended she was able or fond of the everyday routine that might have been expected of a wife in the early 1960s. So it was never going to be totally straightforward for her being married to someone who was meticulous about tidiness, cleanliness and ordered home life. She was a working young woman, not a domestic goddess. Ironing for example was not something she was at all adept at; certainly she did not have Bobby's mother Doris's devotion to the art. Hong Kong Harry took some of the strain, but Bobby liked his smart creases in everything from jeans to shorts and bootlaces.

After Bobby and Tina had been married for a few months, Tina resolved the ironing issue. Sometimes she would visit West Ham to help out in Bobby's sports goods shop. Her mother Betty had given up her job as manageress of a large clothes shop to run it for him. One day Tina took a wander up the road where she discovered a dry cleaner who was made up to be responsible for Bobby Moore's bootlaces, shorts and sock ties. That was the end of her ironing angst. She just took everything there from then on, but never let on to Doris, because for her not doing the ironing would have been a type of domestic blasphemy.

Bobby would not have thought badly about Tina's disposition regarding not taking on the chores of the 'traditional' housewife. In many ways he wasn't like most men of his age, area, era, and class background. He had a deep-set respect for women, likely connected to being, like myself, the child of a female-dominated family and environment. Doris was a matriarch not too far from my grandmother's stripe, similarly Elenore 'Nelly' Belton was protective of her family, but Doris was certainly more benign. This was the foundation of the partnership she had with Bobby's father. That might be said to have been not altogether usual in the district and social situation Bobby grew up in, but I know that it was by no means rare. East London, and perhaps all relatively deprived areas, certainly in wartime conditions, when for the most part, the male population was otherwise engaged, women took on responsibilities and roles that obliged domestic leadership and taking control. Indeed, in Bobby's football world, it was in the war years that the seeds were sown for the burgeoning sport the women's game is today.

It wasn't only the housework which got Tina down. In the first year of marriage, Bobby's England career began to take off big time. That, plus his West Ham commitments, meant he was often away. Bobby and Tina had experienced a very full social life; they were no strangers to the most fashionable West End venues, such as 'The Talk of the Town' and 'London Palladium', seeing all the top acts of the time, the likes Matt Monro, Shirley Bassey and Ella Fitzgerald. The most stylish professional footballers buzzed around in exhilarating circles and in the most exclusive places. This was healthy fun for the young couple at the most exciting stage of their lives.

Johnny Haynes, the first player to be paid £100 a week, introduced Tina to the then fashionable 21 Club, where he was a regular. Bobby had frequented the place with Malcolm Allison. This was really the start of footballers being part of the celebrity culture of London as the 1960s began to swing. There has been no time like it since, or before, when people from 'ordinary' backgrounds, mostly the younger generation, 'war babies', for the first time could, en masse, partake in the highlife previously reserved for those seen as their betters. Music had never been, and would never be, better, as the black and white 1950s gave way to a technicolour age.

Stan Flashman made his fortune as a big-time ticket tout[76]. For some reason he seemed to escape the attentions on the law, as his obese figure became familiar to the general public. He supplied Bobby with almost any ticket he might have wanted, as well as backstage passes to all the top shows. Fat man Stan was also to introduce Bobby and Tina to a range of celebrities, who in turn invited them to every description of party and function. At first this was thrilling and interesting for the couple, but things snowballed, people introduced them to other people, who presented them to yet more people.

Ultimately, the 'faces' of London's nightlife recognised that Bobby was becoming something of a 'show pony' and a lucrative photo opportunity. It was a raw feeling, being used in such a way, but Moore didn't like to think he might disappoint anyone, so he was always polite. However, he had a noticeable way of camouflaging himself with civility. Tina had a strong affection for those, including the club's supporters, who genuinely appreciated Bobby, but disliked him being used, taken advantage of, or exploited by people who only had their own interests in mind. She was strongly protective of her new husband and when things got a bit much, he would look at her in a particular way, at which point she'd dart to his side and vocally remind him they had some other pressing commitment that would demand they leave immediately.

Tina was bright and lively, with a classy taste in fashion. She and Bobby shared a liking for fun. He had at first been drawn to her attractive blonde good looks, but it was her vibrant personality that cemented the deal for him. Effervescent and sociable, and able to hold an intelligent conversation, Jimmy Armfield once had it that, 'Tina wasn't quite a WAG but she may have been the prototype.'

The world got a bit more serious after Tina and Bobby were married. As is the way with many newlyweds, it was a big change of life for the pair, so understandably it took Tina some time to adjust. Bobby had wanted her to give up work, given he trained in the mornings only and came home for lunch. She was an able, assertive, intelligent, and strong young woman, but she began to feel a bit isolated, missing the company and stimulation of working life. At the same time she had become accustomed on the one hand to the fun and a full social calendar that being with

---

76   Flashman, between 1985 and 1995, was the owner Barnet FC. He is best known for employing Barry Fry as manager and sacking and re-instating him on a regular basis.

Bobby entailed, but on the other hand she missed the warmth and security of Christchurch Road, surrounded by family.

A while before Bobby and Tina married, her aunt and her family had moved to Barkingside, so she would drive to their place in her Hillman Minx, which Bobby had bought for her for £100, with Pelé in his cat basket beside her. Gradually things got better and Tina found a routine. From this position of security she became the rock in Bobby's life on which he was able to face an ever more challenging world.

Cap 6

England 1 France 1
Wednesday, 3 October 1962
European Nations' Cup preliminary qualifying round first leg
Hillsborough
Attendance: 35,380
Referee: Frede Hansen (Denmark)

England: Springett, Armfield, Wilson, Moore, Norman, Flowers, Hellawell, Crowe, Charnley, Greaves, Hinton.
France: Bernard, Wendling, Lerond, Chorda, Synakowski, Ferrier, Robuschi, Bonnel, Kopa, Goujon, Sauvage.

This match was Bobby's first senior England appearance on home turf. It was a disappointment, not least for 35,380 paying customers. Johnny Haynes was recovering from injuries, received in a car crash, which would ultimately end his international career, while Bobby Charlton was recuperating from a hernia operation.

Mike Hellawell, Chris Crowe, Ray Charnley, and talented winger Alan Hinton were drafted into a forward line that while ranking as boldly experimental, failed in terms of anything like looking potentially effective. Ron Springett broke Harry Hibbs's record of being his country's most capped goalkeeper, an honour that Harry had held since 1935.

Yvon Goujon had put the visitors ahead after just eight minutes, but a dozen minutes into the second half Ron Flowers scored the penalty that would spare England's blushes.

The French manager Henri Guérin, who was still in charge during the 1966 World Cup, applied a 4-3-3 formation. His men, in their blue crew-necked jerseys, white shorts and red socks, were captained by the cunning old hand Raymond Kopa, had a good game but the same could not be said of the home side. Each time Maurice Norman touched the ball he was booed, perhaps predictably, as he was playing on the home ground of the man he replaced, Sheffield Wednesday's centre-half Peter Swan.

England, running out in their 1959 Bukta kit of white v-necked short-sleeved continental jerseys, blue shorts, white socks with red, white and blue tops, lacked the effective timing and understanding between the ranks that would have allowed them to make headway against what was an able French team.

However, Bobby felt that he was coming into the England side at the end of an era. He liked Winterbottom and remembered Walter as a 'warm, outgoing man who loved talking about techniques, tactics, skills, attitudes … he knew every good player in every country by his Christian name, knew every individual's strength and weakness. The man was a walking education on football.' Personality wise, and in terms of background, Walter was very different to his successor, but the two men had a similar attitude to, enthusiasm for and knowledge of football.

By that time Winterbottom had come to be regarded as a symbol of a bygone, amateur world by many, but also something of a national treasure. Although, he had done much to overcome the archaic system he worked in, and had formed the nucleus of the team that would be victorious in 1966, with players such as Charlton, Wilson, Greaves and, centrally, Bobby Moore.

Part of the outgoing England manager would always be locked in the theoretical – it was part of him and his passion for the game. He was 'donnish' in the best sense, kind and never given to heavy-handed treatment of players. He put on no shows of bombast or ego, but it was clear that the days of the teacher would have to give way to those of the 'pro'.

No place like home

Bobby and Tina started their married life in a three-bedroomed terraced house in Glenwood Gardens, Gants Hill, maybe a 15-minute walk from Ilford High Road, and just under five miles as the cockney crow flies, coughing over the A13, from where Bobby had first kicked a football in Barking.

The Moores' first marital home cost them £3,650 (equivalent to about £100,000 at the time of writing) which today might not get you a decent-sized tent. They had wanted a slightly superior place in the same vicinity, but couldn't make the extra £600.

Not long after they moved in Brylcreem paid Bobby £450 for appearing on an advertising poster, so it was a pity that the cash hadn't come along a bit earlier. However, unlike the football's former 'Brylcreem Boy' Johnny Haynes, Bobby's barnet wasn't really flattered by the 'slicked down' treatment; his naturally wavy locks looked more hemmed in than appropriately coiffured. So that gig was short-lived. Tina and Bobby, along with Martin and Kathleen Peters, for a while appeared in a television campaign for local pubs. Viewing it on YouTube recently the drum where it was filmed looks a right ropey old dive, the likes of which I very much doubt Bobby might ever have chosen to spend any time in, let alone with his classy Mrs. Peters wasn't exactly Albert Tatlock either.

In his early 20s Moore was living in a far superior area and house than the home on the edge of an industrial estate where he had been brought up, and where his parents continued to reside. Tina too had moved up in the world from the flat with an outside toilet in Christchurch Road, Ilford, although by today's standards, in respect of the typical domicile you might find a first-class professional footballer abiding in, a gaff in Gants Hill might be close to humble. However, the Glenwood Road place had French doors at the back that opened on to an attractive garden where the couple planted a magnolia tree. The lounge was of the period, a green carpet festooned with a pattern of pink roses. There was plate rail going round the walls where they placed Bobby's memorabilia.

The household included the feline Pelé, who seemed to double up as an attack dog. He was a somewhat evil looking Siamese cat of dubious mood and cynical intent, who would become infamous for serially assaulting Hammers defender John Bond (Pelé wasn't the first or last to do that, however). John and Janet Bond often went out with Bobby and Tina. John hated even the best of cats, but one night, while the Bonds were waiting for Bobby to get himself ready, which often took a lot longer than Tina, Pelé jumped on John's lap. The cat must have sensed the dislike the man known as 'Muffin' – for his ability to kick like a mule – held for his kind as he decided to inflict a nasty tear in John's best suit trousers. I was to remind John of this incident and he remarked pointedly 'I've never hurt an animal in my life, but given half a chance I'd have kicked that bastard right over the roof!' The power of Bond's boot might well have seen Pelé become the first feline in orbit.

Bobby was always a very generous and thoughtful person. When the pair returned to Gants Hill from a vacation in France, he gave Tina a pink suit, navy blue blouse with pussycat bow and a Paco Rabanne chain mail bag. All very much in vogue at that time and romantically Parisian.

Back to work

The 1962/63 season started badly for the Hammers. The first two home games were lost with ten goals conceded; Wolves left East London as 4-1 winners, while Spurs, with the contribution of an own goal by John Lyall, returned to White Hart Lane on the back of 6-1 triumph.

John Dick was transferred to Brentford. His goals were to help the Bees to win the Fourth Division championship that season.

Things brightened in September with a 6-1 win at Maine Road and a 6-0 League Cup victory over Second Division Plymouth Argyle, getting some vengeance for FA Cup humiliation of the previous season. But it was back to earth with a bump in the next round when Rotherham, who would go on to finish two places below Plymouth in the bottom half of the table, turfed their visitors out with a convincing 3-1 result.

The tough and talented England international winger Peter Brabrook joined West Ham from Chelsea in October, making his debut in a 1-1 draw against Burnley. Costing the club £35,000, a hefty fee at that time, he had grown up in the immediate area around Upton Park, and was one of the many gifted young players, the likes of Jimmy Greaves and Terry Venables, who as boys had fallen through the Hammers' much-vaunted scouting net. He was watched many times by Wally St Pier[77], but despite being picked for East Ham, Essex, and London schoolboys, was openly rejected by the man code named 'Southend' by his fellow scouts. Chelsea scout Jimmy Thompson was quickly to take advantage of St Pier's error.

The list of overlooked and rejected young players on St Pier's watch seems to grow the longer I delve into the history of East London football, to the extent I find myself wondering if Upton Park's 'youth radar', headed up by the sainted Wally, was ever as effective as mythology of the club has it. It seems as many were bypassed or totally missed as were brought into the Upton Park fold.

When Brabrook got to the club, by then with youth, under-23, and full international caps to his credit, as well as the distinction of having been called into the England's 1958 World Cup squad, Tony Scott reverted to outside-left. This led later to Malcolm Musgrove moving to Leyton Orient.

Cap 7

Northern Ireland 1 England 3
Saturday, 20 October 1962
British Home Championship
Windsor Park
Attendance: 55,000
Referee: James Barclay

Ireland: Irvine, Magill, Elder, Blanchflower, Neill, Nicholson, Humphries, Barr, McMillan, McIlroy, Bingham.

---

77   St Pier, as a boy, attended the same school in Dagenham as Alf Ramsey, although some 16 years before Alf got there.

England: Springett, Armfield, Wilson, Moore, Labone, Flowers, Hellawell, Hill, Peacock, Greaves, O'Grady.

As winter drew in, Moore continued to establish his place in the England side and in a well-attended and exciting game in Belfast, against a side with some impressive names in its ranks, Jimmy Greaves opened the scoring, typically pouncing on a rebound.

In the second half the home side drew level as Hugh Barr and Armfield went for the same ball. There was some argument that the England skipper got the final touch, thus being guilty of an own goal. However, Mick O'Grady, fifth son of Irish parentage, picking up a pass from Greaves (who also had some Irish connections) put the visitors ahead.

The game was put beyond the home side when O'Grady netted his second, making the most of Peacock's deft delivery.

Changes

Among the first players Ron Greenwood brought to Upton Park was goalkeeper Lawrie Leslie, from Airdrieonians for £15,000, he would be voted Hammer of the Year in 1962 following some remarkable performances. In November 1962, after Leslie broke a leg against Bolton, Jim Standen was signed from Luton Town. Phil Woosnam moved to Aston Villa, which opened the way for young Ronnie Boyce to find a place at inside-right.

Cap 8

England 4 Wales 0
Wednesday, 21 October 1962
British Home Championship
Wembley
Attendance: 27,500
Referee: S. Carswell

England: Springett, Armfield, Shaw, Moore, Labone, Flowers, Connelly, Hill, Peacock, Greaves, Tambling.
Wales: Millington, Williams, Sear, Hennessey, Nurse, Lucas, Jones, Allchurch, Leek, Vernon, Medwin.

The end of November saw Walter Winterbottom summon Moore to take up a place in his final team. Winterbottom's successor, Alf Ramsey, watched the home international fixture from the stand. The crowd was the lowest up to that point for a Wembley international, but those who took the trouble to make their way to the twin towers saw the home side claim a comfortable win.

As Ivor Allchurch extended his record for the most appearances for Wales, Bobby Tambling, the prolific Chelsea forward, made his debut in the England strike force. Alan Peacock chalked up a brace, with John Connelly and Greaves chipping in a goal apiece as England beat a record set in 1957, going 11 matches unbeaten at Wembley.

After the game Jimmy Armfield, on the players' behalf, gifted Winterbottom with a set of crystal cut-glass goblets. The subsequent toast was to 'Walter Winterbottom, master manager'. Likely his 19 year, 139-game record of 78 wins, 33 draws and 28 losses[78] would have been bettered if he had been less cramped by amateur selectors. With a win/loss ratio of +50 Winterbottom remains second only to Alf Ramsey, with +52, in terms of individual manager performance (at the time of writing Gareth Southgate's record is currently +36).

At that time Bobby was thinking that English football had developed something of an inferiority complex, seeing overseas players as necessarily superior. Starting with the consciousness of the quality of first Hungary and then Brazil, this was a deep and profound change as English teams became losers, if 'gallant' and 'plucky' ones. Pre-war any player or team from outside the British Isles was taken to be logically inferior.

Moore named the Scottish team's attitude as the consideration that changed his perspective, the Caledonians being recognised as fighting for their country, while the English were seen, comparatively, as having less of a stomach for battle. However, Bobby was adamant, 'Nobody is going to tell me that to be English is to be second-best.'

Ramsey shared this resolve and under him, Bobby saw the team develop the contention that they had as much right to expect victory as anyone else. However, this belief did not arise out of just 'getting a grip' – it came, according to Moore, from the recognition that the game had to be approached more as a scientific endeavour, and less reliant on big bollocks alone. For him, the days of 'getting stuck in' were history. He observed, 'We became very bad losers … Anything but victory was a failure.' For Moore, winning or losing had to be the source of learning and so betterment.

Goals on ice

Back on the domestic front two away fixtures in December supplied an avalanche of goals. At White Hart Lane eight were shared equally (Dave Mackay dragged Spurs level in the final minute) and the following week West Ham won 4-3 at Nottingham Forest, with the help of two goals from Peter Brabrook. This was to

---

78   One game was abandoned – England scored 383 goals under Winterbottom, conceding 196.

be the final match the Hammers would contest for six weeks due to violently cold weather, which brought football to a standstill nationally.

The quest for FA Cup glory eventually got under way. Due to the 'big freeze' most third-round ties in the FA Cup had to wait until February. When the much-postponed home meeting with Fulham finally went ahead under the Upton Park lamps the pitch was blanketed in snow, with the temperature well below freezing. The encounter would never have got started today. As it was the match finished goalless, so 18 days later the replay took place in a snowstorm. The Hammers twice got the orange ball past the Fulham keeper Tony Macedo, Ronnie Boyce and a Johnny Byrne spot-kick (after the former had gone down in the box) doing the damage and the Irons opened the gate to the fourth round with a 2-1 victory.

Swansea and former Hammers keeper Noel Dwyer were next up at Upton Park. Dwyer had the game of his life, but Boyce bagged the only goal of the game on a pitch that was just a notch down from a bog.

Cap 9

France 5 England 2
Wednesday, 27 February 1963
European Nations' Cup preliminary qualifying round second leg (France win 6-3 on aggregate)
Parc des Princes
Attendance: 23,986
Referee: Josef Kandlbinder (West Germany)

France: Bernard, Wendling, Lerond, Rodzik, Synakowski, Herbin, Wisniewksi, Bonnel, Goujon, Douis, Cossou.
England: Springett, Armfield, Henry, Moore, Labone, Flowers, Connelly, Tambling, Smith, Greaves, Charlton.

Moore was in the side for Alf Ramsey's first match as England manager, the second leg of a European Nations' Cup qualifier. Tottenham's Bobby Smith and Ron Henry were also brought into the line-up.

The visitors started promisingly enough, but the match was still young when Moore suspected that he was still playing for a relatively poor team. By half-time England were losing 3-0 and trailing 4-1 on aggregate. Bobby recalled that France 'were still going strong and we were diabolical'.

At half-time the players were both wary and curious about how the new manager might respond. Most were surprised how calm Ramsey appeared. Moore recollected that Alf told his team they 'could still win the game' if they 'went out and started to play a bit and believed we could do it'.

That view looked prophetic briefly when Smith pulled one back, and with just over a quarter of an hour to play Tambling brought the overall score to 4-3. But ultimately it was not to be England's or Ramsey's night. For Moore the team had put on 'an awful performance … No organisation, no nothing'.

Ron Springett had something of a 'mare', taking the blame for three of the French goals. The worst error came after England had pulled the game back to 3-2 on the night. Springett offered no excuses for his below-par performance, although Ramsey recounted how his keeper had been kicked in the ribs when conceding the first goal. The floodlights were also decidedly dodgy. Ron continued to keep goal for England occasionally after Paris, but Gordon Banks, being one of the new faces brought into the side, was in the ascendency.

Henry also had not the best of nights up against the soaring winger Maryan Wisnieski. The talented left-back, making his England debut, would never play for his country again.

Of the starting XI for this game only Moore and Charlton would play a part in the 1966 World Cup Final, although Springett was the second-choice goalkeeper in the squad that summer.

The Paris experience was to confirm the wisdom of Ramsey's insistence about the need to do away with the selection committee. This body had chosen the side for the match against the French (Alf had not at that point officially taken the control he would have the following May). Some of the committee members journeyed to France with the team, including the FA chairman Graham Doggart[79], Chelsea chairman Joe Mears and Joe Richards of Barnsley. As Alf was to tell, he could immediately appreciate how hard it had been for Winterbottom. Ramsey saw the men on the selection panel as 'enthusiasts' but lacking any kind judgement or 'worthwhile opinion' he might value. His meeting with these people confirmed him in his position that he had been 'absolutely right' to demand the same sort of authority he had been given as a club manager with Ipswich Town, the team he had taken over in 1955 as an obscure Third Division outfit to lead them to the First Division championship in 1962. He was to baldly tell Mears, 'The panel has been a dead-hand on the England team and must take responsibility for its failure by standing aside'. The

---

79   Doggart died suddenly in 1963 while chairing the annual meeting of the Football Association at Lancaster Gate, Bayswater. He was 66. Educated at Darlington Grammar School and Bishop's Stortford College, an independent school in the historic market town of the same name in Hertfordshire, he was a scholar at King's College at the University, Cambridge – in terms of background about a million miles from the average footballer.

Chair of Chelsea, the son and nephew of founders of that club, Joseph and Gus Mears respectively, whose son Brian would also a Chair the Pensioners, could do nothing but agree

The team the panel had selected gave Ramsey the worst possible beginning to his England career, but the winter of the 'big freeze' was the coldest since 1740. West Ham, for instance, played just one game throughout January and February. The England team thus came to the match with a distinct lack of practice over the previous couple of months.

Ron Henry, who had been with Ramsey at White Hart Lane in 1954, remembered Alf's pre-match talk. Ramsey told the players, 'If you behave yourself and work hard, you'll get on all right with me.'

Bobby was to tell how many of the England players were cautious of Alf, who was more reserved, quieter, more withdrawn than Winterbottom. He wasn't a shouter or prone to rage like some managers. The team were keen to give him a positive start to his new job, but of course, individually, given the new selection regime, they would have also had future selection in mind.

Alf didn't attempt to broach tactics that night, simply telling his side, 'Go on, you know what you have to do.' Although it was unclear that they did. It was a terrible evening; the pitch, blanketed in snow, was like a slice of artic tundra. During the first few minutes Springett appeared literally frozen stiff.

After the game the players were obliged to sit on the edge of the big square bath in the dressing room and dangle their feet in the hot water as their boot laces had frozen solid. Everything about the stadium was sub-standard – the dressing rooms were cramped and the place was grubby.

Ramsey didn't have much to say about the match to the players as a group as he went round shaking the players' hands. He did tell Jimmy Armfield, his skipper that night, 'We don't let Frenchmen beat us at football – at least not like that,' and added, 'We don't want any more performances like that.' Armfield had it that the match should never have been played, 'You could hardly stand up and the floodlights were poor. I remember in the dressing room afterwards, Alf looked round for inspiration and could not find any. So he walked over to me and said, "Do we always play like that?"' Jimmy confirmed that the team had been uncharacteristically poor. Ramsey replied by saying, 'That's the first bit of good news I've had all evening.'

Everton centre-half Brian Labone had to admit that he had not played well, but commented, 'You have a result like that, you look at the keeper and the centre-half because they're meant to be the backbone of the side. I remember after the game going down to some nightclub and getting really sloshed.'

However, Moore was impressed by the new manager in the face of defeat. At that point he was functioning like a traditional right-half, but that wasn't working for the midfield or in defence; he was neither one thing or the other, which meant England were not getting the best out of him.

However, Ramsey had already settled on Moore as his lieutenant, partly because he knew he had not been involved with the England senior side long enough to develop an over-allegiance to Winterbottom's ideas and vision, or store up tight-lipped, blind loyalty to the former manager. Alf probably also saw something of his own steely determination, focus and ambition in Moore, unfettered by sentiment. The foundations were laid for a long relationship which, for the most part, avoided becoming blurred by emotion.

Ramsey was impressed by the way Moore managed himself after the defeat in Paris. On the coach to the airport after that game, Alf had sat beside Moore and they engaged in a non-stop conversation about how Winterbottom had worked with players, the way England had played and might play, and where Bobby saw himself fitting into the side. This left Bobby, despite the poor showing by the team, feeling positive. West Ham's rising star got the impression that the new England manager was 'really going to sort things out'.

During the flight back to London, Ramsey shared his ideas with Armfield about the importance he placed on getting the team playing as a unit and that didn't always translate to picking what might be seen as the best players. Talented performers could not always be accommodated in teams designed to work in a given way. Moore was to be at the heart of Alf's thinking in this respect.

Bit of bovva at the Boleyn

Sitting in mid-table during March, West Ham achieved a couple of notable results at Upton Park, beating Manchester United 3-1 and getting a very creditable 2-0 victory over Sheffield Wednesday.

In the FA Cup, four days after just about getting by Swansea, the fifth round saw the Hammers meet Everton at the Boleyn Ground. The Merseysiders were souped up by their chairman's patronage (John Moore was the founder of the Littlewoods Pools, and thus a multimillionaire). The side boasted full internationals of all the home countries and the Republic of Ireland, providing the Irons with their biggest test so far in that season's competition. Hordes of voluble Everton supporters had rolled up early, lodging themselves on the terraces. All of them looked to be sporting blue and white paper hats with 'Follow Everton with the Daily Express' plastered across them. The overall effect was to make them look reminiscent of a huge flock of newly paint-branded, vacant sheep, but to call the atmosphere tense was like saying things felt a bit edgy just before the charge of the Light Brigade.

It was a nervous scrap, dominated in the first half by the Toffees. However, when Dennis Stevens clogged Moore, distinguished referee Jim Finney (his day job was a 'brewery representative', so part of his role was likely to organise piss-ups in a brewery) awarded the home side what was seen by some as a contentious penalty. The metaphoric shit hit the proverbial fan on the South Bank[80] as Byrne coolly inserted the ball beyond Gordon West in the visitors' goal. The irate travelling fans let loose a reign of bottles and other lumpy detritus pitchward. Play had to be halted and a copper was struck by a huge lump of flying concrete that looked like it would have needed a trebuchet to launch it – you wouldn't bet against the Scousers finding the means to smuggle one of those bad boys in.

As the 'Academy' triumphed over the 'School of Science' and the Irons got their passport to the sixth round, the crowd behaviour was what made the headlines, being depicted as some sort of riot. While it would make recent disturbances at matches (by old fat blokes with their kids on their shoulders) look like a gavotte fest for Weight Watchers rejects, it's a bit of a stretch to name that afternoon, alongside the much exaggerated events of home encounter with Chelsea the previous season, as the blue touch paper for all football crowd agitation that was to follow, as has been suggested by some writers. Both situations were a bit more than storms in teacups, but neither might be compared to the Somme or the rampant blood feuds of South American soccer watchers.

The quarter-final was at Liverpool on Grand National day. West Ham were met by a crowd of 49,036 fervent Reds. 'You'll Never Walk Alone' by the denizens of the Kop, Liverpool's very own Gerry and the Pacemakers, would not be released for another nine months, although the song had been around since 1945. Apparently, and surprisingly, your average Scouser wasn't inclined towards Rodgers and Hammerstein, likely less to the musical *Carousel*, preferring such ditties as 'The Long Day Closes'. So, you could only take it (retrospectively) that Bill Shankly and his lads might indeed have been walking relatively alone at that time. But they did OK on their own, although the Hammers were unfortunate not to bring the Reds back to East London; with just six minutes left to play, Roger Hunt grabbed the deciding goal which sent his side into the last four.

---

80   This would become the Bobby Moore Stand. The North Bank was where I and my compatriots always stood, danced, jumped, sang, shouted, chanted and generally fucked about on from the start of the 1960s. At that time the away support was by and large ensconced on the opposite South Bank (writers commonly get these two corrals confused – you kinda had to be there) with those home supporters that we saw (very unfairly) as 'wankers'. In 1994 the North Bank gave way to the Centenary Stand, which the following year was renamed the Sir Trevor Brooking Stand and is now known as a random block of ugly, light shit-brown yuppie maisonettes.

Moore was livid about the decision that allowed the goal to stand. He had been steering the ball away for a goal kick when Jimmy Melia dragged it away from him, before crossing for Hunt to score. Bobby was adamant that the ball had gone out of play – he was not a dissembler when it came to football, but it was beyond him to call an injustice fair enough. Jim Standen, in the Hammers' goal, hadn't moved because he assessed the situation in much the same way as his captain, and was just waiting to take the goal kick. If the Irons had held on they would have had every chance of winning the replay. As it was Liverpool were beaten by eventual losing finalists Leicester in the semi-final.

Cap 10

As springtime peeped over the London skyline, Bobby was called into the tribal warfare that any England-Scotland sporting confrontation is. I was at a shove-ha'penny match between the two countries in Kirkintilloch sometime in the early 1970s which hospitalised five people!

It was the first game played at the 'new' Wembley; the £500,000 roof encircling the grand old stadium started to pay for itself with record gate receipts for an international game of £76,000

England 1 Scotland 2
Saturday, 6 April 1963
British Home Championship
Wembley
Attendance: 98,606
Referee: Leo Horn

England: Banks, Armfield, Byrne, Moore, Norman, Flowers, Douglas, Greaves, Smith, Melia, Charlton.
Scotland: Brown, Hamilton, Caldow, Mackay, Ure, Baxter, Henderson, White, St John, Law, Wilson.

Scotland hadn't won at Wembley for 12 years, but the side that ran out against England was maybe the finest ever to cross the border, and the tartan-festooned terraces made the encounter as good as a home game for the McVisitors.

Just five minutes into the game both teams were a player short thanks to a collision between Bobby Smith and Eric Caldow, the Scotland captain. Caldow had to be stretchered off, having sustained a triple fracture of the leg, which was to keep him from playing for many months. Left-winger Davie Wilson played 85 minutes as the left-back, Jim Baxter assuming a role in attack. Smith missed most of the first half, returning for the second half at outside-right. But before he was able to hobble back on pitch, his bruised knee heavily bandaged, the wonderfully gifted Baxter had twice bettered Gordon Banks, England's new goalkeeper, who was winning the first of his 73 caps, a record in his playing days[81].

The first goal by the Rangers man was on the cards the moment he had dispossessed Armfield. The England skipper was facing his own goal, about 30 yards out, and instead of turning towards the touchline and clearing the ball upfield, he turned inside to be robbed by Baxter, who had no hesitation homing in on the English goal, drilling the ball home with his left boot. Banks, in frustration, raged at his captain's blunder, while all Armfield could do was put his hands up in apology.

Baxter's second, a cleverly feigned, ground-level shot that went left while Banks went right, came via the penalty spot after Henderson had been decked by Flowers as he dribbled his way into the area.

The game didn't make much of a debut for Liverpool colleagues Gerry Byrne and Jimmy Melia. Bryan Douglas's consolation goal ten minutes from the time was actually very little in the way of consolation, but Scotland well deserved their victory, the major instigator of which was Baxter. 'Slim Jim', typically flamboyant and defiant, strolled off with the match ball up his jersey. This strikingly talented magician of a player had dominated the game, so few would argue that his claim for the ball wasn't justified.

Practically as the final whistle blew, the media were asking if Ramsey, having started his tenure as England manager with two defeats, was the figure to guide the hopes of Albion in the World Cup. The man himself was in a grim mood post-match, finding the idea of losing abhorrent generally, defeat at the hands of Alba was off the grid, Richter scale and Geiger counter, unacceptable. Alf's side had been embarrassed by Baxter ambling at will around Wembley as if it was his back garden.

Alf growled about Baxter being gifted too much space, although likely there wasn't a defence on the planet that might have stymied the Hill of Beath 23-year-old that day. His touch and passing had reached his most exquisite heights of grace and arrogance.

Moore was to reflect that this was the best Scotland team he had ever faced, but the focus of Ramsey's ire was Armfield, who recalled, 'After the game he was walking towards me and I said, "My fault, I know, I know."' Alf responded by asking, 'You'll never do that again will you?' Jimmy said he wouldn't. Darkly, Ramsey answered, 'No, you won't."

---

81   Banks has only ever been bettered by three other custodians of the English net: Peter Shilton (125), David Seaman and Joe Hart (both 75).

That was the analysis concluded. The manager's faith in Armfield was effectively shot.

Back in the league

Nottingham Forest were beaten 4-1 towards the end of April with two goals from Hurst, one from Peters and Bobby's effort in the 79th minute. By this time Greenwood had shifted Hurst from wing-half to inside-left. Geoff scrambled his first goal after the Forest keeper, Peter Grummett, spilled his initial attempt. With Johnny Byrne not available for selection, Hurst was tasked with the responsibility for a couple of penalties in two minutes. The first was awarded when centre-half Bobby McKinlay fouled Alan Sealey. The second was punishment for Doug Baird handling the ball. Hurst lost his chance of a hat-trick when he sent a powerful drive wide, but the result was a mark of the change at Upton Park as Hurst would be top marksman for West Ham with 13 goals that season.

Cap 11

England 1 Brazil 1
Wednesday, 8 May 1963
FA Centenary Celebration Match
Wembley
Attendance: 92,000
Referee: Leo Horn (Netherlands)

England: Banks, Armfield, Wilson, Milne, Norman, Moore, Douglas, Greaves, Smith, Eastham, Charlton.
Brazil: Gilmar, Lima, Eduardo, Zequinha, Roberto Dias, Rildo, Rodrigues, Mengálvio, Coutinho, Amarildo (Oliveira 40), Pepe.

For the match celebrating the centenary of the Football Association, Gordon Milne became the first defensive ball-winning midfield player to be selected by Ramsey, a role that Nobby Stiles would make his own in Alf's seminal England line-ups. This was the 'dark side' of Ramsey's defence/midfield strategy – Bobby Moore was 'yang' to Nobby's 'ying'.

George Eastham followed his father, George senior, as an England international; they were the first father and son to win England caps. While Ramsey was still mulling over who to give the role of captain to, Armfield continued to hold on to the distinction. There had been talk of bringing Johnny Haynes back, to revive his partnership with Jimmy Greaves, which was seen by many as a near perfect inside-forward combination. Alf stuck to his contention that the Fulham maestro was not fit enough, although Haynes, in the mind of the England boss, was the old guard, too imbrued with Winterbottom's approach and attitudes. That said, most of the players saw the non-inclusion of Haynes as a loss.

With Ramsey's contract with Ipswich finished, this was the first time he was free of the shackles of the selection panel.[82] The game was the first in which Bobby wore his favourite number six shirt. He had been playing at right-half for England that season, but for the meeting with Brazil he was switched to left-half. On the morning of the match he was gutted to find out that the great Pelé had failed a fitness test. Brazil turned out with only two of their World Cup-winning team – Gilmar, the goalkeeper, and Amarildo the inside-left. This situation took a bit of shine off the encounter.

However, the presence of José Macia, popularly known as Pepe, did much to compensate. Generally agreed to be among the finest players to turn out for Santos, Pepe can certainly be considered one of the greatest left-wingers of all time. He came to Wembley as a two-time World Cup winner, being part of the Brazilian squad in 1958 and 1962. With his famous club he was also a two-time winner of the Intercontinental Cup, the forerunner of the FIFA Club World Cup, in 1962 and 1963. The former victory involved overcoming the legendary Benfica, spearheaded by the iconic Eusébio. The latter final pitted the *Alvinegro Praiano*[83] against AC Milan, a side that boasted such luminaries as Cesare Maldini, Giovanni Trapattoni, Amarildo, Gianni Rivera and José Altafini.

Pepe spent his entire club career playing for Santos between 1954 and 1969, scoring 405 goals in 750 league outings, making him the second-highest scorer in the history of the club and only bettered by Pelé's 1,091 goals.

To Santos fans Pepe was known as *Canhão da Vila* ('The Village Cannon'), a reference to his powerful left foot (Santos played in the Urbano Caldera Stadium, that is located in the Vila Belmiro district of the municipality of Santos). In jest he often had it that he was 'the greatest Santos striker on the planet – because Pelé is from Saturn'.

Perhaps a little predictably it was Pepe's first-half 'banana' free kick, a 25-yard effort, that bewildered Banks, as it swung into the top of the England net. Douglas scrambled a late equaliser. Banks later recalled, 'Alf gave me a rollocking at half-time for falling for what he called Pepe's three-card trick. But from Alf's position on the touchline he could not have known how much bend Pepe put on the ball. I swear that if it had not gone into the net it would have done a circular tour of the stadium!'

---

82   Winterbottom had left the post in October, but Alf had wanted 'to do the right thing' by his club and see out his contract before taking full-charge of England.
83   'The Black-and-White from the Beach'.

The match concluded in a decent enough result, but it being Ramsey's first since taking up the manager's post full-time, he wanted his first win, and was totally pissed off with his defence, especially Banks, for what he saw as a disregard of Alf's warning about how deadly Brazil could be with a free kick close to the box. However, it is far from clear what one might do (other than guess right) with the kind of unpredictable and malevolent veering shot that gave the visitors the lead. But despite Banks pleading his case in the dressing-room postmortem, that the ball had curved aggressively in flight, Alf remained stubbornly adamant in his opinion that the goalkeeper should have been on the end of it.

Ramsey was later to admit that this was the first time that the England team appreciated he was capable of being annoyed and showing anguish. He insisted that prior to the game he had continually talked to Banks about Pepe's free-kick technique. However, as Bobby once casually intimated, it wasn't unusual for Alf to focus annoyance on an individual. He recollected, 'I don't think I'd ever seen Alf as angry as he was over Gordon letting in that free kick from Pepe. He kept saying like a stuck record, "I told you what he'd do with a free kick … I told you." But in fairness to Banksie, the ball went on a crazy swerve and I doubt if any goalkeeper in the world could have stopped it. All in all, we were pleased with our performance against the world champions, but Alf was still waiting for his first victory.'

For all this, the team looked organised, with a considerable air of confidence that had been noticeable by its absence for a long time. There was also a new hint of optimism in England's game. Nevertheless, many thought it was a match the home side should have won easily, having had most of the play and chances. Morale remained strong and the fact remained that England had only ever been beaten by two foreign teams at Wembley.

Final day

Manchester City were relegated by West Ham on the final day of the season, sunk by a 6-1 hiding at the Boleyn Ground. The Irons finished 12th in the First Division, frustratingly unable to kick on to better their performance of the previous season, but as we know, things were just getting started for West Ham and Bobby Moore – and yes, that's another story.

The young Irons reached the FA Youth Cup Final. Trailing 3-1 to Liverpool after the first leg, in the home tie, Martin Britt struck four times as West Ham won 6- 5 on aggregate. Nine of that side went on to play in the first team. The ground that had been prepared by Malcolm Allison, tended by Ron Greenwood, together with the example of Bobby Moore, was beginning to produce an impressive crop.

19
ROT SETTING IN WITH RON

In the early 1980s, appearing on what turned out to be the transient TV-AM, Bobby told how he loved the early days of Ron Greenwood's tenure at Upton Park, because the side were 'local lads and knew each other like class-mates'. By the end of 1963 all that seemed to have dissipated as the newspapers were reporting that Moore was bound for White Hart Lane, following a transfer request by the 22-year-old international. Greenwood and the club denied the story. The West Ham chair, Reg Pratt, was closer to the facts and responded with a mixture of disbelief and annoyance, asking himself why the player might have become connected with gossip of this kind. He saw Moore as looking to be disruptive. For Pratt, Moore's salary was as good as he might hope for. The previous year his benefit had earned him £750; what more might he want?!

However, Bobby was following in the footsteps, unsurprisingly, of Malcolm Allison, Noel Cantwell, and Frank O'Farrell at Upton Park in terms of being a demanding employee. Pratt convinced himself that Moore was using his contacts and leverage with the media to strengthen his own hand. Maybe he was, but so what? Why shouldn't he? Who wouldn't?

For all the club's denials and Greenwood's angry 'no comment' responses, the very public speculation went on for weeks. Moore felt that the West Ham board lacked both the ambition and the punch to back up a side that might consistently challenge for honours. He commented that he had made it clear to his employers that he was ambitious, and claimed to have told his manager that if the opportunity came along for him to join a bigger club he would want to leave the Boleyn Ground.

One newspaper stated that Pratt, a known poor loser (although one would have thought, being chair of West Ham for 13 years, his skin should have been a little thicker in that respect) was 'angry' about the situation (again, so what?). Moore's position had clearly touched a nerve. Top man Reg remarked, 'It makes me mad that people expect us to part with our best player at the drop of a hat.' You can bet it did, but once more, so what?

Outside of football, Pratt was the owner of a wood yard in Wanstead. My dad ran a similar business in Plaistow for several years, a bit 'down at heel' compared to leafy E12, but at this distance, who the fuck did Pratt think he was – Moore's owner? The answer to that might probably be 'pretty much'. That was the football culture

Pratt emerged from, clubs considering themselves, more or less, the 'masters' of the players, as colonial gentry saw their indentured labour, part of their 'property'. In this respect the 'West Ham family' proposal might be understood in much the same way as the posh Edwardian household, wherein the servants were considered adjuncts to the family, albeit of lowly status, but nevertheless the responsibility of the 'head of the house'. Admittedly, Pratt ultimately looked to move on from this, mostly because it didn't make financial sense in mid-20th century terms, but the culture clearly persisted. Moore was never going to do anything but buck against such circumstances.

For all this, it's probable that if it hadn't been for Greenwood, Moore would have been traded for bigger bucks than the record-breaking fee West Ham had laid out to bring Johnny Byrne to East London from Selhurst Park. The prospective windfall would have been too nice a slice cake for the board not to want to grab. That sort of response, alongside a pervasive inferiority complex, had been in train, and continued for decades, up to the Terry Brown years, to be embedded in the cultural DNA of the Hammers.

However, Greenwood knew that Bobby was too valuable, both on the field and as a symbol of the club, to be allowed to depart Upton Park. Added to this, Moore's exit would likely have led to more requests for transfers, probably Byrne after not too long. By the mid-1960s Moore was the cement between the bricks at the Boleyn Ground and like Allison before him, he was for the players' 'master and commander' of the good ship West Ham United.

Thus, Bobby's relationship with Greenwood was turning sour, as the start of the end of Moore's spiritual association with the Hammers kicked in. He was to say to one or two members of the victorious 1963 FA Youth Cup side that Ron thought more of them then he did the senior team. There might have been something to that, but from around that point on, England became Bobby's club and West Ham something short of a necessary bondage. While he was never less than a consummate performer for club and country, while he always did enough, he would, less and less, play as perfectly and consistently well for West Ham as he did for his nation. As his long-time team-mate Joe Kirkup had it, Bobby was 'ten times the player when he pulled on an England shirt'. It wasn't that he made more mistakes or lacked drive with the Hammers on his chest, it was more a partial loss of spirit; sometimes there was a hint of resignation about his demeanour.

It's important not to misunderstand Moore's attitude. When he turned out for Fulham against West Ham in the 1975 FA Cup Final, at the end of the game he approached us West Ham supporters, having swapped his Cottagers' shirt with Hammers captain Billy Bonds. He stood in front of us and held his hand over the badge that covered his heart. His affection for the Irons fans and the spirit of the club always endured, but if the West Ham board had felt the same about him in 1963 it would have wanted what was best for him, and at that point, as far as Bobby was concerned, that was a move to a bigger club. That he was effectively disallowed from following what he saw as his destiny was bound to impact on his motivation; that was not about peek or sulky intention, it was an understandable psychological response, more likely an unconscious reaction. At the same time this 'withdrawal' was a very gradual process; he did after all captain the Hammers to domestic and European success in the mid-1960s, and was central to that 'golden age' at Upton Park.

I bumped into Bobby several times after he left his playing days behind. The last time I spoke with him at any appreciable length was in the mid-1980s, in the Roots Hall car park during his short spell managing Southend United. I was hobbling around with a stick, recovering from a sports injury, awkwardly trying to change a flat tyre when he asked me if I needed a hand. I had always sensed that he was partial to a bit of an 'in-passing' exchange, but usually of his own instigation. We shared a passion for boxing, and I asked him what he reckoned about the upcoming Hearns-Hagler fight, and it turned out we both rated 'Marvellous Marvin'. He enquired about my dad and we reminisced about Queens Road market, next to Upton Park station, some names, and characters from the past, West Ham dog track and our feelings about the Hammers. He told me he would 'always be West Ham' and that was 'just the way it is'. West Ham opened the world he wanted to be part of when no one else was interested; no West Ham, no Bobby Moore. West Ham gave him Malcolm Allison, Noel Cantwell and Ron Greenwood, the men who had worked with him to shape himself. He saw his best days in football as those early years at Upton Park, and breaking into the England side, a feat West Ham had effectively facilitated for him, not the board, or the hangers-on, but his fellow players and all the people who were really what the club was and remains.

I have a huge fidelity for East London; I am that place, it is me. It's where I was born, brought up, went to school. I attended what was West Ham College and started the work that led to my professional career in the area. The docklands 'made' me. Fairbairn House Boys' Club in Plaistow, the Mayflower Centre in Canning Town, New Cambridge Boys' Club in Bethnal Green, all these places helped mould me as a youth worker. But I didn't just squat in East London for the rest of my days. I have worked in every continent on earth, I have travelled from the Falklands to Hong Kong, from Baltimore to Cape Town. That doesn't mean those places mean more to me than London's docklands and the cockney communities, neighbourhoods and parishes that once saw the Boleyn Ground as the hub of their identity. Bobby's feelings about West Ham and the need for other motivations and inspirations might not have been too far from my own, or perhaps your sentiments now and/or in years gone by.

Johnny Haynes had 'mown the grass ceiling' after the end of the maximum wage, becoming the first ton-a-week player, but few had the weight he welded at Fulham. However, for Moore, Haynes was an example of what could be achieved. For all that, the boardrooms of English football were not going to give up the fruits of their exploitation (dosh) too easily; they had fought tooth and nail and left bollock to hold basic wages at basement level, having more of an appetite to cough up via incentives, bonuses connected to wins, appearances, victories, goals, or stadium attendance. Liverpool had done much to set the standard in this respect, linking extra pay to on-pitch 'performance indicators': the old 'make us a lot richer than we are and we'll make you not so hard-up as you were' riff.

At that stage agents were something allegedly added to washing powder, anything like the role of an informed advisor for players was outlawed by the Football League. So while post-Jimmy Hill it was open season in terms of player wage demands, the worldly wisdom of most footballers was limited, many knowing little of the world of employment beyond their club than what their employers told them. As such, with a few notable exceptions, players were mostly clueless when it came to dealing with the business-savvy directors of the top clubs.[84]

Greenwood detested the bartering around player wages and contracts. He was never comfortable arguing over money. The impression was it was too close to the role of the tradesman for his sophisticated tastes, and/or he didn't really see it as part of his job – he was, after all, by vocation, a coach, happier with balls than bank notes. He had a point. It was never a great idea to expect managers to get into haggling with players about money, their living, what enabled them to pay their mortgages and look after their kids, and thereafter being obliged to ask them, as an employee, to give their all for the club. The whole situation was contradictory in the extreme. Differences of loyalty and interest, as with Moore and Greenwood, were almost bound to evolve into a toxic, brooding disputes, although in the case of Ron and Bobby, made up not of shouting and hollering, but deep, simmering, noxious silences.

Adding to Ron's pain, the player he most valued and needed to build his vision round was the most demanding when it came to the 'wedge'. Moore was to reflect on the commonly held opinion that footballers should not look for higher rewards

---

84   As outlined in Young Bobby, part of the reasoning for club ridding themselves of Jack Turner seems to have been in part, in all but name, him acting as a player agent, peddling his not insubstantial financial shuffling skills to club staff, inevitably at a cost of board profits.

in return for their skills. Moore mixed with celebrities, film stars, artists and performers of every ilk and came to understand himself and his playing colleagues as, at base, entertainers. So it was not surprising he was to make the point that pop stars were far better rewarded for their talents than footballers, often watched by smaller crowds than attended the top football matches. For him, players were convinced into undervaluing themselves, something he had been tutored into not tolerating. A self-doubter by nature, value of self had been a primary development for Moore; without it he would have never broken through. He had learned that if he didn't value and invest in his talent, it would be hard for others to rate or invest in them. This after all was the 'West Ham Way': advance!

By the time Bobby took over the captaincy of West Ham he had become respected and admired by his team-mates, some of whom, like Eddie Bovington, were not easily impressed. However, even Eddie was to say of Moore, 'Whatever you could do, he could do it better. You had to respect him just for that.'

Dignity is a value for self

In February 1962 Ron Greenwood had made a crucial move, perhaps his most powerful commitment to his ideals, signing the mercurial Johnny Byrne for a British record fee. Around the same time, seemingly out of frustration and anger, Ron accused Moore of being 'a weak player' – someone motivated by the weekly wage, because he was asking for some monetary confirmation of his worth to the club. Amazingly, Bobby had asked for just a couple of quid, a raise of about seven per cent. Bobby was looking for something quite a bit less than £30 a week (that'd be worth around £500 today). Gate money at Upton Park would have been approximately £8,000 a game (£160,000 nowadays). But it got to a point when the attrition was more about principles than cash; always a moment of jeopardy for all concerned.

Ron came from a 'respectable working-class' background and, typical of such roots and his generation, he had been brought up never to spend what he didn't have. This gave him the reputation among West Ham players of being 'tight'. For sure, the Hammers weren't among the richest clubs, but neither were they the most impoverished. However, Greenwood accepted being the front line of protection of the board's financial interest and so he was seen by everyone else to be 'the bosses' man'. This, together with his cultural and professional mentality to lean towards prudence and thrift, put him in an isolated position, certainly for someone who habitually had to talk about working as a team.

However, Bobby was adamant about his and his playing colleagues' worth, thus there was to be an annual 'face-off' between him and Ron. Bobby had been tutored by Malcolm Allison about the need to fight your corner – to quote Terry Pratchett, 'There is no justice, just us!' Indicative of Moore's education to this end was him witnessing an ongoing dispute centred on a win bonus promised for a game against the English amateur side. Allison had threatened to call the team out on strike a quarter of an hour before a league encounter with Nottingham Forest unless this money was paid. Ultimately, it was.

All in all, the annual wars between captain and manager were likely a series of battles of wills but also respective values. It was something of a veritable pissing contest and the 'victor' would win the role of the 'alpha male' in the club; the 'big swinging dick'. This was a game Moore wasn't going to lose. Greenwood likely would have been better in the long run just to have taken the hit and let himself be seen as the 'bigger man', or at least not a swingeing tight arse. It made even less sense when you factor in Ron's opinion of Moore as a player. Despite his momentary outburst, for Greenwood, only Franz Beckenbauer was comparable to Bobby. While he conceded that the German had more pace, he understood that Moore could more than compensate for that lack by way of mindfulness and spatial awareness.

Ron saw Moore's capacity to read games as uncanny; at the same time his anticipation consistently appeared to give him an extra yard or two. Bobby was cooler than the coolest of cool cucumbers at points of high stress, while his sense of position was unparalleled. Greenwood had no doubt that Moore was at his best when his best was most required; his concentration was unshakable. For Ron, Bobby made football 'look a simple and lovely art'. But the Hammers manager somehow seemed to forget that obvious fact that such skills come at a premium and have a requisite cost.

Nevertheless, what ensued was not a negotiation at all, with Greenwood merely parroting the same figure over and over and Moore rationally and calmly reiterating it wasn't enough. Neither man was fond of conflict, but Moore was breaking the unwritten rules relating to the 'loyal servant', 'all for the club' forelock-tugging shite that had kept players the poor relations in the feudal football industry practically throughout the first three-quarters of the 20th century.

Moore's rectitude in terms of his own value also betrayed the image built around him. The portrait of a man of angelic quality didn't fit this rebel stance in terms of pay. His unapologetic attitude with regard to his worth belied his usual modesty and humility. But he knew full well that Jimmy Greaves, his friend from early teenage life, had been on £60 a week at Tottenham since 1961.

Not long after he got back from the World Cup, while the rest of the West Ham team settled for the £28, Moore stood fast for the best part of two months.

The situation concluded in the only way it was ever going to: Bobby got the £30, backdated, and on his insistence it meant everyone else in the senior team also got the extra deuce. Consequently, Moore's dressing-room approval soared even higher, while Greenwood's leadership was severely eroded. Bobby grew to be 'the main man'; Ron wouldn't really get over or recover from this. His attempt at the strong man/tough negotiator schtick had left him looking hollow and feeble. Bobby had won as he won on the field, by calmness, a steady eye and cutting focus.

Never again did Moore sign a contract with West Ham without a fight, often an acrimonious one. This was the kernel of the rancour that was to fester quietly between Moore and Greenwood as the skipper pushed the club to its limits and some way beyond. Persistently, the first man on the park was the last of the playing staff to accept terms, once with just hours before the opening game of the season. Bobby was the proverbial pain in the arse for the board and Ron, in much the same way he was for many a striker.

But Moore didn't confine the application of his negotiation skills to West Ham and Greenwood. There was a £22,000 win bonus for the England side after their World Cup victory in 1966. It's unlikely that anyone would have successfully objected if those who had actually played in the final had made the case for receiving the lion's share, perhaps with something extra for those who had missed out on facing West Germany but had been selected for earlier games. However, it was Bobby who immediately spoke up when Alf Ramsey asked the question about how the dough should be distributed. He reasoned that there were 22 players in the squad and so each should get £1,000. This was reinforcing an informal agreement between the players made prior to the tournament about the sharing of bonuses.

All the squad received their equal share, plus £248-15s for six match fees, the daily allowance, which came to £46 in total, and whatever the second-class return train fare was to London for each player (no one paid more than a cockle but it's the principle that matters). The XI for the final did receive an extra £60 each. This was typical of Moore. It was not unusual for him, when negotiating for himself at Upton Park, to insist all other first-team players got an equivalent payment to himself. Predictably, this amplified the affection other players had for him and augmented their loyalty to him.

According to Jimmy Adamson, when playing for England one couldn't just 'roll along' and 'do what you do for your club, and think it's enough … You have to exert yourself in a way you haven't done before because this is a new test, not just of your ability, but of your playing character.' For Jimmy, a player's responsibility increases with the degree of their ability.

A performer like Bobby is expected to play at a high level. If he failed to live up to those expectations and deliver the best of himself, the impact was much more detrimental than if someone less experienced or talented had performed below par. I think Moore shared Adamson's views in this respect, and it is part of the explanation why he nearly always looked better in an England shirt than he did in the claret and blue of the Hammers.

Yes, I know with England he was surrounded by a different class of player, and facing opponents who would have called on him to produce his best game, more so than say a Third Division outfit, on a cold, wet, dark English winter evening in the early rounds of the League Cup. But in truth, Moore was never rewarded his true worth at Upton Park, and West Ham paid a price for this in other ways, as England became his main focus and his form for the Hammers became less and less congruent with his performances at international level. The message 'you get what you pay for in this world' became more and more tangible to everyone involved with West Ham, from supporters to the chair. The directors wanted Moore on the cheap, they knew it, Greenwood knew it, and most of all Moore knew it. The truth was they were never going to get that.

Just to reiterate, I'm not saying that Bobby purposely pulled back playing in any game, he really didn't. However, none of us can control our unconscious feelings of resentment, perpetuated by purposeful injustice. Even at his lowest, Moore was still a giant for the Hammers, but with a little more intelligence and a lot more generosity of spirit, the Boleyn Ground would have got that bit more out of him. In a club seemingly addicted to false economies, West Ham's attitude to Moore took the proverbial hob nob.

Bobby, many times, was to clearly state that West Ham had always been good to him. For all that, he went on to say, 'But the way I saw it was that a footballer's career lasts a comparatively short time, and I felt that I had to do the best for myself and my wife.' And who can make him wrong?

Greenwood should not bear too much culpability in all this. I'm sure he knew the score, but in the last analysis the board employed him to do their bidding, not Bobby's. Without any sense of reason from the board, other than thick-headed, short-term gain, life was made less comfortable and fruitful for Greenwood and everyone else. All that was achieved was distraction from and the effective prevention of the purpose of the club, to play football to a high standard.

The cold war around Moore's wage breaks the myth that player and club are one. They are not. While putting this book together the shit-storm that was the proposed European Super League had about run its course (for now). Radio chat stations and the internet were storming with irate fans vociferously making points on variations on the theme of, 'It's all about money now!' But it's always been all about money, certainly since the domination of the professional game in the early 20th century. The idea that clubs are some sort of extension of the welfare state or philanthropic entities is the height of bollocks. Professional football clubs peddle sentiment and are capitalistic entities naked in tooth and claw. Where is the evidence that there was some halcyon time in living memory when this was not the case?

The struggle between Moore, West Ham and Greenwood was one of the first open and tangible acts in the development of 'player power' that had been going on covertly at Upton Park for more than a decade; in fact the first rumblings were under way as early and the 1930s (but that's another story).

The early 1960s was a point in time and football when the pastiche fell away and the reality peeped through. The game is an industry and constitutes the 'all against all and devil take the hindmost' philosophy of business. While the fans are paying into an emotional fix, the big picture of the football cartels is fostering the rational pursuit of profit, be it by forms of property speculation/investment or legalised money laundering. It's pointless condemning this because in our society, mass consumption of high level football is never going to be offered as a 'free lunch'. It's a nexus of mass transactions with an overall profit motive. What other form might the 'product' take?

This is the point when people generally start shouting 'Borussia Dortmund' at me – the John Lewis of football. But that's just a different incarnation of much the same thing. To an extent, in the early 1960s, Moore 'got' this and from then on it was 'them and us'. This reflects the whole character of the professional game and explains a lot as to why Bobby, unlike the more compliant 'soccer Sirs', was never knighted by Her Maj and why, at the end of his career, he suffered, at every turn, rejection from the sport. But, guess what, that's another story.

Guilt and resentment – destructive symbiosis

Bobby admitted he liked the skipper's role, the sense of responsibility it imposed, that if something occurred on the pitch, it was he who would need to decide what action was to be taken. Others invariably recognised his willingness and skill in this respect; for instance Brian Dear, a Hammers striker of the 1960s, has told of how he would tell Jack Burkett, the team's left-back, 'Just pass it straight to Bobby and make yourself look good.'

Moore had it that, 'In boys' teams the captain is generally the outstanding player – simply because boys are impressed purely by ability and very little by knowledge. But in professional teams the captain – if he means anything at all –

must be a natural leader, the kind of individual whose play and conduct sets an example to the others. If he is slack and cynical and doesn't seem to care much about training, then the rest of the team will take the hint. I try to be the other kind.'

Bobby was indeed a meticulous leader, but I'd say closer to an on-field manager. It was under his direction as *Zulu*, *Dr Strangelove*, and *The Pink Panther* started to draw the crowds at the cinema, West Ham looked like a team beginning to click.

Thus, as Bobby grew in authority, when this was constantly confirmed by the players around him, any attempt to 'manage' Moore was going to ultimately lead to him resenting and resisting efforts to control him and/or curtail his authority.

Few researchers and writers looking at football allow for the fact that the sport is a federal institution. In fact, it is a Russian doll of institutions within institutions. The semi-independent institution of the club fits into a national associational institution (a federation) that is part of a broader continental and global institution. At the same time, clubs are relatively closed entities; the people in them, outside of the boards, know very little else other than football. When Moore stepped into the business and commercial world, it was disastrous for him and amounted to one failed project following another. This is not unusual, and in fact for the bulk of the history of football and that other working-class sport, boxing, it has been typical, with a few exceptions that have proved the rule. Such failure is predictable because if you have no experience but the experience you have, what do you have to call on when novel experiences and different contexts demand different qualities and thinking to what you know? Expecting Moore just to be able to make critically cogent business decisions was like asking someone to drive a car who has only ever sat in a car or seen them driving down the road, never having driven one.

ALL learning is learning ignited and confirmed by experience. You can't learn outside your experience (what would that even be?). ALL thinking is about and for (a response to) something (even if you believe it's not). Learning is ALWAYS about something and purposeful (you can learn about nothing, as even nothing is something). To think someone just 'learns' aimlessly (although there are ideas about 'unconscious learning' and 'blue sky thinking') outside their experience is not to understand what learning is or for. In fact it's not understanding sentient life.

Effective, efficient learning necessarily needs summation (review via recollection and aids to the same) else it is mostly ditched and distorted by the limits and requirements of memory, and your memories interchange with and become 'laundered' by your imagination. This book you are reading is a summation, but if all you know is football, the summation of that learning is going to be limited.

People like Jock Stein and Bill Shankly were never common in the top flight of the game, less so postwar – men who had been obliged to do 'real work', coming in and out of football from the 'outside world'. Greenwood and Moore had the more common biographies in relation to the game. This closed world cuts off certain routes to and eventual destinations of adult development. There are any number of examples of the consequences of this, but pertinent in the story being told here is the cycle of guilt and resentment.

We are all familiar, perhaps especially since the coming of the Premier League, with managers who have a tendency to overtly blame players, or referees for poor results. They might be right, but this 'blame game' invites predictable, unavoidable reactions. The proportioning of blame in the top level of football is the way of things. A manager fails to get what an owner wants, they are gone. The player who loses form is out. Fans and the media ramp up this cycle of destruction that perhaps one could argue is unavoidable in a game that is essentially adversarial: 'them and us',' 'winners and losers', the victorious and the vanquished.

The wiser manager does what they can to avoid piling too much blame on their players. West Ham's John Lyall and Bob Paisley of Liverpool come to mind, and more contemporaneously Jürgen Klopp. By and large such people, in the last analysis, took and take ultimate responsibility when their teams stumble. To be fair, Ron Greenwood did too. He nearly always referred to what 'we' didn't do, and what happened to 'us'. It is also noticeable when these managers get moved on (although that never happened to Paisley or Greenwood) they do so, by and large, without having a go at owners or the board or fans. This can be thought of as mature responses; adult attitudes.

I don't need to name names when looking at managers who pretty much plonk the blame for the failures of their sides squarely on the shoulders of their players, referees, the fans, VAR, the FA, or the club cat. This implies that (usually principally) the players are guilty of some form of neglect by way of low skill, poor attitude, laziness, failure to focus, insufficient application, lack of fitness, or motivation and so on. This is the stuff of the playground – the 'I did nuffin, he did it' scenario (very Billy Bunter/Trump/Johnson).

If I make or even attempt to make you feel guilty, your self-preservation instinct kicks in. Without going into too much detail, this results in you feeling a level of resentment toward me. The expression of your resentment towards me is geared to cause me to consider retracting my accusation; that is the purpose of the expression of your resentment, to make me feel guilty enough to put my hands up and say, 'I was wrong.' That is the only thing that might allay your feeling of guilt. However, that reaction is uncommon; more likely is that I will resent you for your attempt to make me feel guilty - trying to get me to say I was off beam - but I will resent you even more if you are successful and that happens.

This cycle of guilt and resentment often ignites a degenerative spiral of discomfort through frustration, anger and finally hate. At a fundamental level this is the result of brain chemistry that goes right back to our reptilian past. The 'blame game' essentially activates our flight or fight mechanisms, and once that pot is on the boil it is hard to pull up; the old 'red mist' or what the psychologists call 'the amygdala hijack' (our lower brain taking over the higher intellectual capacities). This is the point beyond compromise, negotiation, or reason. We have just the two reactions – flight or fight – and everything else is cut off by a chemical flood of our higher brain.

The only way to short-circuit this is by the engagement of the 'higher' or what one might call the 'adult' or 'reasoning' brain (see Lyall, Paisley, Klopp et al).

However, institutions of any hue or stripe do not encourage the development of the broad range of thinking – a consequence of a wider horizon of experience – that turbo-charges higher brain functions. Much of the latter is done at the control level of the institution (the boardroom for instance). At the same time, in football, as remarked above, the media and the fans are constantly looking to blame someone for any negative outcomes of a particular game or season. Part of the reason for this is the flight or fight mode of the lower brain functioning excites us, sometimes unto frenzy. Most supporters are part of the way there from the outset of any match, competition, or tournament. They are emotionally involved in an adversarial experience – 'them and us'. The more one's emotions are engaged, the more our logical capacities (our higher brain functioning) is closed down; we are ripe for fight or flight.

In 1962 Bobby Moore and Ron Greenwood were locked into this type of dance. It is a toxic collaboration that is ultimately and always destructive. But it was Moore who thought, more than fought, his way through – somewhat contradictorily he learned and habituated that capacity from his experience of playing football, replicating what he did on field to the negotiation situation, keeping his cool, following a logical strategy, playing on strengths. Ron stood no chance really.

CONCLUSION

Ron Greenwood was managing the England under-23 side when they pounded West Germany 4-1 at White Hart Lane in May 1961. Ron had been told late on by the Football Association that he was going to be short of players. He turned to Mike Harrison, a winger who had just finished a training session at Stamford Bridge. Bobby Moore was in that England team along with Johnny Byrne. Together they tore the soul out of the Germans. Byrne was majestic, as Bobby remembered, 'Budgie must have had a hundred touches of the ball, 75 of them from my passes, most of that one-touch, all down to Ron's organisation.'

The FA analysis of that match included the number of passes that came from Bobby to Budgie. Johnny collected 108 passes from Bobby. Hard to fathom, but the stats don't lie, although people have been known to lie about them.

Byrne's was called up for his first under-23 international for the game in which Moore won his second cap at that level, a 2-0 victory over Wales at Goodison Park in February 1961, using a modified 4-2-4 system devised by Ron Greenwood. England were then defeated by Scotland, the Tartan lads' first win against the 'old enemy' since the under-23 games started in 1955. Denis Law had been at his devastating best.

Just four of that England team retained their place for the game against West Germany: George Cohen of Fulham, Mike O'Grady of Huddersfield Town, plus Moore and Byrne. Michael McNeil of Middlesbrough, who had been the captain, was out of the team. Greenwood named Moore as his skipper.

Byrne, the only full international in the side, was elegance personified, his judgement seeming faultless and athleticism towering. His positional sense and timing were poetic. Repeatedly, when Bobby advanced to make a pass, Johnny was on the end of it, perfectly placed to pick up the ball. For sure, Budgie had an uncanny aptitude to be in the right place at the right time, but it was Moore who supplied him. For extended periods it appeared that the two Londoners were taking the Germans apart on their own.

At last, the world had seen what Moore could do and his destiny was set. The 1961/62 season was to be West Ham's fourth in the top flight of English football after a 26-year absence. The eighth-placed finish was their best since their first term back among the elite, after which the East Enders had finished in a very creditable sixth. But subsequent positions of 14th and 16th had made them very much part of the 'also-rans' of the old First Division. This was a critical period for West Ham and Greenwood, so club and manager turned to Moore, beginning the time when Bobby and West Ham started to become synonymous.

To know a man, you must know his influences

Playing for Chelsea, Greenwood had been exposed to the coaching of Arthur Rowe, having, as a teenager, seen him play for Spurs. Greenwood the centre-half (the same position as Rowe played) knew the Tottenham side of the early 1950s well. Rowe does not get the credit he deserves in terms of the development of the modern game. His ideas and vision not only exemplified those elicited by the 'Hungarian renaissance' of football, they pre-empted them. Ron had also worked with Walter Winterbottom and so had shared his razor-sharp insight into the emergence and organisation of that great Hungarian side. Greenwood had been one of the few in a place to recognise the way the eastern Europeans played that day in 1953 when England had been humbled.

That November game, the last Harry Johnston (another centre-half) would play for England, had been something of a dream made manifest for Greenwood. Ferenc Puskás and his men were working according to his own vision of the game; seeing his personal insight literally played out in front of his eyes proved to be a motivating influence that would guide the rest of his life. From then on, Ron was looking for the means to apply that approach himself, to unlock its potential. Moore, for Greenwood, was the key to that realisation.

Being made England's captain perhaps can be understood as the point at which young Bobby became 'Moore the man', the moment when he entered the next and most glittering part of his life and career. He was now the footballer he himself had built, fostered by Allison, nurtured Greenwood, and his final influence would be Alf Ramsey, the person he would walk with to collect football's greatest prize.

Ramsey once had it that when a game was under way it was Moore who made all the decisions, including changing the team formation. He was one of the youngest people to take his FA coaching badge during his era – he was a student of the game, but he was more than that. He commanded the respect that gave him the authority that caused others to follow his directions, as an example. Authority, like power, is never given, it must be taken. The means to take authority is built on one's capacity to influence, and marshal the personal confidence to take authority, and command the faith of others to hand authority over.

The association between Moore and Greenwood started well, but after the first couple of years of the 1960s it progressively deteriorated. Ramsey's aesthetic disposition and personality, not too dissimilar from Greenwood's, was in stark contrast to Moore's comparatively flamboyant outlook, and to an extent permissive lifestyle. That said, by the mid-1960s, Bobby's cultural tastes leaned towards the conservative. If he read a book on an away trip or a tour, he'd favour the likes of one of Ian Fleming's James Bond novels. He was to tell how he had read 'the whole' of *The Carpetbaggers* by Harold Robbins. Musically he was choosing the 'easy listening' genre, the likes of Frank Sinatra, Tony Bennett, and Peggy Lee. Bobby cultivated a sophisticated style, as smooth as silk, but he liked his lager and he enjoyed the London nightlife of the optimistic 1960s – a planet as foreign as Mars to Greenwood and Ramsey.

Bobby certainly would have felt closer to Johnny Byrne than say Bobby Charlton, when it came to an assessment of Alf and Ron. Budgie never fell under Ramsey's spell. One night, after he had retired, he told Moore, 'I can hear his talk now. The same old talk. Let's face it, Bobby, he didn't hold a candle to Ron Greenwood in his knowledge of the game. Not in the same street.'

It's too easy to just take this as a lack of respect, but it's not a complete dismissal – it's a judgement premised on experience, if you like evidence, and effectively more in praise of Ron than a condemnation of Alf.

Johnny told me, 'Alf wasn't a general, he was a sergeant-major[85] type. I found it an effort to take him too seriously. He knew his trade, but he had trouble changing his ideas too much. He chose who he listened to, but you had to have a way of talking to him I didn't have, but Bobby did. Ron was more of a teacher. He was always looking to develop our and his thinking and he would listen to what anybody thought and often take the thinking of others on … Alf was clever, or astute, but stubborn and ruthless. Greenwood was intelligent, he was interested in wisdom … probably a genius.'

Both Byrne and Moore knew what they were talking about and had every justification to come to conclusions about their experiences, including those who effectively had authority over them.

While going with Ramsey's ambition and much of his coaching authority, Moore, like Byrne, didn't totally pay into Alf's authoritarian side. Although he always appreciated Ramsey as a coach, Bobby was much more complicated and, at times difficult than the legend probably too often has it.

Alf, like Moore, was essentially an East Londoner by birth, also like Bobby he came from working-class roots and was skipper of his nation's football team, being possessed of a similar calm authority on the pitch. Both lacked pace as players, but each could read the game much better than most of their peers. Ramsey and Moore shared a gift for distribution, being able to play a crucial ball at the critical

---

85   More than once Ramsey was referred to (behind his back) as 'sergeant-major posh'

moment. Both men were often accused of being aloof and detached.

Alf and Bobby were not at their best with people they didn't know, and you'd call neither 'chatty'; colleagues and team-mates not unusually found them 'distant'. That said, Moore had a sort of radar for genuineness. He seemed to warm to a familiar face, and was amused by innocent interest, although Bobby was able to present a starchy exterior when he sensed someone pushing to get into his company. This was his means of remaining well-mannered. He managed not to appear rude, but put over that he was just not available at that moment. Bobby was uncomfortable turning a handshake away or not returning a greeting, so what was often mistakenly taken to be coldness was Bobby attempting to retreat into a diplomatic carapace.

For all this, as the distinguished journalist Hugh McIlvanney wrote of Moore, 'You felt that there was always another door inside him that you could never reach.' Much the same could be said of Ramsey. A habit of dressing immaculately was something associated with both men, although Bobby was very fussy about his appearance, whereas Alf was more military in that sense – more well turned-out than dapper. They both had a presentational self, as a sort of veil of confidence, sometimes taken as arrogance, that hid a more frail and uncertain side. Greenwood didn't quite need the same sort of barrier, but like Ramsey and Moore, there was an air of 'imposter syndrome' about his manner and the need to compensate for that.

Ramsey was a deeply private person, not a teetotaller, but not one for anything that might have a whiff of carousing. Bobby loved the glamour of mixing with A-list celebrities, the associated nightlife, drinking and clubbing. Not unlike Greenwood, take Alf away from football and he cut an awkward figure. Reticent by nature, he was seemingly always close to embarrassment. In contrast, Jack Charlton recalled Bobby taking him to a club in London's West End. Moore arrived in his red Jaguar, handing the keys to the doorman as he entered the venue. Big Jack had never seen anybody do that before. Ramsey, like Ron, favoured the underground or train in terms of transport.

Bobby had a suite of dispositions, and it's probably true that over the period of his life my two books have focused on, only Tina Moore, the person who more than any perhaps, brought him out of his shell, might be said to have known the man in the middle of his personal complexity, the dimensional array of personality that Ramsey and Greenwood lacked. He had perhaps learned from Malcolm Allison to be, albeit on very rare occasions, cuttingly sarcastic to the point of disparaging someone without them knowing it, or only becoming conscious of the put-down hours later. Greenwood was 'proper,' with a hint of respectable charm. Ramsey was achingly straight, rigidly polite, but often as blunt as a 12lb thump hammer. At core he was earnest, by nature painfully honest and sober to the point of naivety. He was utterly wedded to the values of his generation; a perplexed stranger to the 1960s, although he was capable of constructive deceit and ruthlessness, motivated by ambition, but also the protection of others; he could be loyal to a fault (literally). He struggled, now and then almost pathetically, to be taken as a patriotic English gentleman, but one who, not far under the surface, hid a vortex of vulnerability. Thus he was wary of the consequences of too much familiarity. Moore was, in comparison, sophisticated and more than capable of clever impertinence, that usually fell short of humiliating of others, but got close at times; he could generate a barbed remark, but a distancing gaze, that had a frisson of contempt, was usually enough for people to know when to back off.

Although you could see the influence of Allison and Noel Cantwell, Moore wasn't really 'like' anyone, certainly not a lot of other footballers. He didn't warm to anything crude; he was OK with a risqué comment or joke, but found reference to 'bodily functions' distasteful and considered spitting rude (it was rare for Moore to be seen spreading his sputum on the pitch). His prime teachers as a player in his transition from boyhood to manhood were Cantwell and Allison, although Malcolm was also something of a role model for Moore as a person. Greenwood confirmed and extended Allison's football philosophy. Winterbottom and Ramsey, in parallel, but in different ways, embedded the same. However, of this handful of people who majorly impacted Moore's life, while temporarily captivating, and intellectually stimulating, only Big Mal was possessed of the inspirational enchantment, attractive persona, embodied by a daunting physical presence.

What I know of Bobby Moore isn't some unimpeachable truth, it is however the result of a lifetime of watching him play, reading almost everything written about him, talking to many of those who played and trained alongside him, and some, all too few, treasured moments of chat with him. My impression, and that is all any portrait of Moore might aspire to, is that over the first part of his life Moore appeared to have trusted only three people totally: Tina, Cantwell, and Allison. Tina was his rock and Noel a secure and honest friend, but Malcolm stood like a tower on the horizon of Bobby's experience. Alf and Ron perhaps wanted Bobby as their adopted or professional son, but Allison was Moore's sun, and it was in his gleam that Moore cast his considerable shadow.

Thou shalt not be on your arse

Moore did extend Ron's noble vision of the game practically. He was often to ask if the players he watched after his retirement were ever taught to stay on their feet while tackling. He was firm in his conviction that you are unable to defend while sitting on your arse. Moore believed that the art of the tackle had never been totally appreciated. For Bobby the hygienic dispossession was as commendable as a goal scored by way of a dramatic overhead kick.

Bobby also found lunging unpalatable, not because he saw it as in some way beneath him, but because for him other considerations were more critical: shutting down openings, cutting off angles, closing down opponent opportunities and denying the opposition space, making it difficult for strikers to break through without losing the ball, but everything with converting defence to offence in mind – move forward.

Bobby had it that if a player was obliged to make a last-ditch lunge to save a situation, something had gone wrong previously. According to Moore, defending started with an appreciation of the play as it develops in front of you. Only when this had been grasped could one interpret play and take the appropriate action to dictate it. The lunging tactic was not conducive to responsible defending because in the process one takes oneself out of the game. It was just foolhardy to slide-tackle Di Stéfano and present a free kick on the edge of the penalty area or lunge at Garrincha, with the predictable disastrous results.

The greatest blasphemy of all in the Moore credo was hacking through a player's pins to get to the ball. From Moore's perspective such an act was a mark of ignorance and inherently offensive; his doctrine was one of 'controlled interception' that was always preferable to a ploughing tackle – he wanted players to defend cleanly and correctly, keep on their feet, hold on to the ball, and press forward. Not bad words to live by. Indeed, there is more to these practical coaching guides than meets the eye. Yes, it was the way Moore played, but it reflects his approach to others generally and how he lived his life.

In his final years, Bobby was frustrated and perplexed that the teaching of the defensive craft was apparently neglected. This has had a detrimental effect on football, but it has also impacted on the development of player personality and integrity.

Bobby hung out with people he respected in the game. We talk a lot about respect these days, as if anyone is entitled to be respected, just be 'being'. Apart from that standing out as a signifier of toxic narcissism, if you respect everyone, what is your respect worth? Respect is really something earned, like love or trust. If you have done nothing to be respected and you think people are respecting you, they're not; you are being patronised or subjected to sycophancy. You are also being treated as if you were an emotionally illiterate fool. Of course, if you get respect from someone, like if you get trust or love, you are more likely to return that sentiment.

Moore was respected because he earned it. He was trusted because he put his trust in those worthy of it. He was loved because his love and devotion to his beliefs meant something. Part of the evidence of the respect and trust people had for Bobby was their readiness to learn from him, but he wasn't one for giving lectures or strings of instruction; Moore taught by example. Even as a spectator you could learn from him; I know I did. In part Bobby was one of those who showed me how to gain, use and pass on wisdom. Knowledge is a poor relation of wisdom; the former requires some type of orchestration, the latter is only achieved in the doing, the application, growth and development of knowledge is the fuel of insight, and the midwife of foresight. Wisdom thus emanates from the application of knowledge in the world. Above all though, Moore taught me the value of integrity: how one is valued for having it, but as importantly, the self-worth, the dignity one derives from the effort to be decent and honest.

Bobby had progressed from a relatively ordinary lad from the fringes of East London, and would become the golden captain of the glittering years of the English game. This was a time when the football crafted under the Three Lions banner had never been more supreme, a moment we will perhaps never know again. He did this by his capacity to learn from his experience and pass that on to others; to generate and disseminate wisdom. The stage he walked on to in Bratislava and the central role he took up as a man was what that boy, young Bobby, made of himself, by way of a gift bestowed to many a cockney of his era, the ability to endure and work hard. You have seen how that happened. In the way of the Buddha, Bobby was his own lamp.

Nostalgia ain't what it used to be…

While Bobby had a few very good friends in football, the likes of Jimmy Greaves, he never encouraged a skipper's clique. After the awkwardness of youth, Bobby had a word for everyone – even a few times the likes of me. He was anything but vociferous, but he always came across as having authentic, sometimes amused interest, mature concern, and warmth. From his teenage years, he didn't have to work on projecting authority. It was part of him. He asked about family, if everything was OK with you, and then he'd amble off. Players, during his playing career, told of being assured he would always be around for them. He was a sturdy, but never extravagant voice of command on the pitch and sometimes, when necessary, beyond. Bobby didn't make it hard for people to look up to him.

Being a captain was seemingly in Moore's DNA somewhere. It came and looked natural to him. That said, that last thing managers, the men who played against and alongside him and supporters talk about is the nuts and bolts of his playing qualities, those assets that usually determine the descriptions of the best performers. The apparently innate positional sense is regularly mentioned as something that became instinctive to Bobby. Likewise, his judgement and anticipation, arising from his genius for reading the game, and the consequent capacity to close down potential trouble before it manifested itself, which was essential given his lack of pace, are repeatedly remarked on. But this is all rather ethereal and/or abstract. Few could pin down Moore's talent in any carnal sense.

Moore's alleged deficiencies, which really were the source of his strengths, are consistently reiterated, avoidance of heading the ball and not being in possession of the best left foot ever, but even as people go on yet again about such things, they cannot sensibly talk about the world's greatest players without mentioning Bobby Moore.

I would never fail to be surprised how he placed himself in front of an attacker to win the ball, choosing not to wait at the back, a natural recourse for a player who might lack a turn of speed. At the start of his senior career, the risks were concomitant in that had a propensity to scare the shit out of his team-mates. Later such audaciously became less of a shock and more an expectation of him. Indeed, on the rare occasion things went wrong it was a matter of surprise. This was the essence of Moore – you knew what he did, but not quite, you knew how he did it, but few could replicate it. Such intangibles however are probably the mark of great exponents of any sport or art; how did Shakespeare, Lennon and McCartney or Leonardo da Vinci 'do it'?

So, we've come to the end of the story of young Bobby – two books, more than a quarter of a million words. I'm not sure I know him any better than I did when I started this endeavour something in excess of half-a-century ago, but perhaps you do.

When his then girlfriend Tina Dean discovered that Bobby's mum was a knitter of some renown, she embarked on making him what grew into a hideous green v-neck sweater. When she gifted him with it, he was amused but also delighted. When she went away one weekend, on her return she found Bobby had redecorated her bedroom. Likely calling on his O-level in woodwork, he had also made her a jewellery box, lining the interior. He put his good design and technical skills to use re-upholstering a tub chair in red satin with black buttons. Today that might feel a bit over the top, but at the time the result was strikingly lavish. At heart, Bobby was a kind person who took joy in making others happy, but as Tina was to tell, you only got to understand this fully if you were close to him, and not many people got that close, no matter how many might claim to have achieved that feat.

However, as you might have understood if you have read both books, Moore was single-minded. He was capable of exceptional focus, but that had a cost as it could cause him to shut out what became, or he took to be extraneous considerations. Perhaps the most poignant example of this is how wounded his mum was when, after Bobby had fallen in love with Tina, he increasingly excluded her from his life. As Tina was to put it, 'That was Bobby ... he only ever had one passion at a time.'

Moore is often taken to be something of a conformist, partly perhaps because of his devotion to training and being a perfectionist. But again, the biography of his young life demonstrates that, while not exactly a revolutionary, he had an anti-authoritarian streak; he wasn't that good at doing what he was told. When he understood how possessive his mum was he rebelled against the authority Doris had always had in his family context. He didn't entirely cut all ties with parents, but a while after he and Tina were married, what had been regular visits to Waverley Gardens became less and less frequent. That intimacy that had existed between mother and son dissipated somewhat. The special relationship, wherein he shared everything, shifted from Doris to Tina. Ultimately, Bobby shut his mum out emotionally almost totally. There can be little doubt that hurt her a lot. Moore could appear to be insensitive and ruthless, and while there weren't too many who were to feel the extensive warmth of his love and friendship, there were a few others, including Alf Ramsey and Ron Greenwood, who felt his cold shoulder and were left woundedly numb

Jimmy Greaves once said to me, 'When you start to get old and begin to think things that happened when you were young weren't as good as you thought, you suddenly discover nostalgia.'

Every life, in the end, is just a mist of memories, and on that, out of that, we make our reality. No one can be blamed for any wrongs or mistakes our dodgy faculty of recall makes. The storage faculty to remember is fragile, made up as it is of impressions, themselves brittle and shaped by wishes and imagination. The activity of recall is located in the brain's temporal lobe, this is where episodic memories are formed and indexed for later access. The activity and accuracy of this functioning is curtailed and distorted by fears, anxieties, and broken dreams; it isn't a library of time-proof videos, it is inhabited by unconscious bias and its shadowy products are mediated by the ghost of our emotional selves. Logic within the multidimensional twists and turns of memory has little purchase, it is a patchwork maze in which we rationalise the fleeting expression of all we are and have been. What we recall seems to mean everything, but it comes to nothing. This is our means to make of the world what we will and in there, somewhere, is 'a' Bobby Moore, for any and each of us, that is 'our' Bobby Moore, but it isn't 'the' Bobby Moore, and I cannot and do not boast to have shown him to you, but you have your picture, even if it's only one from 'Charles Buchan's Football Monthly' circa 1963 and perhaps my words have added dimension to that. I hope so.

The world knows much, or thinks it does, of the feats that would follow Moore's initiation as captain of his country's team, playing the national game. You, good reader, have maybe seen him play, YouTube and the like facilitate this, although it ain't the same as being there. Me? I watched Bobby hundreds of times, including all the finals he graced as a senior player. In my memory Bobby is still tackling the likes of Pelé and George Best as he did plenty of times. In his pomp he met them with confidence and surgical precision, more often than not bettering their efforts.

After Moore, football seemed to lack at least some of the class he brought to the pitch; a touch of grace, a degree honour, the measure of honesty, a good deal of dignity and so the spirit of professionality, which is integrity. Worship David Beckham and Wayne Rooney, idolise Cristiano Ronaldo and Lionel Messi, the 'GOATs' in slippers, passing a balloon sideways, but be sure, be oh so sure, Bobby would have ate 'em. Yep, sing me the song of not being able to compare eras and so on, but here I am doing just that; what a bastard eh? I'm not having it. Why? Because I don't want, need, or have to, just because Gary Lineker might think I should. Why should I spare these (to borrow a phrase from the Hulk) 'puny gods'?

Whatever, alongside like all the greats of Moore's era – Denis Law, Rodney Marsh, Stan Bowles, whoever – the 'puny gods' of today would find themselves having run five yards without the ball before they knew Moore had taken it away from them and set up an attack threatening their goal. He was given his football boots by God, but Bobby made them fit.

There's only one Bobby Moore

* * *

The pages you have turned have sauntered through the second part of Bobby's early biography, from his time on the fringes of the West Ham first team to his ascent to the captaincy of England. In this story I have looked to open a vista on those who peopled the world around Moore's maturing as a 'legend to be', his continued becoming and flourishing. In the process, the figure of 'the man in formation' has been depicted, who he was and how he honed the skills and attitudes he had acquired as a boy. But his life is now lodged in the realm of the sentiments, the person he was and who we might want him to be. In that he lives in and mirrors part of us.

Moore himself once said, 'When I think of little Tubby Moore, who wondered if he was going to be the one left behind, I know just how much I owe to this game … It's given me everything. I hope I serve it well.'

You did, mate. You most certainly did.

BIBLIOGRAPHY

Books:

Allen, M., *Jimmy Greaves* (Virgin, 2001)

Allison, M., *Colours of My Life* (Everest, 1975)

Armfield, J., *Right Back to the Beginning* (Headline, 2004)

Belton, B., *Hammerin' Round: East End Speedway* (The History Press, 2002)

Belton, B., *Johnnie the One: the John Charles Story* (The History Press, 2003a)

Belton, B., *Founded on Iron* (Tempus, 2003b)

Belton, B., *Bluey Wilkinson: West Ham's First World Champion* (The History Press, 2003c)

Belton, B., *The Men of 64: West Ham and Preston North End in the FA Cup* (Tempus, 2005)

Belton, B., *West Ham United Miscellany* (Pennant Books, 2006a)

Belton, B., *Black Hammers: The Voices of West Ham's Ebony Heroes* (Pennant Books, 2006b)

Belton, B., *The Lads of '23* (Tony Brown, 2006c)

Belton, B., *Fay Taylour: Queen of Speedway* (Panther, 2006d)

Belton, B., *East End Heroes, Stateside Kings* (John Blake, 2008)

Belton, B., *Burn Budgie Byrne, Football Inferno* (DB, 2012)

Belton, B., *Bubbles, Hammers & Dreams,* (DB, 2013a)

Belton, B., *The First and Last Englishmen* (DB, 2013b)

Belton, B., *Days of Iron: The Story of West Ham United in the Fifties* (DB, 2013c)

Belton, B., *War Hammers: The Story of West Ham United During the First World War* (The History Press, 2014)

Belton, B., *War Hammers II: The Story of West Ham United during the Second World War* (The History Press, 2015)

Belton, B., *Nearly Reached the Sky: West Ham in Europe* (Fonthill Press, 2017)

Charlton, B., *My England Years* (Headline, 2009)

Crane, T., *They Played with Bobby Moore* (Tim Crane, 2014)

Daniels, P., *Moore than a Legend* (Goal Publications, 1997)

Dickinson, M., *Bobby Moore: The Man in Full* (Yellow Jersey, 2014)

Edworthy, N., *England: The Official F.A. History* (Virgin Books, 1997)

Emery, D. (Ed), *Bobby Moore. A Tribute* (Headline, 1993)

Fenton, T., *At Home With the Hammers* (Nicholas Kaye, 1960)

Flowers, R., *For Wolves and England* (Sportsman Book Club, 1964)

Football Association, *The Complete Guide to England Players Since 1945* (Stanley Paul, 1993)

Greaves, J., *Greavsie* (Time Warner, 2003)

Green, G., *Soccer in the Fifties* (Ian Allan, 1974)

Giller, N., *Bobby Moore: The Master* (NGB, 2013)

Goodyear, S., *From Mine to Milan: The Gerry Hitchens Story* (DB , 2010)

Greenwood, R., *Yours Sincerely Ron Greenwood* (Collins Willow, 1984)

Hodgkinson, A., *Between the Sticks* (HarperSport, 2013)

Hugman, B.J., *The PFA Premier & Football League Players Records* (Queen Anne Press, 2005)

Hurst, G., *The World Game* (Sportsmans Book Club, 1968)

Inglis, S., *Soccer in the Dock* (Collins, 1985)

Irving, D., *The West Ham United Football Book* (Stanley Paul, 1968)

Irving, D., *The West Ham United Football Book No.2* (Stanley Paul, 1969)

Johnston, H., *The Rocky Road to Wembley* (Museum Press, 1954)

Korr, C., *West Ham United: The Making of a Football Club* (Gerald Duckworth, 1986)

Lewis, R., *England's Eastenders* (Mainstream, 2002)

Lyall, J., *Just Like My Dreams* (Penguin, 1989)

McDonald, T., *West Ham United: The Managers* (FootballWorld, 2007)

McDonald, T., *West Ham in My Day* (FootballWorld 2007)

McDonald, T., & Roper, T., *West Ham in My Day, Volume 2* (FootballWorld 2008)

McKinstry, L., *Sir Alf* (HarperSport, 2006)

Miles, M., *Ron Greenwood* (Pitch Publishing, 2021)

Moore, B., *My Soccer Story* (Stanley Paul, 1967)

Moore, T., *Bobby Moore: By The Person Who Knew Him Best* (CollinsWillow, 2005)

Morse, G., *Sir Walter Winterbottom: The Father of Modern English Football* (John Blake, 2013)

Moynihan, J., *The West Ham Story* (Arthur Barker, 1984)

Palmer, J. (Ed.), *Bobby Moore: England's Greatest* (Athem, 2006)

Powell, J., *Bobby Moore* (Alpine Books, 1993)

Peters, M., *Goals From Nowhere* (Stanley Paul, 1969)

Roper, T., *West Ham in the Sixties: The Jack Burkett Story* (FootballWorld, 2009)

Stevens, P., *John Lyall. A Life in Football* (Apex, 2014)

Swan, P. & Johnson, N., *Peter Swan: Setting the Record Straight* (Stadia, 2006)

Robson, B., *Bobby Robson. Farewell but not Goodbye* (Hodder, 2005)

Thomas, D., *Jimmy Adamson. The man who said 'no' to England* (Pitch Publishing, 2013)

Tossell, D., *Big Mal* (Mainstream, 2008)

Venables.T., *Venables* (Michael Joseph, 1994)

Journals/newspapers:

Hammers News

Newham Recorder

East Ham Echo

East and West Ham Gazette

East London Advertiser Evening Post

Ex Magazine

Stratford Express

ND - #0253 - 270225 - C0 - 234/156/21 - PB - 9781780916330 - Gloss Lamination